Benjamin Beil, Gundolf S. Freyermuth, Hanns Christian Schmidt (eds.)
Playing Utopia

Studies of Digital Media Culture | Volume 10

The series is edited by Gundolf S. Freyermuth and Lisa Gotto.

Benjamin Beil (PhD) is Professor of Media Studies & Digital Culture at the Department of Media Culture & Theatre at the University of Cologne.
Gundolf S. Freyermuth (PhD) is Professor of Media and Game Studies and a founding director of the Cologne Game Lab at TH Köln-University of Applied Sciences in Cologne, Germany. He also teaches Comparative Media Studies at the *ifs international film school* Cologne.
Hanns Christian Schmidt (PhD) works as a research assistant at the Department of Media Culture & Theater at the University of Cologne and within the project »Literacy of Play / Literacy of Games« at the Cologne Game Lab.

BENJAMIN BEIL, GUNDOLF S. FREYERMUTH,
HANNS CHRISTIAN SCHMIDT (EDS.)
Playing Utopia
Futures in Digital Games

[transcript]

TH Köln-University of Technology, Arts, and Sciences supported the publication of this volume.

Technology
Arts Sciences
TH Köln

Bibliographic information published by the Deutsche Nationalbibliothek
The Deutsche Nationalbibliothek lists this publication in the Deutsche Nationalbibliografie; detailed bibliographic data are available in the Internet at http://dnb.d-nb.de

© 2019 transcript Verlag, Bielefeld

All rights reserved. No part of this book may be reprinted or reproduced or utilized in any form or by any electronic, mechanical, or other means, now known or hereafter invented, including photocopying and recording, or in any information storage or retrieval system, without permission in writing from the publisher.

Cover concept: Kordula Röckenhaus, Bielefeld
Printed by Majuskel Medienproduktion GmbH, Wetzlar
Print-ISBN 978-3-8376-5050-1
PDF-ISBN 978-3-8394-5050-5
https://doi.org/10.14361/9783839450505

Table of Contents

Preface and Acknowledgements | 7

Utopian Futures.
A Brief History of Their Conception and Representation in
Modern Media—From Literature to Digital Games
Gundolf S. Freyermuth | 9

UTOPIAS IN DIGITAL GAMES

Tinkering with Political Utopias and Dystopias in DEMOCRACY 3.
An Educational Perspective
André Czauderna | 69

The Concept of Utopia in Digital Games
Gerald Farca | 99

"Everything is true; nothing is permitted".
Utopia, Religion and Conspiracy in ASSASSIN'S CREED
Lars de Wildt | 149

Beyond the Holonovel.
The Holographic Interactive Digital Entertainment Utopia
of STAR TREK
Tonguc Ibrahim Sezen | 187

UTOPIAS OF DIGITAL GAMES

Feminist Interventions for Better Futures of Digital Games
Alison Harvey | 211

**Ludopian Visions.
On the Speculative Potential of Games in Times of
Algorithmic Work and Play**
Anne Dippel | 235

**Playful Utopias.
Sandboxes for the Future**
Hartmut Koenitz | 253

**Building Utopia, Brick by Brick?
Selling Subversiveness in LEGO DIMENSIONS**
Hanns Christian Schmidt | 267

**We have won this battle ;)
Modding and Swapping as a Utopian Video Game Practice**
Thomas Hawranke | 285

The Utopia of Getting Over It
Benjamin Beil | 315

Contributors | 327

Preface and Acknowledgements

BENJAMIN BEIL, GUNDOLF S. FREYERMUTH,
HANNS CHRISTIAN SCHMIDT

Niklas Luhmann once asked in which forms the future might present itself in the present. One answer is that media narratives inform contemporary ideas of "the shape of things to come."[1] Games are currently making a significant contribution to this medial reservoir. On the one hand, they demonstrate a particular propensity for fantastic and futuristic scenarios. On the other hand, digital games often serve as an experimental field for the latest media technology. However, while dystopias are part of the standard gaming repertoire, games feature utopias much less frequently. Why?

This anthology attempts to provide some answers to this question. The idea of creating such a publication goes back to a Game Studies Summit which took place at the Cologne Game Lab of TH Köln in November 2018 as part of the ninth *Clash of Realities—International Conference on the Art, Technology, and Theory of Digital Games*. Its subject was "Playing Utopia— Futures in Digital Games." This volume documents the keynotes and lectures given at this summit and adds further perspectives and contributions. It collects various analyses of visions of a better world as they are presented in games as well as investigations of the role ludic elements play in such scenarios.

In the introductory essay "Utopian Futures. A Brief History of Their Conception and Representation in Modern Media—From Literature to Digital

---

1 Wells, H.G.: *The Shape of Things to Come. The Ultimate Revolution*, London: Hutchinson & Co. 1933.

Games," Gundolf S. Freyermuth situates the visions of the future that characterize our digital present in the context of media history.² After that, the contributions are divided into two major areas: utopias *in* digital games, and utopias *of* digital games. An overview of the individual contributions to these two parts, their highly diverse topics, methodological approaches, and insights, can be found at the end of the introductory essay.³

ACKNOWLEDGMENTS

This anthology would not have been possible without the hard work of many people and the support of several sponsors. The *Clash of Realities* conference was planned by a Program Board chaired by Björn Bartholdy and Gundolf S. Freyermuth of the Cologne Game Lab (CGL). Cooperating institutions were the Institute for Media Research and Media Pedagogy of TH Köln, the ifs—internationale filmschule köln, and the Institute for Media Culture and Theater of the University of Cologne. The conference was financed through the generous support of TH Köln, Film und Medien Stiftung NRW, the State Chancellery of North Rhine-Westphalia, the City of Cologne, and Electronic Arts Germany. Our sincerest thanks go to these institutions and companies.

Both, the Game Studies Summit "Playing Utopia—Futures in Digital Games" and this volume, were planned and organized by Benjamin Beil, Gundolf S. Freyermuth, and Hanns Christian Schmidt. The summit owes much of its success to the extraordinary staff of the *Clash of Realities* conference, in particular, Rüdiger Brandis, Sebastian Felzmann, Alexandra Hühner, Tobias Lemme, Judith Ruzicka, Su-Jin Song, and the many members of CGL student support groups as well as Mathias Mehr (CGL) who provided technical assistance. The present volume was tirelessly edited and proofread by Alexander Boccia, Leon Freyermuth, Alexandra Petrus, and Raven Rusch. We thank them all for their extraordinary help!

We owe the deepest debt and gratitude, however, to the speakers and presenters who came to Cologne from all over the world, as well as to the authors who wrote additional contributions. Last but not least, we would like to thank the TH Köln for supporting this publication.

---

2   In this volume pp. 9-65.
3   In this volume pp. 51-55.

Utopian Futures

A Brief History of Their Conception and Representation in Modern Media—From Literature to Digital Games

GUNDOLF S. FREYERMUTH

Once upon a time, Western Culture had no utopian future.[1] If you lived in Greek or Roman antiquity, you could dream of a Golden Age which was forever bygone. If you lived later, in the earthly vale of tears that was the Christian Middle Ages, you could look forward to eternal life in the great beyond—paradise, hopefully; or hell. However, there were no utopian hopes that structurally corresponded to the prevalent ideas of the modern age, i.e., the belief that the future should be a better time, which if we did not live to see and experience then at least our direct descendants might.[2]

I will argue that the concept of such utopian futures—their theoretical possibility rather than any details of content—is the result of cultural changes which began with the Renaissance and that media, theoretical and artistic visions, had and still have a decisive role in the development of this new concept.

Telling the history of utopian futures means reading and watching and playing a rich array of stories in which humanity's hopes and desires have manifested themselves. Such research would be exciting and essential at any time. At present, however, there is a further interest: It seems that now, in the

---

[1] Or any other culture that we know of. But in this paper, I will limit myself to the history of utopian hopes in Western culture.

[2] See the more detailed account and debate below in parts V-VII.

first decades of digital culture, we are again creating new utopian blueprints for the future. Their contours indicate that the emerging hopes and desires driven by the potential of 21st-century technologies will be dramatically different from the utopias of the pre-industrial and industrial times.

My investigation will start with a brief outline of contemporary views on the future (*I. Status Quo: Deep Doom and High Hopes*). Next, I venture to define the central terms and concepts—future, utopia, dystopia—and understand their social and cultural function (*II. Utopian Futures as Cultural Constructs*). After considering the challenges associated with the prediction and artistic anticipation of societies, cultures, and ways of life (*III. Problems of Prophecy and Theories of Anticipation*), I will focus on the analysis of the three major historical phases in which Western culture has dealt with hopes of improving human living conditions. For each period, I proceed in two steps: First, I discuss the respective development of the cultural concepts of time and notions of how to achieve a better life (*IV. Utopian Futures in the Pre-Industrial Ages; VI. Utopian Futures in the Industrial Age; IX. Utopian Futures in the Digital Age*). Second, I trace the artistic efforts to aesthetically shape—however distorted, displaced, compressed, encrypted—new utopian (and also dystopian) visions of the future in various media; particularly literature, film, and games (*V. Hieroglyphs of the Future in Pre-Industrial Cultures; VII. Hieroglyphs of the Future in Industrial Culture: Literature; VIII. Hieroglyphs of the Future in Industrial Culture: New Media*). A summary concludes the historical survey, followed by an outlook on the contributions of this volume (*X. Summary and Outlook: Hieroglyphs of the Future in Digital Culture*).

I. STATUS QUO: DEEP DOOM AND HIGH HOPES

Human-made climate change triggers intensifying natural disasters like burning rainforests and water scarcity, thus endangering all biological life. The rise of global and national surveillance in combination with the resurgence of totalitarian systems is jeopardizing our freedom. Worldwide epidemics and biological warfare put our physical survival at stake. Computer viruses, state trojans, and anonymous hackers threaten to compromise the security of our data. Black box artificial intelligence is undermining the dominance of our not-so-sapiens species. And that is just the news reports. According to some of the most popular works of art and entertainment, the future is even worse off. From blockbuster movies like the HUNGER GAMES film series (2012-2015), MAD MAX: FURY ROAD (2015), BLADE RUNNER 2049 (2017), READY, PLAYER, ONE (2018), and TERMINATOR: DARK FATE (2019) to successful TV series like WESTWORLD (2016/2018) and HANDMAID'S TALE (2017/2018) to AAA games like THE LAST OF US (2013), FALLOUT 4 (2015), MAD MAX (2015), THE SURGE (2017), and MASS EFFECT: ANDROMEDA (2017)—nothing but doom and gloom.

Anyone who got to know our present only via the media—whether through news and non-fiction or novels, feature films, and digital games—could hardly doubt that our planet is no longer habitable and that our civilizations are no longer sustainable. We live in the "Golden Age of Dystopian Fiction."[3] Its beginnings, however, date back decades, as Jill Lepore argues. She quotes literary scholar Chad Walsh, who in 1962 observed that a "decreasing percentage of the imaginary worlds are Utopias" and "an increasing percentage are nightmares,"[4] and she also quotes Margaret Atwood, the author of the dystopian novel *The Handmaid's Tale* (1985), who wrote in the 1980s: "It's a sad commentary on our age that we find dystopias a lot easier to believe in than utopias."[5]

We are reaping the harvest that has been sown in the final years of industrial culture and at the dawn of digital culture. Critics claim for quite some time that we are in the grip of a dystopian plague. In 2014, Michael Solana observed: "Certainly dystopia has appeared in science fiction from the genre's inception, but the past decade has observed an unprecedented rise in its authorship. Once a literary niche within a niche, mankind is now destroyed with clockwork regularity […]." He concluded: "The time is fit for us to dream again."[6]

---

3   Lepore, Jill: "A Golden Age of Dystopian Fiction," *The New Yorker*, May 29, 2017; https://www.newyorker.com/magazine/2017/06/05/a-golden-age-for-dystopian-fiction

4   Ibid.

5   Ibid.

6   Solana, Michael: "Stop Writing Dystopian Sci-Fi—It's Making Us All Fear Technology," *Wired*, August 14, 2014; https://www.wired.com/2014/08/stop-writing-dystopian-sci-fiits-making-us-all-fear-technology/—The same issue published an opposing opinion piece by Maloney, Devon: "No, Dystopian Sci-Fi Isn't Bad for

Of course, many do still dream. There are not just dystopias today; there are also widespread hopes, big promises, and positive fictions telling us that we are moving towards the edge of a better tomorrow. According to these visions, we will profit from personalized education and personalized medicine, providing replacement organs and three-digit longevity if not immortality. Nanotech and 3D printing will revolutionize manufacturing. Ubiquitous household robots and artificial intelligences will help us do our work. Powerful human-machine interfaces will make us super-intelligent cyborgs. Space travel has already been jump-started by several private, well-funded companies that will offer affordable holidays in orbit and trips to the moon. That is if we still want to go because the seductive, immersive worlds of VR and holographic entertainment will trump all of reality's offerings. In short: We will experience a world of abundance that is full of magic by any historical comparison.

Such utopian predictions are presented predominantly in scientific research and popular non-fiction books and publicly proclaimed by leaders and 'evangelists' of high-tech industries.[7] In the arts and mass entertainment—or the humanities, for that matter—, future-positive attitudes are harder to come by. When in 2017 Yorgo Lee undertook to draw up a list of "Optimistic Sci-fi: 10 Movies That Think We Have a Chance," he had difficulties finding convincing contemporary examples.[8] Moreover, for the few blockbuster films from the last decade that he does list—HER (2013), INTERSTELLAR (2014)—, it seems doubtful that they convey an unabashedly positive outlook.

The same holds for some of the—imagined—future advances mentioned above, particularly AI or nanotech: What gives hope to some, puts fear into others. More than ever, the demarcation between utopia and dystopia seems to hinge on political positions and moral attitudes. A telling example of this is the reaction of author Stephen Marche to Google co-founder Larry Page's

---

Society. We Need It More Than Ever"; https://www.wired.com/2014/08/no-dystopian-sci-fi-isnt-bad-for-society-we-actually-need-it-more-than-ever/

7   See for example Kurzweil, Ray: *The Singularity is Near: When Humans Transcend Biology*, New York: Viking 2005.

8   Yorgo Lee: "Optimistic Sci-fi: 10 Movies That Think We Have a Chance," *Medium*, March 1, 2017; https://medium.com/@yorgo.douramacos/optimistic-sci-fi-10-movies-that-think-we-have-a-chance-3decac4c1ab4

future visions. Page raved about potential improvements to his memory: "Eventually you'll have the implant, where if you think about a fact, it will just tell you the answer."[9] However, what Page—and not only he—is dreaming of, frightens Marche profoundly:

"That's not a conspiracy theorist babbling outside the toilets in a public library about how Google's going to put a chip in your brain. That's Larry Page. [...] The single most important technologist alive believes the future is brain implants. Literally, I've had nightmares since reading that passage."[10]

The strong and strange mixture of contradictory and opposing views, hopes and fears, which represents the status quo of utopian (and dystopian) thinking has, in spite of all its diversity, a common basis: What we think about the future and believe we know about it, we owe mainly to information and aesthetic-fictional representations that we obtain from media. The same applies, of course, to almost everything. "Whatever we know about our society, or indeed about the world in which we live, we know through the mass media," Niklas Luhmann stated.[11] The future, though, is not yet part of our world, at least not entirely. Before it can be fully realized, it has to be imagined. While the details of the future, whose utopian and dystopian versions we are currently negotiating, will be the result of media productions and engagement with them, the influence of media reaches further. Even the basic notion that utopian futures like these are possible at all—the mental category of such prospects—has been generated through modern media; first written matter, later cinematic narrations, and more recently interaction with and in digital games.

---

9   Larry Page's statement appears in: Levy, Steven: *In the Plex: How Google Thinks, Works, and Shapes Our Lives*, Simon & Schuster 2011. It is cited here after Marche, Stephen: "*Star Trek: The Next Generation* Was the Last Sci-Fi Show Hopeful About the Future. Brave New Worlds have been Replaced by a Google Chip," *Esquire*, May 22, 2014; https://www.esquire.com/entertainment/tv/a31206/star-trek-the-next-generation-future/

10 Ibid.

11 Luhmann, Niklas: *The Reality of the Mass Media: Cultural Memory in the Present*, Stanford: Stanford University Press 2000, p. 1.

II. Utopian Futures as Cultural Constructs

Big History tells us that since the cognitive revolution, our species has the unique "ability to transmit information about things that do not exist at all."[12] Yuval Noah Harari names non-material entities like "gods, or nations, or limited liability companies."[13] To the list of "imagined" but "intersubjective orders,"[14] we can add the future. Its central characteristic is that it is "unwritten," as Cicero and Joe Strummer, lead singer of *The Clash*, equally emphasized.[15] The "facta," the facts that have been established, are categorically separated from the "futura," the 'things' and 'actions' which are about to exist but have yet to be. This notion, however, that the time before us can bring more than the return of the same natural rhythms, seasons and lifetimes, is comparatively recent. Only about 2,500 years ago, "when Greek philosophers were reframing time from its cyclical to its linear shape and developing abstract thinking,"[16] the new tripartite division of time into past, present, and future created the potential for utopian thinking.

Two thousand years later, in 1516, Thomas More coined the term 'Utopia'; denoting either a 'no place' or a 'good place.'[17] The genre that More established is now commonly defined as the attempt to design in media—

---

12 Harari, Yuval Noah: *Sapiens: A Brief History of Humankind,* New York: Harper 2015 (Kindle edition), p. 24.
13 Ibid., p. 31.
14 Ibid., p. 116.
15 For Cicero see Gidley, Jennifer M.: *The Future: A Very Short Introduction*, New York: Oxford University Press 2017 (Kindle edition), loc. 986; for Joe Strummer see Montfort, Nick: *The Future*, Cambridge, Mass.: MIT Press, 2017 (Kindle edition), p. 16.
16 J. M. Gidley: *The Future*, loc. 841.
17 The Greek noun 'topos' means place; the prefix 'ou' means 'not'; the prefix 'eu' means 'good.' More himself plays with the two possible meanings in a short poem that he had prepended to the first edition: "Wherefore not Utopia, but rather rightly, / My name is Eutopie: a place of felicity."—For an analysis of More's fictitious account see below *V. Hieroglyphs of the Future in Pre-Industrial Cultures*, pp. 25-26.—For today's discussion about Utopia and Eutopia see N. Montfort, *The Future*, p. 40: "Those who study utopian thought and writing distinguish, however, between a utopia or 'no place' and a eutopia or 'good place.'"

literature, film, games—a "non-existent society" which is "described in considerable detail and normally located in time and space."[18] Such utopian concepts express not just "hope but desire—the desire for a better way of being."[19]

Dystopic blueprints for the future pursue the opposite objective: to express disapproval of possible societies and primarily undesirable living conditions. The term 'Dystopia'—the Greek prefix 'dis' means 'bad'—was coined in reaction to More's *Utopia* in 1747 by Lewis Henry Younge in his poem "Utopia: or Apollo's Golden Garden."[20] More than a hundred years later and close to the first "dystopian turn from the late 19th to mid-20th century,"[21] the term was popularized by philosopher and economist John Stuart Mill, then prime minister of Great Britain, who used it during a speech in the House of Commons as a warning against false hopes.

Both descriptions of desirable and undesirable non-existent societies seem deeply rooted and confined in their own time—even more so than all artistic expression. Most scholars who have studied utopias and dystopias observed that with some historical distance, visions of the future are revealing the time of their creation in striking ways: unique contemporary concerns, typical longings and fears, the morals and prejudices of their time.[22] Contemporary artists creating utopian or dystopian fiction seem to be well

---

18 Sargent, Lyman Tower: *Utopianism: A Very Short Introduction*, Oxford: Oxford University Press 2010 (Kindle edition), p. 6.

19 Levitas, Ruth: *The Concept of Utopia*, Syracuse, N.Y.: Syracuse University Press 1990, p. 191.

20 L.T. Sargent, *Utopianism*, p. 4.—See also Budakov, Vesselin E.: "Dystopia: an Earlier Eighteenth-Century Use," *Notes and Queries 57.1*, Oxford University Press; March 1, 2010: p. 86-88; https://www.academia.edu/944097/_Dystopia_an _Earlier_Eighteenth-Century_Use_Notes_and_Queries_57.1_March_1_2010_8 6-88_Notes_and_Queries_Oxford_University_Press_first_published_online_on _February_8_2010_doi_10.1093_notesj_gjp235_

21 J.M. Gidley: *The Future*, loc. 1198.

22 Cf. Heilbroner, Robert L.: *Visions of the Future: The Distant Past, Yesterday, Today, Tomorrow*, New York: Oxford University Press 1995 (Kindle edition), loc. 1240: "Visions of the future express the ethos of their times."—L.T. Sargent, *Utopianism*, p. 21: "Utopias are reflections of the issues that were important to the period in which their authors lived."

aware of this fact. Neal Stephenson, for example, says: "[W]hat science fiction writers are really doing is writing a kind of metaphorical story about the present."²³

From this perspective, we can identify several beneficial functions of utopian (and dystopian) thought and artistic creation. Above all, these fictions promote self-awareness. One of the first to recognize that stories about the future are less fantastic than they appear and rather reflect the present, was Darko Suvin. In *Metamorphoses of Science Fiction* he wrote:

"The aliens—utopians, monsters, or simply differing strangers—are a mirror to man just as the differing country is a mirror for his world. But the mirror is not only a reflecting one, it is also a transforming one."²⁴

Similarly, L. T. Sargent remarked that "utopia is a mirror to the present designed to bring out flaws, a circus or funfair mirror in reverse, to illustrate ways in which life could be better."²⁵ In the case of dystopias, this mirroring is usually associated with warnings; "calls to readers to turn in another direction," as science fiction writer Andreas Eschbach says;²⁶ the telling of "cautionary tales for ourselves," according to Jonathan Nolan, one of the creators of the WESTWORLD series.²⁷

---

23 Cowen, Tyler: "Neal Stephenson on Depictions of Reality,'" Conversations with Tyler, Episode 71, *Medium*, July 17, 2019; https://medium.com/conversations-with-tyler/tyler-cowen-neal-stephenson-science-fiction-writer-7fbe020e60b6

24 Suvin, Darko: *Metamorphoses of Science Fiction,* New Haven: Yale University Press 1979, p. 25; cited after: Beil, Benjamin: "'Introducing the All New eyePhone!'—The Future of Mobile Media," WiJournal (8/2), November 28, 2014, http://wi.mobilities.ca/introducing-the-all-new-eyephone-the-future-of-mobile-media/. I am indebted to Benjamin Beil for this information.

25 L.T Sargent: *Utopianism*, p. 112.

26 Haeming, Anne: "'Politik und Science Fiction sind nicht fern voneinander.' Interview mit Bestseller-Autor Andreas Eschbach," *Der Spiegel*, December 21, 2018; https://www.spiegel.de/kultur/literatur/andreas-eschbach-ueber-nsa-es-sind-viele-ungute-zukuenfte-denkbar-a-1244124.html

27 Watercutter, Angela: "Westworld's Creators Know Why Sci-Fi Is So Dystopian," *Wired*, June 8, 2017; https://www.wired.com/2017/06/westworld-wired-business-conference/

No less critical than the function to create self-awareness seems to be an evolutionary function. Arthur C. Clarke once declared: "One of the biggest roles of science fiction is to prepare people to accept the future without pain and to encourage a flexibility of mind ..."[28] Beyond facilitating adaptation to certain changes, utopian fiction can encourage further change, as Robert Anton Wilson used to stress: "Science fiction is liberation. Reality in the old Aristotelian sense is a crutch for those who are afraid to walk alone on their feet, above the Abyss that yaws when we begin to break our mental sets and pause to wonder—really wonder."[29] This potential of utopian thinking and creating to become a catalyst for future developments seems to be its most important social and cultural function. "The influence of SF," writer Thomas M. Disch observed, "can be felt in such diverse realms as industrial design and marketing, military strategy, sexual mores, foreign policy, and practical epistemology—in other words, our basic sense of what is real and what isn't."[30]

However, Disch's—accurate—description poses the question: What special foundations, procedures, and means do utopian (and dystopian) creations command to be able to initiate future affairs through theoretical speculation and artistic anticipation?

---

28 Arthur C. Clarke, quoted in: Agel, Jerome (ed.): *The Making of Kubrick's 2001*, New York: New American Library 1970.

29 Robert Anton Wilson cited after: Neuhaus, Wolfgang: "Science Fiction als Pop-Epistemologie. Ein Sinn für Neuorientierung in der hypermedialen Welt," *Telepolis*, August 30, 2002; https://www.heise.de/tp/features/Science-Fiction-als-Pop-Epistemologie-3426255.html—Also: "Storytelling, according to show co-creator Jonathan Nolan, serves an evolutionary purpose, allowing us to try out different realities." (A. Watercutter, "Westworld's Creators Know Why Sci-Fi Is So Dystopian.")

30 Thomas M. Disch cited after: W. Neuhaus: "Science Fiction als Pop-Epistemologie."

III. PROBLEMS OF PROPHECY AND THEORIES OF ANTICIPATION

In his seminal study *The Principle of Hope*, Ernst Bloch wrote about the essential path from abstract to concrete utopia. While their "dreaminess" characterizes abstract utopias, concrete utopias are "an anticipatory kind."[31] However, finding this path is made difficult by different variants of humanity's future blindness. Again, and again, there have been futures that hardly anyone saw coming. In the past decades, they have ranged from the fall of the Berlin Wall to the exponential growth of the World Wide Web; from the burst of the dot-com bubble to 9/11 and the war on terror; from the rise of global surveillance to the historical relapse of nationalism, isolationism, and anti-democratic stances embodied by political leaders such as Recep Tayyip Erdogan in Turkey, Viktor Orbán in Hungary, and Donald Trump in the United States.

Conversely, we have misidentified a number of futures that never came to pass; from the rise of the Soviet economy that many pundits predicted in the 1970s to the rise of Japan as the dominant world power that even more pundits predicted in the 1980s. "Japan has become the most interesting place for future nostalgia," William Gibson says, "with beautiful futures that never came through."[32] The biggest misjudgment, however, concerned the exploration of space. "When Sputnik and Apollo 11 fired the imagination of the world, everyone began predicting that by the end of the century, people would be living in space colonies on Mars and Pluto."[33]

Space is also at the center of the third kind of future blindness: futures that happened, but of which we have lost sight. Currently, there is a space probe flying in interstellar space, more than 22 billion kilometers away. This

---

31 Bloch, Ernst: *The Principle of Hope*, Cambridge, Mass.: MIT Press 1986 (*1954), p. 146.
32 Cited after: Wegner, Jochen: "William Gibson: 'Ich hoffe, wir sind nicht in negativen Utopien gefangen,'" *Die Zeit*, January 12, 2017; https://www.zeit.de/zeitmagazin/leben/2017-01/william-gibson-science-fiction-neuromancer-cyberspace-futurist. My translation of the German original: "Japan ist zum interessantesten Ort für Zukunftsnostalgie geworden – mit wunderschönen Zukünften, die nie eingetreten sind."
33 Y.N. Harari: *Sapiens*, p. 412.

probe, Voyager 1, left the planet in 1977 and it still works with 64K of data storage on an eight-track tape deck. But we have more or less forgotten about it. Novelist Warren Ellis once asked: "Can you even consider being part of a culture that could go to space and then stopped?"[34] However, this forgotten future is by no means an exception. The history of culture is rich in examples. Gene Wolf, for instance, named these:

"The Greeks had complex gear systems but they didn't make clocks. The Alexandrians had a simple steam engine but they didn't end up making trains [...] They had indoor plumbing in Ancient Crete. It was lost with the fall of that civilization [...] A model airplane, carved from wood, has been found in an Egyptian tomb."[35]

Considering humanity's fundamental future blindness—the long list of futures that we did not expect, or misidentified, or just forgot—, how is it that so many artistic utopian designs, in retrospect, seem to have gotten at least 'something right'? In 1965, Marshall McLuhan was asked on Canadian TV: "What about the future?" He answered: "We are always living a way ahead of our thinking."[36] With that remark, he expressed the insight that most futures begin early, and parts of them can be discovered in the present. Related ideas were advanced already a decade earlier by futurologist Robert Jungk—*Tomorrow Is Already Here*[37]—and in 1999 by William Gibson: "The future

---

34 Ellis, Warren: "How to See the Future," raw text of a keynote given at the conference *Improving Reality*, posted September 7, 2012; http://www.warrenellis.com/how-to-see-the-future/

35 Chu, Charles: "The Future-Altering Technologies We Forgot to Invent. Science Fiction Legend Gene Wolfe Shares His Thoughts," *Medium*, February 24, 2018; https://medium.com/the-polymath-project/gene-wolfe-a-science-fiction-legend-on-the-future-altering-technologies-we-forgot-to-invent-a3103572a352

36 McLuhan, Marshall: "Take 30 Interview with George Garlock and Paul Soles," CBC, April 1, 1965; https://www.youtube.com/watch?v=qABC3_8ai58

37 Jungk, Robert: *Tomorrow Is Already Here*, New York: Simon & Schuster 1954.—The title of the German edition *Die Zukunft hat schon begonnen* translates: "The future has already begun."

is already here—it's just not very evenly distributed."[38] Similarly, Tom Standage noted in *The Economist*: "Technologies have surprisingly long gestation periods; they may seem to appear overnight, but they don't. As a result, if you look in the right places, you can see tomorrow's technologies today."[39] Discovery, however, is only a first step. The second is about deducing from the traces detected 'the shape of things to come.'[40] Given this need for inference and imagination, academics, as well as artists, have long stressed that no other groups in society seem as well-suited to the task of anticipating the future as, of course, academics and artists.

The basic idea that anticipation is possible dates back at least to the 18th century. Immanuel Kant spoke of the aesthetic apparition as prophecy and gave our ability to recognize patterns as one reason why we can anticipate the unknown: It allows us to give shape to the universe even before we were able to observe it.[41] Ernst Bloch and Walter Benjamin, among others, continued this thought. Bloch analyzed the "specific pre-appearance which art shows"[42] and praised the "great work of art" in a quite religious phrase as "a star of anticipation."[43] Walter Benjamin, applying Freud's tools and borrowing from 19th-century historian Jules Michelet, set as the motto of his *Arcades*

---

38 Gibson, William: "The Science in Science Fiction," *Talk of the Nation*, NPR, November 30, 1999, min. 11:55; http://www.npr.org/templates/story/story.php?storyId=1067220

39 Standage, Tom: "A Toolkit for Predicting the Future," *The Economist*, May 31, 2017; https://medium.economist.com/a-toolkit-for-predicting-the-future-2f24757d9699

40 Wells, H.G.: *The Shape of Things to Come. The Ultimate Revolution*, London: Hutchinson & Co. 1933.

41 See for example: "We are actually in possession of *a priori* synthetical cognitions, as is proved by the existence of the principles of the understanding, which anticipate experience." Kant, Immanuel: *Critique of Pure Reason* (1787), Norman Kemp Smith version; "II. Transcendental Doctrine of Method, § II. The Discipline of Pure Reason in Respect of its Polemical Employment." Cited after: https://www.marxists.org/reference/subject/ethics/kant/reason/ch04.htm

42 E. Bloch: *The Principle of Hope*, p.15.

43 Bloch, Ernst: *Spirit of Utopia*, Stanford: Stanford University Press 2000 (*1918), p. 151.

Project: "Each epoch dreams the one to follow."[44] According to Benjamin, the reason for such dreamy clairvoyance is not supernatural but has a material basis: individual perceptions of contemporary life. Mentally processing advanced experiences of the present, artists gain the patterns as well as the raw material they need to anticipate aspects of the future artistically.

In the industrial age, the attitude of many writers and artists corresponded to these theses of the theorists. H.G. Wells published his *Anticipations* in 1902, forecasting "the way things will probably go in this new century."[45] Thirty years later he followed up on his non-fiction bestseller of future telling with the just as successful *Shape of Things to Come*.[46] The assertion that artists are more clairvoyant and far-sighted than most people was by no means limited to authors of utopian writings and science fiction novels. The modernist poet Ezra Pound, for example, claimed: "Artists are the antennae of the race."[47]

There is ample evidence that these promises of being able to anticipate have been and are being met.[48] According to Winston Churchill, H. G. Wells gave the British military "the idea of using aeroplanes and tanks in combat ahead of World War One."[49] In the same vein, Stephen Hawking observed: "Science fiction like *Star Trek* helps inspire the imagination."[50] The spaceship Enterprise is not only superficially connected to the NASA shuttle of

---

44 Benjamin, Walter: *The Arcades Project*, Cambridge, Mass.: Belknap Press of Harvard University Press 2002, p. 5.

45 Wells, H.G.: *Anticipations of the Reaction of Mechanical and Scientific Progress upon Human Life and Thought,* New York and London: Harper. Bros. 1902; online: http://www.gutenberg.org/ebooks/19229

46 H. G. Wells: *The Shape of Things to Come*.

47 Pound, Ezra: "The Teacher's Mission," in: *Literary Essays*, London: Faber and Faber 1954, pp. 58-63; here p. 58.

48 See later examples pp. 21-22 and p. 35.

49 Merchant, Brian: "Nike and Boeing Are Paying Sci-Fi Writers to Predict Their Futures. Welcome to the Sci-Fi industrial complex", *Medium*, Nov 28, 2018; https://onezero.medium.com/nike-and-boeing-are-paying-sci-fi-writers-to-predict-their-futures-fdc4b6165fa4

50 Krauss, Lawrence: "Foreword," in: Finn, Ed/Cramer, Kathryn (eds.): *Hieroglyph: Stories and Visions for a Better Future*, New York: William Morrow 2014 (Kindle edition), loc. 109.

the same name or the STAR TREK tricorder to Motorola's StarTac phone. Neal Stephenson, therefore, claims that good science fiction provides more than "inspiration."[51] It supplies "hieroglyphs of the future": "a plausible, fully thought-out picture of an alternate reality in which some sort of compelling innovation has taken place."[52]

In the following historical parts, I will use this concept of the hieroglyph to demonstrate how emerging utopian visions were transformed into concrete artistic representations of possible futures.

IV. UTOPIAN FUTURES IN THE PRE-INDUSTRIAL AGES

Those who sought better times prior to the Christian Middle Ages usually looked backward. "Most human cultures did not believe in progress. They thought the golden age was in the past, and that the world was stagnant, if not deteriorating."[53] In the culture of ancient Egypt, Henri Frankfort noticed "the emptiness of its views of its future."[54] In Greek antiquity and later in Roman antiquity, the myth of the metal ages dominated, as codified first by the Greek poet Hesiod and then by the Roman poet Ovid. According to their writings, the path of humanity through time led inescapably downwards: from gold, silver, and bronze to iron, Hesiod's and Ovid's own age.[55]

The Christian doctrine of salvation then exchanged the lost Golden Age for the expulsion from the Garden of Eden. Better times, i.e., salvation waited only in the afterlife. Crucial for an understanding of the non-utopian attitude of the Middle Ages is the fact that its people did not think of themselves as living in a middle age—this perspective is modern. They firmly believed that

---

51 Stephenson, Neal: "Innovation Starvation," *Wired*, October 27, 2011; https://www.wired.com/2011/10/stephenson-innovation-starvation/: "The Inspiration Theory. SF inspires people to choose science and engineering as careers. This much is undoubtedly true, and somewhat obvious."
52 Ibid.
53 Y. N. Harari: *Sapiens*, p. 264.
54 R. L. Heilbroner: *Visions of the Future*, loc. 238.
55 Ibid., loc. 247.

their time was the final stage of the world, the Last Days.[56] Consequently, they were more drawn to dystopian than to utopian thinking. "The most common form of utopian writing during this period were apocalypses, which foresaw an imminent cataclysm in which God would destroy the wicked and raise the righteous for a life in a messianic kingdom."[57]

Around 1500, however, a more secular and—anachronistically speaking—almost utopian vision emerged in Northern Italy: the notion of a possible rebirth of ancient culture. *La rinascita*, the Renaissance, marks the beginning of modern times.[58] An early result was the scientific revolution. Yuval Noah Harari calls it history's "most momentous choice, changing not only the fate of humankind but arguably the fate of all life on earth."[59] Scientific insights, especially the discovery of two new worlds, instantaneously altered the horizon of Western humanity. The confrontation with the Americas, unknown to the scriptures as well as to cartographers of antiquity, popularized awareness that the earth offered completely unknown possibilities. The almost simultaneous realization of our planet's position in the solar system shifted the entire human race from the center of the universe to its periphery. Both shocks to the traditional Christian view initiated a gradual process of secularization of thought. In the course of a quarter of a millennium, it was to culminate in the Enlightenment.

To summarize, in pre-industrial times, the notion of a better life was based on the natural life cycle. Desire for a better life attached itself—as in antiquity—to the past, which was thought of as a better youth of humanity to which no return was possible. Or hope clung—as primarily in the Christian Middle Ages—to an afterlife in which human existence was to continue forever. Only in the early modern period did the discovery of hitherto unknown regions of the world undermine both the ancient fixation on the past and the Christian negation of the mundane. Travelogues that appeared 'incredible'

---

56 Geuenich, Dieter: "Zukunftsvorstellungen im Mittelalter. Antrittsvorlesung an der Universität Duisburg," May 30, 1989; https://duepublico.uni-duisburg-essen.de/servlets/DerivateServlet/Derivate-5183/GeuZuk.htm
57 L.T. Sargent: *Utopianism*, p. 92.
58 The term *la rinascita* ('rebirth') was first used in Vasari, Giorgio: *The Lives of the Most Excellent Painters, Sculptors, and Architects*, Florence: Torrentino 1550 and 1558.
59 Y. N. Harari: *Sapiens*, p. 244.

to contemporaries, such as those by Amerigo Vespucci at the beginning of the 16th century, inspired a new orientation towards the unknown and brought about the historical invention of the utopian.

V. Hieroglyphs of the Future in Pre-Industrial Cultures

In Western culture, reflections on the future and its artistic anticipations began in Greek antiquity and primarily in the medium of writing.[60] Plato's *Republic* (380 BCE), fluctuating aesthetically "somewhere between literary imagination and academic scenario,"[61] is regarded as the first essential conception of a society that is 'different' because it is more just. The next change towards utopian thinking came up in Roman antiquity with Virgil's *Eclogues* (approx. 38 BCE). In a radical turn, Virgil shifted the Golden Age from the past to the future. The advent of a better world was also no longer the product of divine powers but owed its existence to human labor. Lyman Tower Sargent writes: "Virgil's images of the simple life in Arcadia are something of a transition between the fantasy of the first tradition and the human-created utopia of the second."[62] The triumph of the Christian religion was to break off this development towards a secular future, or at least interrupt it, for more than a millennium.

The advance to utopian thinking proper, including the term's coinage, then occurred in the context of the scientific revolution and colonial conquests. Both major aspirations at the beginning of the modern era—explore and conquer—were intimately connected; theoretically as well as practically. "For modern Europeans, building an empire was a scientific project, while

---

60 The other media—painting, sculpture, theater as well as the Greek and Roman games—continued to concentrate on the representation and celebration of the past and the present and would remain more or less free of the future until the early modern age.

61 J. M. Gidley: *The Future*, loc.: 785.—The concept is said to have been oriented on Sparta, i.e., it was less utopian and more based on an existing model. See L. T. Sargent: *Utopianism*, p. 16.

62 Ibid.

setting up a scientific discipline was an imperial project."[63] Consequently, colonial expeditions used to include scientists. The Italian cartographer, Amerigo Vespucci, gives a prominent example. Around 1500, he accompanied several Spanish and Portuguese expeditions to the New World[64] and published travelogues between 1504 and 1507, which occupied the imagination of the educated. The success of these publications had two significant consequences. First, the recently discovered New World was named after Amerigo Vespucci—America. Second, Vespucci's travelogues inspired the British philosopher and politician Thomas More to write a travelogue of his own.

In 1516, *Libellus vere aureus, nec minus salutaris quam festivus, de optimo rei publicae statu deque nova insula Utopia* was published.[65] More's travelogue was fictitious, of course. However, he tried to make the existence of the island Utopia more believable by using several literary devices. For one, he wrote himself, the well-known Thomas More, into the story. He also framed the invented narrative with actual correspondence with existing contemporaries. Third, he gave his hero Raphael Hythloday a 'credible' biography: Hythloday was supposedly one of the men who accompanied Vespucci to the New World. Venturing a little further into the South Atlantic than Vespucci, he had discovered the island of Utopia. At the same time, More counteracts these factional strategies of authentication with satirical elements. One has to doubt, for example, Hythloday's description of Utopia as a socialist paradise for the mere reason that the Greek surname of the narrator means "expert of nonsense." In the end, even the prototype of the new utopian genre keeps its readers in the dark as to whether the 'perfect equality' in the society portrayed is indeed desirable or not somewhat dystopian.[66]

---

63 Y. N. Harari: *Sapiens,* p. 297.

64 Two to four; the exact number is in dispute.

65 More, Thomas: *Libellus vere aureus, nec minus salutaris quam festivus, de optimo rei publicae statu deque nova insula Utopia,* Louvain, Habsburg Netherlands 1516.—The Latin title translates to "A truly golden little book, no less beneficial than entertaining, of a republic's best state and of the new island Utopia."

66 The ambivalence that characterizes utopian writings from the outset seems important for the further development of the genre—that one's great desire is another's great fear.

It was to be a century before More's prototype found successors. Then, however, a series of utopian writings began. The most influential include Tommaso Campanella's *The City of the Sun*,[67] Johannes Valentinus Andreae's *Description of the Republic of Christianopolis*,[68] and Francis Bacon's *The New Atlantis*.[69] These early utopias are characterized by the fact that they focus on isolated and manageable venues: islands and city-states. For the first time, the ideal life is not in another age but another place.[70] The connection with the contemporary discovery and conquest of the New World seems evident. Better or perfect societies do not have to be created; they already exist and have for quite some time. However, just like the wonders of the Americas, these utopian places have to be discovered.

Equally evident seems the close relation of the emerging utopian thought to the historical process of secularization. While the authors of the early utopias stay firmly attached to the Christian faith system, their writings at the same time tend to secularize central elements of the religious belief in paradise. The better life, which is supposed to wait in the afterlife, can now be found in this world. A dialectical relationship to the Christian doctrine of salvation will remain constitutive even for the secular utopian designs of the coming centuries. The longing for utopia persists as both a result of but also a reaction to secularization. "Utopianism is often read as the desire to overcome original sin and re-enter Eden, or, with sin gone, create a new utopia."[71]

In summary, two characteristics of the utopian thinking that developed in the early modern period can be identified. First, the good places that in antiquity and the Middle Ages had been considered lost in time—the Golden Age, the Garden of Eden from which humankind was expelled—were relocated from the past to the present and became remote islands or cities waiting to be discovered.[72] While the first characteristic shows itself in comparison

---

67 Campanella, Tommaso: *The City of Sun*, written in 1602 in Italian, published in Latin, Frankfurt 1623.
68 Andreae, Johannes Valentinus: *Description of the Republic of Christianopolis*, Strasburg: Lazarus Zetzner 1619.
69 Bacon, Francis: *The New Atlantis*, published posthumously, London 1627.
70 See for this and the following J. M Gidley, *The Future*, loc. 1,035.
71 L. T. Sargent: *Utopianism*, p. 88.
72 With the development of these new ideas, the old ones of course did not disappear. Both coexist until today. See for example: "W. H. Auden, in a once famous essay,

to the past, the significance of the second reveals itself primarily in contrast to the dominant utopian visions of the following periods. In this first phase of utopian thought, between the Renaissance and Enlightenment, visions of the future were concentrating on radically new ways of organizing society, that is on the making of a better life through the improvement of moral rules and political laws. Later, in the process of enlightenment and industrialization, the focus of utopian desire would shift—from morals and politics to technological innovations and their cultural consequences.

However, this change in emphasis did not come out of nowhere. The utopian interest in technology was annunciated hieroglyphically. Particularly widespread were speculations about future means of transport. Already in the mid-13th century, Roger Bacon envisioned helicopters, just like Leonardo da Vinci in the late 15th century. In the early 17th century, Tommaso Campanella foresaw "vessels able to navigate without wind and without sails,"[73] and a few years later Francis Godwin imagined a voyage to the moon employing a flock of wild swans.[74] In the 18th century, these developments resulted in innovative literary approaches to telling stories of better futures, such as the epistolary novel *The Memoirs of the Twentieth Century* written by Samuel Madden in 1733.[75] "In French, the new genre was called 'roman de l'avenir', in English 'the tale of futurity', and in German, 'Zukunftsroman'."[76]

---

divided all imaginative people into Utopians and Arcadians—makers of the New Jerusalem we want, or seekers of the lost Eden we've been expelled from." (Gopnik, Adam: "What Can We Learn from Utopians of the Past?" *The New Yorker*, July 23, 2018; https://www.newyorker.com/magazine/2018/07/30/what-can-we-learn-from-utopians-of-the-past).—Gopnik is referring to "Dingley Dell & the Fleet," published in W. H. Auden's collection *The Dyer's Hand and Other Essays*, London: Faber & Faber 1962, pp. 407-428; online: https://archive.org/stream/in.ernet.dli.2015.16420/2015.16420.The-Dyers-Hand-And-Other-Essays_djvu.txt

73 N. N.: "Tommaso Campanella," *Stanford Encyclopedia of Philosophy*, Aug 25, 2014; https://plato.stanford.edu/entries/campanella/
74 Godwin, Francis: *The Man in the Moone*, published posthumously, London: John Norton 1638.
75 Madden, Samuel: *The Memoirs of the Twentieth Century*, London: Osborn and Longman, Davis and Batley 1733.
76 J. M. Gidley: *The Future*, loc. 1,111.

VI. Utopian Futures in the Industrial Age

During the Enlightenment, the future became a particular concern. The ostensible reason was profound political change. The old monarchic order, which had been thought to be God-given and eternal, began to crumble. Unknown historical horizons opened up. However, the political revolutions manifesting the search for new orders—the American Revolution (1765-1783) and the French Revolution (1789-1799)—were only the tip of the iceberg. Under the surface of visible changes, fundamental shifts in the tectonics of civilization took place. Walter Benjamin famously described the unprecedented upheaval as an unforeseen climate change that puts the "Angel of History" into distress:

> "[A] storm is blowing from Paradise; it has got caught in his wings with such violence that the angel can no longer close them. The storm irresistibly propels him into the future to which his back is turned, while the pile of debris before him grows skyward. This storm is what we call progress."[77]

This storm of progress, writes Robert L. Heilbroner, was raised by the combined effect of three forces "that had previously existed only in embryo or on the fringes of society."[78] One is the rational investigation of the world, established two hundred years earlier in the scientific revolution, which had since produced groundbreaking insights in the natural sciences and the humanities. The second is "the appearance of an idea utterly absent from all the civilizations [...], namely the legitimacy of the will of the people as the source of their own collective direction."[79] The third, and arguably most influential, force is the emergence of a new economic system reorganizing the production and distribution of material goods. Karl Marx would soon analyze, understand, and criticize its mechanisms. Heilbroner concludes: "Taken together the three forces [i.e., science, democracy, and capitalism] formed

---

77 Benjamin, Walter: "Theses on the Philosophy of History," in: *Illuminations*, New York: Schocken Books, 1969, p. 249.
78 R. L. Heilbroner: *Visions of the Future*, loc. 527.
79 Ibid., loc. 1,247.

the basis of an utterly new conception of the future as embodying Progress."[80]

The fuel feeding the escalating speed of progress was, of course, economic growth; a steady expansion of production and consumption like no civilization before had experienced.[81] Until then, greater prosperity could only be achieved through geographical and social redistribution—war and conquest, slavery, colonization, spoliation, expropriation. With industrialization, the millennia-old economic stasis ended. It is true that the evolving capitalistic order, specifically the reign of the market and the unfamiliar phenomenon of seemingly limitless growth, left many contemporaries uneasy. But already in the late 18th century, the view became popular that economic advances were to be accompanied by a steady improvement in human living conditions.[82] Thus, as a consequence of growth, a gradual cultural re-evaluation of the past commenced. Its idolization, the longing for the Golden Age or the admiring imitation of antiquity, gave way to the understanding that the present was in many respects better than former times; an insight which in turn led to the assumption that the future should be even better than the present.

This cultural reassessment had two effects. First, the future became the preferred vanishing point of utopian hopes. "At the end of the eighteenth century, a significant shift from space to time took place in utopian writing. The typical setting of the ideal society (or its opposite, dystopia) radically changed from a different place at the same time to the same place at a different time."[83] Second, since the future was now the central field for utopian action, various efforts started to foresee and plan progress.

The first attempts were made by leaders of the totalitarian systems rising in Europe after the turn of the 20th century. They aimed to conquer and subjugate the new frontier of the future. Like Karl Marx and Friedrich Engels, who mocked the utopian socialists of their time, Vladimir Ilyich Lenin was decidedly anti-utopian. "In politics utopia is a wish that can never come

---

80 Ibid., loc. 1,252.
81 Y. N. Harari: *Sapiens*, p. 304ff.
82 N. Montfort: *The Future*, p. 28.
83 J. M. Gidley: *The Future*, loc. 801. Gidley summarizes findings of the sociologist Wendell Bell.—I will discuss this 'temporal turn' of utopian visions in the following section.

true," he wrote in 1912. Consequently, the Bolshevists, once they had consolidated their dictatorial regime, undertook to predetermine the economic future of the Soviet Union through a series of five-year plans.[84] In the same way, the German National Socialists insisted that party and state should control all future progress. Their first four-year plan came into force in 1933, the year Adolf Hitler seized power.

Scientific approaches to investigate the future took more time to come to fruition. Already in 1902, H. G. Wells gave a lecture at the Royal Institution of Great Britain on "The Discovery of the Future."[85] His suggestions, however, were so inconsequential that he could complain thirty years later, as Gidley summarizes, "that although there were thousands of professors of history, there was not a single professor of fore-sight in the world."[86] Only after the Second World War, the gradual establishment of scientific research into the future began. Its main objective was to better understand the mechanisms of progress in the interest of forecasting and long-term planning in the context of democratic politics. Robert Jungk,[87] Ossip K. Flechtheim,[88] Herman Kahn,[89] and Alvin Toffler[90] were among the pioneers of Future Studies. Today, the comparatively young transdisciplinary academic field is "combining education, philosophy, sociology, history, psychology, and economic theory with real-life observation."[91] As the three central methods, J. M. Gidley

---

84 The scriptwriters of NINOTSCHKA (USA 1939, D: Ernst Lubitsch), Charles Brackett, Billy Wilder, and Walter Reisch, found prophetic words for the success of this effort: "Comrade. I've been fascinated by your Five-Year Plan for the last fifteen years."

85 Wells, H. G.: *The Discovery of the Future: A Discourse Delivered to the Royal Institution on January 24, 1902*, London: T. Fisher Unwin 1902; online: http://www.gutenberg.org/ebooks/44867

86 J. M. Gidley: *The Future*, loc. 713.

87 R. Jungk: *Tomorrow Is Already Here*.

88 Flechtheim, Ossip K.: "Teaching the Future," *Journal for Higher Education*, 16 (1945), p. 460-65.

89 Kahn, Herman/Wiener, Anthony J.: *The Year 2000. A Framework for Speculation on the Next Thirty-Three Years*, New York: MacMillan 1967.

90 Toffler, Alvin: *Future Shock*, New York: Random House 1970.

91 J. M Gidley: *The Future*, loc. 743.

identifies "the extrapolation of historical experience, the utilization of analytical models, and the use of experts as forecasters."[92]

All forecasting, though, is inherently flawed as every prediction about systems with human actors inevitably changes the process it tries to anticipate. In this regard forecasts of natural processes—weather, earthquakes—differ from, for example, economic forecasts. While nature does not take note of prognoses, market participants do. Exposed to forecasts, they change their behavior accordingly. This is probably one of the reasons why, at least in the long term and in retrospect, the predictive qualities of works of art and entertainment have so far been superior to scientific forecasts: because aesthetic works do not predict the future in plain text, with statistical evidence, and explanatory charts, but in hieroglyphic form, with multifaceted designed worlds, ambivalent characters, and ambiguous actions, all of which must be deciphered before anybody can act upon them.

To summarize, in the 18th century, the Age of Enlightenment and during the transition to an industrial society, political and social, technical and economic development accelerated to such an extent that, for the first time, change could be experienced within individual lifespans. The combination of scientific, political, and economic progress allowed contemporaries to recognize the present improvements over the past. Thus, the belief emerged that life was getting consistently better and, in consequence, the future was the time when utopian desires would be fulfilled.

VII. Hieroglyphs of the Future in Industrial Culture: Literature

In the industrial age, artistic engagement with the future started to differ from earlier times in that it was no longer confined to the medium of print. As early as the 19th century, efforts were made to move beyond theoretical conception and literary description and create a more sensorially perceptible future. World Expositions were the most spectacular vehicle because they combined many media—architecture, model building, graphics, sculpture, theater, music, literature—to create an integrated experience. Later, in the 20th century, technological developments and the needs of the industrial masses

---

92 Ibid., loc. 1317.

led to the successful introduction of new media, in particular silent and sound film, radio and television. They all came to contribute to the increasing popular exploration of the future.

In the early 19th century, however, visions of the future were still more or less limited to the spoken and printed word. At first, two works became extraordinarily influential that do not fall into the literary genre of utopia: Mary Shelley's novel *Frankenstein; or, The Modern Prometheus*,[93] published in 1818, and the *Manifesto of the Communist Party*[94] that Friedrich Engels and Karl Marx published in 1848. In hindsight, though, Shelley's novel was a precursor of the science fiction genre, which a few decades later would at least partially inherit utopia, and the *Manifesto* by now "is regarded by many as one of the most influential utopian visions in human history."[95]

Literary utopias exploring the future potential of the nascent industrial society were only to appear in the second half of the 19th century, but then in high numbers. Among the most influential are Samuel Butler's *Erewhon: Or, Over the Range*,[96] Edward Bellamy's *Looking Backward 2000-1887*[97] and William Morris' *News from Nowhere*.[98] The three novels are representative of the main variants of utopian writing in the last third of the 19th century. Butler's vision was traditionalist. He still stuck to the pre-industrial model established by More. Erewhon—an anagram of 'Nowhere'—is introduced as a newly discovered distant country. Butler compares its society satirically

---

93 Shelley, Mary: *Frankenstein; or, The Modern Prometheus*, London: Lackington, Hughes, Harding, Mavor & Jones 1818; online: http://www.gutenberg.org/files/84/84-h/84-h.htm

94 Engels, Friedrich/Marx, Karl: *Manifest der kommunistischen Partei*: Office der Bildungs-Gesellschaft für Arbeiter: London 1848; online: http://www.gutenberg.org/cache/epub/61/pg61.html

95 J. M Gidley: *The Future*, loc. 1,156.

96 Butler, Samuel: *Erewhon: Or, Over the Range*, London: Trübner and Co., 1872; online: http://www.gutenberg.org/ebooks/1906

97 Bellamy, Edward: *Looking Backward 2000-1887*, Boston: Ticknor & Co 1888; online: https://archive.org/details/lookingbackward200bell

98 Moris, William: *News from Nowhere; or An Epoch of Rest, Being Some Chapters from a Utopian Romance*, Boston: Roberts Brothers 1890; online: http://www.gutenberg.org/ebooks/3261

with Victorian England. At first glance, Erewhon seems utopian, but at second look things become more ambivalent.

Bellamy and Morris were more daring. Their utopian societies are no longer located in the present but in the future. Since Morris' novel was written as a direct response to Bellamy's, the initial situation is similar: both heroes and narrators fall into a deep sleep in the present and wake up in future socialist societies. The two varieties of socialism, however, could not be more different. Bellamy's utopia is the ideal of a coldhearted technocrat. His Boston of the year 2000 is highly developed. Capitalism has been overcome, private ownership of means of production is abolished. A strong centralized state determines the lives of its citizens. Work is strictly regimented and structured according to the requirements of large-scale industrial technology. In return, citizens enjoy free consumption, and their working life ends at the age of 45.[99]

For Morris, who reviewed Bellamy's book, state socialism was not utopia. Quite the opposite, in fact. Associated with the British Arts and Crafts Movement, Morris sought to combine romantic and aesthetic ideals. The socialism his hero experiences in the British future when he wakes up has overcome not only capitalism but also industrialization. Money has disappeared, as have factories and large cities. People's everyday lives are marked by the absence of the alienating division of labor, including the separation of work and private life. In Morris' utopia, people are happy not because they work less but because they work voluntarily and self-determined.

While Bellamy designed an advanced technocratic industrial socialism, Morris imagined a romantic agrarian socialism. From today's perspective, these utopias are blending progressive and retrograde, democratic and authoritarian, liberating, and oppressive elements. In his review of Michael Robertson's, *The Last Utopians: Four Late Nineteenth-Century Visionaries*

---

99 Bellamy's book was not only a sensational literary success, selling hundreds of thousands of copies. It also initiated a political movement. In the United States, hundreds of "Bellamy Clubs" were founded, advocating the nationalization of the means of production, and also some utopian communities, whose members tried to live according to the rules of the novel.

and Their Legacy,[100] Adam Gopnik summarizes the conflicting ideological situation at the end of the 19th century:

"The utopian feminists are also eugenicists and anti-Semites; the men who dream of a perfect world where same-sex attraction is privileged also unconsciously mimic the hierarchy of patriarchy, putting effeminate or cross-dressing 'Uranians' at the bottom of their ladder. The socialists are also sexists, and the far-seeing anarchists are also muddle-headed, mixed-up mystics."[101]

However, by then the time of utopian novels was running out, as the title of Robertson's study indicates. A new variant of writing about a better future developed: science fiction. Although the term science fiction did not come into use until the 1920s, the rise of the new genre began already in the second half of the 19th century.[102] Its pioneer was Jules Verne who published, amongst others, *From the Earth to the Moon* in 1865,[103] and *Twenty Thousand Leagues Under the Sea* in 1869.[104] Around the turn of the 20th century, H. G. Wells distinguished himself as the most influential author in this field, not least because he wrote not only science fiction but also dystopian novels and non-fiction books about the future. His most influential contributions to science fiction were *The Time Machine* in 1895,[105] *The Island of Doctor Moreau* in 1896,[106] and *The War of the Worlds* in 1898.[107]

From a present-day perspective, many of the early works of science fiction stand out for their unusually high ability to anticipate future developments, especially technical inventions. Jules Verne alone described hieroglyphically dozens of later inventions, including air conditioning, television,

---

100 Robertson, Michael: *The Last Utopians: Four Late Nineteenth-Century Visionaries and Their Legacy*, Princeton: Princeton University Press 2018.
101 A. Gopnik: "What We can Learn from the Utopians of the Past."
102 J. M. Gidley: *The Future*, loc. 1,171.
103 Verne, Jules: *De la terre à la lune*, Paris: Hetzel 1865; English title: *From the Earth to the Moon*, first translation into English 1867.
104 Verne, Jules: *Vingt mille lieues sous les mers*, Paris: Hetzel 1870; English title: *Twenty Thousand Leagues Under the Sea*, first translation into English 1872.
105 Wells, H. G.: *The Time Machine*, London: William Heinemann 1895.
106 Wells, H. G.: *The Island of Doctor Moreau*, London: William Heinemann 1896.
107 Wells, H. G.: *The War of the Worlds*, London: William Heinemann 1898.

space travel, automobiles, and submarines.[108] The best science fiction writers who followed Verne were no less visionary. H. G. Wells foresaw nuclear power and nuclear war, Arthur C. Clarke conceived of geostationary satellites, Isaac Asimov wrote of robots, driverless cars, wall screens, and satellite phones, Robert Heinlein of rocket ships and waterbeds, William Gibson of global cyberspace which we have at least started to construct.

The gradual, more than a century-long, implementation of science fiction as a literary genre, its path from the margins of early industrial culture to the center of digital culture, was substantially fostered by the fact that the anticipation of scientific-technical progress expanded from the medium of writing—novels, non-fiction, magazines, and newspapers—into other media.

World fairs and world expositions initiated this process of multi- and transmedialization already at a time when print still dominated the conception of the future. Since the late 18th century and up to the present, more than half a thousand such events have taken place all around the world, more than 110 alone between 1890 and 1910.[109] Their history documents "how the future has been envisioned and how future visions have been shared with the public."[110] The heyday of these exhibitions lay between the "Great Exhibition of the Works of Industry of All Nations," held in London in 1851 and attended by over six million people, and the "New York World's Fair," held 1939 to 1940 and visited by 44 million people. Its theme was "The World of Tomorrow." The main attraction was a ride into the automotive world to come, commissioned by General Motors and realized by the industrial designer Norman del Geddes who was also a renowned theatrical set designer.

---

108 The engineer Simon Lake read Verne's *Twenty Thousand Leagues Under the Sea* when he was eleven years old and went on to construct the first American submarines. He starts the second chapter of his autobiography with the statement: "Jules Verne was in a sense the director-general of my life." (Lake, Simon/Corey, Herbert: *Submarine. The Autobiography of Simon Lake*, New York and London: D. Appleton Century Company 1930, p. 10; online: http://www.submarineboat.com/files/Submarine%20The%20Autobiography%20of%20Simon%20Lak e.pdf)

109 See https://en.wikipedia.org/wiki/List_of_world%27s_fairs

110 N. Montfort: *The Future*, p. 59.

Called "Futurama," the ride transported its visitors—552 people at a time, 28 000 per day[111]—twenty years ahead

"over a huge diorama of a fictional section of the United States that was designed with a stunning array of miniature highways, towns, 500,000 individually designed homes, 50,000 miniature vehicles, waterways, and a million miniature trees of diverse species. These elements of the diorama gradually became larger as the visitors, seated in chairs overhead, moved through the exhibit, until the cars and other elements of the exhibit became life-size."[112]

The accuracy of the prediction of how everyday life would change under the influence of mass motorization remains astonishing to this day. In the 1960s, the United States was to be traversed by exactly the new highways and freeways the Diorama envisioned. Also, in "a convergence of different sorts of future-making, the First World Science Fiction Convention was held at the fair."[113] By then, however, science fiction had long since ceased to be limited to printed matter.[114] Apart from world exhibitions, several other new media popularized the genre beyond literature, though mainly through literary adaptations.

---

111 Fotsch, Paul Mason: "The Building of a Superhighway Future at the New York World's Fair," *Cultural Critique 48*, Spring 2001, pp. 65–97.—The numbers Fotsch provides are taken from a contemporary *Business Week* report.
112 Wikipedia entry "1939 New York World's Fair," https://en.wikipedia.org/wiki/1939_New_York_World%27s_Fair#cite_note-17.—The entry refers to Herman, Arthur: *Freedom's Forge: How American Business Produced Victory in World War II*, pp. 58-65, 338, 343, New York: Random House 2012.—See also General Motor's promotional film about the Futurama TO NEW HORIZONS (USA 1940: O: General Motors); https://publicdomainreview.org/collections/to-new-horizons-1940/
113 N. Montfort: *The Future*, p. 64.
114 The new and popular medium of comics was presented prominently: The exposition offered a *Flash Gordon* Ride using filmed images and vibrating seats, which transported 150 people by rocket to another planet; see https://en.wikipedia.org/wiki/Flash_Gordon#1939_World's_Fair

VIII. Hieroglyphs of the Future in Industrial Culture: New Media

The history of fictional film begins, to a certain extent, with a science fiction film, Georges Méliès' A TRIP TO THE MOON (1902), which makes use of works by two of the most important contemporary authors of that genre: Jules Verne and H. G. Wells. A series of Verne and Wells adaptations, mostly shorts as well, followed in the years up to the First World War. In the 1920s, Fritz Lang directed two groundbreaking feature-length science fiction movies. Both were based on novels, however, presented highly contrasting futures. METROPOLIS (1927) displays a dystopic, highly industrialized and urbanized world with gaping social divides between classes. Two years later, WOMAN IN THE MOON (1929) sketches the future of space travel, anticipating numerous elements that forty years later will actually mark the first flights to the moon.[115]

Comics and radio were two other new media contributing to the popularization of science fiction in the early 20th century. While comics about the technological future appeared since the turn of the century, the period of high growth started in the late 1920s. The first *Buck Rogers* issues came out in 1929, followed by *Flash Gordon* in 1934 and *Superman* in 1938. Radio adaptations were produced only a few years later, with the adaptations of the *Buck Rogers* series, which began in 1932, considered the first science fiction shows on American radio. Radio also adapted many classics of the genre. Orson Welles' 1938 version of H. G. Wells' *The War of Worlds* gained particular notoriety, as the factional 'live broadcast' of the landing of Martians allegedly caused panic among many listeners.[116]

Since the mid-20th century, television became another major source of science fiction entertainment. First, early television served as a kind of cinema museum, broadcasting the classics of film history in ever new reruns, including Hollywood's successful serial adaptations of the *Buck Rogers* and *Flash Gordon* comic series.[117] Second, television soon produced its own

---

115 See below pp. 38-39.
116 For audience reaction see headline *The New York Times*, October 31, 1938: "Radio Listeners in Panic, Taking War Drama as Fact"; see facsimile http://en.wikipedia.org/wiki/Image:WOTW-NYT-headline.jpg
117 BUCK ROGERS (1939, 12 episodes); FLASH GORDON (1936, 13 episodes).

science fiction, including the highly influential STAR TREK (1966-69) franchise from the mid-1960s onwards.[118] Particularly film and television reinforced science fiction's influence on the practical design of the future. The makers of STAR TREK, for example, anticipated not only today's smartphones, tablet PCs, and noninvasive surgery. In the last third of the 20th century, they also inspired young people to realize these imagined innovations.[119]

An even clearer example can be found in the production and reception of DIE FRAU IM MOND. Fritz Lang hired Hermann Oberth, one of the three most important space pioneers of the early 20th century, as a consultant for his film.[120] Like his two competitors, the Russian Konstantin Tsiolkovsky and the American Robert Goddard, Oberth had come to space travel in his youth by reading science fiction novels. Like Tsiolkovsky but independent of him, Oberth had developed the idea of chemical propellants and multistage rocketry. Oberth not only advised Lang on the cinematic design of the moon ride, specifically the design of the rocket and astronaut's capsule. He also proposed to construct his first real multistage rocket and launch it as a marketing tool for the film's launch. While Lang's movie rocket started successfully to the moon—after the first countdown in history—, Oberth's real rocket failed. Nevertheless, it would have a significant historical impact. Members of the civilian German "Verein für Raumschifffahrt" (Society for Space Travel), among them the young engineer Wernher von Braun, got their hands on Oberth's left-over materials and used them to construct a new rocket called Mirak (short for "Minimum Rakete," i.e., minimum rocket).

"In August 1932, a Mirak demonstration helped convince the German Army that rockets could be practical weapons, and when Hitler became Germany's chancellor five months later, the Society for Space Travel was ordered to cease all experiments.

---

118 This original series was followed so far by an animated series, several feature films, and five more TV series.
119 See HOW WILLIAM SHATNER CHANGED THE WORLD (2005).
120 See for the following Benson, Michael: "Science Fiction Sent Man to the Moon," *The New York Times*, July 20, 2019; https://www.nytimes.com/2019/07/20/opinion/sunday/moon-rockets-space-fiction.html

Screenings of WOMAN IN THE MOON were banned, with all prints impounded. The film simply gave too much away."[121]

The rest is war and space history: the Mirak was developed into the so-called "Wunderwaffe," i.e., "miracle weapon" V2 that killed 8,000 to 12,000 British and Belgian civilians while another 12 000 forced laborers died producing it in Germany.[122] SS officer Wernher von Braun, who was in charge of developing and implementing V2, became the man who finally led, in 1969, the United States to the moon. In the process, NASA adopted the countdown that Fritz Lang's film had invented to increase suspense.[123] Rightfully, Science Fiction writer Michael Solanas asks: "Has there been any major technological advancement that wasn't dreamt up first in man's imagination?"[124]

In summary, three changes mark the artistic engagement with utopian hopes in the industrial age. First, designs of better life shifted from faraway places to faraway times. The future became the core action space for the narrative expression of utopian desires. Second, the designs of utopian changes were no longer limited to printed matter. In the 20th century, ideas of a better life were expressed in many media, especially the new industrial media of film and television. Third, the new genre of science fiction began to compete successfully with the established genre of utopia. The focus shifted from questions of morality and better political organization of a static society to the aspect of technological improvement, which is now understood as the central basis of new, better ways of life in societies subject to rapid progress.

---

121 Ibid.

122 Leicht, Johannes: "'Die Wunderwaffen' V1 und V2," *Deutsches Historisches Museum*, Berlin, May 19, 2015; https://www.dhm.de/lemo/kapitel/der-zweite-weltkrieg/kriegsverlauf/die-wunderwaffen-v1-und-v2.html

123 See M. Benson, "Science Fiction Sent Man to the Moon": "As for Oberth's six-foot-long liquid-fueled rocket, developed in 1929 from the budget of Fritz Lang's WOMAN IN THE MOON, it served as a kind of acorn to the 363-foot-tall Saturn 5, directly linking the first big-budget science fiction film to depict a lunar voyage to the actual landing four decades later."—It should be noted that director Fritz Lang refused to work for the Nazi film industry and fled the country. He went on to have a distinguished Hollywood career.

124 M. Solana: "Stop Writing Dystopian Sci-Fi."

While in popular culture science fiction literature almost supplanted the genre of classical utopia, in high literature and culture a modification of this form prevailed: dystopias.[125] Their establishment began with the horrors of the First World War, which demonstrated to humanity the worst of technological progress. Yevgeny Ivanovich Zamyatin's *We* is regarded as the prototype, anticipating many themes of later dystopias. Written in Russian in 1921 and banned in the Soviet Union, the novel was published three years later in English.[126] It depicts a high-tech police state based on mass surveillance. In *We*'s distant future, numbers have replaced names, and every individuality is suppressed. The closeness of the two most significant dystopias of the 20th century—Aldous Huxley's *Brave New World* and George Orwell's *Nineteen Eighty-Four*[127]—to this forerunner is evident; even though both novels describe futures that are even more different than Bellamy's and Morris' once were.

Huxley wrote *Brave New World* in 1931, at the height of the economic depression. Located in the year 2540, the novel evokes the dangers of advanced technology and the liberal capitalist consumer society whose contours emerged in the 1920s and early 1930s. Orwell wrote his novel after the end of World War II. *Nineteen Eighty-Four* portrays possible further developments of the repressive mechanisms introduced by the totalitarian states of the 1930s and 1940s, in particular, Stalin's Soviet Union and Hitler's Germany. Neil Postman summed up the difference between both dystopias: "In short, Orwell feared that what we hate will ruin us. Huxley feared that what we love will ruin us."[128]

In retrospect, we can see that in the dystopias of the first half of the 20th century a change in Western consciousness loomed—an anti-progressive

---

125 See Shiau, Yvonne: "The Rise of Dystopian Fiction: From Soviet Dissidents to 70's Paranoia to Murakami," *Electric Literature*, July 26, 2017, https://electricliterature.com/the-rise-of-dystopian-fiction-from-soviet-dissidents-to-70s-paranoia-to-murakami/

126 Zamyatin, Yevgeny Ivanovich: *We,* New York: E. P. Dutton, 1924.

127 Huxley, Aldous: *Brave New World*, London: Chatto & Windus 1932; Orwell, George: *Nineteen Eighty-Four*, London: Secker & Warburg 1949.

128 Postman, Neil: *Amusing Ourselves to Death: Public Discourse in the Age of Show Business*, New York: Viking 1985, p. xiii.

shift from optimism to pessimism—that with the decline of industrial civilization would soon take hold in the culture and specifically in science fiction.

IX. UTOPIAN FUTURES IN THE DIGITAL AGE

The last decade marks a crisis of the future as we knew it. Critics and science fiction writers have noticed and lamented it. In 2013, Graeme McMillan wrote in *Time Magazine*: "Science fiction seems to have become stuck in a rut of hopelessness."[129] A year later, cultural critic Mark Fischer noticed "the slow cancellation of the future."[130] In 2017, William Gibson remarked that "we are in a historic phase in which we are losing the future per se. Like people in the Middle Ages."[131] The same year, the American band Dead Cross released a song titled "The Future Has Been Canceled," and the European band Palais Ideal released an album of the same title.[132] In 2018, science fiction writer Tom Hillenbrand observed that "when we talk or think about the future, dystopia seems to have become the standard."[133] And Maria Far-

---

129 McMillan, Graeme: "Where Are Our Bright Science-Fiction Futures?" *Time*, March 29, 2013; http://entertainment.time.com/2013/03/29/where-are-our-bright-science-fiction-futures/

130 Fisher, Mark: *The Ghosts of My Life*, London: Zero Books 2014; the first chapter is titled "The Slow Cancellation of the Future."

131 Cited after: J. Wegner. "William Gibson: 'Ich hoffe, wir sind nicht in negativen Utopien gefangen.'" My translation of the German original: "Wir sind jetzt aber in einer historischen Phase, in der wir die Zukunft an sich verlieren. Wie die Menschen im Mittelalter."

132 Dead Cross: "The Future Has Been Canceled," *Dead Cross* (USA 2017, Label: Ipepac); Palais Ideal: *The Future Has Been Canceled* (Netherlands 2017, Label: Dark Vinyl Records).

133 Hillenbrand, Tom: "Dystopien im Film: Science-Fiction und sein Einfluss auf unser Zukunftsdenken," *Berliner Zeitung*, October 27, 2018; https://www.berliner-zeitung.de/kultur/dystopien-im-film--science-fiction-und-sein-einfluss-auf-unser-zukunftsdenken-31478062

rell quipped in allusion to William Gibson's famous quote, "The apocalypse is already here. It's just unevenly distributed."[134]

Two factors have been suggested as the primary cause of the prevailing pessimistic view of the present and the future. First, what Neal Stephenson called "innovation starvation," a perceived slowdown or even absence of progress. In an opinion piece, aptly titled: "The Dystopic Leftist Youth of Reddit and Facebook. A Look into the Spaces Where Young People Mock the 'Boring Dystopia' that Capitalism has Built," Corin Faife describes the current stagnation:

"In the 40-year period from 1950 to 1990, consumers were introduced to the microwave oven, color television, ATM and credit card, contraceptive pill, cellphone, and personal computer, and, in 1989—the year marking the fall of the Berlin Wall—the World Wide Web itself was invented. [...] Besides the smartphone (which is ultimately a miniaturized computer plus the internet), there have been very few inventions in the nearly three decades since the fall of communism that have so fundamentally changed our lives."[135]

This sense of a historical standstill, at least of technological progress, is reinforced by the feeling of being unable to act, to change anything. Neal Stephenson calls it "a general failure of our society to get big things done."[136] Second, then, the dystopian zeitgeist is supposed to stem from a dramatic loss of agency. It seems to paralyze not only the average citizens of Western

---

134 Farrell, Maria: "How to Cope with the End of the World," *Medium*, June 7, 2018; https://medium.com/s/how-to-cope-with-the-end-of-the-world/how-to-cope-with-the-end-of-the-world-2520ef9d3dbc

135 Faife, Corin: "The Dystopic Leftist Youth of Reddit and Facebook. A Look into the Spaces Where Young People Mock the 'Boring Dystopia' that Capitalism has Built," in: *Medium*, January 22, 2018; https://medium.com/s/darkish-web/the-dystopic-leftist-youth-of-reddit-and-facebook-cbe4e35dfd6f—See also N. Stephenson, "Innovation Starvation": "My parents and grandparents witnessed the creation of the airplane, the automobile, nuclear energy, and the computer to name only a few. Scientists and engineers who came of age during the first half of the 20th century could look forward to building things that would solve age-old problems [...]."

136 N. Stephenson: "Innovation Starvation."

democracies but also the elites. Media theorist Douglas Rushkoff reports how in the summer of 2018 he was invited by hedge fund managers to talk about the future.[137] He had to quickly realize, however, that his hosts had long since resigned themselves to the fact that the world was coming to an end. "For all their wealth and power, they don't believe they can affect the future."[138] They did not invite him to learn anything about the future; they just wanted to find out how they as individuals could survive the inevitable apocalypse. Their view of the world was, Rushkoff writes, "a reduction of human evolution to a video game that someone wins by finding the escape hatch."[139]

The paralysis, which is often triggered by dystopian world views, can of course also be observed outside the circles of the super-rich. It has become pervasive. "We are collectively losing faith in our future at the precise moment humanity as a whole needs to think decades and centuries ahead,"[140] Maria Farrell states and summarizes the consequences in her subtitle: "Thinking the Future Is a Dystopia Is Helping to Make It One."[141] Similarly, J. M. Gidley warns how young people, in particular, can be "very deeply affected by the negative images of the future portrayed in the media and dystopian movies."[142] French philosopher Pascal Bruckner analyzed the effects of the contemporary popularization of catastrophic scenarios:

"Day after day the children are accustomed to catastrophism, they are told [...] that we humans pay the price for our activities and will die out. This is how we raise fearful generations: The children are not actually mobilized but rather paralyzed."[143]

---

137 Rushkoff, Douglas: "Survival of the Richest. The Wealthy Are Plotting to Leave Us Behind," *Medium*, July 5, 2018; https://onezero.medium.com/survival-of-the-richest-9ef6cddd0cc1—For his advice Rushkoff received an enormous fee, as he reveals, more than he earns in half a year as a professor.

138 Ibid.

139 Ibid.

140 M. Farrell: "How to Cope with the End of the World."

141 Ibid.

142 J. M. Gidley: *The Future*, loc.: 2,556.

143 Bruckner, Pascal: "Klimaproteste: Alt und Jung in Unreife vereint," *Neue Zuercher Zeitung*, April 26, 2019; https://www.nzz.ch/meinung/klimaproteste-alt-und-jung-in-unreife-vereint-ld.1476994—My translation of the German original:

Likewise, writer Ilija Trojanov recently stressed "that the dream of a good world is the basis for its improvement. Without utopias, we are at the brink of hopelessness."[144]

Of course, there are also significant efforts in contemporary culture to counter the dystopian mood and attitude. Three seem to be gaining a particular tack and influence. First, the academic study of the future, which began around the middle of the 20th century and focused on theoretical analysis, is taking an artistic-practical turn. Under various buzzwords such as "design fiction"[145] and "science fiction prototyping,"[146] attempts are made to combine the previously separate approaches to forecasting in the sciences, arts, and literature.[147] Using the tools of media production for "systematic imagination"[148]—especially iterative design, world-building, and storytelling—, mixed teams of futurists, artists, and writers try "to explore different possible

---

„Tag um Tag gewöhnt man die Kinder an den Katastrophismus, man sagt ihnen, […] dass wir Menschen den Preis für unser Treiben bezahlen und aussterben werden. So ziehen wir angsterfüllte Generationen heran: Die Kinder werden nicht eigentlich mobilisiert, sondern eher gelähmt."

144 Trojanov, Ilija: "Schlagloch: Nie gut, aber besser," *taz*, April 18, 2019; https://taz.de/Kolumne-Schlagloch/!5585265/; German original: "dass der Traum von einer guten Welt die Grundlage für ihre Verbesserung bildet. Ohne Utopien droht uns die Hoffnungslosigkeit."

145 See N. Montfort: *The Future*, p. 113.—Montfort traces the origin of the term to Sterling, Bruce: *Shaping Things*. Cambridge, Mass.: MIT Press 2005.

146 Johnson, Brian David: Science Fiction Prototyping. Designing the Future with Science Fiction, San Rafael, CA.: Morgan & Claypool 2011.

147 See Bouée, Charles-Edouard: "Creating the Present by Imagining the Future: The Power of Science Fiction," *LinkedIn*, April 15, 2019; https://www.linkedin.com/pulse/creating-present-imagining-future-power-science-fiction-bouée/; Ettel, Anja, "Science Fiction: Wo deutsche Unternehmen an der Zukunft arbeiten," *Die Welt,* April 20, 2019; https://www.welt.de/wirtschaft/article192166549/Science-Fiction-Wo-deutsche-Unternehmen-an-der-Zukunft-arbeiten.html; B. Merchant: "Nike and Boeing Are Paying Sci-Fi Writers"; Nordberg, Anna: "Silicon Valley, It's Time to Hire Science Fiction Writers," *Ozy*, March 19, 2019; https://www.ozy.com/immodest-proposal/silicon-valley-its-time-to-hire-sci-fi-writers/93038

148 N. Montfort: *The Future*, p. 136.

scenarios for the future."[149] One of the pioneers of this new method of forecasting is former film production designer Alex McDowell, presently Director of the World Building Media Lab at the University of Southern California. The building of future worlds, McDowell says is not just about "prediction and trends": "We are looking for arcs of history through present to future at multiple scales that properly represent each unique world. From the past and present, we extrapolate forward to immediate, near, or far future horizons."[150]

While the academic-artistic approach confronts present stagnation—whether real or imagined—with pragmatic designs of possible better futures, two more radical concepts are outlining, when taken together, an entirely new variant of a utopia. What the twin ideas of *transhumanism* and the advent of a *singularity* are proposing is as radically different from the utopias of the industrial age as the industrial ideas of a better life once were from those of the pre-industrial ages.

The origins of the philosophy, or ideology, of transhumanism go back to the second half of the past century, to writings of biologist Julian Huxley,[151] Jesuit philosopher Pierre Teilhard de Chardin,[152] and AI pioneer Marvin Minsky,[153] among others. However, transhumanist thoughts gained popularity only in recent decades, in the context of digital culture.[154] Transhumanism shifts the focus of the utopian desire once again: The better life is no longer primarily sought by improving the moral values and political organization of society, as in the utopias of the pre-industrial modern age. Also, the better life is no longer primarily sought, as in the industrial era, by improving technologies to control external nature like in production or transport. Instead, the better life is sought by improving the natural shortcomings of humanity itself: through technical and biological self-enhancement, self-modification,

---

149 C.-E. Bouée: "Creating the Present by Imagining the Future."
150 Cited after B. Merchant: "Nike and Boeing Are Paying Sci-Fi Writers."— McDowells clients include corporations such as Nike, Ford and Boeing.
151 See Huxley, Julian: "Transhumanism," in: *New Bottles for New Wine*, London: Chatto & Windus 1957; pp 13-17.
152 Teilhard de Chardin, Pierre: *The Phenomenon of Man*, New York: Harper 1959.
153 Minsky, Marvin: *The Society of Mind*, New York: Simon and Schuster 1986.
154 For the pioneering role of Max More and the Extropy Institute in the 1990s see my book *Cyberland*, Berlin: Rowohlt 1996.

and finally, a complete upgrade of humanity to a new species with a higher life span and significantly increased intelligence.

This possible—or impossible—transformation of the species leads to the second new concept, which is about to replace the Enlightenment narrative of gradual progress: the idea of a singularity, a sudden rupture in human history.[155] The basic idea goes back to mathematician and physicist John von Neumann, who while working on the atomic bomb in Los Alamos suggested in talks with his colleague Stanislaw Ulam that we are "approaching some essential singularity in the history of the race beyond which human affairs, as we know them, could not continue."[156] The concept became more widely known half a century later through Vernor Vinge, mathematician and science fiction author, who presented it at a NASA congress in 1993.[157] The vision that regular progress is over and life on earth will experience a rupture was finally popularized by inventor Ray Kurzweil, today Google's Director of Engineering, who predicted in his 2005 bestseller *The Singularity is Near: When Humans Transcend Biology* that the singularity would occur by 2045.[158]

While it is true that the term singularity suggests that it is or will be a unique event, human understanding of the unknown requires comparison with something known. To explain the term singularity, Yuval Noah Harari speaks of the Big Bang as a comparable event in the realm of nature.[159] Kevin Kelly has even related the—possible—singularity to an earlier incident in human history: the "creation of language." He calls it "the first singularity for humans. It changed everything. Life after language was unimaginable to

---

155 For a short overview and arguments against a coming singularity see Walsh, Toby: "The Singularity May Never Be Near," *AI Magazine*, (38/3), 2017, pp. 58-62; here p. 58; https://aaai.org/ojs/index.php/aimagazine/article/view/2702

156 Ulam, Stanislaw: "Tribute to John von Neumann," *Bulletin of the American Mathematical Society* 64 (3), 1958; cited after Bostrom, Nick: *Superintelligence: Paths, Dangers, Strategies*, Oxford: Oxford University Press 2015 (Kindle edition), loc. 6,063.

157 Vinge, Vernor: "What is the Singularity?" Presentation at the VISION-21 Symposium sponsored by NASA Lewis Research Center and the Ohio Aerospace Institute, March 30-31, 1993; https://mindstalk.net/vinge/vinge-sing.html

158 R. Kurzweil: *The Singularity Is Near*.

159 Y. N. Harari: *Sapiens*, p. 411.

those on the far side before it."[160] In the case at hand, the question is whether upgraded transhumanist individuals will still be able to understand or at least communicate with unenhanced Homo sapiens.

To summarize, the first decades of the digital age are shaped by sharply conflicting perceptions of the future: on the one hand, a widespread dystopian view of stagnation and loss of agency and, on the other hand, the just as widespread utopian assumption that humanity will be facing rather sooner than later a massive evolutionary leap. Contemporary anticipations of humanity's future express this contradiction.

X. Hieroglyphs of the Future in Digital Culture

Four fundamental changes resulting from the process of technical digitization and cultural digitalization seem to be of particular importance for the artistic exploration of the future and specifically utopian visions. Together, they indicate a new role for and relevance of media. First, the basic technological innovation of digitization—the virtualization of hardware, i.e., the functional substitution of hardware by software—is creating a common signal basis. The material diversity of analog media, and in particular the heterogenous multimediality of industrial media, transforms into the homogenous transmediality of software. In this transfer, all content that used to be fixed in specific materials—on paper, canvas, celluloid—, becomes changeable ad indefinite and can be copied onto new storage media without generational loss. Objects and processes stored in the new digital transmedium are defined by their creators' as well as their users' ability to arbitrarily manipulate them.

The impact of this shift is particularly profound in film and television. Under the conditions of analog production, cameras had the ability—and imperative—to redeem reality, as Siegfried Kracauer wrote, in his seminal *Theory of Film: The Redemption of Physical Reality*.[161] Digital technology now adds the capability to post-process photographically recorded images as well

---

160 Kevin, Kelly: *What Technology Wants*, New York: Viking 2010 (Kindle edition), loc. 441.

161 Kracauer, Siegfried: *Theory of Film: The Redemption of Physical Reality*. New York: Oxford University Press 1960.

as generate seemingly photorealistic images from scratch. Under the conditions of digital production, film and television no longer have to reproduce the real. For example, still and moving images of people who are alive or once lived can be altered at will and seemingly photorealistic images of people who never lived can be created. This potential to generate photorealistic images (and corresponding sounds) without index, i.e., a direct reference to physical reality, marks the transition from photorealism to hyperrealism. The consequences for the design of future worlds—worlds that do not exist and cannot be captured by cameras—are evident.[162]

The second fundamental change results from the experience of virtualization as well: the understanding that constitutive elements of the real world that seemed purely material are actually shaped and controlled by software codes. The most dramatic example, of course, is the discovery of the DNA double helix by James Watson and Francis Crick in 1953,[163] just a few years after John von Neumann and Claude Elwood Shannon outlined the fundamentals of digital technology.[164] In the wake of Watson's and Crick's finding, the assumption gradually prevailed that humans are "an assemblage of organic algorithms."[165] As such, we are like all algorithms "not affected by the materials from which the calculator is built."[166] With the fusion of genetic research and computer science, the techno-biological manipulation of the human body (and mind) approaches that of the human gestalt in audiovisual hyperrealism. Thus, as part of the transition to digital culture, we are

---

162 In the 1990s and 2000s, however, the new digital hyperrealism primarily served the creation of spectacular apocalyptic worlds and dystopian futures.

163 Watson, James D., and F. H. C. Cricks: "A Structure for Deoxyribose Nucleic Acid," *Nature* 171, April 25, 1953, pp. 737-738; https://www.nature.com/articles/171737a0.pdf

164 Neumann, John von: "First Draft of a Report on the Edvac," University of Pennsylvania 1945. https://sites.google.com/site/michaeldgodfrey/vonneumann/vnedvac.pdf?attredirects=0&d=1; Shannon, Claude Elwood: "A Mathematical Theory of Communication," *The Bell System Technical Journal* (27/1948), July/October, pp. 379–423, 623–56; http://www.math.harvard.edu/~ctm/home/text/others/shannon/entropy/entropy.pdf

165 Harari, Yuval Noah: *Homo Deus: A Brief History of Tomorrow,* New York: Harper 2017 (Kindle edition), loc.: 5,332.

166 Ibid.

experiencing an escalating process of medialization. DNA code seems to become editable and reprogrammable, and transferrable onto different storage systems. Accordingly, quite a few scientists are predicting a "second genesis," a subsequent total rewrite of the code of life.[167]

The medialization of the biological realm points ahead to the third fundamental change. We appear to be in the process of not only altering the essence of what it means to be human but also of physical reality. With advanced technology, from augmented reality to nanotechnology, we have begun to transform the world in which we live into a medium; that is, something we can design, shape, and modify at will. In the early 20th century, at the height of industrialization, Pierre Teilhard de Chardin famously observed that by wrapping the planet with—analog—networks of transportation and communication, humanity was building something like a global nervous system.[168] Currently, this long-term process is advancing to the next level. Physical reality is turning into a hybrid of hard- and software, matter and media. Information that can be retrieved and interactively manipulated overlays the material world. As a result, the production of the future in reality is increasingly becoming indistinguishable from the production of the future in media.

The fourth fundamental change resulting from digitalization is brought about by digital games. In their analog form, mainly as games of chance, they have been linked to the future since the beginnings of Western civilization.[169] However, in contradistinction to almost all of their analog predecessors, from antiquity to postmodernity, digital games are an audiovisual medium.[170] As such, they play a pivotal role in the current simulative and hyperrealistic exploration of the future. Games owe this outstanding position to the "four prin-

---

167 See for the term and an early critique Rifkin, Jeremy: "Dazzled by the Science Biologists Who Dress up Hi-Tech Eugenics as a New Art Form are Dangerously Deluded," *The Guardian*, January 14, 2003; http://www.ekac.org/rifkin.html

168 P. Teilhard de Chardin: *The Phenomenon of Man.*—See also Cobb, Jennifer J.: "A Globe, Clothing Itself with a Brain," *Wired*, January 6, 1995; http://www.wired.com/wired/archive/3.06/teilhard_pr.html

169 "Casting lots was the way to hand over the decision to divine agency." (N. Montfort: *The Future*, p. 22.)

170 The notable exception being game shows on analog television.

cipal properties" or affordances of the digital transmedium which Janet Murray analyzed first.[171]

The first affordance is procedurality: the ability not only to describe or show systems—as literature and film do—but represent them as dynamic simulations. Since games and classical utopias both have in common that they design systems, digital games seem more suited than older media to create and convey utopian experiences.[172] Second, digital games (or at least certain genres) are employing the encyclopedic potential of the digital transmedium in the sense that they can provide considerably more information for possible retrieval than older audiovisual media. Third, unlike film and television, digital games are not primarily time-based but can offer the unique ability to freely navigate narrative spaces. Thus, as a medium, in a privileged way they shape the postmodern experience of "the displacement of time, the spatialization of the temporal."[173] Almost two decades ago, Steven Poole remarked that "a videogame is liquid architecture."[174] Henry Jenkins later argued famously "for an understanding of game designers less as storytellers and more as narrative architects."[175] In this respect, games like no other medium have the affordance to simulate non-existent places—utopias—and render them accessible to individual experience and exploration.

This observation leads to the fourth affordance Janet Murry identified: Digital environments are participatory; they are "inviting human action and

---

171 See Murray, Janet Horowitz: *Hamlet on the Holodeck: The Future of Narrative in Cyberspace*. New York: Free Press, 1997, chapter "The Four Essential Properties of Digital Environments," pp. 71-90.

172 See Domsch, Sebastian: "Dystopian Video Games: Fallout in Utopia," in: Voigts, Eckart/Boller, Alessandra (eds.): *Dystopia, Science Fiction, Post-Apocalypse Classics—New Tendencies—Model Interpretations*, Trier: Wissenschaftlicher Verlag Trier 2015, pp. 395-409; here p. 398.

173 Jameson, Fredric: "Utopianism After the End of Utopia," in: *Postmodernism, or, The Cultural Logic of Late Capitalism*, Durham: Duke University Press, pp. 154-180; here: p. 156.

174 Poole, Steven: *Trigger Happy: Videogames and the Entertainment Revolution*, New York: Arcade Publishing 2000, p. 226.

175 Jenkins, Henry: "Game Design as Narrative Architecture," in: Wardrip-Fruin, Noah/Harrigan, Pat (eds.): *First Person: New Media as Story, Performance, and Game*, Cambridge, Mass.: MIT Press 2004, pp. 119-29, here p. 121.

manipulation of the represented world."[176] Users can try out the designed systems—whether these are fictitious realms or representations of real places—and 'test' their functioning. Games, of course, surpass in this regard not only the older media but also other digital genres because they not just offer but almost always require agency. Without the players acting, there is no progress in gameplay. The ludic emphasis on (inter-) action correlates with the fact that the question of human agency is at the center of all utopian hopes (and the absence of such agency at the center of most dystopian fears).[177] Sebastian Domsch has highlighted this special connection between digital games and utopian worlds:

"This sense of agency is then—besides video games' general nature as systems—what so strongly relates them to utopian and dystopian thinking: both are concerned with the extent to which human/player agency is able to influence and change a system."[178]

Thus, due to their specific affordances, digital games can function as a virtual training ground for utopian (or dystopian) change. More than other media, games allow us to test alternative scenarios. Such a playthrough of possible futures seems particularly worthwhile, since right now—in the first decades of digital culture—our cultural expectations are undergoing a radical transformation in regard to both what the future will bring as well as the notion in which way the coming change is supposed to arrive.

***

Both aspects are the subject of this anthology. Its first part deals with utopian futures as they are anticipated *in* games, the second part with the future *of* games.

The first part, "Utopias in Digital Games," opens with André Czauderna's paper on "Tinkering with Political Utopias and Dystopias in DEMOCRACY 3."[179] In the analyzed turn-based political simulation, players take on

---

176 Murray, Janet H.: "Four Affordances," on: *Humanistic Design for an Emerging Medium*, undated; https://inventingthemedium.com/four-affordances/
177 See S. Domsch: "Dystopian Video Games", p. 403.
178 Ibid., p. 401.
179 In this volume, pp. 69-98.

the role of the prime minister of a Western democracy and are given the opportunity to go beyond the constraints of everyday politics and test the consequences of radical concepts of society. In a detailed interpretation of the gameplay, Czauderna identifies the learning processes and outcomes. He recognizes the potential of the game "as applied political philosophy which might be utilized in political education."[180] As a result, he recommends the game for use in upper secondary school.

This exemplary analysis of a single game is followed by an exploration of the full spectrum of utopian and dystopian games. In "The Concept of Utopia in Digital Games," Gerald Farca presents a comprehensive typology addressing the expression and design of the utopian impulse in digital games.[181] As the central effect of playing with the future, he recognizes a particular form of "regenerative play" which allows players to "see beyond the inoculating powers of the status quo, differentiate societal issues, and explore potential solutions to these through play."[182]

In "'Everything is true; nothing is permitted.' Utopia, Religion, and Conspiracy in ASSASSIN'S CREED,"[183] Lars de Wildt traces how a central change in cultural perception has inscribed itself into Ubisoft's popular game franchise: the transition from modern paranoia, which places the enemy outside one's own society, to postmodern paranoia, which suspects the enemy inside society. By blurring the boundaries between the two factions in the game, the Assassins and the Templars, the binary distinction between utopia and dystopia gradually dissolves as well. The "straightforwardness of utopian projects"[184] is challenged and "the 'not-place' of Utopia is increasingly mapped over every-place, to be found all around us, if only we learn to unveil its conspiratorial hiddenness."[185]

Tonguc Ibrahim Sezen's "Beyond the Holonovel. The Holographic Interactive Digital Entertainment Utopia of STAR TREK,"[186] concludes the first part of the anthology by addressing a central utopian ideal for the future of

---

180 Ibid., p. 69.
181 In this volume, pp. 99-147.
182 Ibid., p. 103.
183 In this volume, pp. 149-185.
184 Ibid., p. 179.
185 Ibid., p. 177.
186 In this volume, pp. 187-207.

media in digital culture: the holodeck. This fictitious entertainment medium has influenced—and continues to influence—science fiction writers, filmmakers, and game designers as well as inventors, scientists, and scholars. The paper examines its double evolution: the development of the vision of a holodeck since the 1960s and the development of the holodeck within the many TV episodes and feature films of STAR TREK. On the one hand, the various 'fictional' and 'non-fictional' applications of the holodeck are quantitatively assessed and analyzed, with an emphasis on the genre of the "holonovel." On the other hand, the author discusses the cultural connotations of the holodeck and its "prominent role in academic discussions [...] as a utopia for interactive digital entertainment,"[187] in particular the impact on media and game studies and the scholarly debate about the future of narration.

The second part, "Utopias of Digital Games," starts with an assessment of the problematic working conditions within the games industry as well as the heteronormative, neoliberal and meritocratic value system of many popular games. In "Feminist Interventions for Better Futures of Digital Games"[188], Alison Harvey confronts these "dark realities."[189] Her interim verdict "Games are Dystopias"[190] is supposed to serve as a wake-up call. Stressing that "feminist game studies is premised on a utopian methodology, driven by the desire to transform inequitable systems for better futures for all,"[191] she promotes cultural criticism and political action playing together to bring about urgently needed changes in the industry as well as gaming culture.

The relation between work and digital play is also the starting point for Anne Dippel's "Ludopian Visions. On the Speculative Potential of Games in Times of Algorithmic Work and Play."[192] Based on Walter Benjamin's concept of the "Spiel" as an 'ur-phenomenon' of artistic creation, Dippel explores the ludopian vision "whether computers and computer games may

---

187 Ibid., p. 194.
188 In this volume, pp. 211-233.
189 Ibid., p. 224.
190 Ibid., p. 214.
191 Ibid., p. 224.
192 In this volume, pp. 235-252.

open up spaces of possibility to envision utopian societies."[193] The discussion of possible interrelationships between ideologies and the architecture of software and workspaces leads to the realization that games offer "spaces to rethink the society" and that this turn from mere representation to reflectivity "opens a gate to possible worlds and utopias."[194]

Taking the contentious effectiveness of so-called Serious Games or Persuasive Games as a starting point, Hartmut Koenitz, in "Playful Utopias—Sandboxes for the Future," comes to a comparable understanding of games "as vessels for utopias."[195] Many current social problems are extremely complex, from the radicalization of the political climate to the public debates on climate change, and traditional narrative media have obvious problems to represent these multifaceted discourses adequately. Games, however, as an interactive medium of simulation and narration seem particularly suited to make it possible to experience and reflect our current challenges in their complexity. Koenitz' analysis leads to the proposal of "three concrete ideas for utopian sandboxes."[196]

Utopian discourses surrounding the products of one of the world's most famous toy manufacturers are the focus of Hanns Christian Schmidt's contribution. In "Building Utopia, Brick by Brick? Selling Subversiveness in LEGO DIMENSIONS,"[197] he investigates what happens when analog play turns digital. Physical Lego bricks allow children "to construct their very own spaces of the imagination: places that were literally non-existent before—and are therefore 'utopian' (no-places) in the original sense of the word."[198] In the digital realm, however, the company is not granting its players the ability to build an actual digital utopia. Instead, Lego is selling a remix of different popular entertainment properties, thereby creating a deconstructive playfulness. As a consequence, Schmidt concludes, "LEGO DIMENSIONS becomes a sort of super-structure [...] that modifies and preserves [...] older games within Lego's own specific language of form."[199]

---

193 Ibid., p. 235.
194 Ibid., p. 249.
195 In this volume, pp. 253-265, here 261.
196 Ibid., p. 262.
197 In this volume, pp. 267-283.
198 Ibid., p. 267.
199 Ibid., p. 278.

Another popular variant of remediation is 'modding,' i.e., the adaptation or extension of the content and structures of digital games by individual users or teams of hobby programmers. In "'We have won this battle ;)' Utopian Practices in Video Games,"[200] media artist Thomas Hawranke explores this practice both theoretically and artistically. Using the example of two mod projects—the exchange of male and female characters, so-called gender-swapping, and a human-animal swap, in which chimpanzees replace human passers-by in the game world—, Hawranke demonstrates the subversive and critical function of modding. The changeability of games, he declares, constitutes their utopian potential. Like reality, games offer two categorically different options for action. On the one hand, the execution of expected behavior, which means in games: what was implicitly intended by the designers. On the other hand, the discovery of potentially feasible actions, utopian possibilities which are unexpected and unplanned and have yet to be realized.

"The Utopia of Getting Over It" concludes the anthology.[201] On the basis of Jesper Juul's "paradox of failure"— that we avoid failure in everyday life but like to play games in which we fail again and again—, Benjamin Beil reflects on the appeal of the game GETTING OVER IT WITH BENNETT FODDY. Its interface and mechanics are not 'fair,' so most players keep on failing, and the unsatisfactory ending does not offer any rewards. Still, the game attracts players. To understand this fact, Beil refers to Bernard Suits' idea that in a utopian society which has satisfied all basic needs, play is all that remains to fight boredom. Players of GETTING OVER IT, Beil claims, resemble the hero of Albert Camus' "Myth of Sisyphus": a modern everyman trapped in a situation of failure and futility who is nevertheless happy. "Playing GETTING OVER IT is not a Utopia, but it is a remarkably consistent utopian practice in regard to its inefficiency and unnecessariness. It is just a little utopian game in an (as it seems) increasingly dystopian world [...]."[202]

---

200 In this volume, pp. 285-313.
201 In this volume, pp. 315-325.
202 Ibid., p. 324.

Literature

Agel, Jerome (ed.): *The Making of Kubrick's 2001*, New York: New American Library 1970.

Andreae, Johannes Valentinus: *Description of the Republic of Christianopolis,* Strasburg: Lazarus Zetzner 1619.

Auden, W. H.: "Dingley Dell & the Fleet," in: *The Dyer's Hand and Other Essays*, London: Faber & Faber 1962, pp. 407-428; online: https://archive.org/stream/in.ernet.dli.2015.16420/2015.16420.The-Dyers-Hand-And-Other-Essays_djvu.txt

Bacon, Francis: *The New Atlantis*, published posthumously, London 1627.

Beil, Benjamin: "'Introducing the All New eyePhone!'—The Future of Mobile Media," WiJournal (8/2), November 28, 2014, http://wi.mobilities.ca/introducing-the-all-new-eyephone-the-future-of-mobile-media/

Bellamy, Edward: *Looking Backward 2000-1887*, Boston: Ticknor & Co 1888; online: https://archive.org/details/lookingbackward200bell

Benjamin, Walter: "Theses on the Philosophy of History," in: *Illuminations*, New York: Schocken Books 1969, p. 249.

Benjamin, Walter: *The Arcades Project*, Cambridge, Mass.: Belknap Press of Harvard University Press 2002.

Benson, Michael: "Science Fiction Sent Man to the Moon," *The New York Times*, July 20, 2019; https://www.nytimes.com/2019/07/20/opinion/sunday/moon-rockets-space-fiction.html

Bloch, Ernst: *The Principle of Hope*, Cambridge, Mass.: MIT Press 1986 (*1954).

Bloch, Ernst: *Spirit of Utopia*, Stanford: Stanford University Press 2000 (*1918).

Bostrom, Nick: *Superintelligence: Paths, Dangers, Strategies*, Oxford: Oxford University Press 2015 (Kindle edition).

Bouée, Charles-Edouard: "Creating the Present by Imagining the Future: The Power of Science Fiction," *LinkedIn*, April 15, 2019; https://www.linkedin.com/pulse/creating-present-imagining-future-power-science-fiction-bouée/

Bruckner, Pascal: "Klimaproteste: Alt und Jung in Unreife vereint," *Neue Zuercher Zeitung*, April 26, 2019; https://www.nzz.ch/meinung/klimaproteste-alt-und-jung-in-unreife-vereint-ld.1476994

Budakov, Vesselin E.: "Dystopia: an Earlier Eighteenth-Century Use," *Notes and Queries 57.1*, Oxford University Press; March 1, 2010: p. 86-88; https://www.academia.edu/944097/_Dystopia_an_Earlier_Eighteenth-Century_Use_Notes_and_Queries_57.1_March_1_2010_86-88_Notes_and_Queries_Oxford_University_Press_first_published_online_on_February_8_2010_doi_10.1093_notesj_gjp235_

Butler, Samuel: *Erewhon: Or, Over the Range*, London: Trübner and Co., 1872; online: http://www.gutenberg.org/ebooks/1906

Campanella, Tommaso: *The City of Sun*, written in 1602 in Italian, published in Latin in Frankfurt 1623.

Chu, Charles: "The Future-Altering Technologies We Forgot to Invent. Science fiction legend Gene Wolfe shares his thoughts," *Medium*, February 24, 2018; https://medium.com/the-polymath-project/gene-wolfe-a-science-fiction-legend-on-the-future-altering-technologies-we-forgot-to-invent-a3103572a352

Cobb, Jennifer J.: "A Globe, Clothing Itself with a Brain," *Wired*, January 6, 1995; http://www.wired.com/wired/archive/3.06/teilhard_pr.html

Cowen, Tyler: "Neal Stephenson on Depictions of Reality," Conversations with Tyler Episode 71, *Medium*, July 17, 2019; https://medium.com/conversations-with-tyler/tyler-cowen-neal-stephenson-science-fiction-writer-7fbe020e60b6

Domsch, Sebastian: "Dystopian Video Games: Fallout in Utopia," Eckart Voigts, Alessandra Boller (eds.), *Dystopia, Science Fiction, Post-Apocalypse Classics – New Tendencies – Model Interpretations*, Wissenschaftlicher Verlag Trier.

Ellis, Warren: "How to See the Future," raw text of a Keynote given at the Conference *Improving Reality*, posted September 7, 2012; http://www.warrenellis.com/how-to-see-the-future/

Engels, Friedrich/Marx, Karl: *Manifest der kommunistischen Partei*: Office der Bildungs-Gesellschaft für Arbeiter, London 1848; online: http://www.gutenberg.org/cache/epub/61/pg61.html

Ettel, Anja, "Science Fiction: Wo deutsche Unternehmen an der Zukunft arbeiten," *Die Welt,* April 20, 2019, https://www.welt.de/wirtschaft/article192166549/Science-Fiction-Wo-deutsche-Unternehmen-an-der-Zukunft-arbeiten.html

Faife, Corin: "The Dystopic Leftist Youth of Reddit and Facebook. A Look into the Spaces Where Young People Mock the 'Boring Dystopia' that Capitalism has Built," in: *Medium*, January 22, 2018; https://medium.com/s/darkish-web/the-dystopic-leftist-youth-of-reddit-and-facebook-cbe4e35dfd6f

Farrell, Maria: "How to Cope with the End of the World," *Medium*, June 7, 2018; https://medium.com/s/how-to-cope-with-the-end-of-the-world/how-to-cope-with-the-end-of-the-world-2520ef9d3dbc

Fisher, Mark: *The Ghosts of My Life*, London: Zero Books 2014.

Flechtheim, Ossip K.: "Teaching the Future," *Journal for Higher Education*, 16 (1945), pp. 460-65.

Fotsch, Paul Mason: "The Building of a Superhighway Future at the New York World's Fair," *Cultural Critique* 48, Spring 2001, pp. 65-97.

Freyermuth, Gundolf S.: *Cyberland*, Berlin: Rowohlt 1996.

Geuenich, Dieter: "Zukunftsvorstellungen im Mittelalter. Antrittsvorlesung an der Universität Duisburg," May 30, 1989; https://duepublico.uni-duisburg-essen.de/servlets/DerivateServlet/Derivate-5183/GeuZuk.htm

Gibson, William: "The Science in Science Fiction," *Talk of the Nation*, NPR, November 30, 1999, min. 11:55; http://www.npr.org/templates/story/story.php?storyId=1067220

Gidley, Jennifer M.: *The Future: A Very Short Introduction*, New York: Oxford University Press 2017 (Kindle edition).

Godwin, Francis: *The Man in the Moone*, published posthumously, London: John Norton 1638.

Gopnik, Adam: "What Can We Learn from Utopians of the Past?" *The New Yorker*, July 23, 2018; https://www.newyorker.com/magazine/2018/07/30/what-can-we-learn-from-utopians-of-the-past

Haeming, Anne: "'Politik und Science Fiction sind nicht fern voneinander.' Interview mit Bestseller-Autor Andreas Eschbach," *Der Spiegel*, December 21, 2018; https://www.spiegel.de/kultur/literatur/andreas-eschbach-ueber-nsa-es-sind-viele-ungute-zukuenfte-denkbar-a-1244124.html

Harari, Yuval Noah: *Sapiens: A Brief History of Humankind*, New York: Harper 2015 (Kindle edition).

Harari, Yuval Noah: *Homo Deus: A Brief History of Tomorrow*, New York: Harper 2017 (Kindle edition).

Heilbroner, Robert L.: *Visions of the Future: The Distant Past, Yesterday, Today, Tomorrow*, New York: Oxford University Press 1995 (Kindle edition).

Herman, Arthur: *Freedom's Forge: How American Business Produced Victory in World War II*, pp. 58-65, 338, 343, New York: Random House 2012.

Hillenbrand, Tom: "Dystopien im Film: Science-Fiction und sein Einfluss auf unser Zukunftsdenken," *Berliner Zeitung*, October 27, 2018; https://www.berliner-zeitung.de/kultur/dystopien-im-film--science-fiction-und-sein-einfluss-auf-unser-zukunftsdenken-31478062

Huxley, Aldous: *Brave New World*, London: Chatto & Windus 1932.

Huxley, Julian: "Transhumanism," in: *New Bottles for New Wine*, London: Chatto & Windus 1957; pp 13-17.

Jameson, Fredric: "Utopianism After the End of Utopia," in: *Postmodernism, or, The Cultural Logic of Late Capitalism*, Durham: Duke University Press, pp. 154-180.

Jenkins, Henry: "Game Design as Narrative Architecture," in: Wardrip-Fruin, Noah/Harrigan, Pat (eds.): *First Person: New Media as Story, Performance, and Game*, Cambridge, Mass.: MIT Press 2004, pp. 119-29.

Johnson, Brian David: *Science Fiction Prototyping. Designing the Future with Science Fiction*, San Rafael, CA.: Morgan & Claypool 2011.

Jungk, Robert: *Tomorrow Is Already Here*, New York: Simon & Schuster 1954.

Kahn, Herman/Wiener, Anthony J.: *The Year 2000. A Framework for Speculation on the Next Thirty-Three Years*, New York: MacMillan 1967.

Kant, Immanuel: *Critique of Pure Reason* (1787), Norman Kemp Smith version; https://www.marxists.org/reference/subject/ethics/kant/reason/ch04.htm

Kevin, Kelly: *What Technology Wants*, New York: Viking 2010 (Kindle edition).

Kracauer, Siegfried: *Theory of Film: The Redemption of Physical Reality*. New York: Oxford University Press 1960.

Krauss, Lawrence: "Foreword," in: Finn, Ed/Cramer, Kathryn (eds.): *Hieroglyph: Stories and Visions for a Better Future*, New York: William Morrow 2014 (Kindle edition).

Kurzweil, Ray: *The Singularity is Near: When Humans Transcend Biology*, New York: Viking 2005.

Lake, Simon/Corey, Herbert: *Submarine. The Autobiography of Simon Lake*, New York and London: D. Appleton Century Company 1930.

Lenin, Vladimir Ilyich: "Two Utopias" (written October 1912), *Lenin Collected Works*, Progress Publishers, [1975], Moscow, Volume 18, pp. 355-359.

Lepore, Jill: "A Golden Age of Dystopian Fiction," *The New Yorker*, May 29, 2017; https://www.newyorker.com/magazine/2017/06/05/a-golden-age-for-dystopian-fiction

Levitas, Ruth: *The Concept of Utopia*, Syracuse, N.Y.: Syracuse University Press 1990

Levy, Steven: *In the Plex: How Google Thinks, Works, and Shapes Our Lives*, Simon & Schuster 2011.

Luhmann, Niklas: *The Reality of the Mass Media: Cultural Memory in the Present*, Stanford: Stanford University Press 2000.

Madden, Samuel: *The Memoirs of the Twentieth Century*, London: Osborn and Longman, Davis and Batley 1733.

Maloney, Devon: "No, Dystopian Sci-Fi Isn't Bad for Society. We Need It More Than Ever," *Wired*, August 14, 2014; https://www.wired.com/2014/08/no-dystopian-sci-fi-isnt-bad-for-society-we-actually-need-it-more-than-ever/

Marche, Stephen: "*Star Trek: The Next Generation* Was the Last Sci-Fi Show Hopeful About the Future. Brave New Worlds have been Replaced by a Google Chip," *Esquire*, May 22, 2014; https://www.esquire.com/entertainment/tv/a31206/star-trek-the-next-generation-future/

McLuhan, Marshall: "Take 30 Interview with George Garlock and Paul Soles," CBC, April 1, 1965; https://www.youtube.com/watch?v=qABC3_8ai58

McMillan, Graeme: "Where Are Our Bright Science-Fiction Futures?" *Time*, March 29, 2013; http://entertainment.time.com/2013/03/29/where-are-our-bright-science-fiction-futures/

Merchant, Brian: "Nike and Boeing Are Paying Sci-Fi Writers to Predict Their Futures. Welcome to the Sci-Fi Industrial Complex," *Medium*, Nov 28, 2018; https://onezero.medium.com/nike-and-boeing-are-paying-sci-fi-writers-to-predict-their-futures-fdc4b6165fa4

Minsky, Marvin: *The Society of Mind*, New York: Simon and Schuster 1986.

Montfort Nick: *The Future*, Cambridge, Mass.: MIT Press, 2017 (Kindle edition).

More, Thomas: *Libellus vere aureus, nec minus salutaris quam festivus, de optimo rei publicae statu deque nova insula Utopia*, Louvain, Habsburg Netherlands 1516.

Morris, William: *News from Nowhere; or An Epoch of Rest, Being Some Chapters from a Utopian Romance*, Boston: Roberts Brothers 1890; online: http://www.gutenberg.org/ebooks/3261

Murray, Janet H.: *Hamlet on the Holodeck: The Future of Narrative in Cyberspace,* New York: Free Press 1997.

Murray, Janet H.: "Four Affordances," on: *Humanistic Design for an Emerging Medium*, undated; https://inventingthemedium.com/four-affordances/

Neuhaus, Wolfgang: "Science Fiction als Pop-Epistemologie. Ein Sinn für Neuorientierung in der hypermedialen Welt," *Telepolis*, August 30, 2002; https://www.heise.de/tp/features/Science-Fiction-als-Pop-Epistemologie-3426255.html

Neumann, John von: "First Draft of a Report on the Edvac," University of Pennsylvania 1945; https://sites.google.com/site/michaeldgodfrey/vonneumann/vnedvac.pdf?attredirects=0&d=1

N.N.: "Tommaso Campanella," *Stanford Encyclopedia of Philosophy*, August 25, 2014; https://plato.stanford.edu/entries/campanella/

Nordberg, Anna: "Silicon Valley, It's Time to Hire Science Fiction Writers," *Ozy*, March 19, 2019; https://www.ozy.com/immodest-proposal/silicon-valley-its-time-to-hire-sci-fi-writers/93038

Nowlan, Philip Francs: *Buck Rogers*, New York: Amazing Stories 1928.

Orwell, George: *Nineteen Eighty-Four*, London: Secker & Warburg 1949.

Poole, Steven: *Trigger Happy: Videogames and the Entertainment Revolution*, New York: Arcade Publishing 2000.

Postman, Neil: *Amusing Ourselves to Death: Public Discourse in the Age of Show Business*, New York: Viking 1985.

Pound, Ezra: "The Teacher's Mission," in: *Literary Essays*, London: Faber and Faber 1954, pp. 58-63.

Raymond, Alex: *Flash Gordon*, New York: King Features Syndicate 1934.

Rifkin, Jeremy: "Dazzled by the Science Biologists Who Dress up Hi-Tech Eugenics as a New Art Form are Dangerously Deluded," *The Guardian*, January 14, 2003; http://www.ekac.org/rifkin.html

Robertson, Michael: *The Last Utopians: Four Late Nineteenth-Century Visionaries and Their Legacy*, Princeton: Princeton University Press 2018.

Sargent, Lyman Tower: *Utopianism: A Very Short Introduction*, Oxford: Oxford University Press 2010 (Kindle edition).

Shannon, Claude Elwood: "A Mathematical Theory of Communication," *The Bell System Technical Journal* (27/1948), July/Oktober, pp. 379–423, 623–56. Online reprinted with corrections from *The Bell System Technical Journal* http://www.math.harvard.edu/~ctm/home/text/others/shannon/entropy/entropy.pdf

Shelley, Mary: *Frankenstein; or, The Modern Prometheus,* Lackington, Hughes, Harding, Mavor & Jones: London 1818: online: http://www.gutenberg.org/files/84/84-h/84-h.htm

Shiau, Yvonne: "The Rise of Dystopian Fiction: From Soviet Dissidents to 70's Paranoia to Murakami," *Electric Literature*, July 26, 2017, https://electricliterature.com/the-rise-of-dystopian-fiction-from-soviet-dissidents-to-70s-paranoia-tomurakami/

Siegel, Jerry/Shuster, Joe: *Superman*, New York: DC Comics 1938.

Solana, Michael: "Stop Writing Dystopian Sci-Fi—It's Making Us All Fear Technology," *Wired*, August 14, 2014; https://www.wired.com/2014/08/stop-writing-dystopian-sci-fiits-making-us-all-fear-technology/

Stephenson, Neal: "Innovation Starvation," *Wired*, October 27, 2011, https://www.wired.com/2011/10/stephenson-innovation-starvation/

Sterling, Bruce: *Shaping Things*. Cambridge, Mass.: MIT Press 2005.

Standage, Tom: "A Toolkit for Predicting the Future," *The Economist*, May 31, 2017; https://medium.economist.com/a-toolkit-for-predicting-the-future-2f24757d9699

Suvin, Darko: *Metamorphoses of Science Fiction,* New Haven: Yale University Press 1979.

Teilhard de Chardin, Pierre: *The Phenomenon of Man*, New York: Harper 1959.

Toffler, Alvin: *Future Shock*, New York: Random House 1970.

Trojanov, Ilija: "Schlagloch: Nie gut, aber besser," *taz*, April 18, 2019; https://taz.de/Kolumne-Schlagloch/!5585265/

Vasari, Giorgio: *The Lives of the Most Excellent Painters, Sculptors, and Architects*, Florence: Torrentino 1550 and 1558

Verne, Jules: *De la terre à la lune*, Paris: Hetzel 1865.

Verne, Jules: *Vingt mille lieues sous les mers*, Paris: Hetzel 1870.

Vinge, Vernor: "What is the Singularity?" Presentation at the VISION-21 Symposium sponsored by NASA Lewis Research Center and the Ohio Aerospace Institute, March 30-31, 1993; https://mindstalk.net/vinge/vinge-sing.html

Walsh, Toby: "The Singularity May Never Be Near," *AI Magazine*, (38/3), 2017, pp. 58-62; https://aaai.org/ojs/index.php/aimagazine/article/view/2702

Watercutter, Angela: "Westworld's Creators Know Why Sci-Fi Is So Dystopian," *Wired*, June 8, 2017; https://www.wired.com/2017/06/westworld-wired-business-conference/

Watson, James D., and F. H. C. Cricks: "A Structure for Deoxyribose Nucleic Acid," *Nature* 171, April, 25, 1953, pp. 737-738; https://www.nature.com/articles/171737a0.pdf

Wegner, Jochen: "William Gibson: 'Ich hoffe, wir sind nicht in negativen Utopien gefangen,'"*Die Zeit*, January 12, 2017; https://www.zeit.de/zeitmagazin/leben/2017-01/william-gibson-science-fiction-neuromancer-cyberspace-futurist

Wells. H.G.: *Anticipations of the Reaction of Mechanical and Scientific Progress upon Human Life and Thought*, New York and London: Harper. Bros. 1902; online: http://www.gutenberg.org/ebooks/19229

Wells, H.G.: *The Time Machine*, London: William Heinemann 1895.

Wells, H.G.: *The Island of Doctor Moreau*, London: William Heinemann 1896.

Wells, H.G.: *The War of the Worlds*, London: William Heinemann 1898.

Wells, H.G.: *The Discovery of the Future: A Discourse Delivered to the Royal Institution on January 24, 1902*, London: T. Fisher Unwin 1902; online: http://www.gutenberg.org/ebooks/44867

Wells, H.G.: *The Shape of Things to Come. The Ultimate Revolution*, London: Hutchinson & Co. 1933

Yorgo Lee: "Optimistic Sci-fi: 10 Movies That Think We Have a Chance," *Medium*, March 1, 2017; https://medium.com/@yorgo.douramacos/optimistic-sci-fi-10-movies-that-think-we-have-a-chance-3decac4c1ab4

Zamyatin, Yevgeny Ivanovich: *We,* New York: E. P. Dutton, 1924.

Radio

Buck Rogers in the 25th Century (USA 1932-1947, O: CBS)
War of the Worlds (USA 1938, O: Orson Welles/CBS); online: https://www.mercurytheatre.info

Filmography

Blade Runner 2049 (USA 2017, D: Dennis Villeneuve)
Die Frau im Mond. (English titles: By Rocket to the Moon / Woman in the Moon; D 1929, D: Fritz Lang).
Her (USA 2013, D: Spike Jonze)
Hunger Games (USA 2012-2015, D: Gary Ross-1/Francis Lawrence-2-4)
Interstellar (USA 2014, D: Christopher Nolan)
Le Voyage dans la Lune (F 1902, D: Georges Méliès)
Mad Max: Fury Road (Australia/USA 2015, D: George Miller)
Metropolis (D 1927, D: Fritz Lang)
Ninotschka (USA 1939, D: Ernst Lubitsch)
Ready, Player, One (USA 2018, D: Steven Spielberg)
Terminator: Dark Fate (USA 2019, D: Tim Miller)
To New Horizons (USA 1940: D: N.N.; i.e., General Motors)

Series

Buck Rogers (USA 1939, O: Universal Pictures)
Flash Gordon (USA 1936, O: Universal Pictures)
How William Shatner Changed the World (USA 2005, O: Discovery Channel; two-part documentary)
Star Trek (USA 1966-69, O: Gene Roddenberry)
The Handmaid's Tale (USA 2017- 2018; O: Hulu / Bruce Miller)
Westworld (USA 2016-2018; O: HBO / Jonathan Nolan, Lisa Joy)

Gamography

FALLOUT 4 (Bethesda Softworks 2015, O: Bethesda Game Studios)
MAD MAX (Warner Bros. Interactive 2015, O: Avalanche Studios)
MASS EFFECT: ANDROMEDA (Electronic Arts 2017, O: Bioware)
THE LAST OF US (Sony Computer Entertainment 2013, O: Naughty Dog)
THE SURGE (Focus Home Interactive 2017, O: Desk13)

Utopias in Digital Games

Tinkering with Political Utopias and Dystopias in DEMOCRACY 3
An Educational Perspective

ANDRÉ CZAUDERNA

The present contribution looks at the possibility of tinkering with political utopias and dystopias in the turn-based political simulation DEMOCRACY 3 (2013), which offerws players the opportunity to slip into the role of a Western democracy's president or prime minister and to govern the selected country as long as they are not thrown out of office. In contrast to many articles of the present volume, this one focuses on utopias and dystopias as non-fiction.

Political utopias are understood as coherent sets of political ideas and/or policies following a particular theory of justice, such as political philosophies, political ideologies, or manifestos from political parties. Political dystopias refer to political utopias that do not suit the player's ideological standpoint or that went objectively wrong in the practice of playing. In this sense, playing DEMOCRACY 3 is read as applied political philosophy which might be utilized in political education.

After a brief overview of the field of digital games for political education and a short introduction to the topic of political utopias and dystopias with a special focus on the perspective of political philosophy, the present contribution reconstructs DEMOCRACY 3's gameplay. Afterwards, the game's implicit learning possibilities in regard to political philosophy will be outlined. The article will then exemplify observable learning processes and outcomes elicited by DEMOCRACY 3, which become visible in "affinity spaces" around the game, for example, on platforms such as YouTube, when players present and discuss their own realizations of utopian or dystopian policies in Let's Play videos. Finally, the article argues for an application of the game in political education in upper secondary school.

DIGITAL GAMES FOR POLITICAL EDUCATION

The use of games in political education is not only a phenomenon of the digital age. The "Model United Nations," for example, in which the players take on the role of diplomats and simulate the work of the United Nations, has been part of the repertoire of political education in and outside schools for decades.

The potential of digital games for political education has also been discussed for some time. According to Motyka and Zehe, digital games can be used to illustrate complex relationships as well as to investigate values and norms. They furthermore enable players to change their perspective. The authors conclude that digital games could expand the methodological repertoire of teachers and counteract the often-criticized lack of methods in political education.[1]

Among the more well-known serious games (i.e., digital games that pursue a purpose beyond pure entertainment) with relevance for political education are games such as ENERGETIKA 2010 (2010), FOODFORCE (2005), and PEACEMAKER (2007). ENERGETIKA 2010 deals with energy policy in the Federal Republic of Germany, FOODFORCE with the United Nations World Food Program, and PEACEMAKER with the Middle East conflict, which the player must resolve either as representative of the Israelis or as representative of the Palestinians. While these games refer to single fields of policy, other games, such as GENIUS. IM ZENTRUM DER MACHT (2007), supported by the German Federal Agency for Civic Education (*Bundeszentrale für politische Bildung/bpb*), represent political processes in general.

A large part of the present studies measuring the learning effects of serious games with relevance for political education relate to their effect on

---

[1] Motyka, Marc/Zehe, Mario: "Lernen mit Computerspielen im Politikunterricht. Empfehlungen und Fallbeispiele für die Praxis," *Politik unterrichten* 29/2 (2014), pp. 37-43.

political attitudes.[2] The effect on the understanding of political processes is less well investigated. However, studies on digital games relating to other domains of knowledge—including studies on commercial games such as CIVILIZATION III (2001)—suggest that digital games might support the understanding of political processes in general.[3]

POLITICAL UTOPIAS AND DYSTOPIAS

Political utopias have been developed for millennials—starting in ancient times with philosophers such as Plato and Aristotle. According to the *Routledge Encyclopedia of Philosophy*, "Utopianism is the general label for a number of different ways of dreaming or thinking about, describing or attempting to create a better society."[4] The term utopia as such has been coined by Thomas More in his book of philosophical fiction, *Utopia*, published in 1516[5]—in which he

> "described a society significantly better than England as it existed at the time, and the word utopia (good place) has come to mean a description of a fictional place, usually a society, that is better than the society in which the author lives and which functions as a criticism of the author's society."[6]

---

2 E.g. Cuhadar, Esra/Kampf, Ronit: "Learning About Conflict and Negotiations through Computer Simulations: The Case of PeaceMaker," *International Studies Perspectives* 15/4 (2014), pp. 509-524; Alhabash, Saleem/Wise, Kevin: "Playing Their Game: Changing Stereotypes of Palestinians and Israelis through Videogame Play," *New Media & Society* 17/8 (2015), pp. 1358-1376; Gonzalez, Cleotilde et al.: "Learning to Stand in the Other's Shoes: A Computer Video Game Experience of the Israeli-Palestinian Conflict," *Social Science Computer Review* 31/2 (2013), pp. 236-243.

3 E.g. Squire, Kurt: "Changing the Game: What Happens When Video Games Enter the Classroom," *Innovate: Journal of Online Education* 1/6 (2005).

4 Sargent, Lyman Tower: "Utopianism," *Routledge Encyclopedia of Philosophy Online*, Thames: Taylor and Francis 1998; https://www.rep.routledge.com/articles/thematic/utopianism/v-1

5 More, Thomas: *Utopia*, Kindle 2012 [1516].

6 L. T. Sargent: "Utopianism."

Thereby, utopias cannot only be understood as dreams, but also as objectives of social reform: "In some cases it is intended as a direction to be followed in social reform, or even, in a few instances, as a possible goal to be achieved."[7]

The antonym of utopianism is dystopianism which paints the future in a pessimistic fashion. Huntington's well-known book *The Clash of Civilizations and the Remaking of World Order*, published in 1997, is just one example for writings (including monographs and essays) that predict an undesirable and frightening future and thus can be interpreted as dystopias. In the case of this monograph, the author develops the hypothesis that future post-cold war conflicts will be about cultural and religious identities.[8]

Utopias and dystopias are two sides of a coin. It depends on one's perspective whether one perceive a certain political state and/or its effects as utopia or dystopia; someone's utopia is someone else's dystopia. And each (theoretical) utopia might end in (practical) dystopia.

Both of these genres of non-fictional writing—utopias and dystopias—have their twins in fiction throughout the media: from literature to digital games telling stories about a better or worse society. In fiction, today, dystopias are more common than utopias. This might be because the description of a fictional dystopian scenario alone seems to imply an enormous appeal to readers, viewers, players as well as it offers a more interesting background for plot and character development. As all utopias imagine an ideal community or society including an assumed ideal life for its citizens, the god place, and all dystopias are about undesirable communities or societies, the not-god place, politics are central in both genres by definition—even though the respective story does not have to be about politics in the first place, but the life of people living in the depicted society. A few dystopias became literature classics, among them Huxley's *Brave New World* (1932) and Orwell's *Nineteen Eighty-Four* (1949), to mention only two famous examples. Although fictional utopias and dystopias are interesting for political education as well, this contribution looks in particular at utopias and dystopias as non-fiction.

---

7   Ibid.
8   Huntington, Samuel P.: *The Clash of Civilizations and the Remaking of World Order*, New York City: Simon & Schuster 1997.

The academic discipline that systematically develops non-fictional political utopias—in terms of outlining their normative theory and claiming their justice—is called political philosophy. According to Miller in the *Routledge Encyclopedia of Philosophy*, "Political philosophy can be defined as philosophical reflection on how best to arrange our collective life—our political institutions and our social practices, such as our economic system and our pattern of family life."[9] Historical figures in political philosophy include, for instance, Thomas Hobbes and Karl Marx. Contemporary political philosophy is very much influenced by John Rawls and Jürgen Habermas, for example.

Political philosophy aims

"to establish basic principles that will, for instance, justify a particular form of state, show that individuals have certain inalienable rights, or tell us how a society's material resources should be shared among its members. This usually involves analyzing and interpreting ideas like freedom, justice, authority and democracy and then applying them in a critical way to the social and political institutions that currently exist."[10]

While "[s]ome political philosophers have tried primarily to justify the prevailing arrangements of their society," others have developed utopias: they "have painted pictures of an ideal state or an ideal social world that is very different from anything we have so far experienced."[11] The latter branch of political philosophy is called utopianism.

When players experiment with political utopias in DEMOCRACY 3, it can be seen as an application of "normative political philosophy", i.e., "recent theories of a just or free or good society."[12] Consequently, the game might be a useful tool for political education. In political education, political philosophy helps students to evaluate historical and contemporary policies and politics. Upper secondary school seems to be a good place to discuss political

---

9   Miller, David: "Political Philosophy," *Routledge Encyclopedia of Philosophy Online*, Thames: Taylor and Francis 1998; https://www.rep.routledge.com/articles/overview/political-philosophy/v-1
10 Ibid.
11 Ibid.
12 Kymlicka, Will: *Contemporary Political Philosophy: An Introduction*, Oxford: Oxford University Press 2002, p. 1.

philosophies—as the moral development during late adolescence includes systematic thinking about concepts such as justice and a good society.[13]

In his introduction to Anglo-American contemporary political philosophy, Will Kymlicka outlines the following schools of thought: utilitarianism, liberal equality, libertarianism, Marxism, communitarianism, citizenship theory, multiculturalism, and feminism. All of them are principally relevant for applied political philosophy in DEMOCRACY 3—though some of them might be easier to implement in a digital game than others and not all of them are equally important for the curricula of political education in upper secondary school.

Political dystopias are interesting for political education too, but in a more implicit way. In political discourse, the prediction of dystopian scenarios is a common rhetoric tool to discredit political opponents, especially in times of increasing political antagonisms, e.g. when it comes to the topic of immigration in general and refugees in particular. Therefore, it seems to be important for students, as citizens, to critically assess the value of those dystopian scenarios. In addition to non-fictional dystopias, fictional ones, such as the above-mentioned classics by Huxley and Orwell might also play a role in political education—especially, when political education is perceived as an interdisciplinary endeavor which spans other subjects such as literature as well.

GAMEPLAY OF DEMOCRACY 3

In DEMOCRACY 3, which is the third installment of a series of turn-based government simulations developed by the British indie studio Positech Games, in fact almost single-handedly by the programmer Cliff Harris, the players slip into the role of a head of state or government, i.e., the role of president or prime minister. At the beginning of the game, the player decides which country they want to govern. They can choose between Australia, Germany, France, Great Britain, Canada, and the United States of America. The player takes over his or her government office immediately after winning an

---

13 Kohlberg, Lawrence: *The Philosophy of Moral Development: Moral Stages and the Idea of Justice*, Vol. 1, San Francisco: Harper & Row 1931.

election. The main goal of the game is to win the approval of a majority of the voters in elections.

DEMOCRACY 3 is a turn-based game. This also means that there are no time-critical components in the game. The players can make their decisions without any rush. They decide for themselves when they want to finish a round of the game. Each round represents a period of three months.

Interestingly, the game cannot be won. The players always lose—either because they lose an election or fall victim to an assassination. In the manual of the game it says aptly: "All political careers end in failure."[14]

As shown in figure 1, the main interface of the game is based on a complex network of relationships between numerous political and economic variables. These are represented in the interface as circles and sorted according to policy fields. DEMOCRACY 3 distinguishes between seven policy fields: tax, economy, public services, welfare, transport, law and order, and foreign policy.

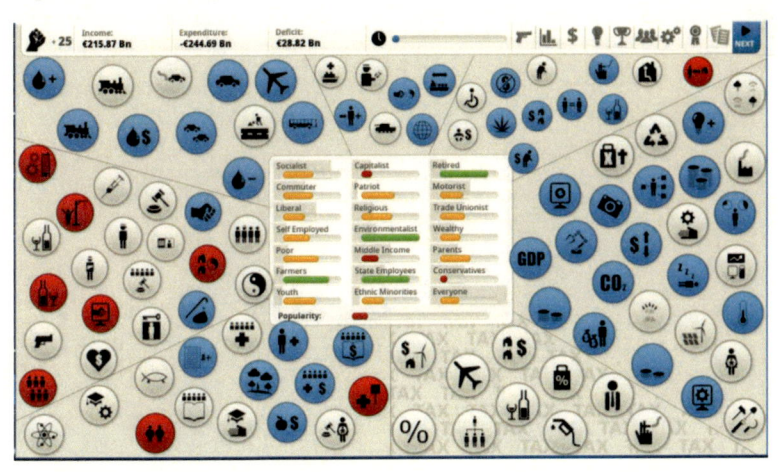

Figure 1: Main Interface

Source: Screenshot from DEMOCRACY 3

---

14 Positech: "Democracy 3. Institute of Effective Government: Briefing Notes. Version 1.0," 2013; http://cdn1.macgamestore.com/macgamesarcade/manuals/Democracy3_Manual.pdf

The grey circles represent policies that can be designed by the player. The blue circles contain additional data or statistics that cannot be influenced by the player. The green and red circles are good situations, such as a technology advantage over other countries, or bad situations such as alcohol abuse prevalent in the population.

Statistics and situations result directly from the player's policies. To be successful in DEMOCRACY 3, both statistics and situations must be permanently monitored. A selection of the most important statistics is presented to the player after each round in the respective quarterly report. These are data on gross domestic product, health, education, unemployment, crime and poverty.

The relationships between different variables become visible in the interface when the mouse pointer is moved over a specific item. Animated, connecting lines appear between the selected variable and other variables. A green line means a positive effect; a red line a negative effect. The small characters on the lines indicate the direction of the effects. The faster the lines move, the stronger the effects between the variables. Figure 2 illustrates the complex interrelationships of the gross domestic product.

Figure 2: The relationship between variables using the example of gross domestic product

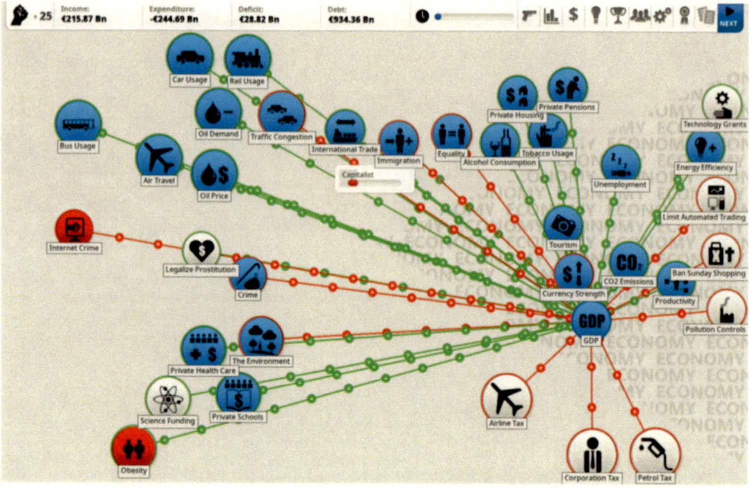

Source: Screenshot from DEMOCRACY 3

If the game refers to positive and negative effects, it does not make any valuations. A positive effect on unemployment implies rising unemployment. A negative effect on pollution means decreasing pollution. Whether the effects are desirable or undesirable does not matter.

Players who want to be successful in DEMOCRACY 3 must first and foremost satisfy their voters, because it is they who decide after the end of each legislative period whether the player may continue to govern or whether the game is over for him or her.

In DEMOCRACY 3 voters represent a cross-section of society in their entirety. Each voter has different characteristics: They are more or less liberal or conservative, they are more or less socialist or capitalist, and they belong to a certain income group: low, middle, or wealthy. In addition, each voter belongs to other groups, such as parents or motorists. The degree of attachment to the respective group varies.

The affiliation of individual voters to groups is subject to change: it is influenced by the policies of the player insofar as successful policies implying a certain ideology or favoring a certain group might convince individual voters to 'switch over' and thus increase the number of voters affiliated with the respective group of voters (and the other way round). The distribution of voters among these groups differs from country to country.

The happiness of the 20 voter groups with the policies of the respective player is shown in the middle of the main menu (Fig. 1). For the player it is important to understand that the happiness of a certain voter group is always only an abstract value—because the happiness of a single real voter is not only based on his or her belonging to one group. Accordingly, even a voter who, as a socialist, agrees with the player's policies can ultimately decide not to vote for the player—because they dislike the player's policies in other respects.

Players who would like to get a closer look at their own voters in the game can use the focus group feature. In the focus groups of the game, the player can look at individual, randomly selected voters in detail. A diagram shows the player how strongly the individual voter identifies with the voter groups to which they belong. In addition, the player receives information on the effect that the individual membership to a particular group is currently having on his potential voting decision.

The central gameplay in DEMOCRACY 3 is the implementation of policies. This includes, for example, the passing of laws as well as modifying of budgets and investing in various policy areas. Political actions are paid in the game with the currency of "political capital." With this concept, the political effort involved in a certain policy is symbolically represented. Smaller, less controversial projects cost less political capital than large, controversial projects. At the beginning of each round, the player receives new political capital. The amount of political capital per round is linked to the player's popularity among the electorate and the quality of his or her cabinet government.

The player changes a policy with the so-called "policy slider." With the slider, they determine the intensity of a policy in a certain area. In the case of laws, the slider usually regulates something like the severity of punishment for non-compliance with this law. In the case of expenditures and investments, it determines the amount of the invested sum. And in the case of taxes, the player regulates the respective tax rates via the slider.

Some policies are easy to implement. They come into effect immediately. These include, for instance, tax changes that can take effect as early as the next quarter. Other policies, such as the construction of new railway lines or the establishment of a space program, require several quarters in order to be implemented. Investments in science and education also only pay off in the long term.

The costs and revenues of a policy depend not only on the actions of the player, but also on other factors. For example, the costs and revenues are influenced by the effectiveness of the respective minister. External factors play a role as well. If, for example, certain diseases occur more frequently in the population, the costs for the state health system can skyrocket. Last but not least, the player has to deal with a global economy that is subject to economic cycles and is not directly influenced by the player.

In addition to adapting (or abolishing) existing policies, the player can also introduce new policies. DEMOCRACY 3 has its own menu for this purpose under the heading "policy ideas." Again, the player can choose from the above-mentioned policy fields: Foreign policy, welfare, economy, tax, public services, law and order, and transport.

In the game, the national budget plays a special role, with the player initially being confronted with a certain degree of national debt in all countries. In principle, there is no obligation to pay off the mountain of debt. As long as the state can afford the interest, the debts will not get the player into any major difficulties. However, a financial imbalance can arise if interest rates rise significantly. This is the case, for instance, in certain economic situations, or when the credit rating of the state governed by the player is downgraded because of concerns about the stability of the government or the solvency of the state.

While in DEMOCRACY 3 the players normally decide for themselves which policy areas they want to pursue at which point in time, they are occasionally confronted with so-called dilemmas. These are time-critical issues or debates that require a player's positioning or decision.

The length of a legislative period, i.e., the duration until the next election, depends on the country selected. In each country, however, there are only two parties: that of the player and that of the opposition. The election itself is then always carried out as a direct election of the president or prime minister.

According to the logic of political processes, the elections in DEMOCRACY 3 have a special significance. Thus, each election can lead to the end of the player's political career, i.e., to the end of the game. Following the simulation of the election by the computer, the player is informed of the turnout and the result of the election. Immediately thereafter, the game is either over or continues with the next legislative period.

Another way to lose the game is to fall victim to an assassination attempt by a terrorist organization. Terrorist organizations are formed in the game especially when the player's policies do not adequately consider a particular interest group at all. For example, if patriots feel permanently disadvantaged, a small proportion of them will join terrorist organizations, increasing the risk for the player of losing the game as a result of an assassination. This is another reason why it is important for players to keep an eye on internal security. In the game, terrorist organizations are monitored via the so-called "security screen." Terrorist groups can be fought at short notice by intelligence services. In the medium term, a change in policy can help.

The power of the player as president or prime minister is great. Political negotiations and control processes between the executive, legislative, and judicial branches are not simulated. Nevertheless, the power of the player is restricted by a limited amount of political capital and the player has to deal with a cabinet government made up of ministers from different departments.

First, the ministers generate political capital that enables the player to implement his or her policies in general. Second, they specifically influence the success of policies in their ministry. And thirdly, they help the player to make a good impression on certain groups of voters. If the player is dissatisfied with the performance of ministers or considers a strategic repositioning necessary, they can dismiss and reappoint ministers or reshuffle the entire cabinet government. It is important to stress that in DEMOCRACY 3 ministers do not make their own decisions. The government's policies lie solely in the hands of the player as head of state or government.

All in all, the mechanics (and narration) of DEMOCRACY 3 allow players to play with political utopias as well as dystopias. Players can freely try out a certain set of coherent set of ideal policies, implement them and test its effects, check whether they lead (inside the system of the game) to an expected utopian or dystopian outcome. In other words, players can tinker with political ideologies and philosophies—at least as long as they get re-elected and not assassinated, i.e., as long as their experimental play is approved by the rules of the game.

In contrast to narrative games discussed in other contributions of this volume, in the political simulation of DEMOCRACY 3, the appearance of utopias or dystopias is not a necessity initiated by the game in any case. Instead, utopias and dystopias can be created by the players themselves—as an option. The game is not telling a pre-defined utopian or dystopian story, but the player is creating this story voluntarily, by his or her own choice, including a significant creative freedom in terms of the direction of this story. However, of course, players cannot control the course of the game, which includes that they might end up in utopia or dystopia accidently. Furthermore, the effects of their policies depend on biases of the game.

From time to time, DEMOCRACY releases expansions that extend the existing game in a certain direction. The extension EXTREMISM (2014) is of particular interest for the context of this article because it supports the design of more extreme political ideologies and philosophies. The game's website describes the expansion as follows:

"This expansion for DEMOCRACY 3 adds 33 new situations and policies that reflect the more extreme side of politics, all within the framework of a democracy. Fed up with just adjusting taxes and government spending in the conventional sense? Perhaps you think your people need the national anthem sung at the start of every news broadcast? or maybe what they are crying out for is a ban on divorce, or same-sex relationships? Alternatively, you might like to close your countries [sic.] airports to save the environment, or maybe outright ban private education? How far to the extremes can you take your country and still maintain the support of the people (and avoid some of them putting a gun to your head)."[15]

Another interesting expansion relevant for the topic of utopias and dystopias is CLONES & DRONES (2014):

"What challenges are to come for the politicians of the future? Mass unemployment due to the automation of factories? Or will this lead to a leisure society and equality? Will ubiquitous drones lead to better law enforcement and less traffic congestion or to widespread crime and infringement of privacy? Should we give the go-ahead to human cloning? Will climate change cause problems for our country? Are we going to run out of rare earth metals? Or oil...? The people look to YOU for leadership in these turbulent times. Can you keep the country happy and prosperous as we head to the 2020s and beyond?"[16]

Finally, from an educational perspective, it is worth mentioning that the game is open to modding. The central mechanics of the game can easily be changed by everyone. This offers players the opportunity to become co-designers of the game. A selection of DEMOCRACY 3 mods is published on the official website of the game. The featured mods introduce, for instance, new countries or new factors such as inflation/deflation. Interestingly, there are also mods that might be facilitated to support players by implementing several political ideologies and philosophies, in other words, working/playing towards political utopias:

"Keynesian Economic POlicy (by nikosb1995): Change: Adds Stimulus Package as a policy to help stimulate the economy (if played under USA the stimulus costs 800 billion just like the most recent US stimulus)."

"The Happy Capitalists Mod (by Gikgik): This mod makes Capitalists a little happier. They do no longer react to child or disability benefits. They get happy from private pensions, housing, healthcare, schools, and relaxed border controls, and angry from inheritance tax."

---

15 http://www.positech.co.uk/democracy3/extremism.html
16 http://positech.co.uk/democracy3/clonesanddrones.html

"Migration (by Gikgik): Three new policies: Immigrant Language Courses, Immigrant Welfare and Work Visas. Two situations: Emigration and Labor Shortage. Balancing of Immigration causes and effects. Six dilemmas related to ethnic and racial issues. Complexity: + (Marginally more complex) Difficulty: + (Marginally harder) Version 1.22."[17]

The first two above-mentioned mods, for example, would increase players' scope when it comes to economics—by offering the possibility to implement a stimulus package, a tool of Keynesian economics (Keynesian economic policy), and by allowing players to easier increase the happiness of capitalists which might be useful in scenarios that favor, but also disfavor that particular group of voters (The Happy Capitalists Mod). The third mod could help players to create a multicultural utopia.

LEARNING POLITICAL PHILOSOPHY BY TINKERING WITH POLITICAL UTOPIAS AND DYSTOPIAS

In the following, I will look at learning possibilities offered by DEMOCRACY 3 with a special focus on the application of political philosophy. However, I will start with a broader perspective: What can players learn in DEMOCRACY 3 in general?

First of all, by assuming the role of prime minister or president, players have to deal with the effects of political actions. In the course of the execution of their government business, the players are directly confronted with the consequences of their political decisions for the economic, social, and cultural situation of the governed country. Furthermore, the players experience the effects of their policies on the approval of the electorate, i.e., they will find out whether they can win elections with the implemented set of policies.

In the course of the game, the player is made aware of the complexity of political decisions. Ultimately, the player is given the opportunity to realize how difficult it is to reconcile the various demands placed on a government, such as meeting the needs of as many voter groups as possible, presenting an appropriate state budget, and increasing the gross national product.

---

17 http://www.positech.co.uk/democracy3/mods.html

In general, the players can govern in three (strategic) ways: (a) they can act based on ideology and/or philosophy, i.e., play with a coherent set of policies which are implicitly or explicitly influenced by certain kinds of professional or amateur political philosophies, (b) they can follow a form of 'Realpolitik' from the very beginning, or (c) opt for a pragmatic combination of aforementioned forms of governance, i.e., balance ideological or philosophical preferences and coherence on the one hand, and political success (i.e., re-election) on the other hand—in order to prevent that their adopted direction of political ideology or philosophy fails in practice, in other words, that his or her policies ends in dystopia.

The availability of options (a) and (c) indicates that DEMOCRACY 3 offers learning possibilities in terms of an application of political philosophies. Actually, the game makes it pretty easy to implement ideal and even extreme forms of political programs, at least in the first place—because, in the logic of the game, the player, as government, is actually not really controlled by other political institutions, such as the parliament. However, even in the game, change requires time—because the implementation of policies must be paid with resources that are limited: political capital as well as money. In the longer run of the game, over a couple of rounds, change furthermore warrants the support of the electorate including many groups of voters. The player must make the electorate happy to stay popular. One-sided radical policies imply the constant risk of failing, i.e., losing the game due to not being re-elected or being assassinated.[18]

DEMOCRACY 3 can be understood as a test laboratory or experimental field for political ideas, ideologies, philosophies. The game enables the player to implement political philosophies in an ideal way and to observe its consequences directly. Political philosophies might mean (a) professional political philosophies—in various grades of abstraction starting from simplified versions of socialism or liberalism to theories of justice from contemporary political philosophy as described e.g. by Kymlicka,[19] or (b) amateur

---

18 As the distribution of people to voter groups differ between countries, at the beginning of the game (which is however subject to change)—the US has a higher amount of capitalists than Germany, for instance—the selection of the country matters. It is, for example, more difficult to pursue social democratic policies in the US than in Germany.

19 W. Kymlicka: *Contemporary Political Philosophy*.

political philosophies envisioned by the player—i.e., their own ideas about a just society, which might be (consciously or unconsciously) influenced by (one or more) professional political philosophies.

Of course, the game's evaluation of the player's set of policies cannot be fully unbiased. The system has been designed and programmed by a human and humans cannot be completely neutral by nature—although in this case the designer/programmer, Cliff Harris, who owns a degree in Economics from the London School of Economics, consciously reached for realism and political neutrality.[20] While he based the game/system on political, societal, and economic realities, it is certainly his interpretation of reality. Furthermore, the system, as a game, must necessarily imply a significant reduction of complexity. Therefore, players should not understand the outcomes of their policies as absolute truth, but as one legitimate interpretation of reality.

In addition to tinkering with normative political philosophies, players might also play with ideas suggested by political parties for implementation, as e.g. outlined in manifestos. These are in many cases built around a particular ideological standpoint, but somehow already shaped by the constraints of reality including economic, cultural, and political conditions. Even though these sets of policy suggestions are not purely ideal, they are still relatively pointed—since political parties know that due to the logics of politics in parliamentary democracy, they will never have to implement a pure version of it.

Manifestos from radical political parties might be of particular interest. As these will not necessarily reflect the player's own ideas, applying them might be like playing with dystopia (rather than utopia) for them. As already said, political utopias and dystopias are two sides of a coin. It depends on your perspective whether you perceive a certain set of ideological policies as utopia or dystopia. And utopia can end in dystopia.

The journalist Dan Griliopoulos actually tested a consistent implementation of manifestos in DEMOCRACY 3 several times. Among others, he applied the Tory manifesto for the 2017 United Kingdom general election. In an article, published in the political weekly *The New Statesman*, he outlines that "the results were terrifying":

---

20 Benson, Julian: "Programming Prejudice and Why Democracy 3 is So Hard to Rip Off," *Kotaku UK*, 2017; http://www.kotaku.co.uk/2017/02/21/programming-prejudice-and-why-democracy-3-is-so-hard-to-rip-off

"Events, dear boy, events. She [the British Prime Minister] couldn't shake off the general strike, which pushed GDP down, which in turn pushed up unemployment, and high unemployment just destroys everything—I didn't go into the detail, but there were armed gangs on the streets, horrible alcoholism everywhere, and poverty galore."[21]

It ended, somehow, in dystopia.

At this point, reference should be made to a feature of the game: the "political compass." This tool shows the player, with the help of a coordinate system, where his or her own policies can be located in the political field. The horizontal axis locates the player's policies in the spectrum between socialism and capitalism. The vertical axis refers to the spectrum between liberal and conservative policies. In the case of a won election, the player can then compare the ideological positioning of his policies with the election victories in previous rounds and, if applicable, with the election victories of his friends (Fig. 3).

Another way of the game of offering its players feedback on the direction of their policies and encouraging them to tinker with political philosophies is the conferment of awards, which include, among others: "Socialist Utopia," "Egalitarian Miracle," and "Green Utopia."

Although players are relatively free to set up their ideal states, in the course of the game, reality usually strikes back: players need to win a majority in the elections as well as they have to avoid to get assassinated by minorities they have isolated, who organize themselves in terrorist groups. Most utopias based on a polar political philosophy end up being voted out or collapse due to counter-revolution. In the course of implementing radical policies, the player may find that the goal of the game—not to be voted out and not to fall victim to an assassination attempt—cannot be achieved with such a polarizing policy. At least, the player would then have learned that the political, economic, and cultural realities could stand in the way of the realization of political ideals.

---

21 Griliopoulos, Dan: "We Ran the Tory 2017 Manifesto Through a Video Game … and the Results Were Terrifying," *The New Statesman*, 2017; http://www.newstatesman.com/2017/05/simulection-we-ran-tory-2017-manifesto-through-video-game-and-results-were-terrifying

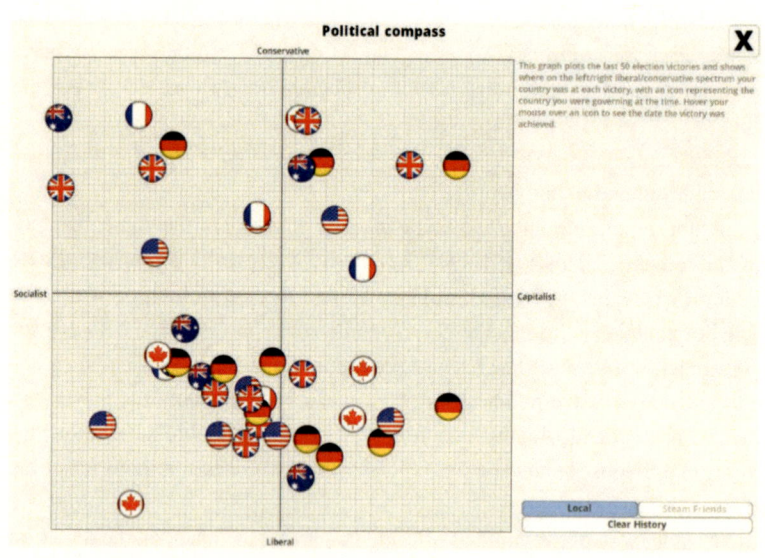

Figure 3: The political compass feature

Source: https://store.steampowered.com/app/245470/Democracy_3/

As a reaction to the failure of such a polarizing set of policies, the player may then change his or her tactics by implementing a more moderate version of his or her idealistically shaped policies in order to satisfy the needs of different groups of voters and ultimately achieve a political majority. In other words, they might add a certain degree of 'Realpolitik' to their strategy. Alternatively, players might keep on tinkering with political utopias or dystopias in further rounds of the game—independent of his or her political success, respectively, the goal of the game. In the end, as we know from player research, players of digital games are not always following (solely) the goal of winning. Playing with the system, experimenting, tinkering, and even destroying can be interesting too—depending on a player's motivations and characteristics, as e.g. described by Nick Yee's in his taxonomy of player types.[22]

---

22 Yee, Nick. "The Gamer Motivation Profile: What We Learned From 250,000 Gamers," in: *Proceedings of the 2016 Annual Symposium on Computer-Human Interaction in Play*, ACM 2016, pp. 2-2.

It can be concluded that DEMOCRACY 3 offers players the possibility to learn about political philosophy by tinkering with political utopias and dystopias, in other words, by playing with ideas and ideologies. The processes and outcomes of this learning becomes visible when players document their play online, on video platforms or in their blogs, for instance. The next section takes a closer look at this phenomenon.

EXAMPLES FROM AFFINITY SPACES AROUND THE GAME

Educational researcher James Paul Gee uses the concept of "affinity spaces" to situate those interactions and learning processes that take place between players outside the actual space of the game, in discussion boards, wikis, blogs, or video platforms, for example.[23] An observation in affinity spaces around DEMOCRACY 3 reveals that the above-reconstructed learning possibilities offered by the game indeed initiates various learning processes and outcomes in the area of political ideas. In YouTube, for instance, players upload Let's Play videos showcasing their utopian or dystopian policies, respectively, demonstrating how they reached their own utopias or dystopias. The presented sets of policies are mostly based on simple interpretations of one or more professional political philosophies or their own thought-out amateur political philosophy (which might be inspired by one or more of the aforementioned normative theories of justice). In some cases, the publication of one player's video essay leads to a discourse in the comments. There are, for instance, discussions about the adequate and/or consistent application of a particular theory, or about the correct interpretation of crucial terms such as "liberal." In the following, I will refer to several examples from YouTube and one example from a player's blog in order to exemplify the learning processes and outcomes that can be elicited by DEMOCRACY 3.

A selection of relevant titles of YouTube videos alone uncovers the phenomenon that players of DEMOCRACY 3 tinker with political ideologies and utopias throughout the political spectrum:

---

23 E.g. Gee, James Paul: "Semiotic Social Spaces and Affinity Spaces: From The Age of Mythology to Today's Schools," in: Barton, David/Tusting, Karin (eds.), *Beyond Communities of Practice: Language, Power and Social Context*, Cambridge, UK: Cambridge University Press 2005, pp. 214-232.

- "DEMOCRACY 3—All DLC—Canada—1—Capitalist Utopia"[24]
- "Niko plays DEMOCRACY 3—turning United states into a utopia for liberals"[25]
- "DEMOCRACY 3: Creating a Social Democratic Utopia and trying to Balance the Budget!"[26]
- "M Plays DEMOCRACY 3: Socialist Utopia"[27]
- "Challenge: DEMOCRACY 3—Make the USA Communist"[28]
- "DEMOCRACY 3—Communist USA 01—Max Difficulty"[29]

The following text written by the YouTube user "Socialist Progressive Games" as a teaser for his video "DEMOCRACY 3: Creating a Social Democratic Utopia and trying to Balance the Budget!" shows that players deliberately follow a political ideology/philosophy as well as that they explain their policy choices with a systematic argument (in opposition to other political ideologies/philosophies):

"In my first gaming episode, I show you the Social Democratic policies I have implemented such as strict rent controls and a large state housing program! I also implement new laws such as raising the corporation tax to 50 %, legalizing cannabis and LSD, and I implement the 'Welfare Fraud Department' I also ramble on about why Liberalism is ineffective on combating contradictions within the Capitalist system."[30]

A lot of posts reveal that players autonomously determine creative and/or difficult goals and pursue (partly humorous) thought experiments, in other words, that they tinker with political ideas, ideologies, and philosophies. "The Educational Gamer," for example, introduces his video "DEMOCRACY 3—Communist USA 01—Max Difficulty" as follows:

---

24 https://www.youtube.com/watch?v=5fePpdyH9m4
25 https://www.youtube.com/watch?v=isSI3bPbcpU
26 https://www.youtube.com/watch?v=qIqciTW2LkI
27 https://www.youtube.com/watch?v=1ooBtHlvfuI
28 https://www.youtube.com/watch?v=UMkW4RWfYKE
29 https://www.youtube.com/watch?v=B_zeDmv2T8&list=PLBCKdXwKFwSh0AtuNXyfnxxaFaN_61Zw1
30 https://www.youtube.com/watch?v=qIqciTW2LkI

"We are trying to turn the USA into a communist dictatorship in DEMOCRACY 3. Our goal is to unlock the 'Socialist Paradise' and the 'Surveillance' achievements at the same time."[31]

Other players systematically apply their own thought-out political philosophy, i.e., they design a set of policies and test their effects in the system of the game. The blogger Matthias Schulze offers insights into this process in a longer post. He starts by outlining his approach to government as well as his ideas of just policies:

"You can govern completely ad-hoc in a Merkelian style (which did not work out for me!) or have a plan for a communist, neoliberal or surveillance utopia in mind. To test the extreme types and see what happens was the most fun for me. [...] This got me thinking: What would be the BEST for my digital voters, for me as a digital politician, for the country itself and for the world? I decided on the following political goals and principles:

- Increase economic growth and reduce debts in order to finance the following initiatives.
- Get the best education and free education in the world, with free university access and high science and research funding which results in being a high-tech nation.
- Decrease crime rates.
- Decrease unemployment rates.
- Have a high degree of social equality and a high basic income and minimum wage.
- The economy must be environmentally friendly and as green as possible.
- Increase foreign aid for third party countries. Change to voluntary military service.
- Have the best welfare system with high degrees of public health.
- Stay in office as long as possible.
- Do not engage in any surveillance practices and stick to the rule of law.
- Separate church and state and ban creationism from public schools.

---

31 https://www.youtube.com/watch?v=B_zeDmv2T8&list=PLBCKdXwKwSh0AtuNXyfnxxaFaN_61Zw1

- Get a space program! Because? Spaaaace, final frontier, developing mankind etc. You get the idea!"

In his blog post, Schulze afterwards summarizes the effects of his consequent implementation of the above-mentioned set of ideas:

"To sum up: I managed to achieve all of my goals and the game awarded me several achievements. I reduced unemployment, got a stable, egalitarian (Egalitarian Miracle Award) and green economy (Green Utopia & Kyoto Award)). My finances were solid (Economic Miracle, Sovereign Wealth and Budget Balancer Award). My state had the best education (Intelligentsia Award) with several Nobel prizes, a space program and leadership in the high-tech market (Technological Superiority Award). With the help of taxes I managed to create a healthy society (Healthy Minds and Bodies Award). My electorate loved me (Legitimate Leader, Elder Statesmen Award) and in several elections I obliterated the opposition (Landslide Award and One-Party State Award), gaining 94 % in popularity ratings. This was also because I established a Crime Free Utopia (Award) without even touching any surveillance measures. In sum: I created a role model democracy and most of my voters where happy, except one type: the capitalists. In order to build my green, socialist, intelligent & health, technology utopia I had to adopt several policies which capitalists didn't like: minimum wages, education standards, housing initiatives, inheritance and corporation taxes, food & consumption standards, CO_2 tax and several more. In the end, I realized everything that is good for a society and the world in general but got assassinated by a radical capitalist Battenberg group of which my secret service warned me several times."

Finally, the blogger reflects on his own learning experience—among other things, in terms of the relationship between political ideology/philosophy and 'Realpolitik:'

"The moral of this story is: the world won't become greener, more educated, more peaceful because in the end, capitalist interest will assassinate you. This was really an astonishing insight: even though the economy was thriving and I reduced public debt and also adopted several investor-friendly policies, capitalists hated me whereas the rest of the people (except the Catholics) were happy. This is the second lessons: you have to listen to the people equally and do not favor one type of interest over another for the whole time. In some cases, it is necessary to adopt policies against the short-term interest of the voter and adopt policies with a long-term effect (education grants, drug taxes, CO2 tax). This requires you to adopt a certain 'basta!' mentality: giving a damn about the next election and hoping for positive effects in the future. I observed myself saying: f*ck the election, this is good for the people (increasing welfare coverage), the country (increasing education) or the planet (CO2 Tax)."[32]

Assessing this blogger's contribution in context of a discussion of DEMOCRACY 3's educational merit, it certainly has to be taken into account that the player/author is a political scientist himself, at the time of writing a Ph.D. student, and thus his playing/reading of the game does not necessarily have to be representative for the average player's practices (though it can be assumed that players of DEMOCRACY 3 are rather well-educated in general). However, his postings clearly disclose *possible* learning processes and outcomes the game can elicit.

Dystopian scenarios are also being presented in the affinity space of YouTube. "Allohmon," for instance, tried to set up an "Orwellian nightmare." In the beginning of his video titled "UK—Let's make an Orwellian nightmare!", he massively increased the police force, community policing, and intelligence services. He also supported the proliferation of CCTV cameras. In order to save money in his budget, he backed out of state pensions, which led to the development of a system of private pensions. He furthermore raised military spendings. As an innovation (policy idea), he introduced technology grants. At this time, the human rights society already said that it actively encourages its members to oppose the current government. Then the player implemented strict alcohol laws (including strong restrictions) as well as another policy idea in maximum capacity: robotics research grants. Inbetween two of his rounds, he banned same sex marriage in a so-called event which asks the player for a decision. Afterwards, the player introduced compulsory work for all the unemployed living in his state. In addition, he encouraged the building of gated communities. The combination of all his policies yielded among other things an extremely low gross domestic product, massive deficits, and a recession, as well as homelessness and a stress epidemic, which means according to the game itself "dangerously high levels of stress for people with full time jobs" diagnosed by medical doctors. As a

---

32 Schulze, Matthias: "What I Learned Playing Democracy 3 or Why the World Will Not Change," 2015; https://percepticon.wordpress.com/2015/01/07/what-i-learned-playing-democracy-3-or-why-the-world-will-not-change/

reaction, i.e., to get rid of that deficit, the player cut the country's public health service. The final end of the game/story is not reported.[33]

A discussion of DEMOCRACY 3's affinity spaces must mention that there is another sophisticated practice of tinkering with the political simulation outside of the game: modding, i.e., a manipulation of the game's system, in other words, a contribution to game design. Sometimes, the process of modding considers political philosophies as well. The community, for instance, creates mods which support players to set up particular political philosophies, such as the previously mentioned "Migration" mod which fosters the implementation of multiculturalism.

Since the learning possibilities of DEMOCRACY 3 are used by players in the informal setting of affinity spaces, from the perspective of education, the question arises how the same processes can be harnessed in the formal setting of political education, in which players could be asked to follow a more structured and professional way of playing with political utopias and dystopias.

PLAYING DEMOCRACY 3 IN SCHOOLS

Although DEMOCRACY 3 was not designed as a serious game, the developer of the game regularly receives requests from teachers who are interested in using the game in school. To meet this demand, the developer offers licenses to schools and other educational institutions at reasonable prices. A license for 40 students costs 100 British pounds. According to the developer, the game is already used by more than 70 schools and universities to teach politics and economics.[34]

In view of the complexity of the game, I assume that it is particularly suitable for use in upper secondary education. A meaningful play of DEMOCRACY 3 presupposes basic knowledge of politics and economics. Otherwise, players will not understand many of the concepts and interrelationships that appear in the game.

Since DEMOCRACY 3, as a game, is based on an *oversimplified* simulation of politics in parliamentary democracies, which implies that the player can govern with an unrealistic amount of power (i.e., without being dependent

---

33 https://www.youtube.com/watch?v=3iuRHc94kok.

34 http://positech.co.uk/democracy3/educational.html

on negotiations and approvals of other political instances such as the parliament), the teacher should make sure that students understand the difference between the simulation of the game on the one hand and real politics on the other hand. In another article, I have rendered these deficits of the simulation as a didactic opportunity. I have argued that the empty and weak points of the game's simulation of political processes are actually offering special learning possibilities for a school context, because they virtually challenge a critical analysis of the simulation, i.e., a comparison with the reality of politics—which could lead to a deep engagement with political processes in general.[35]

The game furthermore requires a certain ability to concentrate as well as frustration tolerance. The players do not receive immediate feedback on each of their actions, as it is common in other (e.g. more action-oriented) genres. Instead, the players have to deal with a complex system to which they have to devote themselves over a longer period of time without receiving direct rewards after each and every action.

From an educational point of view, the game offers various learning possibilities when it comes to political education in a formal school setting.[36] However, in the context of this volume, I will solely emphasize those learning opportunities related to the study of political philosophies as well as ideologically connotated concepts of political parties (such as manifestos) which are relevant when it comes to the overall topic of utopias and dystopias.

As outlined throughout this paper, DEMOCRACY 3 invites players to tinker with political ideas, ideologies, and philosophies in various forms. Upper secondary education, in which students are already in their late adolescence, seems to be a good time to discuss the normative questions of political philosophy—because the moral development during this time includes systematic thinking about concepts such as justice and a good society.[37] While experimenting with political philosophies, students will ultimately also deal

---

35 Czauderna, André: "Unvollständigkeit als didaktische Chance. Überlegungen zum Einsatz von DEMOCRACY 3 im Politikunterricht," in: Möhring, Sebastian/Riemer, Nathanael (eds.), *Videospiele als didaktische Herausforderung*, Potsdam: Potsdam University Press 2019.
36 Ibid.
37 L. Kohlberg: *The Philosophy of Moral Development*.

with the possibly disenchanting question of what effects, including associated difficulties, the consistent implementation of political philosophies could provoke.

In contrast to the informal learning environment of affinity spaces, formal education in schools will probably aim for a more systematic way of applying political philosophies as well as a stricter and more appropriate interpretation of textbook knowledge.

The observed applications of political philosophy in affinity spaces around the game are based on oversimplified professional political philosophies or amateur political philosophies, which include individual conceptions of players, i.e., personal utopias which are sometimes an unconscious merger or remix of several professional political philosophies. They mostly refer to political ideas from socialism, liberalism, and capitalism. Although some of them might be quite sophisticated, i.e., may include a coherent set of political ideas and in case they are presented in Let's Play videos sometimes even an intelligent and/or humorous discussion, they usually lack academic rigor, e.g. an explicit link to textbook political philosophies or an explicit discussion of the underlying theories of justice. While these video playthroughs show an application of a set of policies following one or more directions of political philosophy, they do not display a discussion of reasons why this set of policies is better than other sets of policies in terms of its justice. They also do not depict the diversity of normative theories discussed in political philosophy.

For a school context, it would be necessary to apply political philosophies more accurately as described in textbooks including an acknowledgment of their complexity as well as to cover the broadness of the field—although, in addition, teachers might let students develop and then tinker with their own amateur political philosophies. As a starting point, it would be worthwhile to look into contemporary political philosophies as summarized by Kymlicka: utilitarianism, liberal equality, libertarianism, Marxism, communitarianism, citizenship theory, multiculturalism, and feminism.[38] More recent developments in normative political theory such as multiculturalism and feminism, following the cultural turn in the humanities and social sciences, might bring different perspectives than the usual applied classical theories focused on economic conditions. Teachers' selection of adequate philosophies for

---

38 W. Kymlicka: *Contemporary Political Philosophy*.

application in DEMOCRACY 3 must also consider which ones are most relevant for the respective curriculum as well as easier to grasp and (re)construct in a digital game. As playing the game as such does not require a reflection of the chosen political philosophies' justifications and reasonings, their discussion must take place prior to and/or after the gaming sessions.

In addition to textbook normative political philosophies, ideological connotated concepts of political parties, such as manifestos, which are relevant when it comes to the overall topic of utopias and dystopias, are also interesting for political education in schools. For example, it might be worthwhile to let students replay current manifestos of radical political parties (which are situated on the poles of the political spectrum rather than being a plan for 'Realpolitik' already shaped by political negotiations) and thus let them test their effects, which might include that they end in dystopia. This could be followed by a critical discussion of political ideology on the one hand and 'Realpolitik' on the other hand.

The previously mentioned feature of the political compass could be a very helpful tool for the use of DEMOCRACY 3 in political education—since it grants students a visual overview of the field of political ideas while also facilitating reflection and discussion. The political compass situates the players' policies in the coordinate system of political ideas. It furthermore allows a comparison with previous rounds of the game as well as with the rounds of other players.

The role of teachers during the application of DEMOCRACY 3 in schools should not be underestimated. They must, among other things, embed the educational tool of the game in a broader teaching unit and its didactic approach as well as assisting students to fill the apparent gaps of the game. The game does not stand alone. According to many authors contributing to the literature on digital game-based learning, the processing of the gaming experience within the framework of a so-called "debriefing" is absolutely necessary in order to initiate sustainable learning processes.[39] Thus, for the use of

---

39 E.g. Crookall, David: "Serious Games, Debriefing, and Simulation/Gaming As a Discipline," *Simulation & Gaming* 41/6 (2010), pp. 898-920; Arnab, Sylvester et al.: "Framing the Adoption of Serious Games in Formal Education," *Electronic Journal of e-Learning* 10/2 (2012), pp. 159-171; Kolb, Alice Y./Kolb, David A.: "The Learning Way: Meta-Cognitive Aspects of Wxperiential Learning," *Simulation & Gaming* 40/3 (2009), pp. 297-327.

DEMOCRACY 3 in education, in line with the 'experiential learning' approach, it is recommended that, after a certain period of play, a comprehensive debriefing—e.g. a class discussion or group work—should be provided. Afterwards, the students would play again and then participate in another debriefing—and so on and so forth. In short, play and reflection phases should alternate.[40]

To sum up, the application of DEMOCRACY 3 in a school context allows students to tinker with political utopias and dystopias as well as to experiment with political ideas, ideologies, and philosophies. It could thus contribute to a deeper understanding of normative political philosophy in particular and an active and critical examination of politics in general. And perhaps even more important: It could stimulate utopian thinking, i.e., encourage students to envision a significantly better society than the one they are currently living in. Thereby, it might motivate political commitment.

LITERATURE

Alhabash, Saleem/Wise, Kevin: "Playing Their Game: Changing Stereotypes of Palestinians and Israelis through Videogame Play," *New Media & Society* 17/8 (2015), pp. 1358-1376.

Arnab, Sylvester et. al: "Framing the Adoption of Serious Games in Formal Education," *Electronic Journal of e-Learning* 10/2 (2012), pp. 159-171.

Benson, Julian: "Programming Prejudice and Why Democracy 3 is So Hard to Rip Off," *Kotaku UK*, 2017; http://www.kotaku.co.uk/2017/02/21/programming-prejudice-and-why-democracy-3-is-so-hard-to-rip-off

Crookall, David: "Serious Games, Debriefing, and Simulation/Gaming as a Discipline," *Simulation & Gaming* 41/6 (2010), pp. 898-920.

Cuhadar, Esra/Kampf, Ronit: "Learning About Conflict and Negotiations through Computer Simulations: The Case of PeaceMaker," *International Studies Perspectives* 15/4 (2014), pp. 509-524.

Czauderna, André: "Unvollständigkeit als didaktische Chance. Überlegungen zum Einsatz von DEMOCRACY 3 im Politikunterricht," in: Möhring, Sebastian/Riemer, Nathanael (eds.), *Videospiele als didaktische Herausforderung*, Potsdam University Press 2019.

---

40 A. Y. Kolb/D. A. Kolb: "The learning way."

Gonzalez, Cleotilde et al.: "Learning to Stand in the Other's Shoes: A Computer Video Game Experience of the Israeli-Palestinian Conflict," *Social Science Computer Review* 31/2 (2013), pp. 236-243.

Gee, James Paul: "Semiotic Social Spaces and Affinity Spaces: From The Age of Mythology to Today's Schools," in: Barton, David/Tusting, Karin (eds.), *Beyond Communities of Practice: Language, Power and Social Context*, Cambridge, UK: Cambridge University Press 2005, pp. 214-232.

Griliopoulos, Dan: "We Ran the Tory 2017 Manifesto Through a Video Game . . . and the Results Were Terrifying," *The New Statesman*, 2017; http://www.newstatesman.com/2017/05/simulection-we-ran-tory-2017-manifesto-through-video-game-and-results-were-terrifying

Huntington, Samuel P.: *The Clash of Civilizations and the Remaking of World Order*, New York City: Simon & Schuster 1997.

Huxley, Aldous: *Brave New World*, London: Vintage 1998 [1932].

Kolb, Alice Y./Kolb, David A.: "The Learning Way: Meta-Cognitive Aspects of Experiential Learning," *Simulation & Gaming* 40/3 (2009), pp. 297-327.

Kohlberg, Lawrence: *The Philosophy of Moral Development: Moral Stages and the Idea of Justice*, Vol. 1, San Francisco: Harper & Row 1931.

Kymlicka, Will: *Contemporary Political Philosophy: An Introduction*, Oxford: Oxford University Press 2002.

Miller, David: "Political Philosophy," *Routledge Encyclopedia of Philosophy Online*, Thames: Taylor and Francis 1998; https://www.rep.routledge.com/articles/overview/political-philosophy/v-1

More, Thomas: *Utopia*, Kindle 2012 [1516].

Motyka, Marc/Zehe, Mario: "Lernen mit Computerspielen im Politikunterricht. Empfehlungen und Fallbeispiele für die Praxis," *Politik unterrichten* 29/2 (2014), pp. 37-43.

Orwell, George: *Nineteen Eighty-Four*, City of Westminster: Penguin 2018 [1949].

Positech: "Democracy 3. Institute of Effective Government: Briefing Notes. Version 1.0," 2013; http://cdn1.macgamestore.com/macgamesarcade/manuals/Demoracy3_Manual.pdf

Sargent, Lyman Tower: "Utopianism," *Routledge Encyclopedia of Philosophy Online*, Thames: Taylor and Francis 1998; https://www.rep.routledge.com/articles/thematic/utopianism/v-1

Squire, Kurt: "Changing the Game: What Happens When Video Games Enter the Classroom," *Innovate: Journal of Online Education* 1/6 (2005).

Schulze, Matthias: "What I Learned Playing Democracy 3 or Why the World Will Not Change....," 2015; https://percepticon.wordpress.com/2015/01/07/what-i-learned-playing-democracy-3-or-why-the-world-will-not-change/

Yee, Nick: "The Gamer Motivation Profile: What We Learned from 250,000 Gamers," in: *Proceedings of the 2016 Annual Symposium on Computer-Human Interaction in Play*, ACM 2016, pp. 2-2.

GAMOGRAPHY

CIVILIZATION III (Infogrames 2001, O: Firaxis Games)

DEMOCRACY 3 (Positech Games 2013, O: Positech Games)

DEMOCRACY 3: CLONES & DRONES (Positech Games 2014, O: Positech Games)

DEMOCRACY 3: EXTREMISM (Positech Games 2014, O: Positech Games)

ENERGETIKA 2010 (Bundesministerium für Bildung und Forschung 2010, O: Takomat)

FOODFORCE (United Nations World Food Programme 2005, O: Playerthree and Deepend)

GENIUS. IM ZENTRUM DER MACHT (Cornelsen 2007)

PEACEMAKER (ImpactGames 2007, O: 2007)

The Concept of Utopia in Digital Games

GERALD FARCA

In a talk at the Swedish Game Awards Conference 2018, Ubisoft Massive's COO Alf Condelius expressed that with TOM CLANCY'S THE DIVISION 2 (2019) the company refrains from making political claims and that the game is simply a product for entertainment.[1] To give context to his precise statement below, one has to be aware that THE DIVISION 2 is set in a post-apocalyptic Washington DC, where a virus outbreak has plunged the country into chaos. This virus is also known as the Doller Pox because it was distributed on Black Friday via infected dollar bills and spread like wildfire. In the meantime, the Capitol building is on fire, and the situation has become so severe that the Mexican government has decided to build a wall to protect Mexico from streams of U.S. refugees. Only small resistance groups, referred to as the Division, aim to restore order to the anarchy that prevails.

"It's a balance because we cannot be openly political in our games [...] So, for example in THE DIVISION, it's a dystopian future and there's a lot of interpretations that it's something that we see the current society moving towards, but it's not—it's a fantasy. [...] It's a universe and a world that we created for people to explore how to be a good

---

1   This paper is a critical expansion of my work conducted in my dissertation and book, *Playing Dystopia*. Whereas the book rather focused on dystopian games, I am now integrating a discussion of utopian games and how a utopian impulse manifests in game fiction in general and in the games industry. Farca, Gerald: *Playing Dystopia: Nightmarish Worlds in Video Games and the Player's Aesthetic Response*, Bielefeld: transcript 2018.

person in a slowly decaying world. But people like to put politics into that, and we back away from those interpretations as much as we can because we don't want to take a stance in current politics. [...] It's also bad for business, unfortunately, if you want the honest truth."[2]

Such a statement necessarily evokes discussion, given the state of the games industry in which developers (more often than not) feel responsible to cater to the tastes of certain gamer communities.[3] This may be an attempt to avoid losing large groups of customers (and satisfy the financial pressure of publishers) or to prevent outrageous outcries in forums—but it is also worth observing from a different yet connected point of view.

In recent history, game developers and academics alike have described video games as forms of art,[4] as showing the potential to affect players emotionally and aesthetically by making them ponder life, culture, and societal developments (and, in general, the many connections between the fictional gameworld and their empirical surroundings).[5] To do so is to approach the video game medium's aesthetic function as an implicit but subversive commentary on contemporary issues and ways of life—and one cannot but pose the question whether game developers, as artists they claim to be, assume a certain (utopian) *responsibility*. Of course, this responsibility may be two-sided: one the one hand, to ensure the success of the product and secure (their own) working places, while on the other hand, it is the artist's desire to question, comment, and meticulously unveil societal wrongs, to destabilize the

---

2   Taylor, Haydn: "Ubisoft Massive COO: 'We Don't Want to Take a Stance in Current Politics,'" *GamesIndustry*, October 17, 2018; https://www.gamesindustry.biz/articles/2018-10-17-ubisoft-massive-coo-we-dont-want-to-take-a-stance-in-current-politics

3   Mortensen, Torill: "Anger, Fear, and Games: The Long Event of #GamerGate," *Games and Culture* 13, no. 8 (April 2016); https://journals.sagepub.com/doi/abs/10.1177/1555412016640408

4   Tavinor, Grant: "Art and Aesthetics," in: Wolf, Mark J. P./Perron, Bernard (eds.), *The Routledge Companion to Video Game Studies*, New York: Routledge 2014, pp. 59–66.

5   With empirical surroundings/world, I refer to the extratextual surroundings (outside of the gameworld) and to what is usually meant when saying the 'real world,' the 'actual world,' and so on.

status quo in precarious times, and to suggest potential ways out of these dilemmas.[6]

In this context, George Orwell was very blunt about his *Nineteen Eighty-Four*[7] in which he describes the world situation back in the 1940s:

> "I think that, allowing for the book being after all a parody, something like *Nineteen Eighty-Four could* happen. This is the direction in which the world is going at the present time, and the trend lies deep in the political, social and economic foundations of the contemporary world situation. ... The moral to be drawn from this dangerous nightmare situation is a simple one: *Don't let it happen. It depends on you.*"[8]

Granted, Condelius' desire to leave the interpretation to players[9] is fundamentally important—and games certainly speak on their own. However, comparing his statement to the openness of Orwell's raises the question of whether game developers should succumb (so easily) to the influence of the status quo or the opinions of gaming communities. Shouldn't they rather promote their works as artists, and as the subversive products they are? For is the function of modern art "to reveal and perhaps balance the deficiencies resulting from prevailing systems,"[10] and to "propose [...] *trial runs* for approaches to what is."[11] This allows players, readers, spectators "to see everyday norms and conventions, social habits of thinking and feeling, in a different light [...] [and] to explore, in a kind of *trial action in a virtual*

---

6 Jameson, Fredric: *Archaeologies of the Future: The Desire Called Utopia and Other Science Fictions*, London: Verso 2005, p. 11-16.
7 Orwell, George: *Nineteen Eighty-Four*, United Kingdom: Secker & Warburg 1949.
8 Crick, Bernard: "Introduction," in: George Orwell, *Nineteen Eighty-Four*, New York: Clarendon Press, 1984, pp. 152-153, quoted in Kumar, Krishan: *Utopia and Anti-Utopia in Modern Times*, Oxford: Basil Blackwell 1987, p. 291.
9 H. Taylor: "Ubisoft Massive COO."
10 Iser, Wolfgang: *The Act of Reading: A Theory of Aesthetic Response*, trans. Wilhelm Fink, Baltimore: John Hopkins UP 1978, p 13.
11 Iser, Wolfgang: *The Fictive and the Imaginary: Charting Literary Anthropology*, trans. Frankfurt a.M.: Suhrkamp, original: Baltimore: John Hopkins UP 1993, p. 143, emphasis added.

environment, the consequences of breaking and transgressing norms without having to fear sanctions in real life."[12]

Specifically, science fiction (SF) and the utopian genre[13] (to which THE DIVISION 2 pertains as a variant of dystopia) do so in a reinforced manner. By having players engage with a gameworld that is both *strange* (a virus outbreak has transformed Washington DC into an anarchical sight) and *familiar* (places and objects, norms, ethics, social and cultural conventions that are generally known), THE DIVISION 2 involves them in a *feedback oscillation* between the fictional gameworld and their empirical surroundings. This allows players to not only comprehend the gameworld by comparing it to the empirical world (based on their cultural knowledge) but also to gain insight into the latter from a different point of view (in its cultures, norms, and politics).[14] Consequently, to deny that any game dealing with such a delicate topic is political is based on an incomprehension of art's creative faculties, or fueled by alternative motives.

This article aims to underline video games' aesthetic potential as art: as forward-looking, subversive commentaries on our contemporary world that meticulously unveil societal wrongs through play and introduce players to different cultures and ways of living. Specifically, I will focus on how digital games *negotiate the concept of Utopia*[15] and involve players in a form of play

---

12　Berensmeyer, Ingo: *Literary Theory: An Introduction to Approaches, Methods and Terms*, Stuttgart: Klett Lerntraining 2009, p. 79, emphasis added; cf. Perron, Bernard: *Silent Hill: The Terror Engine*, Ann Arbor: University of Michigan Press 2012, p. 12.

13　I regard science fiction as a broad genre that encompasses subgenres such as the posthuman, space opera, cyberpunk, steampunk, or post-apocalypse. Although I do not subordinate utopia and dystopia to SF (because of the genres' long traditions), there are many affinities between them. Suvin, Darko: *Metamorphoses of Science Fiction: On the Poetics and History of a Literary Genre*, New Haven: Yale UP 1979, p. 4, p. 61; Sargent, Lyman T.: "The Three Faces of Utopianism Revisited," *Utopian Studies* 5, no. 1 (1994), p. 11; http://www.jstor.org/discover/10.2307/20719246?uid=3737864&uid=2129&uid=2&uid=70&uid=4&sid=21101560295713

14　D. Suvin: *Metamorphoses of Science Fiction*, p. 4, p. 71.

15　Following Baccolini and Moylan, I use capitalisation to refer to the philosophy of Utopia (utopianism) and Anti-Utopia and to specific Utopias—a certain

that is *regenerative* in different ways: in that it helps them see beyond the inoculating powers of the status quo, differentiate societal issues, and explore potential solutions to these through play. By playing utopian and dystopian games, in other words, players implicitly compare the gameworld to what they know from the empirical world in acts of ideation (Ideenbildung).[16] They thus become involved in a *trial action* that may reveal their world's darkest secrets and hidden agendas, but through which they may as well explore ways to cope with contemporary dilemmas (such as capitalism, human greed, totalitarianism, ecological issues) and, potentially, move beyond them.

While utopian and dystopian games follow a similar purpose in this regard—as a strategy of Utopia to promote social change and transformation[17]—they employ adjusted strategies in how they negotiate the issue of *hope*. Whereas utopian fiction starts with a positive premise (showing us a fantastic world that is described as superior to ours), dystopian fiction aims to shock players by involving them in visions of nightmares. This diverse spectrum of possibilities results in a plethora of potential subgenres—and to categorize these in a typology will be the main task of this article while explaining how regenerative play is afforded by them.

To do so, I will begin with a discussion on the concept of Utopia and how a utopian (and anti-utopian) impulse permeates the games industry. This is a first, important step, for it discusses the tensions between a highly capitalist, profit-oriented industry and works of art that shall criticize these machinations and point to ways beyond them. Second, I will scrutinize how this utopian impulse manifests itself in digital games in general and involves players in regenerative ways through 1) the exploration of space, 2) the experience

---

imaginary, virtual, or real place that fulfils the necessary aspects of a Utopia. Lowercase will be used for Utopia's manifestations, such as the literary utopia/dystopia or video game utopia/dystopia. Baccolini, Raffaella/Moylan, Tom: "Introduction. Dystopia and Histories," in: Baccolini, Raffaella/Moylan, Tom (eds.), *Dark Horizons: Science Fiction and the Dystopian Imagination*, New York: Routledge 2003, pp. 1-12, here p 11.

16 W. Iser: *The Act of Reading*, p. 35.

17 Vieira, Fátima: "Introduction," in: Vieira, Fátima (ed.), *Dystopia(n) Matters: On the Page, on Screen, on Stage*, Newcastle-upon-Tyne: Cambridge Scholar Publishing 2013, pp. 1-7, here p. 1.

of plot and thematics, 3) the interaction with characters and communities, and 4) systemic and creational aspects. This will finally lead to the main discussion of utopian and dystopian games. As multi-layered artifacts, these oscillate in function between entertainment and emancipation and involve players in either paradisiac or nightmarish gameworlds. Thereby, all of the discussed subgenres negotiate the spectrum between Utopia and Anti-Utopia (and the issue of hope)[18] in different ways, which results in a comprehensive typology of utopian and dystopian games. This typology includes 1) the classical utopia, 2) the critical utopia of variant I and II, 3) the critical dystopia of variant I and II, 4) the classical dystopia, and 5) the anti-utopia.

1.1 THE UTOPIAN IMPULSE IN DIGITAL GAMES AND BEYOND

"Utopia is forward-looking, yes. Always just around the corner, always on the other side of the horizon, Utopia is 'not yet,' elusive, glimpsed but never grasped. That's one of the things I love about Utopia. And yet, like you [Ruth Levitas], I want the world to be very different from the way it is now. I want to ride the wave of utopian impulse toward a new now."[19]

The philosophy of Utopia, as Lucy Sargisson refers to it, fundamentally revolves around the principle of hope and the dream of a better world. It begins with the *act of imagination* itself when the utopian thinker explores real or fictional alternatives to the contemporary present and induces a "transformative process"[20] that will grasp the recipient's attention.[21] This process begins

---

18 Moylan, Tom: *Scraps of the Untainted Sky: Science Fiction, Utopia, Dystopia*, Boulder, Colorado: Westview Press 2000, p. 147, p. 157.
19 Levitas, Ruth/Sargisson, Lucy: "Utopia in Dark Times: Optimism/Pessimism and Utopia/Dystopia," in: Baccolini, Raffaella/Moylan, Tom (eds.), *Dark Horizons: Science Fiction and the Dystopian Imagination*, New York: Routledge 2003, pp. 13-27, here p. 20.
20 R. Levitas/L. Sargisson: "Utopia in Dark Times," p. 16.
21 Ibid., p. 13, p. 16; Seeber, Hans Ulrich: *Die Selbstkritik der Utopie in der Angloamerikanischen Literatur*, Münster: LIT 2003, p. 58.

"in the now,"[22] as the Utopian scrutinizes empirical reality for potential ills and composes a vision of the future in which these issues are either solved or have turned into a nightmare.[23] Notwithstanding the direction of Utopia, whether it results in a *utopia* or *dystopia*, "the desire"[24] for it is deeply anchored in the human psyche and looks forward. However, there is a pitfall here, as Slavoj Žižek warns: for if the desire is tipped out of balance, it may indeed be the greatest enemy to human happiness.[25]

Utopians have become aware of this peril, and the concept underwent critical changes mainly because of Utopia's abuse, which occurred with the totalitarian regimes of the 20th century.[26] Consequently, moving away from ideas of perfection and from blindly following noble ideals, Utopia is today rather understood as a *cautious desire* and indicates "a direction for man to follow, but never a point to be reached."[27] It takes on "the shape of a process" and "a programme for change and for a gradual betterment of the present."[28] Such an understanding of Utopia lays the focus on a *transformative discourse* and a *creative dialectic* between various parties, while it upholds Utopia's primary function as a *warning*.

Notwithstanding these claims, some scholars (such as Frederic Jameson) still regard the function of Utopia as a more radical one. In *Archaeologies of the Future*, Jameson describes a *utopian impulse* that permeates human society and comes to the fore in many aspects such as social struggle, communitarian projects, and fictional artworks.[29] Thereby, the imagination of a better future must be a radical one (although Jameson understands that this

---

22 R. Levitas/L. Sargisson: "Utopia in Dark Times," p. 17.
23 Booker, M. Keith: *The Dystopian Impulse in Modern Literature: Fiction as Social Criticism*, Westport Conn.: Greenwood Press 1994, p. 15; F. Jameson: *Archaeologies of the Future*, pp. 11-12.
24 Ibid., 84.
25 Žižek, Slavoj: *Welcome to the Desert of the Real! Five Essays on September 11 and Related Dates*, London: Verso 2002, pp. 58-59.
26 R. Levitas/L. Sargisson: "Utopia in Dark Times," p. 25.
27 Vieira, Fátima: "The Concept of Utopia," in: Claeys, Gregory (ed.), *The Cambridge Companion to Utopian Literature*, Cambridge: Cambridge UP 2010, pp. 3-27, here p. 22.
28 Ibid., p. 23; cf. pp. 22-23.
29 F. Jameson: *Archaeologies of the Future*, p. 53.

might be difficult to imagine), which leads to the following conclusion. To Jameson, Utopia shows us "the future as *disruption* (*Beunruhigung*) of the present, and as a radical and systematic break with even that predicted and colonized future which is simply a prolongation of our capitalist present."[30] Given this phrasing, Utopia functions as "a critical and diagnostic instrument,"[31] but it also helps us imagine ways out of current dilemmas and gridlocked societal systems.

Such a conception of the future stands in stark contrast to what scholars have described as the anti-utopian imagination. "Throughout modernity [...] the anti-utopian persuasion has systematically worked to silence and destroy Utopia, but Utopia [...] has always offered a way to work against and beyond these attacks."[32] To Tom Moylan, the anti-utopian persuasion is a strategy of the dominant ideology. It postulates the end of history and discredits Utopia to safeguard "the status quo and the satisfactions that it delivers to its beneficiaries."[33] In other words, the anti-utopian describes the empirical present as "the best of all possible worlds"[34] to keep societal change to a minimum.

Such views may be a matter of perspective, of course, and in need of precise differentiation. However, specifically today, dominant ideology follows a strict anti-utopian strategy. With authoritarian and totalitarian regimes strengthening their power by any means necessary and a capitalist, consumerist way of living that grants few to none alternatives, George Orwell's and Aldous Huxley's visions of nightmare in *Nineteen-Eighty Four* and *Brave New World*[35] have become a combined reality in the 21st century. One may ask now whether these fictions have missed their purpose (since their described futures have become a reality in some ways) or refocus one's interest in modern utopian and dystopian fiction and its regenerative appeal.

In fact, the 21st century has spurred on a new utopian countermovement which (steadily) breaks open the dystopian imagination and its post-apocalyptic fantasies. Noteworthy in this regard is the increase in ecological fiction, which expresses the current needs for climate protection, the struggle

---

30 Ibid., p. 228.
31 Ibid., p. 148.
32 T. Moylan: *Scraps of the Untainted Sky*, p. 104.
33 Ibid., p. 131; cf. p. 129, p. 157.
34 Jameson, Fredric: *The Seeds of Time*, New York: Columbia UP 1994, p. 8.
35 Huxley, Aldous: *Brave New World*, United Kingdom: Chatto & Windus 1932.

against human pollution, and a fresh start on faraway planets due to a lack of alternatives. This function of Utopia (to counter-act problematic aspects of society and point to alternatives) has prevailed since Thomas More's *Utopia*[36] and its response to 16th century Europe. In the *Utopia*, More imagined a quasi-socialist society that has done away with capitalist greed and its resultant hierarchical structures,[37] which creates a *tension* between how things are and how things could be.

1.1.1 The (Anti-)Utopian Impulse in the Games Industry

This aspect, of a conceptually open future, is worth discussing in the larger context of digital games and the games industry. Specifically, if one regards the games industry as a piece of highly profited-oriented machinery (with global revenue of $135 billion in 2018),[38] several tensions between utopian and anti-utopian potentialities arise. Consequently, the following part will describe an (anti-)utopian impulse that permeates game design and address tensions such as games as capitalist products vs. games as art, AAA productions vs. independent games, and the struggle for heterogeneity and diversity vs. a male-dominated industry. These issues will not necessarily be answered here but shall inspire critical thought and utopian solutions to them.

To begin with, the example of THE DIVISION has already unveiled a fundamental tension concerning the status of *games as capitalist products* and *their critique of the capitalist system*. This aspect is noteworthy in many commercially successful games that also aim for artistic diversity—including the BORDERLANDS (2009-) and BIOSHOCK (2007-) series—and formulates an ethical problem to be addressed. For in buying these games, players contribute to the capitalist production machinery that regulates the games industry (and the same is true for Hollywood blockbusters and commercially

---

36 More, Thomas: *Utopia*, Habsburg Netherlands: More 1516.
37 Booker, M. Keith: *Dystopian Literature: A Theory and Research Guide*, Westport, Conn.: Greenwood Press 1994, pp. 53-54.
38 Batchelor, James: "Global Games Market Value Rising to $134.9bn in 2018: Revenues Grew by Over 10 %, Mobile Accounts for Almost Half at $63.2 Billion," *Gamesindustry*, December 18, 2018; https://www.gamesindustry.biz/articles/ 2018-12-18-global-games-market-value-rose-to-usd134-9bn-in-2018

successful literature). This may come to the detriment of developers, who often suffer from precarious working situations and must endure crunch-times during the development process. Such games are highly commercialized products that aim to affect broad audiences while trying to make them aware of the central problems of their times. However, this social criticism lies also in the artist's desire—and to reach a conclusion here is difficult. Maybe, one could argue that the benefit of AAA games (the subversive potential they offer to a large crowd) outweighs their negative impact as capitalist products. Yet, there might be an additional, connected train of thought worth mentioning.

In the recent decade, a new trend of independent games has given way to a utopian movement in game design.[39] These games are produced with a low budget (to AA) and developed by smaller groups of people. In their partial rejection of AAA productions (and the connected limitations in design), independent games offer the possibility for artistic diversity and experimentation. People often gather in creative communities and find like-minded in specific conventions and festivals. Independent games are thus not restrained by the pressures of big publishers (yet alternative means of funding are necessary) and are a means of creative expression to move the medium in different directions. Although often a retro-trend in design can be discerned (2D aesthetics and gameplay), these games nonetheless look forward. In taking up older ludic genres (such as 2D platforming and adventure games) and intermingling them with variants of storytelling, new forms of ludic expression become possible. One example is FEZ (2012) in which a supposedly 2D world and gameplay perspective are later expanded to a 3D realm. People in FEZ have forgotten about three of the four sides of their world, and players have to restore order by solving puzzles and rotating between four 2D perspectives. FEZ is thus a brilliant example of how old gameplay conventions (2D platform and adventures games) are creatively expanded to the modern era. By breaking away from ludic conventions as wells as linear worldviews, the game creates an open-minded environment in which many (cultural) perspectives are negotiated—not only to expand the horizon of game design but also the philosophical impact of digital games.

---

39 Juul, Jesper: *Handmade Pixels: Independent Video Games and the Quest for Authenticity*, Cambridge, MA.: MIT Press 2019.

An additional game worth mentioning is THE STANLEY PARABLE (2013) which has players experience the confinements of an office job and game design alike. During the game, the main character, Stanley, reaches a room with two open doors, which confronts him with a profound choice. This choice is not only representative for branching structures in games and players' lack of agency, but it also addresses the confines of bureaucratic consumer capitalism and the pettiness of the individual worker. Meta-games, such as THE STANLEY PARABLE, negotiate the current status of the medium and offer valuable perspectives on it. They follow on the function of independent games to explore creative ways of expression and attempt to create new ludo-narrative experiences.

While the effect of independent games may be limited to fewer consumers (due to their niche status), they affect AAA productions indirectly. They inspire AAA design and are a trial space for the development of big-budget productions, to test out what methods and forms of ludic expression are successful.

Yet, the move from AAA studios to smaller ones is also due to a different but connected reason. Although the video game industry is striving for diversity and heterogeneous working spaces, it remains a partially hostile environment for minorities. This may be so because of many reasons (and the negative influence of Gamergate shall not be neglected) and can often be discerned in the resulting games. One problem is the severe lack of women working in the games industry—and the success of violent actions games (mostly created by men)[40] may speak on its own. This anti-utopian and confining trend needs to be addressed in the foreseeable future, not only to create balanced and healthy working environments but also to push the creative boundaries of game design and include many different perspectives into the development process.

In this vein, a games industry that moves into a utopian direction should create a balanced and safe environment for the creative mind to thrive. It should embrace diversity and heterogeneity while overcoming linear worldviews and the hostility often to be found in it. Finding expression through games while retaining commercial sustainability is a difficult task,

---

40 Stuart, Keith: "The Last of Us, BioShock: Infinite and why all Video Game Dystopias Work the Same," *The Guardian*, July 1, 2013; https://www.theguardian.com/technology/gamesblog/2013/jul/01/last-of-us-bioshock-infinite-male-view

there is no doubt here. Yet if one values the individual developer and her or his artistic creation, this is the inevitable route to take.

1.1.2 The Utopian Impulse in Digital Games and its Regenerative Appeal

The tension between commercial success and creative artifacts naturally translates to the game product. While any game needs to be successful to ensure commercial stability, one must not forget a game's aesthetic function. For digital games (as works of art and cultural artifacts) may evoke change by subversively commenting (directly or indirectly) on real-world issues and ways of life. Play induces a reflective and transformative process in players. It grants them the ability to enter a safe space for experimentation, pleasure, and relaxation, to escape reality, but also to see real-world issues from another vantage point. In this utopian sense, one clearly demands more from digital games than being commercial products to fuel corporate business. Specifically, if seen in Jameson's context of a utopian impulse (which permeates society and humankind's artistic creations), a particular *regenerative* dimension comes to the fore.

This dimension is implied by a game's structure (its implied player) and rests as a *potentiality* in it. Of course, different players will actualize this potential in different ways, and regenerative play is thus a result of the creative interaction between *game, player,* and *empirical world.* This is not to say that one cannot locate its origins in the game itself and as a structure that affords participation; in fact, this approach is most valuable when discussing games from a structuralist point of view that anticipates participation.

In the following, I will thus describe how a utopian impulse manifests itself in digital games as a regenerative force, before moving on to particular video game utopias and dystopias and how these negotiate the issue of hope. Thereby I will describe regenerative play as originating in a game's structural peculiarities and how these are negotiated by players—1) in the exploration of space, 2) the experience of plot and thematics, 3) the interaction with characters and communities, and 4) systemic and creational aspects—and explain how these elements afford utopian enclaves.

A first, indispensable source of utopian pleasures are types of *game spaces* that evoke specific emotions in players: for instance, those influenced by "expressionism (which maps emotions onto physical space)[41] and romanticism (which endows landscapes with moral qualities)."[42] Both find their way into many digital games, such as the posthuman fantasies of NIER: AUTOMATA (2017) that juxtaposes natural spaces with the ruins of human civilization and consumption, while reflecting on the emotions of androids as they move through these. By embedding such spaces within the gameworld, utopian microcosms shine with marvelous scenery, architecture, and labyrinthine structures. They create a near-perfect design and behavior that result in delightful yet thought-provoking possibilities for play.[43] One could imagine here PROTEUS (2013), with its serene ambiance and myriad of colors pleasuring our vista, or FLOWER (2009), which contrasts dreamlike nature sections that have a calming effect on players to its bleak menu, depicting a rainy city. Such spaces may, however, transform into dystopian ones through inappropriate player behavior—Steffen Walz mentions SHADOW OF THE COLOSSUS (2005), where players disrupt the tranquil scenery by killing behemoths.[44]

A further type of utopian spaces is an environment of untamed wilderness, of a world opaque to players in its totality,[45] which evokes in them the primordial affect of the sublime. Sublime experiences make players feel petty in contrast to the gameworld they explore and trigger imaginings about life, nature, and culture, which gives way to new insights into existence.[46] The result is not only a sentiment for the natural world but also the creation

---

41 Domsch calls such spaces "Seelenlandschaft," which depict "landscapes that reflect the mood of a protagonist, a scene, or a whole narrative (e.g. the fact that it is raining at a funeral)." Domsch, Sebastian: *Storyplaying: Agency and Narrative in Video Games*, Berlin: De Gruyter 2013, p. 103.

42 Jenkins, Henry: "The Art of Contested Spaces," in: *Publications Henry Jenkins*, 2002; http://web.mit.edu/~21fms/People/henry3/contestedspaces.html

43 Walz, Steffen P.: *Toward a Ludic Architecture: The Space of Play and Games*, Pittsburgh, PA: ETC Press 2010, pp. 137-138.

44 Ibid., pp. 140.

45 Vella, Daniel: "No Mastery Without Mystery: Dark Souls and the Ludic Sublime," *Game Studies* 15, no. 1 (2015); http://gamestudies.org/1501/articles/vella

46 Burke, Edmund: *A Philosophical Enquiry into the Origins of the Sublime and Seautiful*, Calgery: Anodos Books 2017, p. 35-37; Garrard, Greg: *Ecocriticism*, New York: Routledge 2004, p. 70-75.

of a utopian enclave as "a place of freedom in whicsh we can recover our true selves we have lost to the corrupting influences of our artificial lives."[47] One example of this is Hello Games' NO MAN'S SKY (2016), which has players explore an infinite, procedurally created universe. The game thereby creates an experience of loneliness, known from robinsonades, and juxtaposes this with the sheer vastness of outer space and the unfamiliarity of alien planets, which players may explore at their own peril.

Similar, though with a focused magnitude, is FIREWATCH (2016). The game sets players into the role of Henry, who struggles because of his wife's sickness and involves them in a journey of self-discovery that leads into the depths of the human unconscious (underlined by the spreading of the June fire). Most noteworthy, thereby, are players' long strolls in nature. These take on the function of an escape from everyday routines as well as they are reflections on them. Nature, in other words, calms players through its serene ambiance and sounds yet terrifies by evoking feelings of loneliness and mystery. It assumes a sublime character, which endows the experience with a feeling of pettiness.[48]

There is no doubt that space creates an indispensable source of utopian pleasures, which in many cases is reinforced by the *plot* and its *thematics*. A good example of this is FIREWATCH, which intertwines nature experiences with the themes of personal loss and suffering. Such an experience potentially affects players on an affective and aesthetic level and has them move away from the game pondering. Plot, in fact, has since Aristotle been ascribed a *purifying*, cathartic effect. It sensualizes the abstract[49] and immerses us in fictional storyworlds, in the fate of characters or entire worlds, to show us different perspectives on the empirical world and have us leave the

---

47 Cronon, William: "The Trouble with Wilderness; or, Getting Back to the Wrong Nature," in: Cronon, William (ed.), *Uncommon Ground: Toward Reinventing Nature*, New York: W. W. Norton & Company 1995, pp. 69-90, quoted in G. Garrard: *Ecocriticism*, p. 77.

48 This is reinforced by Henry's relation to Delilah, who keeps him company on the radio. Although standing in close contact to her, the relative distance to her watch tower seems insurmountable, while a potential romance is frustrated by every day live closing in.

49 H. U. Seeber: *Die Selbstkritik der Utopie in der Angloamerikanischen Literatur*, p. 70.

fictional scenery pondering. Plot and the experience of a fictional world thus affect our habitual dispositions, the way we perceive things and the outside world.[50]

The effect of the plot is discernible in many games, and particular utopian energy is actualized while playing THE LEGEND OF ZELDA: BREATH OF THE WILD (2017).[51] The game involves players in a dreamlike gameworld in which their unconscious desires for an ecological sustainable Utopia and romantic imagery of nature are evoked, exposed to distress, and eventually saturated. By sending players on the journey of a hero to restore order in a polluted but majestic world, the game connects the hero's desire to restore balance in Hyrule to the struggle for Utopia and ecological issues: to appease the four elements disturbed by Ganon and have a restorative influence on the land's ecosystems. For as Joseph Campbell would say: It is the task of the hero "to retreat from the world of secondary effects to those causal zones of the psyche where the difficulties really reside, and there to clarify the difficulties, eradicate them in his own case."[52] Yet this individual level (of a re-enactment of the Oedipus complex and the unconscious desire for a return to the mother's womb)[53] is connected to a repression greater than the individual. This wish-fulfillment lies in our relation to Mother Nature, her ecosystems and elements, and human and animal cultures.

In BREATH OF THE WILD, this plot structure and its thematic have a regenerative effect on players. It not only sensitizes them to the utopian space of a vast, natural gameworld but also reinforces this process by sending players on the journey of the hero to restore balance in a polluted world. Plot, in this sense, is a fundamental aspect of utopian pleasures. It calms, excites, and terrifies players (for instance in tragedies such as NIER AUTOMATA), thus purifying their inner selves by having them involved in the fate of the gameworld, its races, and characters.

---

50 W. Iser, *The Fictive and the Imaginary*, p. 17, p. 297.
51 Farca, Gerald et al.: "Regenerative Play and the Experience of the Sublime in The Legend of Zelda: Breath of the Wild," *Proceedings of The Philosophy of Computer Games Conference* (2018); http:// gameconference.itu.dk/papers/06% 20-%20farca%20et%20al%20%20regenerati ve%20play.pdf
52 Campbell, Joseph: *The Hero with a Thousand Faces*, Bollingen Series 18, 3rd ed., Novato: New World Library 2008, p. 12.
53 Ibid., p. 4, p. 11.

Figure 1: The experience of the sublime is arguably the most prominent form of regenerative play in THE LEGEND OF ZELDA: BREATH OF THE WILD—*when players are astounded by Hyrule's natural wonders.*

Source: THE LEGEND OF ZELDA: BREATH OF THE WILD, location: Hyrule Field

The discussion of plot, now, inevitably leads to players' interaction with *in-game characters*, entire *civilizations,* and *ideologies*, or *other players* themselves—which shows particular utopian energy. Specifically, online communities are highly interesting in this regard. Massive multiplayer online role-playing games, like Blizzard's WORLD OF WARCRAFT (2004), enable the creation of online communities where players come together to experience adventures in a make-believe world.[54] These allow for the negotiation of potential alternatives to the empirical present in that players explore different forms of social interaction "and collective forms of organization."[55]

Yet also single-player games that can be played cooperatively, like JOURNEY (2012), allow for utopian interactions between players. In JOURNEY, this not only includes the choice of taking the route towards the

---

54 Inderst, Rudolf: *Vergemeinschaftung in MMORPGs*, Boizenburg: Werner Hülsbusch 2009.
55 Jagoda, Patrick: "Digital Games and Science Fiction," in: Link, Eric C./Canavan, Gerry (eds.), *The Cambridge Companion to American Science Fiction*, New York: Cambridge UP 2015, pp. 139-152, here p. 146.

mountaintop together but also of performing actions such as communicating via music tunes, waiting for the additional player, or helping her out in dangerous parts of the gameworld—a fact that Fahlenbrach and Schröter attribute to the social dimension of the game, which affords a feeling of solidarity between the players.[56] As such, these potential events shape a community between two people who share the way of life together, help each other out, die together in a freezing blizzard, and become resurrected in a frenzy of emotions (but of course, also the opposite is possible). Similar social interactions can be found in games such as FALLOUT 4 (2015), although the interactions are here geared towards NPCs in that players can build a community of egalitarian settlements in the midst of a nuclear wasteland and create utopian communities in between the Commonwealth's anarchy (see next part).

FALLOUT 4 is also a good example to illustrate a last utopian quality of digital games I want to lay focus on, which the primordial force of *creation* and players interaction with *game systems*. Player agency, also defined as "the satisfying power to take meaningful action and see the results of our decisions and choices,"[57] shows particular regenerative energy, specifically in the interaction with utopian or dystopian processes. In FALLOUT 4, for instance, players may create vast structures and intentional communities within the wasteland. They may gather resources and use these in creative ways to promote either utopian or dystopian fantasies—for the communal well or to strengthen their own power. In this regard, MINECRAFT (2011) goes even further. Here players' imagination knows no bounds as they create a myriad of worlds out of Lego blocks, construct intricate structures and machines, found social communities, enact dramatic plot lines, and design game maps that detail players' creativity. This creational aspect, in negotiating a nearly perfect system of rules and its underlying system, shows a decisively utopian character in that it spurs on players' imagination and grants them a trial space to act out their inner fantasies, and to approach their inner self.

---

56 Fahlenbrach, Kathrin/Schröter, Felix: "Game Studies und Rezeptionsästhetik," in: Sachs-Hombach, Klaus/Thon, Jan-Noël (eds.), *Game Studies: Aktuelle Ansätze der Computerspielforschung*, Köln: Herbert von Harlem Verlag 2015, pp. 165-208, here pp. 198-200.

57 Murray, Janet H.: *Hamlet on The Holodeck: The Future of Narrative in Cyberspace*, Cambridge, Mass.: MIT Press 1998, p. 126.

Given all these facets, *regenerative play* can be regarded as an expression of the utopian impulse. It is afforded by a combination of game elements (space, plot, characters, system) and the players' (cultural) knowledge, and manifests itself in the act of play—and thus in the interaction between *game, player,* and *world* (*culture*). Thereby, 1) *spatial aspects* evoke several emotions in players and have them reflect on the environment they traverse while experiencing the presence of an infinite, unknown Other. 2) Most often, these spaces are held together by the *plot* and its *unifying themes*. Becoming involved in an ongoing story can be purifying and cathartic. The plot helps players identify with characters, get to know cultures, their dilemmas, ideologies, and forms of belief. It thus shows particular utopian energy that makes players familiar with different ways of life, changing their stock of knowledge and dispositions in that it helps them gain a different perspective on their empirical surroundings. 3) Deeply intertwined with the notion of plot are *characters* or entire *communities*. Besides the aspects mentioned above, the creation of online communities and the interaction with other players can be regenerative in that helps players negotiate different forms of living and explore utopian (and also dystopian) possibilities while doing so. 4) Lastly, one must not forget the primordial force of *creation*, of leading the world into a utopian direction, refraining from doing so, or simply trying out different forms of interaction with the gameworld. This trial action shows fundamentally utopian energy, an impulse that may spur on players to effect change in the real world while showing them potential ways to do so.

However, one need to be cautious here, for misuse of utopian images may run contrary to this impulse—and several games use utopian images in a thwarted way. These include, for example, AQUA MOTO RACING UTOPIA (2009) and THE SIMS (2000), which use Utopia either for commercial purposes as a brand mark or in an anti-utopian manner to promote capitalist, consumerist ways of living.

1.2 THE UTOPIAN AND DYSTOPIAN GENRE IN DIGITAL GAMES: A TYPOLOGY

It has become clear that a utopian impulse manifests itself in video game fiction and comes to the fore in the act of play. However, this is not to say that all these games pertain to the genres of the *video game utopia* and *dystopia*. For specific utopias and dystopias negotiate the spectrum between "the historical antinomies of" Anti-Utopia and Utopia[58] in a reinforced manner and need to fulfill certain prerequisites. Consequently, based on previous definitions of utopian and dystopian subgenres in literary works and film, the following part will detail the necessary conditions of games that fall under the utopian and dystopian genre. These endeavors will result in a typology that illustrates how each sub-genre and its specific plot structure negotiate the issue of hope. Thereby, the typology critically expands on previous definitions of utopian and dystopian genres in non-ergodic fiction to cater to the participatory and spatial medium of the video game.[59] It is ordered from optimism to pessimism and will be complemented by illustrative examples.[60]

---

58 T. Moylan: *Scraps of the Untainted Sky*, p. 157.
59 A rather uncritical attempt to differentiate utopian sub-genres based on Lyman Tower Sargent's categories has been conducted by Michał Kłosiński, directly taking the definitions of utopia from literature and simply exchanging the terms 'author' with 'developer,' 'reader' with 'player' without pondering the peculiarities of the game medium and its specific utopian and dystopian subgenres. Kłosiński, Michał: "Games and Utopia," *Acta Ludologia* 1, no. 1 (2018); http:// actaludologica.com/wp-content/uploads/2018/04/01.-KLOSINSKI%E2%80%93-AL-1-2018.pdf
60 As with any typology, the boundaries between the subgenres are rather permeable than fixed, and often based on subjective dispositions of players. In fact, one has to underline that "one man's utopia" may easily be "another man's dystopia." M. K. Booker: *The Dystopian Impulse in Modern Literature*, p. 15. And that in order to declare a particular society—be it fictional or real—utopian, dystopian, or something in between largely depends on the personal disposition of the reader/observer. H. U. Seeber: *Die Selbstkritik der Utopie in der Angloamerikanischen Literatur*, p. 27; Sargent, Lyman T.: "Do Dystopias Matter?" in: Vieira, Fátima (ed.), *Dystopia(n) Matters: On the Page, on Screen, on Stage*, Newcastle-upon-Tyne: Cambridge Scholar Publishing 2013, pp. 10-13, here p. 11; K. Kumar: *Utopia and Anti-Utopia in Modern Times*, p. 105, p. 125.

Table 1: Typology of utopian and dystopian games

classical utopia	Outlines a gameworld whose society can be regarded as (or shows the potential of being) considerably better than the developer's empirical present. In this society, players become involved in a trial action to witness or construct more perfect alternatives to the current capitalist system, or at least tinker with it in sustainable ways.
critical utopia variant I	Outlines a gameworld whose society can be regarded as (or shows the potential of being) considerably better than the developer's empirical present, but in which difficult problems arise, which may or may not be solved, and that is critical of utopianism. Thereby, variant I of the critical utopia emphasizes plot over interactivity and moves towards a fixed yet ambiguous ending where both utopian and dystopian possibilities seem imaginable. Examples include games such as MASS EFFECT: ANDROMEDA (2017) and HORIZON ZERO DAWN (2017).
critical utopia variant II	Outlines a gameworld whose society can be regarded as (or shows the potential of being) considerably better than the developer's empirical present, but in which difficult problems arise, which may or may not be solved, and that is critical of utopianism. Thereby, variant II of the critical utopia is most often found the real-time strategy genre, which emphasizes interactivity over plot. Here, players become endowed with the role of founding fathers and are responsible for an entire society and which direction this society may develop. Examples include games such as SURVIVING MARS (2018), STELLARIS (2016), and ANNO 2070 (2011).

critical dystopia variant II	Outlines a gameworld whose society can be regarded as considerably worse than the developers' empirical surroundings, but which may move in a utopian (or further dystopian) direction through player action. Players enjoy the choice of being a catalyst, and every playthrough may result in either an optimistic, ambiguous, or pessimistic ending (or actualized world). This variant of the critical dystopia thus lays specific emphasis on the malleability of the gameworld and its future and foregrounds the need for change by suggesting several routes out of the dystopian dilemma (which players may actualize or not). Moreover, many critical dystopias lay emphasis on how the dystopian situation came about by embedding information about the gameworld's past into it. Examples includes games such as BLADE RUNNER (1997), BIOSHOCK, DEUS EX: HUMAN REVOLUTION (2011), PAPERS, PLEASE (2014), METRO 2033 (2010), and FALLOUT 4.
critical dystopia variant I	Outlines a gameworld whose society can be regarded as considerably worse than the developers' empirical surrounding, but which nonetheless moves in a utopian direction by locating utopian enclaves (as spaces of imaginative and ergodic resistance) within the gameworld. The prospect of hope thus lies within the bounds of the gameworld but is predetermined by the game's dynamic system. Players follow a linear trajectory (with the emphasis laid on plot over interactivity) towards one or more utopian horizons or ambiguous endings and are assigned the role of a catalyst without enjoying the choice to be one. Examples include games such as THE LAST OF US (2013), WATCH DOGS (2014), BIOSHOCK INFINITE, and MIRROR'S EDGE (2008).

classical dystopia	Outlines a gameworld whose society can be regarded as considerably worse than the developers' empirical surroundings and where the prospect of hope lies beyond the bounds of the gameworld. The counter-narrative results in failure and the gameworld's diegetic characters (and, figuratively, the player) are crushed by the dystopian regime, enclosing them in a rigid system of rules from which there is no escape. Contrary to the anti-utopia, this type aims to trigger a militant reaction in players. It evokes anger and a rejection of the confining system they have just experienced and may thus drive players to act in the real world. Examples include games such as MANHUNTER: NEW YORK (1988), THE STANLEY PARABLE, EVERY DAY THE SAME DREAM (2009), I HAVE NO MOUTH, AND I MUST SCREAM (1995), and NIER: AUTOMATA.
anti-utopia	Seeks to deceive players about its critical nature and involves them in pleasurable action to attenuate the system it represents. The anti-utopia thus forecloses the possibility for change and transformation and remains caught up in a resigned, nihilistic view of the current social order. Examples include games such as CALL OF DUTY: ADVANCED WARFARE (2014), CIVILIZATION (1991), and digital variants of MONOPOLY (2008).

1.2.1 The Lack of Classical Utopian Games

In order to determine what makes a utopian or dystopian game, one needs to take a closer look at how the genre was described before and at its obligatory conditions. For such an enterprise, the definition of Lyman Tower Sargent appears particularly useful. He defines *u/eutopia* as follows:

"A non-existent society described in considerable detail and normally located in time and space. In standard usage utopia is used both as defined here and as an equivalent for eutopia or a non-existent society described in considerable detail and normally located in time and space that the author intended a contemporaneous reader to view as considerably better than the society in which that reader lived."[61]

Most important to Sargent's definition is utopia's need to describe *a society*, "a condition in which there is human (or some equivalent) interaction."[62] However, this society does not refer to any empirical one but is *non-existent*—a fact that underscores utopia's imaginary and fictional nature. In the case of utopia, though, the fictional place shows a specific quality: "All fiction describes a no place," and "utopian fiction generally describes good or bad no places."[63] Consequently, a certain utopia *describes in detail* (owing this part to its verbal form) an imaginary society that *contemporaneous readers* shall view as *considerably better* than their empirical one. Through this juxtaposition of worlds—and the dialectic quality it implies—utopia holds a critical attitude, which arises out of the connection between a specific historical moment (that is to be considered problematic) and an imagined solution in fictional narrative form.

A similar definition is Darko Suvin's, who regards utopia as a fictional genre:[64]

"Utopia is the verbal construction of a particular quasi-human community where sociopolitical institutions, norms, and individual relationships are organized according to a more perfect principle than in the author's community, this construction being based on estrangement arising out of an alternative historical hypothesis."[65]

Like Sargent, who speaks of a society that is considerably better than the present one, there is no hint of *perfection* in Suvin's definition either, and he prefers the term *more perfect*. Both scholars thus explicitly stress that the

---

61 Sargent, Lyman T.: *Utopianism: A Very Short Introduction*, Oxford: Oxford UP 2010, p. 6.
62 L. T. Sargent, "The Three Faces of Utopianism Revisited," p. 7.
63 Ibid., p. 5.
64 D. Suvin: *Metamorphoses of Science Fiction*, p. 46.
65 Ibid., p. 49.

literary utopia, although sometimes near to it, does not aim for perfection. It is something "not inherent in the genre"[66] and has primarily been used by opponents of Utopia (anti-utopians) as ammunition for their attacks.[67]

The second aspect worth mentioning is Suvin's notion of 'cognitive estrangement' that arises out of an 'alternative historical hypothesis.' Such a quality fundamentally links the SF genre to utopia and excludes the fantasy genre, the fairy tale, and other noncognitive genres. This is so because both utopia and SF start with "a cognitive hypothesis"[68] that is *extrapolated* into the future "with totalizing ('scientific') rigor"[69] and in "a wide-eyed glance from here to there."[70] Through this creative approach, a fictional alternate world is created—both familiar and unfamiliar to the appreciator—that works around the logic of "*a fictional 'novum' (novelty, innovation) validated by cognitive logic.*"[71] During this process, called estrangement, the reader shall confront "a set normative system—a Ptolemaic-type closed world picture—with a point of view or look implying a new set of norms,"[72] and thus gains a fresh perspective on the empirical world.[73] From this view, "utopia is a possible impossible,"[74] a fictional alternate world that nevertheless retains a strong connection to the empirical present from which it originates.

Given this function of the utopian genre, it comes as no surprise that one of its primary targets is found in the capitalist system—and the genre has imagined alternatives to it since More's *Utopia*. From this perspective, it is quite difficult to find classical utopias in video game fiction. Some games, like UTOPIA (1981) and UTOPIA: THE CREATION OF A NEW NATION (1991), virtualize hypothetical fictional scenarios that are concerned with the creation of a future society that can be described as considerably better than the empirical world. However, they fall short of letting players tinker with

---

66 Ibid., p. 45.
67 Ibid., p. 45; L.T. Sargent, "The Three Faces of Utopianism Revisited," pp. 9-10.
68 D. Suvin, *Metamorphoses of Science Fiction*, p. 75.
69 Ibid., p. 6.
70 Ibid., p. 37.
71 Ibid., p. 63.
72 Ibid., p. 6.
73 Ibid., p. 6, p. 70, p. 71, p. 75.
74 Ibid., p. 43.

systems outside of capitalism and the current status quo. UTOPIA, for example, is a turn-based strategy game with RTS elements. It sets two players in a competition to build an efficient society on adjacent islands, spend gold bars in order to build types of buildings (factories, schools, hotels, and so on), and finance rebellions of the adversary island. Instead of imagining a just and alternative world system (or at least sustainable ways within capitalism), the game remains caught up in a hunt for high scores and a consumerist way of thinking to keep its populace happy and well-fed.

Figure 2: Whereas Thomas More's Utopia (1516) is critical about the capitalist system, the game UTOPIA (1981) simply functions as a prolongation of it by having players engage in a hunt for high scores.

Source: UTOPIA (left); Cover image of Thomas More's *Utopia*, colorized, illustrator Ambrosius Holbein (right)

Similarly works UTOPIA: THE CREATION OF A NATION which has players colonize an unknown planet and manage growth, taxes, trade, as well as the population to create a better future. The game thereby simulates a conflict between ideologies (in this case with an alien race) and grants players no choice for alliances. As such, both games fail to engage players in the imagination of alternatives systems, those that strive for Utopia in creating sustainable futures by negotiating differing perspectives. In fact, one could even argue that such games are a misuse of utopian images—and thus anti-utopias. They strengthen the status quo through play and foreground the inevitability of the current belief system in which players are caught up. Of course, one could argue that there might be utopian solutions within capitalism, but these games fail to negotiate such possibilities.

1.2.2 The Critical Utopia

There is, however, a more modern utopian genre that has made its ways to video game fiction and that allows for the exploration of alternative forms of life. In overcoming claims of near-perfection and laying the focus on a continual struggle for Utopia, which requires the negotiation between many different perspectives, the *critical utopia* is a highly suited for the interactive medium of the video game. Although its premise is quite positive (the exploration of a supposedly better world or the promise of a fresh start), the critical utopia involves players in a constant oscillation between utopian and dystopian possibilities. Thereby, both imaginative and ergodic possibilities are thinkable, and players assume the roles of founders, who may choose in which direction the gameworld shall develop (variant II of the critical utopia). Sometimes, however, player choices lead to a fixed, ambiguous ending of the game, and only imaginative possibilities remain an option (variant I of the critical utopia).

One example of this first variant is MASS EFFECT: ANDROMEDA, a game that invites players to explore faraway worlds and foreign cultures and places them at the forefront of the struggle for Utopia. MASS EFFECT: ANDROMEDA thus follows a new utopian (ecological) trend in contemporary SF. It moves away from dystopian dreams of nightmare and envisions a positive premise in a faraway future in which humankind searches for a new home in the depths of space. The game endows players (in the form of Sara or Scott Ryder) with the task to transform the Heleus Cluster of the Andromeda Galaxy into a habitable space of co-existence with different races—for the supposedly Golden Worlds are not the promised Utopias the Initiative expected. A dark phenomenon, called the Scourge,[75] has made life on the planets unbear-

---

75 When players arrive in the Andromeda Galaxy, the planets of the Heleus Cluster suffer from an ecological catastrophe, called the scourge. This dark phenomenon and inexplicable web of energy is the result of an ancient conflict (the usage of a powerful weapon) between the Jardaan and an unknown race. The scourge not

able, and it is up to the players to restore these ecosystems. This *attempt at a fresh start* confronts players with a conflict between ideologies and (alien) ethnicities they have to mitigate—the Angara/Roekaar (natives), Krogans (military), kett (colonizers), Initiative (colonizers)—and involves them in a regenerative but precarious struggle for Utopia.

Figure 3: MASS EFFECT: ANDROMEDA allows players to explore faraway places and culture and involves them in a struggle for Utopia that runs into many hindrances.

Source: MASS EFFECT: ANDROMEDA

As such, MASS EFFECT: ANDROMEDA foregrounds the encounter with the Other (known from postcolonial SF) and builds on the plot framework of the critical utopia. As described above, this variant of utopia has the protagonists/players encounter a promising but flawed world, where arising issues aggravate the struggle for a better future and demand the negotiation between many parties.[76] The critical utopia is thus neither caught up in pessimism nor pure optimism but negotiates the spectrum between Utopia and Anti-Utopia

---

only sets the habitats into strife but is also a sublime phenomenon for players to ponder about.

76 L. T. Sargent: "The Three Faces of Utopianism Revisited," pp. 8-9.

on neutral, cautious grounds.[77] It is, as Davis claims, "capable of pointing the way" by breaking "open a horizon of possibilities"[78] while it remains aware "of utopian limitations." In rejecting naïve "blueprints," the critical utopia, therefore "initiates a process of critique and change"[79] and posits an imaginative openness that may lead to many possible outcomes.[80] To put it in Lyman Tower Sargent's words: the critical utopia represents

"a non-existent society described in considerable detail and normally located in time and space that the author intended a contemporaneous reader to view as better than contemporary society but with difficult problems that the described society may or may not be able to solve and which takes a critical view of the utopian genre."[81]

Given these facts, the *notion of regenerative play* is here linked to players' interaction with a conceptually open gameworld and its malleability in imaginative and ergodic terms. Players of MASS EFFECT: ANDROMEDA may choose, for example, whether to pursue military or scientific routes, which planets to terraform, and (how) to mitigate conflicts between different races and ideologies. Based on these choices, they will experience an imaginatively open ending to the game, which leaves room for speculation of how this world will develop further. In finding solutions to problems that plague the Heleus Cluster, players, therefore, participate in a trial action that may translate to their struggle for Utopia in the real world.

Each planet, thereby, is diverse in its ecosystems and confronts players with several (ecological) issues. Whether it is Habitat 7 and H-047c's hostile atmosphere, the scorching heat of Elaaden and Eos, or the tropical paradises of Aya and Havaarl, players directly experience the extent of the Scourge and its ecological consequences—but they are equally fascinated by this

---

77 Fortunati, Vita: "Why Dystopia Matters," in: Vieira, Fátima (ed.), *Dystopia(n) Matters: On the Page, on Screen, on Stage*, Newcastle-upon-Tyne: Cambridge Scholar Publishing 2013, pp. 28-36, here p. 28.

78 Davis, Laurence: "Dystopia, Utopia and Sancho Panza," in: Vieira, Fátima (ed.), *Dystopia(n) Matters: On the Page, on Screen, on Stage*, Newcastle-upon-Tyne: Cambridge Scholar Publishing 2013, pp. 23-27, here p. 25.

79 T. Moylan: *Scraps of the Untainted Sky*, pp. 82-84.

80 Ibid.; R. Baccolini/T. Moylan: "Introduction," p. 2.

81 L. T. Sargent: "The Three Faces of Utopianism Revisited," p. 9.

Otherness and its unfathomable appeal. This presence of sublime phenomena in the Andromeda Galaxy evokes the feeling of pettiness and *astonishment*[82] in players—standing face-to-face to a strange and hostile wilderness—and foregrounds the need for sustainable ways of transforming the Helius Cluster in a prosperous environment.

Especially interesting in this regard are two conflicts in the Heleus Cluster, which players may choose to mitigate. One of these is a long-lasting problem with the Krogans, a warmonger race that reproduced easily, gained in numbers and plunged the Milky Way into chaos. Salarian scientists found a radical solution to the Krogan issue in the Genophage, a biological weapon that robbed them of their ability to reproduce. The Krogans were thus not only pushed to the edge of extinction, but they were also isolated in political affairs. In MASS EFFECT: ANDROMEDA players may now choose whether to repeat history (and isolate the Krogans on political and cultural grounds) or give them a say in the Initiative—specifically, whether to hand them a Drive Core to accelerate the terraforming of their planet, Elaaden, or use the core's power for the Nexus (an option preferred by Director Tann, a Salarian). Whatever players choose has the ending of the game shine in an imaginative ambiguity due to an unknown future of the Krogan society and how things will develop further.

A further conflict is that between the kett, the Initiative, and the Angara. When players arrive in the Heleus Cluster, they come across two indigenous races that seem to repeat human history: the Angara and the kett. The Angara are a friendly, colorful, and intelligent species that remind one of the Native American population. They welcome the Initiative but retain a skeptical distance. The kett, on the other hand, represent the colonizers of this galaxy. Their appearance resembles those of the Angara but in a much darker form. Indeed, players will learn that the kett are Angara themselves, changed through the method of exaltation (genetic manipulation, re-education camps, and tortures) into the horrible selves they have now become. The kett only choose the healthy, whereas weak Angarans are sent to working facilities. As a result of this colonization of the Other, the Angara forget their pasts and become metaphorical fanatics. It is no coincidence, thereby, that the kett

---

82 E. Burke: *A Philosophical Enquiry into the Origins of the Sublime and Seautiful*, pp. 35-37.

resemble Catholic missionaries and priests that drive the native population into a loss of identity by imposing their culture on them.

In MASS EFFECT: ANDROMEDA, the Initiative and players alike are exposed to the demons of (their own) history, when white colonizers and missionaries imposed their culture on natives. Players may now choose to embark on this path of colonization in that they treat the Angara as inferior and exclude them from political issues or emancipate themselves from this by choosing a more post-colonial route. Here, the Angara will be included in the council founded at the game's end (main quest), and players may aid them in their endeavors to rebuild Havaarl (side quest). Notwithstanding these efforts, the colonizing aspect of games remains in the foreground—the dominant helping the supposedly weak—but utopian routes into a different future seem possible.

Figure 4: The conflict with the kett represent the Initiative's (and players') unconscious struggle against dark past when white colonizers and missionaries imposed their culture on natives.

Source: MASS EFFECT: ANDROMEDA

Choosing between a colonial and post-colonial way prepares the game's final act on Meridian, when the Initiative finds the first truly habitable planet. Although seemingly a hopeful ending, how players dealt with interracial conflicts gives it either an optimist or pessimistic touch. An imaginative openness marks this final act, as to how interracial relationships will develop further, whether humankind may repeat history and purse linear worldviews or emancipate themselves from these to strive towards post-colonial negotiations between many races.

Besides MASS EFFECT: ANDROMEDA, there a many critical utopian games that allow for player involvement that decisively changes their endings and the route to get there. These are mostly located within the real-time strategy genre, which because of its world and society buildings aspects seems a perfect fit for the critical utopian genre. In SURVIVING MARS, for example, players are endowed with the task to colonize the red planet, to build infrastructures (housing, water, oxygen, and nutrition supply, etc.), and to survive environmental hazards (such as sandstorms, freezing temperatures, and meteor showers). In addition, players may choose a sponsor from Earth to fund their project. But this sponsor also has ramifications on their playthrough and on ethical or ecological decisions which may move the game in a fundamentally utopian or dystopian direction (or something in between).

There are several ways to play SURVIVING MARS, and most of these are very hard indeed, which simulates the struggle for Utopia in a beautiful manner. This foregrounds the inherent difficulties to attain a better future and the many pitfalls on this route. As a critical utopia of variant II, the game emphasizes the structural openness and malleability of such worlds and the many different plotlines players may embark on. This opens a vast array of potential endings and to hopeful, ambiguous or pessimistic outcomes. In this regard, games like SURVIVING MARS and STELLARIS—which expands this struggle for Utopia (but also for dystopia) to an entire universe—negotiate the spectrum of utopian and anti-utopian possibilities in a careful manner and confront players with the decision which potential world they deem best.

1.2.3 The Critical Dystopia

Very close to the critical utopia, in the negotiating of utopian and dystopian possibilities but starting with a negative premise, is the *critical dystopia*. The critical dystopia is a newer genre than the classical dystopia and emerged within the 1980s and 1990s in tandem with film and the literary works of these times. Even though it involves players in nightmarish gameworlds, the critical dystopia is not about pure survival in a dystopian society, as it prompts a search for alternatives to the system.[83] This it does by locating *utopian enclaves* as spaces of collective resistance within its gameworlds—to change the hegemonic order, individual resistance is not enough and a collective upheaval becomes imperative.[84] Correspondingly, Sargent defines the critical dystopia as

"a non-existent society described in considerable detail and normally located in time and space that the author intended a contemporaneous reader to view as worse than contemporary society but that normally includes at least one eutopian enclave or holds out the hope that the dystopia can be overcome and replaced with eutopia."[85]

Holding out the prospect of hope within the gameworld, the critical dystopia explores potential routes through the nightmare and towards a utopian horizon.[86] In these more "optimistic dystopias" players become responsible for finding the "flaw" within a "seemingly stable" system, triggering a chain of events that will "lead towards its destruction."[87]

---

83 T. Moylan: *Scraps of the Untainted Sky*, p. 189.
84 Ibid., pp. 189-190, pp. 193-194; R. Baccolini/T. Moylan: "Introduction," pp. 7-8; Baccolini, Raffaella/Moylan, Tom: "Conclusion. Critical Dystopia and Possibilities," in: Baccolini, Raffaella/Moylan, Tom (eds.), *Dark Horizons: Science Fiction and the Dystopian Imagination*, New York: Routledge 2003, pp. 233-249, here p. 246; Fitting, Peter: "Unmasking the Real? Critique and Utopia in Recent SF Films," in: Baccolini, Raffaella/Moylan, Tom (eds.), *Dark Horizons: Science Fiction and the Dystopian Imagination*, New York: Routledge 2003, pp. 155-166, here p. 161.
85 Sargent, Lyman T.: "U.S. Eutopias in the 1980s and 1990s: Self-Fashioning in a World of Multiple Identities," in: Spinozzi, Paola (ed.), *Utopianism/Literary Utopias and National Culture Identities: A Comparative Perspective*, COTEPRA/University of Bologna 2001, p. 222.
86 R. Baccolini/T. Moylan: "Conclusion," pp. 239-240; T. Moylan: *Scraps of the Untainted Sky*, pp. 105-106, p. 147, p. 188.
87 Domsch, Sebastian: "Dystopian Video Games: Fallout in Utopia," in: Voigts, Eckart/Boller, Alessandra (eds.), *Dystopia, Science Fiction, Post-Apocalypse: Classics–New Tendencies–Model Interpretations*, Trier: Wissenschaftlicher Verlag Trier 2015, pp. 395-410, here p. 401; cf. pp. 401-402.

Given this plot structure and its applicability to ludic conventions (a bad enemy and players as heroines and heroes who may save the world), the critical dystopia is the dominant form of utopia and dystopia in video game fiction. It is present in games from the mid-1980s and 1990s such as STRIDER (1989), REVOLUTION X (1994), ROBOTICA (1995), BENEATH A STEEL SKY (1994), CRUSADER: NO REMORSE (1995), and in the optimistic sequels to their literary forebears NEUROMANCER: A CYBERPUNK ROLE-PLAYING ADVENTURE (1988) and FAHRENHEIT 451 (1984). All these games end on a hopeful or ambiguous notion and negotiate the spectrum between Utopia and Anti-Utopia on more neutral grounds than classical dystopian games[88] (to which I will come shortly).

This tradition of critical dystopian games continues in the 2000s and 2010s, with only a few classical dystopian games emerging, such as THE STANLEY PARABLE. Most popular are first- and third-person shooters: for example CRACKDOWN (2007), DISHONORED (2012), BIOSHOCK INFINITE, and WOLFENSTEIN: THE NEW ORDER (2014), as well as action-adventure games including ENSLAVED: ODYSSEY TO THE WEST (2010)—and there only few game that explore more diverse ludic routes like MIRROR'S EDGE and PAPERS, PLEASE. In addition, while targeting totalitarianism and theocratic regimes, the negative impacts of capitalism, and the misuse of technology, a considerable amount of these games discuss environmental catastrophes and the end of the world. Most often these are imagined in post-apocalyptic worlds where either nuclear fallout has given way to barren wastelands and anarchical structures—MAD MAX (2015)—or where nature has reclaimed the planet in a nostalgic return. In the latter instance—THE LAST OF US (2014), ENSLAVED: ODYSSEY TO THE WEST—one often encounters a juxtaposition between an ancient, technology-dependent capitalism that has failed and new forms of societies that develop. Such environmentally-focused games show a strong utopian impulse and move the critical dystopian genre into a decisively ecotopian direction.

Variant II of the critical dystopia, now, involves players directly in the struggle for Utopia. Not only do these games posit an imaginative openness to their gameworld, but they also allow players a say in the choice of utopian and dystopian possibilities. This is also to say that ergodic failure or

---

88 Ibid., p. 147, p. 157.

unwillingness to attain a better future are an option—but the potentiality of a militant response on the side of players remains in the foreground.

One brilliant example of the critical dystopia variant II is PAPERS, PLEASE, which involves players in the mechanisms of a totalitarian regime and sets them in a precarious situation between duty and death. Players assume the job of an immigration inspector and are responsible for safeguarding the country of Arstotzka from terrorists, spies, or smugglers, but often encounters people begging for help. This task confronts them with ethical dilemmas since granting entrance to immigrants without proper documents puts the player-character's family at risk.

The game thereby makes use of the classical and critical dystopian plot structure: the clash between "the official narrative," the depiction of the dystopian society, "and the oppositional counter-narrative," which brings forth a rebellion against the ruling order conducted by dissident thinkers.[89] Consequently, the official narrative involves players in the bureaucratic routine of an unnamed immigration officer whose job revolves around the task of inspecting documents. For every processed individual, players receive credits, which they can use to provide for their family. If they make mistakes, however, penalties are enforced, which deprive players of the much-needed money.

In the course of the game, a counter-narrative to this oppressive system potentially emerges (that is if players choose so). It starts on an individual level, where players may help immigrants reunite with their loved ones, and potentially moves forward to a collective struggle for Utopia—once players choose to work with a resistance group called The Order of the EZIC Star. The resulting constellations give rise to *twenty different endings*, most of which result in the player-character's punishment—he is either condemned to hard labor for disobeying the rules or killed for helping EZIC. On day 31, however, EZIC attempts to overthrow the government, and players may contribute to this cause. Having actualized this ending, the player-character is offered a home and contributes to building a new Arstotzka. This ending is ambiguous, however, for EZIC's revolution was brutal, and it remains uncertain whether they succeed in building a better Arstotzka. In addition, there are endings where players flee to Obristan (with or without their family) and those in which they fight EZIC and contribute to the consolidation of the

---

89 Ibid., p. 152; cf. Ibid., xiii; R. Baccolini/T. Moylan: "Introduction," p. 5.

status quo.[90] In the latter case, players side with the official narrative and are rewarded with an endless code, enabling them to play the game in an infinite loop.

PAPERS, PLEASE is a magnificent example of the critical dystopia variant II, because it not only warns of the dangers of totalitarian regimes and the mind-numbing tasks of bureaucracy but also offers a possibility space in which utopian horizons lay hidden and may be actualized through ergodic effort.

This aspect of the critical dystopia variant II is also discernible in FALLOUT 4. The game involves players in a densely polluted gameworld, where vibrant colors and weather phenomena (such as radiations storms or deep mist) depict the Commonwealth as a destroyed yet picturesque environment where a fresh start seems imaginable. This regenerative appeal was never realized in previous games and transforms FALLOUT 4 not simply into a warning of nuclear disaster but also into an experience that suggests ways to cope with it and move forward in different directions. The game is set in 2287 (210 years after the Great War) and involves players in the role of the Sole Survivor who embarks on a mission to search for his lost son. Players may choose a female or male character (mother or father), but the focus soon shifts from the private sphere of the family to a societal struggle for Utopia. On their journey through the Commonwealth, players encounter memorable locations such as Diamond City (where people have found refuge from the surrounding dystopia), Abernathy Farm (a small, peaceful agricultural society), and Goodneibor (a community of ghouls and criminals exiled from Diamond City). All of these seek help in different ways, and players may choose to intervene. In Diamond City, for example, a strange paranoia infests people's mind, making them believe they are being swapped by identical-looking Synths (artificial beings that are created by the ominous Institute). This thematic links FALLOUT 4 to American science fiction films such as Don Siegel's INVASION OF THE BODY SNATCHERS (1956) and foregrounds the game's satirical tone in conveying Cold War anxieties (particularly the fear of a hidden communist invasion).

---

90 Liwinski, Mateusz: "Nostalgia for Dystopia: Critical Nostalgia in Lucas Pope's *Papers, Please*," in: Klonowska, Barbara et al. (eds.), *(Im)perfection Subverted, Reloaded and Networked: Utopian Discourse Across Media*, Frankfurt a.M.: Internationaler Verlag der Wissenschaften 2015, pp. 223-234, here p. 232.

Figure 5: The creational aspect of FALLOUT *4 is foregrounded in players' ability to build a network of settlements. Thereby creative applications are possible—such as in this instance, where several doors metaphorically point to the malleability of the gameworld and players' agency in choosing a future for the Commonwealth.*

Source: FALLOUT 4

The Synth issue and fear of the Institute are widespread in the Commonwealth, and several factions have their own ideas of how to deal with the supposed threat and chart ways into the future. Whereas the nationalist Brotherhood of Steel regards them as dangerous (as things that do not deserve to live), the Railroad functions as the humanitarian opposite. In their attempt to save the Synths and hide them in safe houses until they are integrated into society, a clear connection to the real-world Underground Railroad (that helped African American slaves to escape to the north) from the mid-19th century can be established. The Institute, on the other hand, pursues a different agenda. They are the underground bogeyman of the Commonwealth and aim to replace the anarchical filth from above with artificial beings so that they can establish a society of scientists. Lastly, there are the Minutemen, a faction with clear references to the independently formed, eponymous militia in the American Revolutionary War. Their agenda is to restore order to the Commonwealth by establishing a network of egalitarian communities and dealing with the Raider threat.

All these factions take inspiration from American history (but also create allusions to contemporary trends such as the refugee crises in Europe) and urge players to create imaginative connections between both worlds. This manifests as well in how players may deal with the factions, for whom they will conduct missions, with whom they will side, and eventually how they will decide which of these ideologies they deem best to control the Commonwealth. A particular utopian (or dystopian) energy is thereby placed on the creational aspects of the game. Players may choose to build a network of egalitarian settlements dispersed throughout the Commonwealth where people of all races and ethnicities are welcome. However, they may also choose to do nothing or spend the resources they encounter to create phallic symbols of power to fuel their selfish desires.

Whereas the critical dystopia variant II lays emphasis on an ergodic and imaginative openness, *variant I* rather focuses on a densely structured plot that moves players in an ambiguous but nonetheless utopian direction. Here, players have no say in how the main plot develops but their imagination may still lead to utopian and dystopian possibilities (specifically concerning the interpretation of these games' endings). Irrational Games' BIOSHOCK INFINITE, for instance, sends players to the floating city of Columbia and targets a variety of issues, including theocratic regimes, a rapturous form of capitalism leading to a culture of Disneyfication, and humankind's unrelenting desire for power. To warn players of such potentialities, BIOSHOCK INFINITE entices them with a quest to save a mysterious woman by the name of Elizabeth as they come to uncover society's true nature. To do so, the game involves players in a struggle for forgiveness that is both personal and universalized. Whereas on a basic level, this struggle revolves around Booker DeWitt's guilt for having committed racist atrocities and losing his daughter Anna as a gambling debt, this guilt is transposed to players' current objective of saving Elizabeth. Here, they face the loss of Utopia by participating in hectic combat and an estranged form of capitalism. This gamist playstyle (which is focused on spectacle and gathering points) is aligned with consumer conduct in the empirical world (buying goods one is not in need of while ignoring the atrocities of the capitalist production machinery). In an intricate story of multiverses and negative potentialities, BIOSHOCK INFINITE's ambiguous ending reunites the thematic strands of the BIOSHOCK games and fortifies their attempt to denounce human nature. Yet it also expresses the possibility to break free from this vicious circle in the protagonists' struggle for forgiveness through self-sacrificial acts.

Although players have no saying in this ending, the imaginative possibilities of interpretation remain open to negotiation. Similarly works Naughty

Dog's THE LAST OF US, which allows a variety of interpretations to its ending and the ongoing plot. The game sets players in a world where humankind has been decimated by the Cordyceps Brain Infection and where nature has made a majestic return. THE LAST OF US warns about the ramifications of uncontrolled capitalism that extends into most ecospheres and disrupts nature's intimate balance. Thereby, it involves players in a dialectical opposition between confining city spaces and liberating outdoor spaces. Whereas the former reminds one of the shortcomings of bureaucratic consumer capitalism and the scientific hubris of man, the latter offer a safe haven from the intense gameplay of the city and suburban areas. Although seemingly a didactic opposition, the journey is one of gradual realization, where Ellie aids both Joel (the player-character) and the players in savoring aspects of the natural world they might otherwise have forgotten.

Having gone through this ecological counter-narrative, players are confronted with a decision about the future, which the game takes for them. The plot's logic dictates Joel's decisions (the choice for Tommy's settlement and against the Fireflies) and illustrates his reversion to the loving father he once was and the choice for a sustainable future in balance with nature. This view is however up to interpretation, which ends THE LAST OF US on a decisively ambiguous note.

1.2.4 The Classical Dystopia

The history of the dystopian genre (in games) and its plot structure are closely tied to dystopia's function as a *warning*. Video game dystopias involve players in confining rule systems and nightmarish gameworlds that often seem "beyond redemption"[91] and, by doing so, address contemporary trends prevalent in a specific historical period. Nonetheless, hope, in the sense of "gloomy optimism, fearing for the worst, hoping for the best"[92] is always an option—otherwise, these games would be pointless (other than serving as a

---

91 Schulzke, Marcus: "The Critical Power of Virtual Dystopias," *Games and Culture* (2014), p. 330.
92 Geoghegan, Vincent: "Darkness and Light," in: Vieira, Fátima (ed.), *Dystopia(n) Matters: On the Page, on Screen, on Stage*, Newcastle Upon Tyne: Camebridge Scholars Publishing 2013, pp. 46-48, here p. 48.

product for consumption). The critical dystopia is thereby a sub-genre that moves in a strong utopian direction, whereas *classical dystopian games* aim to shock their players most forcefully by involving them in a world where escape and rebellion are out of range.

This sense of agitation about the future is palpable, for example, in MANHUNTER: NEW YORK, where Earth's population has been robbed of their freedom by a race called the Orbs. Players take on the role of an operative for the Orbs, tracking down human rebels, but eventually become wary of the Orbs' true objectives (to harvest humans as a source of food). This is when players change sides and work to liberate Earth, which nonetheless ends with destruction and mass murder. The pessimism of MANHUNTER: NEW YORK is beyond doubt and can be found in many games of the 1980s and 1990s. There is, for instance, SYNDICATE (1993), where players are unknowingly in charge of a corporation in a ruthless struggle for dominance; SHADOWRUN (1993); A MIND FOREVER VOYAGING (1985); and I HAVE NO MOUTH, AND I MUST SCREAM; the latter of which involves players in a journey through infernal punishment without the possibility of winning the game. All the above-mentioned games tackle fears of the era in different ways: including cold war anxieties, the American population's desire for entertainment (with cable TV going mainstream), electronic innovations and the appearance of the Internet (evoking fears of Artificial Intelligence and robotics), as well as a reinvigorated capitalism governed by multinational corporations. They thus stand in the tradition of classical dystopian fiction such as E. M. Forster's short story "The Machine Stops,"[93] Aldous Huxley's *Brave New World*, and the genre's prime example, George Orwell's *Nineteen Eighty-Four*. Hope in these stories lies outside the story- or gameworld (the diegetic characters are doomed to failure) and is left to readers and players: to learn from the fictional experience and not let it happen in their world.[94]

Another frightening example of this genre is THE STANLEY PARABLE, whose official narrative involves players in the oppressive structures of corporate powers and video game design alike. Thereby, an unnamed narrator guides the players through the branching plot alongside the pre-established path. Following his orders, Stanley comes to experience a heroic story in

---

93 Forster, E.M.: "The Machine Stops", in: *The Oxford and Cambridge Review* (1909).
94 F. Vieira: "The Concept of Utopia," p. 17.

which he discovers the machinations of the system—by encountering a Mind Control Facility and a Panopticon-style observation room that monitors the workers—and eventually comes to destroy it. As a reward, Stanley is led to a gate that opens on to a lush environment. His dreams of freedom are about to come true. However, happiness comes at a price, and the player who wishes to explore her newly found freedom is frustrated when the game triggers a cutscene that strips her of control.

This ending aligns the game with films such as THE MATRIX (1999) or DARK CITY (1998) which thematize life in a *simulacrum*. Yet it also speaks to a more fundamental tendency in society that Michel Foucault describes as the steady change from the practices of public *torture* as a "theatre of hell"[95] to a "system of punishment"[96] that works in disguise but nonetheless subjugates the individual.[97] Through *discipline*—the "methods [...] which made possible the meticulous control of the operations of the body, which assured the constant subjugation of its forces"[98]—the design of punishment extended not only to prison designs but also explained how society operates as a whole. These "general formulas of domination"[99] produce "'docile' bodies"[100] that are well equipped to execute the tasks of social demand.[101]

In light of these arguments, THE STANLEY PARABLE's official narrative virtualizes a gameworld that can be considered a microcosm of the larger Panopticon of game design[102] and of empirical society. It refers to both the *meticulous rule system of a game* that subjugates players by having her execute repetitive tasks and follow pre-established lines of orientation, and to the *confinements of a worker's experience* in a bureaucratic consumer soci-

---

95 Foucault, Michel: *Discipline and Punish: The Birth of the Prison*, 2nd ed., trans. Alan Sheridan, New York: Random House 1995, p. 46.
96 Ibid., p. 89.
97 Ibid., pp. 7-8, p. 138, p. 264.
98 Ibid., p. 137.
99 Ibid.
100 Ibid., p. 138.
101 Ibid., pp. 137-138.
102 de Wildt similarly views games as "power structures in a Foucaultian sense." de Wildt, Lars: "Precarious Play. To Be or Not to Be Stanley," *Press Start* 1, no. 1 (2014); http://press-start.gla.ac.uk/index.php/press-start/article/view/10/4

ety, which is geared to profit while neglecting the self-expression of the individual.

However, THE STANLEY PARABLE is not entirely resigned to such a negative view of society and grants players the possibility of a *counter-narrative* that depends on their actions. This counter-narrative begins once Stanley *chooses the door on his right* and acts contrary to the narrator's instructions. Infuriated by the players' decision to ruin his well-crafted story, the narrator attempts to bring Stanley back on track by closing off allies, rebooting parts of the game, or triggering *The Stanley Parable Adventure Line*, which guides the player to catharsis. Breaking away from these pre-established pathways describes an act of *transgression* and an attempt to escape the confines of the office building and the plot alike. Yet it is exactly this transgression that is about to fail in THE STANLEY PARABLE. None of the endings suggests a hopeful outcome for Stanley—one time he is stuck in a room with the sole option of committing suicide, while on another occasion he turns mad and winds up dead on the pavement outside the building.

Considering this helplessness, *utopian enclaves* are not discernible for Stanley, and hope lies solely with players themselves. In one playthrough, for example, a second narrator reminds players that the only escape is to stop playing the game, while on another occasion they end up in a sequence where their ghost hovers over the paralyzed Stanley. Consequently, it is only by refusing to play the games of larger power structures that players may liberate themselves from them. In the vein of the classical dystopia, THE STANLEY PARABLE thus evokes the shocking insight that players might not be so far from Stanley—and that, if this is so, they should change their lifestyle by refusing to participate in bureaucratic madness.

1.2.5 The Misfit of the Anti-Utopia

Although classical dystopias involve players in confined spaces that are far beyond redemption, they nonetheless evoke a militant response in players and a rejection of the systems they experienced. This is different for the misfit of the anti-utopia, which as Moylan puts it

"remain[s] in the camp of nihilistic or resigned expressions that *may appear to challenge* the current social situation but in fact *end up reproducing it* by ideologically inoculating viewers and readers against any form of anger or action, enclosing them within the very social realities they disparagingly expose."[103]

In other words, the anti-utopia seeks to deceive players about its critical nature or involves them in pleasurable action to attenuate the system it represents. This is discernible, for example, in CIVILIZATION, which Frans Mäyrä describes as an "[i]deological simulation" that involves players in the inner mechanisms of colonization which have them adopt the hegemonic point of view of Western cultures (specifically that of the U.S).[104] The game, therefore, exerts "hidden influence on its player" and can be seen as a strategy of the status quo to justify their ideology.[105] A further example is CALL OF DUTY: ADVANCED WARFARE. By participating in hectic combat and blindly following orders, players devolve into faceless participants in the wars of greater powers. Thereby, the antagonist (the corporation ATLAS) is a direct extrapolation of the U.S. military-industrial complex on whose side (in the form of the resistance group SENTINEL) players are fighting.

1.3 CONCLUSION

This paper has described digital games in their function as creative artworks and cultural artifacts that subversively comment on real-world issues and gradually change players' habitual dispositions and worldviews. It thereby focused on how a *utopian impulse* permeates human society and their creations. This impulse oscillates between utopian and anti-utopian possibilities and manifests itself not only in the games industry but also in digital games in general and video game utopias and dystopias in a reinforced manner.

The issue hope is therefore of essential importance and how utopian enclaves (spaces of imaginative and ergodic resistance) are ingrained into the gameworld as potentialities. Players may choose to actualize these and become involved in a form of play that is fundamentally *regenerative*. This utopian energy comes to the fore in the act of play (in the dialectic between

---

103 R. Moylan: *Scraps of the Untainted Sky*, pp. 195-196, emphasis added.
104 Mäyrä, Frans: *An Introduction to Game Studies: Games in Culture*, London: SAGE, 2008, p. 94.
105 Ibid., p. 98; cf. pp. 95-101.

game, *player*, and *empirical world (culture)* and is outlined by the sensualizing powers of fiction and the different forms of involvement digital games allow: through their spaces, dramatic plot frameworks, characters and cultures, the primordial force of creation, and players' negotiation of the game system.

Regenerative play can thus be desired as a manifestation of the utopian impulse in digital games and is apparent in a reinforced manner in utopian and dystopian games. These function as warnings of contemporary trends and tendencies that may lead the world into negative directions and involve players in different ways in the negotiation of hope. The resulting *typology* has disclosed several strategies and plot frameworks to do so and has shown the diversity of the utopian and dystopian genre in digital games. Besides the misfit of the anti-utopia, all of these subgenres function as strategies of Utopia: to promote a continual society struggle for a better future but also warn of its potential loss.

LITERATURE

Baccolini, Raffaella/Moylan, Tom: "Introduction. Dystopia and Histories," in: Baccolini, Raffaella/Moylan, Tom (eds.), *Dark Horizons: Science Fiction and the Dystopian Imagination*, New York: Routledge 2003, pp. 1-12.

Baccolini, Raffaella/Moylan, Tom: "Conclusion. Critical Dystopia and Possibilities," in: Baccolini, Raffaella/Moylan, Tom (eds.), *Dark Horizons: Science Fiction and the Dystopian Imagination*, New York: Routledge 2003, pp. 233-249.

Batchelor, James: "Global Games Market Value Rising to $134.9bn in 2018: Revenues Grew by Over 10 %, Mobile Accounts for Almost Half at $63.2 Billion," *Gamesindustry*, December 18, 2018; https://www.gamesindustry.biz/articles/2018-12-18-global-games-market-value-rose-to-usd134-9 bn-in-2018

Berensmeyer, Ingo: *Literary Theory: An Introduction to Approaches, Methods and Terms*, Stuttgart: Klett Lerntraining 2009.

Booker, M. Keith: *Dystopian Literature: A Theory and Research Guide*, Westport, Conn.: Greenwood Press 1994.

Booker, M. Keith: *The Dystopian Impulse in Modern Literature: Fiction as Social Criticism*, Westport Conn.: Greenwood Press 1994.

Burke, Edmund: *A Philosophical Enquiry into the Origins of the Sublime and Seautiful*, Calgery: Anodos Books 2017.

Campbell, Joseph: *The Hero with a Thousand Faces*, Bollingen Series 18, 3rd ed., Novato: New World Library 2008.

Crick, Bernard: "Introduction," in: Orwell, George, *Nineteen Eighty-Four*, New York: Clarendon Press 1984, pp. 152-153.

Cronon, William: "The Trouble with Wilderness; or, Getting Back to the Wrong Nature," in: Cronon, William (ed.), *Uncommon Ground: Toward Reinventing Nature*, New York: W. W. Norton & Company 1995, pp. 69-90.

Davis, Laurence: "Dystopia, Utopia and Sancho Panza," in: Vieira, Fátima (ed.), *Dystopia(n) Matters: On the Page, on Screen, on Stage*, Newcastle-upon-Tyne: Cambridge Scholar Publishing 2013, pp. 23-27.

de Wildt, Lars: "Precarious Play. To Be or Not to Be Stanley," *Press Start* 1, no. 1 (2014); http://press-start.gla.ac.uk/index.php/press-start/article/view/10/4

Domsch, Sebastian: *Storyplaying: Agency and Narrative in Video Games*, Berlin: De Gruyter 2013.

Domsch, Sebastian: "Dystopian Video Games: Fallout in Utopia," in: Voigts, Eckart/Boller, Alessandra (eds.), *Dystopia, Science Fiction, Post-Apocalypse: Classics–New Tendencies–Model Interpretations*, Trier: Wissenschaftlicher Verlag Trier 2015, pp. 395-410.

Fahlenbrach, Kathrin/Schröter, Felix: "Game Studies und Rezeptionsästhetik," in: Sachs-Hombach, Klaus/Thon, Jan-Noël (eds.), *Game Studies: Aktuelle Ansätze der Computerspielforschung*, Köln: Herbert von Harlem Verlag 2015, pp. 165-208.

Farca, Gerald et al.: "Regenerative Play and the Experience of the Sublime in The Legend of Zelda: Breath of the Wild," *Proceedings of The Philosophy of Computer Games Conference* (2018); http://gameconference.itu.dk/papers/06%20-%20farca%20et%20al%20%20regenerative%20play.pdf

Farca, Gerald: *Playing Dystopia: Nightmarish Worlds in Video Games and the Player's Aesthetic Response*, Bielefeld: transcript 2018.

Fitting, Peter: "Unmasking the Real? Critique and Utopia in Recent SF Films," in: Baccolini, Raffaella/Moylan, Tom (eds.), *Dark Horizons: Science Fiction and the Dystopian Imagination*, New York: Routledge 2003, pp. 155-166.

Fortunati, Vita: "Why Dystopia Matters," in: Vieira, Fátima (ed.), *Dystopia(n) Matters: On the Page, on Screen, on Stage*, Newcastle-upon-Tyne: Cambridge Scholar Publishing 2013, pp. 28-36.

Foucault, Michel: *Discipline and Punish: The Birth of the Prison*, 2nd ed., trans. Alan Sheridan, New York: Random House 1995.

Garrard, Greg: *Ecocriticism*, New York: Routledge 2004.

Geoghegan, Vincent: "Darkness and Light," in: Vieira, Fátima (ed.), *Dystopia(n) Matters: On the Page, on Screen, on Stage*, Newcastle Upon Tyne: Camebridge Scholars Publishing 2013, pp. 46-48.

Huxley, Aldous: *Brave New World*, United Kingdom: Chatto & Windus 1932.

Inderst, Rudolf: *Vergemeinschaftung in MMORPGs*, Boizenburg: Werner Hülsbusch 2009.

Iser, Wolfgang: *The Act of Reading: A Theory of Aesthetic Response*, trans. Wilhelm Fink, Baltimore: John Hopkins UP 1978.

Iser, Wolfgang: *The Fictive and the Imaginary: Charting Literary Anthropology*, Frankfurt a.M.: Suhrkamp 1993.

Jagoda, Patrick: "Digital Games and Science Fiction," in: Link, Eric C./Canavan, Gerry (eds.), *The Cambridge Companion to American Science Fiction*, New York: Cambridge UP 2015, pp. 139-152.

Jameson, Fredric: *Archaeologies of the Future: The Desire Called Utopia and Other Science Fictions*, London: Verso 2005.

Jameson, Fredric: *The Seeds of Time*, New York: Columbia UP 1994.

Jenkins, Henry: "The Art of Contested Spaces," *Publications Henry Jenkins*, 2002; http://web.mit.edu/~21fms/People/henry3/contestedspaces.html

Juul, Jesper: *Handmade Pixels: Independent Video Games and the Quest for Authenticity*, Cambridge, MA.: MIT Press 2019.

Kłosiński, Michał: "Games and Utopia," *Acta Ludologia* 1 (2018); http:// act aludologica.com/wp-content/uploads/2018/04/01.-KLOSINSKI%E2%80%93-AL-1-2018.pdf

Kumar, Krishan: *Utopia and Anti-Utopia in Modern Times*, Oxford: Basil Blackwell 1987.

Levitas, Ruth/Sargisson, Lucy: "Utopia in Dark Times: Optimism/Pessimism and Utopia/Dystopia," in: Baccolini, Raffaella/Moylan, Tom (eds.), *Dark Horizons: Science Fiction and the Dystopian Imagination*, New York: Routledge 2003, pp. 13-27.

Liwinski, Mateusz: "Nostalgia for Dystopia: Critical Nostalgia in Lucas Pope's *Papers, Please*," in: Klonowska, Barbara et al. (eds.), *(Im)perfection Subverted, Reloaded and Networked: Utopian Discourse Across Media*, Frankfurt a.M.: Internationaler Verlag der Wissenschaften 2015, pp. 223-234.

Mäyrä, Frans: *An Introduction to Game Studies: Games in Culture*, London: SAGE 2008.

More, Thomas: *Utopia*, trans. Paul Turner, London: Penguin Group 2009.

Mortensen, Torill: "Anger, Fear, and Games: The Long Event of #Gamer Gate," *Games and Culture* 13, no. 8 (April 2016); https://journals.sagepub.com/doi/abs/10.1177/1555412016640408

Moylan, Tom: *Scraps of the Untainted Sky: Science Fiction, Utopia, Dystopia*, Boulder, Colorado: Westview Press 2000.

Murray, Janet H.: *Hamlet on The Holodeck: The Future of Narrative in Cyberspace*, Cambridge, Mass.: MIT Press 1998.

Orwell, George: *Nineteen Eighty-Four*, United Kingdom: Secker & Warburg 1949

Perron, Bernard: *Silent Hill: The Terror Engine*, Ann Arbor: University of Michigan Press 2012.

Sargent, Lyman T.: "Do Dystopias Matter?" in: Vieira, Fátima (ed.), *Dystopia(n) Matters: On the Page, on Screen, on Stage*, Newcastle-upon-Tyne: Cambridge Scholar Publishing 2013, pp. 10-13.

Sargent, Lyman T.: "The Three Faces of Utopianism Revisited," in: *Utopian Studies* 5, no. 1 (1994); http://www.jstor.org/discover/10.2307/20719246?uid=3737864&uid=2129&uid=2&uid=70&uid=4&sid=2110156029513

Sargent, Lyman T.: "U.S. Eutopias in the 1980s and 1990s: Self-Fashioning in a World of Multiple Identities," in: Spinozzi, Paola (ed.), *Utopianism/Literary Utopias and National Culture Identities: A Comparative Perspective*, COTEPRA/University of Bologna 2001, pp. 221-232.

Sargent, Lyman T.: *Utopianism: A Very Short Introduction*, Oxford: Oxford UP 2010.

Schulzke, Marcus: "The Critical Power of Virtual Dystopias," *Games and Culture* (2014).

Seeber, Hans Ulrich: *Die Selbstkritik der Utopie in der Angloamerikanischen Literatur*, Münster: LIT 2003.

Stuart, Keith: "The Last of Us, BioShock: Infinite and why all Video Game Dystopias Work the Same," in: *The Guardian*, July 1, 2013; https://www.theguardian.com/technology/gamesblog/2013/jul/01/last-of-us-bioshock-infinite-male-view

Suvin, Darko: *Metamorphoses of Science Fiction: On the Poetics and History of a Literary Genre*, New Haven: Yale UP 1979.

Tavinor, Grant: "Art and Aesthetics," in: Wolf, Mark J. P./Perron, Bernard (eds.), *The Routledge Companion to Video Game Studies*, New York: Routledge 2014, pp. 59-66.

Taylor, Haydn: "Ubisoft Massive COO: 'We Don't Want to Take a Stance in Current Politics,'" *GamesIndustry*, October 17, 2018; https://www.gamesindustry.biz/articles/2018-10-17-ubisoft-massive-coo-we-dont-want-to-take-a-stance-in-current-politics

Vella, Daniel: "No Mastery Without Mystery: Dark Souls and the Ludic Sublime," *Game Studies* 15, no. 1 (2015); http://gamestudies.org/1501/articles/vella

Vieira, Fátima: "The Concept of Utopia," in: Claeys, Gregory (ed.), *The Cambridge Companion to Utopian Literature*, Cambridge: Cambridge UP 2010, pp. 3-27.

Vieira, Fátima: "Introduction," in: Vieira, Fátima (ed.), *Dystopia(n) Matters: On the Page, on Screen, on Stage*, Newcastle-upon-Tyne: Cambridge Scholar Publishing 2013, pp. 1-7.

Walz, Steffen P.: *Toward a Ludic Architecture: The Space of Play and Games*, Pittsburgh, PA: ETC Press 2010.

Žižek, Slavoj: *Welcome to the Desert of the Real! Five Essays on September 11 and Related Dates*, London: Verso 2002.

GAMOGRAPHY

A MIND FOREVER Voyaging (Infocom/Activision 1985, O: Infocom)
ANNO 2070 (Ubisoft 2011, O: Related Designs/Ubisoft Bluebyte)
AQUA MOTO RACING UTOPIA (Resolution Interactive 2009,
BENEATH A STEEL SKY (Virgin Interactive Entertainment 1994, O: Revolution Software)

BIOSHOCK (2K Games 2007, O: 2K Boston)
BIOSHOCK 2 (2K Games 2010, O: 2K Marin)
BIOSHOCK INFINITE (2K Games 2013, O: Irrational Games)
BLADE Runner (Virgin Interactive 1997, O: Westwood Studios)
BORDERLANDS (2K Games 2009, O: Gearbox Software);
BORDERLANDS 2 (2K Games 2012, 2014, O: Gearbox Software);
BURIAL AT SEA: EPISODE 1 and 2 (2K Games 2013, 2014, O: Irrational Games)
CALL OF DUTY: ADVANCED WARFARE (Activision 2014, O: Sledgehammer Games)
CIVILIZATION (MicroProse 1991, O: MicroProse)
CRACKDOWN (Microsoft Game Studios 2007, O: Realtime Worlds)
CRUSADER: NO REMORSE (Electronic Arts 1994, O: Origin Systems)
DEUS EX: HUMAN REVOLUTION (Square Enix 2011, O: Eidos Montreal)
DISHONORED (Bethesda Softworks 2012, O: Arkane Studios)
ENSLAVED: ODYSSEY TO THE WEST (Namco Bandai Games 2010, O: Ninja Theory)
EVERY DAY THE SAME DREAM (Molleindustria 2009, O: Molleindustria)
FAHRENHEIT 451 (Trillium 1984, O: Trillium)
FALLOUT 4 (Bethesda Softworks 2015, O: Bethesda Game Studios)
FEZ (Trapdoor 2012, O: Polytron)
FIREWATCH (Panic/Campo Santo 2016, O: Campo Santo)
FLOWER (Sony Interactive Entertainment/Annapurna Interactive 2009, O: Thatgamecompany)
I HAVE NO MOUTH, AND I MUST SCREAM (Cyberdreams 1995, O: The Dreamers Guild)
JOURNEY (Sony Computer Entertainment/Annapurna Interactive 2012, O: Thatgamecompany)
MAD MAX (Warner Bros. Interactive 2015, O: Avalanche Studios)
MANHUNTER: NEW YORK (Sierra Online 1988, O: Evryware)
MASS EFFECT: ANDROMEDA (Electronic Arts 2017, O: Bioware)
METRO 2033 (THQ 2010, O: 4A Games)
MINECRAFT (Mojang 2011, O: Mojang)
MIRROR'S EDGE (Electronic Arts 2008, O: EA Dice)
MONOPOLY (Hasbro 2008, O: Electronic Arts)
NERUOMANCER: A CYBERPUNK ROLE-PLAYING ADVENTURE (Mediagenic 1988, O: Interplay Productions)

NIER: AUTOMATA (Square Enix 2017, O: Platinum Games)
NO MAN'S SKY (Hello Games 2016, O: Hello Games)
PAPERS, PLEASE (3909 2014, O: 3909)
PROTEUS (Curve Digital/Twisted Tree 2013, O: Ed Key/David Kanaga)
REVOLUTION X (Midway 1994, O: Midway)
ROBOTICA (Sega 1995, O: Micronet Genki)
SHADOW OF THE COLOSSUS (Sony 2005, O: Team ICO)
SHADOWRUN (Data East 1993, O:Beam Software)
STELLARIS (Paradox Interactive 2016, O: Paradox Development Studio)
STRIDER (Capcom 1989, O: Capcom)
SURVIVING MARS (Paradox Interactive 2018, O: Haemimont Games)
Syndicate (Electronic Arts 1993, O: Bullfrog Productions)
TALES FROM THE BORDERLANDS (Telltale Games 2014, O: Telltale Games).
THE LAST OF US (Sony Computer Entertainment 2013, O: Naughty Dog)
THE LAST OF US: REMASTERED (Sony Computer Entertainment 2014, O: Naughty Dog)
THE LEGEND OF ZELDA: BREATH OF WILD (Nintendo 2017, O: Nintendo)
THE PRE-SEQUEL (2K Games 2014, O: Gearbox Software);
THE SIMS (Electronic Arts 2000, O: Maxis)
THE STANLEY PARABLE (Galactic Cafe 2013, O: Galactic Cafe)
TOM CLANCY'S THE DIVISION (Ubisoft 2017, O: Massive Enternainment)
TOM CLANCY'S THE DIVISION 2 (Ubisoft 2019, O: Massive Entertainment)
UTOPIA (Mattel 1981, O: Mattel, Don Daglow)
UTOPIA: THE CREATION OF A NATION (Gremlin Interactive 1991, O: Celestial Software)
WATCH DOGS (Ubisoft 2014, O: Ubisoft Montreal)
WOLFENSTEIN: THE NEW ORDER (Bethesda Softworks 2014, O: Machine Games)
WORLD OF WARCRAFT (Blizzard Entertainment 2004, O: Blizzard Entertainment)

FILMOGRAPHY

DARK CITY (USA 1998, D: Alex Proyas)
INVASION OF THE BODY SNATCHERS (USA 1956, D: Don Siegel)
THE MATRIX (USA 1995, D: The Wachoswkis)

"Everything is true; nothing is permitted"
Utopia, Religion and Conspiracy in ASSASSIN'S CREED

LARS DE WILDT

> Rodrigo [de Borja, Pope Alexander VI, LdW] looked surprised: Don't you know what lies within? Hasn't the great and powerful *Order of the Assassins* figured it out? […] Are you really so naive? I became Pope because the position gave me access. It gave me power! […] It's all lies and superstition. […] Ezio, we *Templars* understand humanity, and that is why we hold it in such contempt! OLIVER BOWDEN, ASSASSIN'S CREED: RENAISSANCE

INTRODUCTION

The ASSASSIN'S CREED series has always framed religion as a dystopian power play. Starting with one game in 2007, the series now (in 2019) includes 21 games, four movies, various books and other media—each more or less taking place in another historical period and place. Throughout all of those, two secret societies (the Assassins and Templars) fight throughout history to find a sacred artefact that will help themselves shape the world as they see fit, while keeping the other party from doing the same. The Order of the Assassins are initially presented as a liberating secularizing force, utopian in its plan to free the minds of historical societies from the (Catholic) Templar mind-controllers.

This chapter will challenge that initial conception. It will start with a review of the relevant literature on Utopia, religion and conspiracy, and then proceed in two sections. The first section argues that the series' original premise monopolizes the Assassins' project as utopian. The Utopia of the Assassins' secularized secret society tries to create space for its 'not-place' (Utopia) in the Holy Land of Jerusalem in the year 1191. This secular Utopia is set against the outside invasion of the Catholic dystopian Templar crusaders. The second section of the paper will trace the development of the series' characters, settings and stories between the first game in 2007 and its most recent release (at time of writing) in 2018 to argue that the idea of Utopia comes increasingly to overlap with the dystopia of the other. That is, that the Assassins' dystopia is the Templar's Utopia and vice versa. Cynically put, both sides are equally legitimate in their striving toward contrasting Utopia, by vying for full control over historical societies: everything is true. Nothing is permitted.

CONSPIRACY, FAITH, AND UTOPIA

Two paratexts shed light on how the basic idea of Utopia comes to fruition in the game series. In the advertisement for ASSASSIN'S CREED SYNDICATE (2015), a nobleman dreams of blades erupting from every surface of Victorian London, as he is chased by them. Waking up, his assistant, in a decidedly upper-middle class British accent asks him: "Is there a problem, my lord?"— "No, nothing that concerns you." As the camera tracks the faces of several conspiring standers-by, Depeche Mode's *Personal Jesus* ("Reach out and touch faith") plays in the background. Assassins appear on the rooftops and a line of text appears full-screen, in all capitals:

OPPRESSION HAS TO END

The advertisement, titled "Blades" and filmed by the agency BETC France for Ubisoft, ends with Depeche Mode's titular lyric "Your own personal Jesus," framing the Assassins as Christ-like liberators. The ad contains all the elements of the series that this paper focuses on: conspiracy, faith, and a utopian project: "oppression has to end." Similarly, the advertisement for ASSASSIN'S CREED III (2012, "Rise," by Sid Lee) shows revolutionaries before the American Revolution noting their moments of resistance ("When I say no to a law we never voted for. When I stop feeding an Empire a world away [...] When I ask God to look the other way"), culminating in another full-screen, all capital slogan:

RISE

Just as the advertisements, reviews too have framed ASSASSIN'S CREED as revolving around an aspiration toward some kind of better world. ASSASSIN'S CREED, according to Games Radar, is about "restoring peace to the region."[1] ASSASSIN'S CREED III, according to Kotaku's Stephen Totilo is about "Connor creating his own better society."[2] Others note that in ASSASSIN'S CREED: UNITY (2014) "revolution is in the air and it's time for you to take a step up and aid the change for a better world,"[3] and in ASSASSIN'S CREED: LIBERATION (2012), players will "be infiltrating plantations, guiding slaves to freedom, and generally fighting to *create a better world*."[4]

Utopia

This sort of discourse (diegetically, in surrounding media and in game culture's reception of the games) strongly suggests that ASSASSIN'S CREED can be, and is being read, as utopian. Before going into how the game presents its utopian project(s), it is valuable to go over what that entails.

---

1 Reparaz, Mikel: "Assassin's Creed Review," *Gamesradar*, 2007; https://www.gamesradar.com/assassins-creed-review/
2 Totilo, Stephen: "The Controversial Assassin's Creed III Is More Impressive in 2019," *Kotaku*, 2019; https://kotaku.com/the-controversial-assassin-s-creed-iii-is-more-impressi-1833676354
3 Milner, Jarred: "Review: Assassin's Creed Unity," *SA Gamer*, 2014; https://sagamer.co.za/review-assassins-creed-unity-xbox-one
4 Rosenberg, Adam: "Assassin's Creed 3: Liberation Review: Flawed, But Realized Potential," *Digital Trends*, 2012; https://www.digitaltrends.com/gaming/assassins-creed-3-liberation-review-realized-potential/, [emphasis added].

Most originally, as most chapters in this book will in some way state, the idea of Utopia—as a non-place on which to find, project or potentially realize an ideal world—comes from Thomas More's *Utopia*, first published in Leuven, Belgium in 1516. In it, in front of Antwerp's Onze-Lieve-Vrouwekathedraal [*Cathedral of Our Lady*], More's protagonist starts relating a story of a perfect state called Utopia (οὐ [not] + τόπος [place]). Gerald Farca, writing about such utopian projects in videogames in his book *Playing Dystopia*, argues that the "*act of imagination,*"[5] [emphasis original] which is at the root of all utopian thinking "induces a transformative process."[6] What this means for videogames, and fiction in general, is that an utopian narrative is always a "concrete fictional portrayal" of Utopia in action,[7] leading Farca to conclude that videogames particularly:

"involves the player in a playful trial action in which she may ergodically and imaginatively explore an alternative societal mode through play that is considerably worse than the game designers' empirical present."[8]

Put simply, the player gets to actively engage with ('ergodically,' i.e., through non-trivial input on the game)[9] as well as imagine Utopia. Typically, in videogames, this means one of two things. Either the player works toward establishing a Utopia, such as, arguably according to some, the cases of WORLD OF WARCRAFT (2004), SIMCITY (1989), or BLACK & WHITE (2001).[10] Or the player works to dismantle the opposite of a Utopia: dystopia, i.e.,

---

5 Levitas, Ruth/Sargisson, Lucy quoted in: Farca, Gerald. *Playing Dystopia: Nightmarish Worlds in Video Games and the Player's Aesthetic Response*, Bielefeld: transcript 2018, p. 37.
6 G. Farca: *Playing Dystopia*, p. 37.
7 Ferns, Christopher S.: *Narrating Utopia: Ideology, Gender, Form in Utopian Literature*, Liverpool: Liverpool University Press 1999, p. 34.
8 G. Farca: *Playing Dystopia*, p. 403.
9 Aarseth, Espen J.: *Cybertext: Perspectives on Ergodic Literature*, Baltimore: JHU Press 1997, p. 1.
10 Galloway, Alexander: "Warcraft and Utopia," *Ctheory* 2/16 (2006); Kłosiński, Michał: "Games and Utopia," *Acta Ludologica* 1, no. 1 (2018), pp. 4-14; Markocki, Miłosz: "Creating Utopian or Dystopian Worlds in Digital Games," *More After More* (2016), pp. 118-133.

usually a hopeless future vision of an autocratic, oppressive state, such as in the cases of HALF-LIFE (1998), FALLOUT (1997), BIOSHOCK: INFINITE (2013), CART LIFE (2010),[11] and so on.[12]

Religion

Often one person's heaven is another's hell. So, too, it seems to be in the Utopia games literature. What Gerald Farca reads as "a Utopia based on the principles of religious piety and American exceptionalism,"[13] leads Frank Bosman to the opposite conclusion about the same game: to him, "the religious based American exceptionalism of [BIOSHOCK INFINITE] is the firm ground on which Ken Levine has created his second dystopian society."[14] Religion, Bosman notes, occurs throughout dystopian games in various ways, although all of the ones he analyses—in the games BIOSHOCK (2007), its successor INFINITE, the DISHONORED (2012) games and BRINK (2011)—start off as Utopian projects.[15]

Christian religion, especially, is historically framed as a utopian project. This goes beyond the description of Eden or the promise of Heaven as perfect, just no-places as alternatives to the current society—whether oppressed by Romans, or others. As Bosman also notes, Puritans fleeing to the United States framed their project as utopian, "trying to establish a new Eden."[16]

---

11 It should be noted that, while CART LIFE seems to portray to many parts of the world a classic dystopian vision of dehumanized hopelessness under an oppressive state; it is elsewhere read as an accurate satire of, if not an actual portrayal of North-American neoliberalism, for which see, e.g., de Wildt, Lars: "On the Subject of Play: Digital Game-Play as Models of Ideologies," 2014, Leiden University; https://openaccess.leidenuniv.nl/handle/1887/28571

12 Tulloch, Rowan: "Ludic Dystopias: Power, Politics and Play," *Proceedings of the Sixth Australasian Conference on Interactive Entertainment* (2009), pp. 1-4; Bosman, Frank G.: "'The Lamb of Comstock.' Dystopia and Religion in Video Games," *Online. Heidelberg Journal of Religions on the Internet* 5 (2014), pp. 162-182.

13 G. Farca: *Playing Dystopia*, p. 326.

14 F. Bosman: "The Lamb of Comstock," p. 177.

15 Ibid., p. 178.

16 Bremer, Francis J. quoted in F. Bosman: "The Lamb of Comstock," p. 175.

Regardless, the presence of religion in contemporary Western media is odd. That is, it is *at odds* with the decline of religion in (Western) cultures and their public spaces. The prediction that religion is in decline is at least as old as the social sciences, in which secularization has been a defining concern as old as its founding fathers. Auguste Comte called "l'état théologique, ou fictive [*the theological, or fictive state*]" of humanity its most primitive state, of which the scientific is its "état fixe et définitif."[17] Marx famously predicted that "alles Heilige wird entweiht [*all that is holy is profaned*]" at the coming of capitalist modernity,[18] and Durkheim wrote that "le domaine de la religion [...] va de plus en plus en se rétrécissant [*the sphere of religion is continually diminishing*]".[19] Max Weber, lastly, spoke (in his inaugural reason at Munich University) about the "Entzauberung der Welt [*disenchantment of the world*]" by which technology and rationality now perform what the savage needed religion and magic for.[20] And indeed, statistics do show a decrease in church attendance, baptism and other institutional religious rituals over the course of the 20th century, especially in the case of Western youngsters.[21] The resulting argument is that either religions' social and

---

17 "Cette loi consiste en ce que chacune de nos conceptions principales, chaque branche de nos connaissances, passe successivement par trois états théoriques différents: l'état théologique, ou fictif; l'état métaphysique, ou abstrait; l'état scientifique, ou positif [...] la troisième, [est] son état fixe et définitif. [*This law consists in that each of our principle conceptions, each branch of our knowing, passes successively through three different theoretical states: the theological or fictive state; the metaphysical or abstract state; the scientific or positive, state [...] the third one is humanity's fixed and definitive state.*]" Comte, Auguste: *Cours de philosophie positive: première et deuxième leçons*, Hatier 1982.
18 Marx, Karl/Engels, Friedrich: "Manifest der Kommunistischen Partei," in: *Marx-Engels: Werke* 4, 1848, pp. 459-493, here p. 462.
19 Durkheim, Emile: *De la division du travail social*, Quadrige: Presses Universitaires de France 1991, p. 144.
20 Weber, Max: *Wissenschaft als Beruf*, Vol. 1., Berlin: Duncker & Humblot 1919.
21 Dobbelaere, Karel/Voyé, Liliane: "Religie en kerkbetrokkenheid: ambivalentie en vervreemding, " *Verloren zekerheid De Belgen en hun waarden, overuigingen en houdingen*, Tielt: Lannoo 2001, pp. 117-152.

cultural significance diminishes as a whole,[22] or that institutional religion shows at least a retreat from the public sphere.[23]

Yet we see a subversive occupation with religion as a mainstay in popular culture, specifically videogames. In such cases, religious symbology either serves to add mystery (or indeed magical re-enchantment)[24] through what religious scholar Christopher Partridge calls a "re-enchantment" through "occulture."[25] We see specific examples of this in, for instance, the use of the occult to bring magic and tension to BUFFY THE VAMPIRE SLAYER, in the popularity of bestsellers such as Dan Brown's *Da Vinci Code* or, indeed, ASSASSIN'S CREED.

Conspiracy

In such cases as the *Da Vinci Code* or ASSASSIN'S CREED, religion—or more specifically the church or any other established, intransparent institution—serves as a black box on which to project, or map, the unknown. As Fredric Jameson insists,

---

22 Wilson, Bryan R.: *Religion in Secular Society*, London: Penguin 1969; Wallis, Roy/Bruce, Steve: "Secularization: The Orthodox Model," in: Bruce, Steve (ed.), *Religion and Modernization: Sociologists and Historians Debate the Secularization Thesis*, Oxford: Oxford University Press 1992; Bruce, Steve: *God Is Dead: Secularization in the West*, Vol. 3, Oxford: Blackwell 2002; Norris, Pippa/Inglehart, Ronald: *Sacred and Secular: Religion and Politics Worldwide*, Cambridge: Cambridge University Press 2011.

23 Dobbelaere, Karel: "Some Trends in European Sociology of Religion: The Secularization Debate," *Sociology of Religion* 48, no. 2 (1987), pp. 107-137, here p. 107; Dobbelaere, Karel: "Towards an Integrated Perspective of the Processes Related to the Descriptive Concept of Secularization," *Sociology of Religion* 60, no. 3 (1999), pp. 229-247; Habermas, Jürgen: „Die Dialektik der Säkularisierung," *Blätter für deutsche und internationale Politik* 4 (2004), pp. 33-46. In English: Habermas, Jürgen: "Notes on Post-Secular Society," *New Perspectives Quarterly* 25, no. 4 (2008), pp. 17-29.

24 Aupers, Stef: "'Better Than the Real World.' On the Reality and Meaning of Online Computer Games," *Fabula* 48, no. 3-4 (2007), pp. 250-269.

25 Partridge, Christopher: *The Re-Enchantment of the West*, Vol. 2, London: A&C Black 2006.

"Conspiracy, one is tempted to say, is the poor person's cognitive mapping in the postmodern age; it is a degraded figure of the total logic of late capital, a desperate attempt to represent the latter's system, whose failure is marked by its slippage into sheer theme and content."[26]

Conspiracy is, in other words, seen as a layman's theorization of what happens in complex systems to which they have no access or insight—such as global capitalism, governments, or the Vatican. According to Jaron Harambam and Stef Aupers, such "conspiracy theories particularly compete with those formulated by social scientists"[27] by providing accounts of social control,[28] and "claim[ing] to uncover (supposedly) 'hidden' plots or machineries which have caused a particular state of affairs or events to take place."[29]

In the 20th century, however, the threat of such systems has always been that of an invader on the 'outside,' whereas the postmodernist conspiracy of the 21st century is of a paranoia pointed inward. Peter Knight argues that

"Where conspiracy-minded narratives of the individual and national immune system under threat might once have served to bolster a sense of (albeit restricted) communal identity, they now regularly register the far more scary anxiety that we can no longer tell the difference between Them and Us."[30]

Conspiracy then, according to authors like Jameson, Knight, Aupers and Harambam, arises as a way of dealing with the complexity of postmodern systems—interconnected, interrelated, intransparent bodies. Consider the presence of mistrust at every level of our public sphere. News and social media

---

26 Jameson, Fredric: *Postmodernism, or, the Cultural Logic of Late Capitalism*, Durham: Duke University Press 1991, p. 356.
27 Harambam, Jaron/Aupers, Stef: "Contesting Epistemic Authority: Conspiracy Theories on the Boundaries of Science," *Public Understanding of Science* 24, no. 4 (2015), pp. 466-488, here p. 2.
28 Melley, Timothy. *Empire of Conspiracy: The Culture of Paranoia in Postwar America*, Ithaca: Cornell University Press 2000, p. 42.
29 Parker, Martin: "Human Science as Conspiracy Theory," *The Sociological Review* 48.2 (2000), pp. 191-207, here p. 191.
30 Knight, Peter (ed.): *Conspiracy Nation: The Politics of Paranoia in Postwar America*, New York: NYU Press 2002, p. 5.

show growing groups of people with no trust in 'their own' climate scientists, vaccines, spherical earth, 'their own' United States Government, 'the Washington swamp,' the Deep State, the European Commission, Parliament and Council, the ones behind it all *actually* running everything; whether they are lizard people, the illuminati or whomever is spraying chem trails. It's all related, and you can't know what is true, but once you go down the rabbit hole, everything is significant. Harambam & Aupers stress this normalization of conspiracy through its pervasive presence in popular fiction, arguing that:

"[Conspiracy] not only features in popular culture—for example, films like The Matrix, bestsellers like *The Da Vinci Code*, or TV-series like THE X-FILES—but conspiracy theories have become an increasingly normalized idiom to account for seemingly inexplicable phenomena in contemporary society. From narratives about the 'real truth' behind the attacks of 9/11, the deaths of John F Kennedy, princess Diana, and Bin Laden, or collective vaccinations like against the Swine flu—official explanations are increasingly challenged, reconstructed, and contested by a discourse of conspiracy."[31]

ASSASSIN'S CREED: A CASE STUDY

Across the literature, a pivotal point for conspiracy culture in the 21st century appears to be September 11; such as through the 9/11 truth movement.[32] The case study for this chapter, ASSASSIN'S CREED, came up in exactly that time. While the United States was still very much pre-occupied with the War on

---

31 J. Harambam/S. Aupers: "Contesting Epistemic Authority," p. 2.
32 Harambam, Jaron J.: *'The Truth Is Out There:' Conspiracy Culture in an Age of Epistemic Instability*, Rotterdam: Erasmus University Rotterdam 2017; Stempel, Carl et al.: "Media Use, Social Structure, and Belief in 9/11 Conspiracy Theories," *Journalism & Mass Communication Quarterly* 84, no. 2 (2007), pp. 353-372; de Wildt, Lars: "Entwining the National and Personal: Art Spiegelman's Post-9/11 Shapeshifting," in: Folio, Jessica/Luhning, Holly (eds.), *Body Horror and Shapeshifting: A Multidisciplinary Exploration*, Leiden: Brill 2013, pp. 123-136; Wood, Michael James/Douglas, Karen M.: "'What About Building 7?' A Social Psychological Study of Online Discussion of 9/11 Conspiracy Theories," *Frontiers in Psychology* 4 (2013), p. 409.

Terror, carrying the traces of September 11 in North-America, the world also saw a rise of Islamophobia and religion-based conflict across the European continent. It is the period that has been called "post-relativist,"[33] exacerbating a "clash of civilizations,"[34] whose news cycle brought the importance of religion back into the public sphere to the point that Jürgen Habermas declared it "post-secular."[35]

Yet, ASSASSIN'S CREED was set in the Middle-East during a period defined by religious turmoil. It was originally a continuation of the PRINCE OF PERSIA IP, but in an open-world Middle-Eastern setting in order to show off the (then) 'next-generation' of consoles' computing powers. The game's developers, Ubisoft, added a disclaimer presumably in order to distance themselves from any perceived bias in the 'clash of civilizations'—Islamophobia would have surely meant horrible sales for a promising title. Thus, the first screen upon starting the game reads, now famously:

Figure 1: Religious disclaimer in the first ASSASSIN'S CREED opening titles

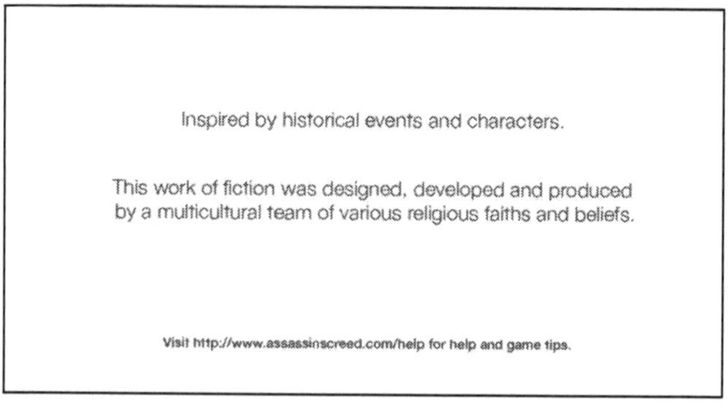

> Inspired by historical events and characters.
>
> This work of fiction was designed, developed and produced by a multicultural team of various religious faiths and beliefs.
>
> Visit http://www.assassinscreed.com/help for help and game tips.

Source: Screenshot from ASSASSINS'S CREED

---

33 Fish, Stanley: "Don't Blame Relativism," *The Responsive Community* 12, no. 3 (2002), pp. 27-31; Rothstein, Edward: "Moral Relativity is a Hot Topic? True. Absolutely," *New York Times* 7 (2002), p. 13.

34 Huntington, Samuel P.: *The Clash of Civilizations and the Remaking of World Order*, London: Simon & Schuster 1996; Eagleton, Terry: *Reason, Faith, and Revolution: Reflections on the God Debate*, New Haven: Yale UP 2009; Boletsi, Maria: *Barbarism and its Discontents*, Stanford: Stanford University Press 2013.

35 J. Habermas: "Die Dialektik der Säkularisierung."

The formula of the game has more or less stayed the same, with a small shift toward more open adventuring in 2017—much akin to Nintendo's new ZELDA game of that same year. That is: as an Assassin—or sometimes a Templar—the player exists in a duality between the present time and the past. This past is where most of the games take place, and it is re-lived by entering a machine called the Animus which digs up the ancestral experiences of the framing story's character's forefathers. In the first game, Altaïr Ibn-La'Ahad [*The Bird, Son of None*] during the Third Crusade; in the second game Ezio Auditore in 15th century Italy; and so on. Players learn about the Assassins' and Templars' secret orders in each period, weaving a historical tapestry of 'speculative fiction:' all this time, the stories of ASSASSIN'S CREED tell us, all the great conflicts and inventions of human history were a result of these two groups' search for the 'Apple of Eden.'

The Apple of Eden, originating from that original 'no-place' (Utopia) of happiness, the Garden of Eden, is the central element of ASSASSIN'S CREED's universe. Every main and supplementary game or paraludic content revolves around this key to re-establishing Utopia—and that transmedial universe currently (as per April 2019) unfolds over 21 games of which 11 'main' entries (see Table 1), one full-length movie, three short films, 13 graphic novels, nine books, a board game, and three editions of an encyclopedia.

Table 1. The ASSASSIN'S CREED games as per April 2019, with main entries in bold.

Setting	Period	Title	Release
Third Crusade	1191 AD	**ASSASSIN'S CREED**	2007
	1190 AD	AC: ALTAÏR'S CHRONICLES	2008
	1191 AD	ASSASSIN'S CREED: BLOODLINES	
Italian Renaissance	1476-1499 AD	**ASSASSIN'S CREED II**	2009
	1491 AD	ASSASSIN'S CREED II: DISCOVERY	
	1499-1507 AD	**ASSASSIN'S CREED: BROTHERHOOD**	2010
	1511-1512 AD	**ASSASSIN'S CREED: REVELATIONS**	2011

Colonial era	1754-1783 AD	ASSASSIN'S CREED III	
	1765-1777 AD	ASSASSIN'S CREED III: LIBERATION	2012
	1715-1722 AD	AC IV: BLACK FLAG	
	1716-1718 AD	ASSASSIN'S CREED: PIRATES	2013
	1735-1737 AD	ASSASSIN'S CREED: FREEDOM CRY	
	1752-1776 AD	ASSASSIN'S CREED ROGUE	
Italian Renaissance	1501-1506 AD	ASSASSIN'S CREED IDENTITY	
French Revolution	1776-1800 AD	ASSASSIN'S CREED UNITY	2014
Ming Dynasty	1526-1532 AD	AC CHRONICLES: CHINA	
Victorian era	1868 AD	ASSASSIN'S CREED SYNDICATE	2015
Sikh Empire	1841 AD	AC CHRONICLES: INDIA	
October Revolution	1918 AD	ASSASSIN'S CREED CHRONICLES: RUSSIA	2016
Ptolemaic Egypt	49-43 BC	ASSASSIN'S CREED ORIGINS	2017
Peloponnesian War	431-404 BC	ASSASSIN'S CREED ODYSSEY	2018

The following analysis will use a variety of material to, whenever possible, stress the argument is as much rooted in the games' diegesis through formal analysis—primarily through gameplay setting and citations of dialogue—as well as extradiegetically through studying the game's reception: i.e., how game culture (reviewers, players on forums) and game studies (academics) support the ideas discussed. Throughout, I will focus primarily on the main games, and their switch over time from an aesthetics of a modernist-conspiratorial secular Utopia versus religious Dystopia, to those of a postmodernist conspiracy of decentralized utopian visions. Additionally, I base myself broadly (when theoretically or empirically necessary) on material from across and around the ASSASSIN'S CREED universe: supplementary games, books, surrounding lore, journalistic commentaries, and of course academic work.

CENTRALIZED UTOPIA

The central struggle of the ASSASSIN'S CREED series described above, is initially presented as that of a dystopian force entering from the outside. Through giving privileged access to Assassin ideology, the series' initial focalization monopolizes the utopian project of the Assassins, thereby casting the Templars as dystopian, Catholic conspirators.

Assassin Utopia

A utopian narrative is always a "concrete fictional portrayal" of Utopia in action,[36] or in the case of ASSASSIN'S CREED, a fictional portrayal overlaying human history in a speculative fiction. Scholar of videogames and cultural memory Emil Hammar insists, for instance, that ASSASSIN'S CREED FREEDOM CRY is a "potentially cathartic power fantasy within a historical struggle," in this case against transatlantic chattel slavery.[37] In such readings, it is clear that the Assassins are on the 'good side' of history. They resist the Templar crusaders in the first game, they unravel a plot by corrupt Templar pope Rodrigo Borgia in the second game (but nobly spare his life), they fight the Templar colonial powers as a half-Mohawk Assassin in ASSASSIN'S CREED III, they fight for the French Revolution in UNITY, and so on.

By contrast, the Templar project opposes that of the Assassins'. Or rather, as the Assassin project is framed as a reaction to the Templars' injustice, the Assassin utopian project is always in response to a dystopian project by the Templars. As one reviewer describes them:

"the Templar order [is] an ancient and secretive sect of wealthy and powerful individuals whose goal is literally world domination. They remind me of the Mayflowers in the criminally underrated Bruce Willis movie Hudson Hawk. They don't believe in individual freedom, [Templars] believe people are too stupid and dangerous to have

---

36 C. Ferns: *Narrating Utopia*, p. 34
37 Hammar, Emil Lundedal: "Counter-Hegemonic Commemorative Play: Marginalized Pasts and the Politics of Memory in the Digital Game Assassin's Creed: Freedom Cry," *Rethinking History* 21, no. 3 (2017), pp. 372-395, here p. 389.

freedom. This is the complete opposite of the Assassin Order which believes in liberty and collaboration for building a better world."[38]

The words of the first game's protagonist Altaïr, stress the Assassin perspective on this opposition of Assassin Utopia against Templars' dystopia:

"I have realized, that so long as The Templars exist, they will attempt to bend reality to their will. They recognize there is no such thing as an absolute truth—or if there is—we are hopelessly under-equipped to recognize it. And so in its place, they seek to create their own explanation. It is the guiding principle of their so-named "New World Order;" to reshape existence in their own image. It is not about artifacts. Not about men. These are merely tools. It's about concepts. Clever of them. For how does one wage war against a concept? It is the perfect weapon. It lacks a physical form yet can alter the world around us in numerous, often violent ways. You cannot kill a creed. Even if you kill all of its adherents, destroy all of its writings—these are a reprieve at best. Some one, some day, will rediscover it. Reinvent it. I believe that even we, the Assassins, have simply re-discovered an Order that predates the Old Man himself..."[39]

There are three things to note about this. First, Altaïr has a certain authority within the universe, receiving, throughout most of the games, a special status as the first and in many ways 'original' Assassin for players to embody. Altaïr was the introduction for all players to the universe, being their first "avatar," i.e., "the primary interface between the user and the world, in the sense that the player of the game acts on the world of the game through the avatar."[40] His formulation of the Assassin project, in other words, is semi-

---

38 Quake, John: "Assassin's Creed 2 Review," *Rebel Gaming Canada*, 2017; https://www.rebelgamingcanada.com/assassins-creed-2-review/
39 Altaïr Ibn-La'Ahad in the ASSASSIN'S CREED II Codex, an in-game encyclopedia.
40 Apperley, Thomas/Justin, Clemens: "The Biopolitics of Gaming: Avatar-Player Self-Reflexivity in Assassin's Creed II," in: Kapell, Matthew (ed.), *The Play Versus Story Divide in Game Studies Critical Essays*, Jefferson: McFarland 2015, pp. 110-124, here p. 113. Additionally, those and other authors have noted that care must be taken to acknowledge the sensitive genealogy of the concept 'avatar' with both its roots in sacred Hindu tradition and its entanglement to contemporary videogame culture, industry and theory since at least the 1960s, for which see: de

nal—underlined by the fact that this citation appears in the "codex" of ASSASSIN'S CREED II, the fourth game—making it into something of a founding document for the Assassins. Secondly, the ideological position of Altaïr himself is formulated in opposition to the Templars' dystopian ambitions to "reshape existence" into a "New World Order."

Thirdly, Altaïr stresses the abstract ideal of both the Templar and Assassin project: it is "about concepts," and "lacks a physical form:" the Assassins' (reactive) project is of an ideal world to be imagined and realized, not a political interest or a material, contained struggled but a concept, a Utopia.

Secular Creeds

The Utopian project of the Assassins has its roots in both a religious conflict (the Crusades), and a religious organization (the Ismāʿīlī hashashin), yet it is subsequently presented in the game as a secularizing project. The religious roots of the game are clear: the invading crusaders of the first game are a quintessentially religious force. The Templar Order was historically a Catholic Military order, recognized by the Pope from 1139 until 1312. The games unambiguously present the Templars in this historical light: they invade the Holy Land. (The sequel would figure a Templar as the aforementioned pope, Rodrigo Borgia). The speculative fiction adds only more religiosity to the theme of the game: the Templar Order conspires to create a society in which they control and manipulate the totality of its subjects through the Apple of Eden.

This promise of Eden and the ability to reconstitute it in different historical ages run through the series. For the Assassins, too, historically and in the game, Eden is an important figure. Consider that historically, assassins were offered a specific hallucinogen-induced vision of Utopia to motivate them, in the shape of a garden of Eden. As one common folk etymology explains pertaining to the *hash* in the original *Hashashin* from which Assassin was derived, young assassins were made to become high on hashish and shown a vision of Eden. As El-Nasr, et al., explain:

Wildt, Lars et al.: "(Re-)Orienting the Video Game Avatar," *Games and Culture* (OnlineFirst).

"According to the tale, Al-Sabbah constructed a heaven, often referred to as the 'garden of paradise' furnished with their interpretation of heavenly delights and women. The followers were drugged, taken to the garden, and later awakened to be told that they were in paradise. After they were able to fathom the luxury of such paradise, they were drugged again and taken away from the garden to a cave-like dwelling. They were then told that God had given them a preview of paradise, but in order to return to it, they needed to carry out some important tasks, including assassination, justifying such action by saying that their targets are evil men. The assassins that went on these missions were very dedicated, believing that they were Martyrs killing for God."[41]

In the game, however, despite their Ismāʿīlī background, the Assassins take a turn with Altaïr's story to present a secularizing vision of Utopia. Many of the themes of Utopia in the game are about liberating the world from the dogma and control of organized religion. The titular 'creed' of the Assassin's, *'Nothing is True, Everything is Permitted'* is explained by Arno, the protagonist of UNITY as a creed that "teaches us that nothing is forbidden to us" while also stating that:

"The Creed is a warning. Ideals too easily give way to dogma. Dogma becomes fanaticism. No higher power sits in judgement of us. No supreme being watches us to punish us for our sins. [...] All that we do, all that we are, begins and ends with ourselves."

The rhetoric of the Assassins is one of personal responsibility for actions and ideas, without a divine appeal to a super-human truth. Or, as Nick Dinicola summarizes his reading of the game: "The Assassins represent rationalism, humanism, and logic; the Templars represent leadership based on blind faith."[42] Again, in the words of Altaïr himself:

"I have studied the ancient pagan faiths that came before this more recent obsession with a single, divine creator. They seem to have focused more on the fundamental forces at play in the world around us and less on arbitrary moral rules... [...] But no

---

41 El-Nasr, Magy Seif et al.: "Assassin's Creed: A Multi-Cultural Read," *Loading...* 3/2 (2008), pp. 1-32.

42 Dinicola, Nick: "The 'Assassins' Religion," *Pop Matters*, 2010; https://www.popmatters.com/118104-rationalizing-faith-in-assassins-creed-2496143914.html.

more. Now we are asked to succumb to a far more simplified explanation. How naive to believe there might be a single answer to every question. Every mystery. That there exists a lone divine light which rules over all. They say it is a light that brings truth and love. I say it is a light that blinds us—and forces us to stumble about in ignorance. I long for the day when men turn away from invisible monsters and once more embrace a more rational view of the world. But these new religions are so convenient—and promise such terrible punishment should one reject them—I worry that fear shall keep us stuck to what is surely the greatest lie ever told."

The Greatest Conspiracy

"[T]he greatest lie ever told" is presented by Altaïr as religion. It is this mystery of religion—is it man-made? Whose interests does it serve?—that is leveraged by the developers as a drawing point to the game's setting. As Jade Raymond (who led the creation of the first ASSASSIN'S CREED as a producer) explains in an interview with Magy Seif El-Nasr:

"People are also fascinated by 'History's Mysteries,' and the Templar Treasure was ripe for exploring. What did the Templars find beneath Solomon's Temple? Why did they want it? Where is it today? The same can be said for the Assassins themselves. We know a little bit about them, but their very nature made them a secretive bunch. Most of what's known comes from third hand accounts. These were very likely orchestrated events, carefully planned by the Assassins to ensure a specific, controlled image was portrayed. Who were they really? What motivated them? What secrets were members given accesses to as they rose through the ranks? These were all questions we get to play within the story. And the answers are pretty interesting."[43]

Coming out at the top of Dan Brown's rising popularity, the game seemed to game culture what the *Da Vinci Code* was to over 80 million readers (in 44 languages) and $758 million worth of cinema-goers in the film adaptation's opening weekend in 2006. Both engage in speculative fictions that suggest more is going on beneath the surface of our own societies' history, by suggesting to unearth all types of plots and conspiracies around the mystery of the Catholic church. It was indeed picked up as such by popular commentators, one of whom wrote about ASSASSIN'S CREED III that "the game indulges

---

43 M. El-Nasr, et al.: "Assassin's Creed: A Multi-Cultural Read," pp. 6-7.

a cartoonishly oversimplified revisionist conspiracy history, and frequently sidelines some inconvenient truths."[44]

These 'fast' and loose aesthetics of conspiracy centres purely around the draw of finding mystery in an outside 'other.' Whether it fetishes Europe from a North-American perspective—as Dan Brown's Robert Langdon or Tom Hanks visits the old churches of France to unearth the secrets of Opus Dei—or whether, instead, it focuses on the outside crusader from a Middle-Eastern perspective—as the Assassin's Altaïr unearths the secrets of the Templars.

These aesthetics of pervasive conspiracy are drawn out throughout the series so that the Templar other is at the helm of every major plot and turning point throughout history. The 'Order' had its hand in every power grab in every time. Alternatively: the Templars are associated with the Vatican, Abstergo, the Children of Cain, Cult of Kosmos, Order of the Ancients, the Roman Senate, the Crusaders, the House of Borgia, the Byzantine, Spanish, and British Empires, and so on. ASSASSIN'S CREED greedily relates them all and projects it on top of factual religion. You can't know what is true. But once you 'go down the rabbit hole,' or 'take the red pill'—or whichever pop reference the discourse of conspiracy bases itself on, 'the truth is out there,' and everything is shown to be significantly related.[45]

In short, the surface premise of ASSASSIN'S CREED sets out, at first, to show us that the Assassins have a utopian project, set in defiance of the Templars' opposite, dystopian project. The Assassins set themselves up as a secular alternative to the Templars' religious, conspiratorial 'New World Order.'

---

44 Dray, Colin: "Look at You, You Big Silly, Says Assassin's Creed 3," *Pop Matters*, 2015; https://www.popmatters.com/194103-assassins-creed-man-against-the-machine-2495523043.html

45 The three references are, in order, to ALICE IN WONDERLAND, THE MATRIX, and THE X-FILES, all of which are in frequent use in conspiracy milieus, cf. J. Harambam: *The Truth is Out There*.

DECENTRALIZED UTOPIA

However, once the series includes Templar perspectives, the binary of Templar dystopia—Assassin Utopia is broken, and their projects are increasingly decentralized.

Breaking the Binary

While it is easy to dismiss the utopian-dystopian binary in ASSASSIN'S CREED as a Manichaean distinction between Assassins and Templars, the assassins are originally already a third actor. As Jade Raymond in the same interview by Magy Seif El-Nasr reminds us:

"As the Saracens and Crusaders battle one another for control, the Assassins are working to find a way to end the hostilities. They see the war as pointless. There is no reason Crusaders and Saracens should not co-exist in peace. The Assassins are not allied with either side of the conflict, nor are they driven by a desire for profit or power. In ASSASSINS' CREED, Crusaders (and the Saracens) are not the Assassins' true enemy. War is—as are those who exploit it."[46]

While this caveat keeps intact the idea that Assassins are unambiguously on the side of historic 'good,' (they are, after all, against war and exploitation), Adrienne Shaw is quick to dispel this claim. Shaw critiques the way in which the series presents itself as a "historically and visually realistic game, yet realism is more often used to pre-empt criticism than it is to reconsider the telos of history."[47] Using ASSASSIN'S CREED III and its American Revolution-setting as an example, she notes that despite its emancipatory framing, it always conforms to the established hegemonic perspective of history, offering no "critique [on] the inevitableness of those historical events,"[48] beyond "the extent of the British and Patriot atrocities against [the various

---

46 M. El-Nasr et al.: "Assassin's Creed: A Multi-Cultural Read," p. 13.
47 Shaw, Adrienne: "The Tyranny of Realism: Historical Accuracy and Politics of Representation in Assassin's Creed III," *Loading...* 9/14 (2015), pp. 4-24, here p. 5.
48 Ibid., p. 19.

indigenous peoples of North-America]."⁴⁹ Just as with the Saracens and Crusaders, then, the Assassins (and their players) are thus positioned outside of history's main actors. In ASSASSIN'S CREED III's case, the half-Mohawk main player-character, "Ratohnhaké:ton/Connor's position in the colonial world is made unexceptional despite the fact that the game uses his "outsider" perspective to tell the story."⁵⁰ In so doing, Assassins are positioned as outsiders to allow the player a spectatorial and uncritical role in the predetermined fate of history.

Furthermore, when we look more closely at the Templar project, we see a similar hopeful rhetoric as with their Assassin equivalent, *when* they are given a voice. The first time these Templars are given a voice they are also already (subversively) shown to believe in their own utopian project. The nine Templars to be assassinated as the main structure of the first game do, as a reviewer noted already in 2007, "defend their seemingly despicable work as good and just, leaving you to wonder just what the hell is going on."⁵¹ Tamir, the weapons dealer and Altaïr's first target, states in a conversation preceding his assassination:

Altaïr: "You believe yourself different then?"
Tamir: "Oh but I am, for I serve a far nobler cause than mere profit. Just like my brothers."

And Abu'l Nuqoud, a Damascan merchant and the fourth target declares:

"I've pledged myself to another cause. One that will bring about a new world in which all people might live, side by side, in peace. A pity none of you will live to see it."

For Abu'l Nuqoud, most poignantly, his subversion of Altaïr's mission offers a sub-narrative to humanize them, which some players take up. Nuqoud is often read as queer, stating diegetically: "How could I finance a war in service to the same god that calls me an abomination?" and declaring: "Look at me! My very nature is an affront to the people I ruled, and these noble robes did little more than to muffle their shouts of hate." Based on such cues, at least one fan source (the Fandom.com wiki) offers the reading that:

---

49 Ibid., p. 18.
50 Ibid., p. 16.
51 M. Reparaz: "Assassin's Creed Review."

"Because of some of his mannerisms, such as his style of dress, his speech about people of all kinds living together, his words about not serving the 'same god that calls me an abomination,' the way he caresses one of his guards, and the fact that many characters refers to him as 'different,' it can be inferred that Abu'l was homosexual."[52]

As much as there is to say about fans' readings (especially on an open platform such as a wiki), the series' original creative director, Patrice Désilets, echoes such an analysis. In a commentary containing production notes on the first game, Désilets adds that the production team called Abu'l—in their words—their "she-male."[53]

Yet none of these Templars are initially given any agency or place in history, despite such subtextual humanizations, or their subversive voice set against the Assassin project. This has been changing in several ways. In recent games, organizations such as the Cult of Kosmos, a proto-Templar organization, presents the main force of opposition to its proto-Assassin adversary—a loose collection of mercenaries referring to themselves individually as "misthios," including the main protagonist. The Cult would later canonically merge together with the Order of the Ancients (a similar organization in 2017's ASSASSIN'S CREED: ORIGINS) into the Templars. This is relevant only because the plot of the game presents the choice between the two organisations (Assassins and Templars) as an almost arbitrary twist of fate. When the player chooses their protagonist (Kassandra, or her brother Alexios), they follow the plot to find out that their sibling has ended up in the other organisation: Alexios (or Kassandra) is the main muscle of the Cult of Kosmos.

That is: whomever the player chooses, their near-identical sibling will end up serving a pivotal role for the Templars. This interchangeability we see increasingly throughout the series. Before introducing a choice of characters, the main games had already offered three Templar focalizers for the

---

52 Abu'l Nuqoud, Assassin's Creed fandom wiki; https://assassinscreed.fandom.com/wiki/Abu%27l_Nuqoud.

53 "Patrice Desilets (Creative Director): My favorite character is the merchant king, Abu'l Nuqoud. We call him, affectionately, our 'she-male.' You know it's fun to put a target like that in the game. I like him. […] You've got to go and reach him and kill him from behind." In: Hodgson, David/Knight, David: *Assassin's Creed Limited Edition Art Book*, Roseville: Prima Games 2007.

player to become. In UNITY, players enter a genetic memory of the advisor to Jacques de Molay, a Templar Grand Master—diegetically in ASSASSIN'S CREED as well as in extradiegetic history.[54] The memory is introduced within the game as "the final tragic hours of Jacques de Molay, through the eyes of his closest friend," upon which the player defends de Molay against a group of assassins' whose Utopia is described as "their anarchic delusions [which] are virulent as the plague, and less easily eradicated.

In the ROGUE (2014) game, players take control of Shay Cormac, who starts out as an Assassin in the Colonial Brotherhood of New York city. As the game progresses, he is betrayed, and declares his allegiance to the Templar Order instead, stating

"Uphold the principles of our Order, and all for that for which we stand. Never share our secrets nor divulge the true nature of our work. Do so until death—whatever the cost. This is my new creed. I am Shay Patrick Cormac. Templar of the Colonial of the American Rite. I am an older man now, and perhaps wiser. A war and a revolution have ended, and another is about to begin. May the Father of Understanding guide us all."

It should be noted for the current argument, that Shay continues life as a Templar, including by killing Assassin Charles Dorian—in turn the father of Arno Dorian, Assassin protagonist of ASSASSIN'S CREED UNITY—and by inducting both his son and grandson into the Templar Order after him. Arno, to make matters more confusing, was adopted by François de la Serre: a Templar Grand Master. All of this genealogical detail serves to show how entangled the two Orders become as the series' speculative fiction.

The consequence of this entanglement is that while the Templar and Assassin orders are originally presented as binary opposite lineages, the games' universe offers many counter-examples to destabilize this indisputably and exclusively in binary opposition. One more example: the aforementioned Shay works with Templar Grand Master Haytham Kenway, the protagonist

---

54 Demurger, Alain: *Jacques de molay: le crépuscule des templiers*, Payot 2002; in English: Demurger, Alain. *The Last Templar: The Tragedy of Jacques de Molay, Last Grand Master of the Temple*, Profile 2004; Barber, Malcolm: *The New Knighthood: A History of the Order of the Temple*, Cambridge: Cambridge University Press 2012.

of ASSASSIN'S CREED III. That is: he is the first introduced character (*protos + agonistes*, the first actor), traditionally the main or 'good' character—as opposed to the antagonist (*anti*, against) who fights against the protagonist. In other words, the third trilogy of the game (set in the colonial era) effectively opens with a Templar 'good guy.' From the genealogical perspective of lineages: Kenway's son Connor becomes an Assassin, while Kenway's father Edward (the protagonist of BLACK FLAG (2013), the next main game) was also an Assassin.

What we need to take away from this is that Templar and Assassin lineages are increasingly presented as actually interchangeable throughout history, and within the same families. Rather than two opposing sides, they are two sides of the same coin: two warring secret societies trying to control the world to enact their own Utopia—almost interchangeable in which to pursue, and more importantly: always opposed to the other as dystopian. Thus, not only is the Templar vision dystopian to Assassins, the Assassin's vision is dystopian to Templars. At the same time, players are called to follow and enact their lives, invited to regard the Templar project as their own.

As a consequence, the utopia/dystopia distinction is dissolved as a matter of position. A position, furthermore, that is easily interchanged over the course of a game; and within lineages and between games throughout the fictional universe.

Post-secular Order

Three things happen that further mess up the distinction between the secular Assassins and the Catholic Templars. First, the Assassin Order develops a distinctly religious aesthetic, including temples, rituals and elaborate hierarchies. Second, the game introduces its own 'true' religion, revealed to the Assassin player-characters, usually at the end of the game. Third, depending on the historical period and place (most pointedly SYNDICATE's Victorian England), religion as an institution is supplanted by other systems, such as capitalism.

Figure 2: Assassin Arno Dorian, facing his initiation ceremony in the 'Sanctuary' in ASSASSIN'S CREED UNITY

Source: Screenshot from ASSASSIN'S CREED UNITY

To take a scene from ASSASSIN'S CREED UNITY as an example, the series saw an increased codification of Assassin rituals, with a catholic-like aesthetic, as the series progressed (both in terms of year of release, as well as the time period within the universe). Arno Dorian, adopted son of a Templar and born of an Assassin father, enters into the 'Sanctuary' to undergo an initiation ritual (Figure 2). Dorian is led into the basement of a church. Arriving in the hidden sanctuary, we see a high semi-circle: its walls (about 2.5 times the height of Dorian), adorned with a large marble fountain bearing, in its centre, the Assassin crest in marble and gold; at the sides of the fountain are two griffons looking outward; above the fountain, at the middle of the wall, stand marble, saint-like figures. Large, orange, open fires of various heights light the room. On top of the semi-circle, ornamental bordeaux-coloured drapes are displayed, hung over a balcony. On the platform behind it, four white hooded figures emerge: Master Assassins, their faces mostly hidden, wearing their cloaks and entering the scene toward four tall, thin thrones; behind them a backdrop of ornate stained glass and long bordeaux-coloured curtains hanging from the ceiling to cover parts of the dark stone walls.

The aesthetic is arguably church-like. The Masters speak Arabic to each other, and eventually ask Dorian: "From the light you will return to the darkness; are you prepared to travel the eagle's path?" Upon his affirmation, he drinks a potion from the gold-inlaid crest-shaped marble fountain, and starts to hallucinate—much like the folk histories of the historical hashashin portray their initiation rites. Throughout various time periods in the series, there are some variations—notably whether a finger is amputated or not. Each ends with a back and forth formula, rehearsing the creed:

Assassin: "Where other men blindly follow the truth, remember..."
Initiate: "Nothing is true."
Assassin: "Where other men are limited by morality or law, remember..."
Initiate: "Everything is permitted."
Assassin: "We work in the dark to serve the light. We are Assassins."

Again, words delivered by Altaïr to the Codex ring true:

"What follows are the three great ironies of the Assassin Order: (1) Here we seek to promote peace, but murder is our means. (2) Here we seek to open the minds of men, but require obedience to a master and set of rules. (3) *Here we seek to reveal the danger of blind faith, yet we are practitioners ourselves.*" [emphasis added]

Not only do the Assassins structure their own paradoxically secular Order along religious aesthetics, hierarchies and rituals; but another pantheon is additionally revealed to them, that undermines both Templar and Assassins' religious positions. Without a need for much elaboration here, suffice to be said that the 'Isu,' or 'ones that came before' are an advanced species that created the pieces of Eden, as well as the human race. The main three are Minerva, Juno, and Jupiter, who together created Adam and Eve, and were revered by earlier human societies as gods (hence the names). As early as ASSASSIN'S CREED II, much of the secular nature of the Order crumbles, with the protagonist stating "You are... gods." As is the nature of videogame gods, it is indeed difficult to deny them once they appear unmistakably before you to hand over items, or quests.[55]

---

55 For which, see: Schaap, Julian/Aupers, Stef: "'Gods in World of Warcraft Exist:' Religious Reflexivity and the Quest for Meaning in Online Computer Games," *New Media & Society* 19, no. 11 (2017), pp. 1744-1760.

Thirdly, finally, the religious-secular distinction is occasionally replaced entirely. Although ASSASSIN'S CREED (initially) places the onus of dystopia on religion, and that of Utopia on the secular; we find these patterns reflected elsewhere in different systems within the series. ASSASSIN'S CREED SYNDICATE, for instance, briefly shifted the series' focus from feudal-religious hierarchies to capitalist class struggle. As Montréal-based advertisement agency Bleublancrouge explains, when describing their ad campaign for SYNDICATE:

"Created as part of the campaign for the ASSASSIN'S CREED SYNDICATE video game, which is set in Victorian England, this poster illustrates that society at the time was no longer controlled by kings, emperors, politicians or religious figures, but rather by money. Capitalism was perceived as the economic model that would improve everyone's lives, when in fact it primarily served rich financiers who took advantage of it to rule over the lower classes. We featured a banker dressed as a king to show this shift in power."[56]

Similarly, other, later, iterations of the game have de-emphasized the presence on religion to more period-suitable systems of hegemony.

Postmodern Conspiracy

Finally, the nature of ASSASSIN'S CREED's aesthetics of conspiracy changes, too. So far, this paper has shown that there are possible readings of the series—formally; by academics; and by game culture—in which the binary Utopia-dystopia distinction and its concurrent secularism-religion distinction are increasingly destabilized.

As a consequence, distrust is scattered. What was once a clear inside-outside distinction (i.e., the Holy Land being invaded by European-Christian Templars) has been increasingly muddied. The dissolution of these distinctions enact a postmodern development, in which binaries dissolve and things like truth and power are displaced. Again, however, the seeds of such postmodern doubt had been marginally apparent in the games' earliest utterances. Again from Altaïr:

---

56 Print advertisement created by Bleublancrouge, Canada for Ubisoft; https://www.adsoftheworld.com/media/print/ubisoft_assassins_creed_finance.

"Over time, any sentence uttered long and loud enough becomes fixed. Becomes a truth. Provided, of course, you can outlast the dissent and silence your opponents. But should you succeed—and remove all challengers—then what remains is, by default, now true. Is it truth in some objective sense? No. But how does one ever achieve an objective point of view? The answer is you don't. It is literally, physically impossible."

As the above readings have shown, the certainty of truth, the centralization of power, the clear threat of the outsider, and their clear distinction to the (powerless) insider have dissolved since. Templars and Assassins become increasingly intermingled, and both appear to have Utopian projects with good intentions, that present itself to the other side as a dystopia, and vice versa.

By thus placing the manipulator—regardless of which side of the coin—inside our own history, Assassin's Creed enacts an increasingly postmodern aesthetics of paranoia and conspiracy as the series develops. To remind us of Peter Knight's words:

"Where conspiracy-minded narratives of the individual and national immune system under threat might once have served to bolster a sense of (albeit restricted) communal identity, they now regularly register the far more scary anxiety that we can no longer tell the difference between Them and Us."[57]

The title of this chapter, of course, is an inversion of the Assassins' creed: "Nothing is true, Everything is permitted." The series, other than its titular Assassins, do not follow this credo. Indeed, increasingly, 'Everything is true,' depending on whom you listen to—whether it is the subversive words of the Templars in the first game; or the full identification allowed to players when they are cast in the role of the incidental Templar protagonists of later games. As if to follow this call for doubt, player communities take note: data gathered on forums show that players for various reasons and from various positions choose to question who is right.[58] Increasingly, modern discussion topics are titled: "Some thoughts on the assassins vs templars conflict,"

---

57 P. Knight: *Conspiracy Nation*, p. 5.
58 de Wildt, Lars/Aupers, Stef: "Pop Theology: Forum Discussions on Religion in Videogames," *Information, Communication & Society* (2019), pp. 1-19.

"Templar or Assassin (choose your side and give a reason)," "Who are right The Templar Order or the Assassin Brotherhood?" All of those were made in August 2018, approaching the release of the latest game, ODYSSEY (2018). They show an increasing willingness among players to identify with the Templar side, seen less as the 'bad' 'Other' and more as an equally interesting secret order. Rather than a full empirical analysis, here is one indicative example:

"I'm about halfway through my first play through of ROGUE, and I ask myself this question, who is right? The Templars or the Assassins? I mean, The Templars seek order and control through the Pieces of Eden. Why do they want control? To basically have peace right? Now that to me seems like a noble cause. While playing AC3 I seriously began to think why are the Templars so bad? I dunno if that was down to Haytham's silver tongue or Connor's naivety tbh."[59]

CONCLUSION

Religion, Utopia and the aesthetics of conspiracy run throughout the ASSASSIN'S CREED series. Through it runs a fundamental development from a unidirectional conflict between the secular utopian project of the Assassins against the religious dystopian Templars; to a decentralized conflict between two parties whose own Utopia constitutes the other's dystopia. In so doing, ASSASSIN'S CREED enacts two aesthetics of conspiracy: a modernist and a post-modernist one. First, its premise and early iterations present a modernist conspiracy: one that fears an enemy from 'without,' against which a utopian project must be leveraged to protect ourselves against it—such as a foreign invasion of Templar Crusaders. Secondly, it moves toward a postmodern aesthetics of conspiracy, which places the enemy 'within' our own society and history, whose 'topos' of Utopia overlaps with our dystopia, and vice versa. In other words, the 'not-place' of Utopia is increasingly mapped over every-place, to be found all around us, if only we learn to unveil its conspiratorial hiddenness.

---

59 Joshbear_1: "Who are right The Templar Order or the Assassin Brotherhood?" *Reddit r/Assassinscreed*; https://www.reddit.com/r/assassinscreed/comments/96y gdk/who_are_right_the_templar_order_or_the_assassin/

In this light, I must do some concessions after having presented such a grand, all-too-clean evolution of three central concepts (Utopia, religion and conspiracy) over the course of over 10 years of ASSASSIN'S CREED. Due to its scope, the series is bound to invite various readings, as it spans about 2450 years of speculative history throughout eleven main games (within a total of 21), and much more paraludic material—as described in the Case/Material section. While this reading is consistent with both the series' premise, its recent iterations and the paraludic material throughout, it is nonetheless inevitable (and important) that these texts themselves offer diegetic resistance and contradictions to these readings. In fact, I argue that both readings will hold, next to each other—as postmodernist thought and aesthetics do inevitably include modernist thought and aesthetics.[60] To bring more concrete nuance to the claims made above: first, research on online discussions has shown that groups of players can perform completely different, mutually exclusive readings of games such as ASSASSIN'S CREED, specifically in the case of religion as this author's previous work has elaborately shown.[61] Second, while there is notable ambivalence both in the content and reception of the series; the majority of the games, books and other materials still take the Assassin perspective as their primary, if not their sole focalizer. There are only three notable exceptions, as stated: Haytham Kenway in ASSASSIN'S CREED III, Shay Cormac in ROGUE and an unnamed Templar advisor in *The Tragedy of Jacques de Molay*.

---

60 See for instance: Haber, John: "The Postmodern Paradox," *Haber Arts: Art Reviews from Around New York*; https://www.haberarts.com/postdox.htm; Berg, Lawrence D.: "Between Modernism and Postmodernism," *Progress in Human Geography* 17.4 (1993), pp. 490-507; Clegg, Stewart R./Kornberger, Martin: "Modernism, Postmodernism, Management and Organization Theory," *Post Modernism and Management* 21 (2003), pp. 57-88; Curry, Michael R.: "Postmodernism, Language, and the Strains of Modernism," Annals of the Association of American Geographers 81, no. 2 (1991), pp. 210-228; Harvey, David: "Postmodern Morality Plays," *Antipode* 24, no. 4 (1992), pp. 300-326.

61 See on this consequently: de Wildt, Lars/Aupers, Stef: "Bibles and BioShock: Affording Religious Discussion on Video Game Forums," *Proceedings of the Annual Symposium on Computer-Human Interaction in Play* (2017), pp. 463-475; de Wildt, Lars/Aupers, Stef: "Playing the Other: Role-Playing Religion in Videogames," *European Journal of Cultural Studies* (2018).

However, I argue that a clear thread can nonetheless be found, that reveals much of how aesthetics of Utopia, religion and conspiracy are presented to modern audiences. Indeed, the topoi of dystopian forces and the suspicion of conspiracy in our own historical world has until recently been classically placed outside of our society, as much as that of the modernist Utopian reading of ASSASSIN'S CREED at the start of the paper—the Communists of the red scare, the fascists, the Jew, the Church. And just so do we increasingly see paranoia about actors placed inside of our culture—a supposed migrant re-structuring of our society from within; lizard people controlling our institutions; the dangers of party-political entryism and cultural Marxism;[62] much like the two sides of the Assassin-Templar coin. Having said that, the conclusion should be exactly the place to expand beyond the reading of one text, and to theorize outward on the state of Utopia in 21st century popular culture beyond ASSASSIN'S CREED.

In its process of decentralizing religious Utopia and conspiracy, ASSASSIN'S CREED enacts the development of conspiracy theories in the West from a modernist binary to a postmodern paranoia within society. The resulting idea is to trust no-one: neither Assassin, Templar, whether they are secular or religious. We see this decentralization of conflict, I argue, in other postmodern cultural artefacts: the warring factions, and on-going interfactional conflict of HBO's GAME OF THRONES, for instance, have in most cases no clearly good or bad side to them—excluding the non-human white walkers, all other factions are humanized to trivialize such binary distinctions: the Lannisters, the Targaryens, and even the Wildlings.

It is in examples such as these that we see the postmodern development from binary oppositions in fictional conflicts to 'messier,' complex webs of contrasting interests. They should also quintessentially be read as aestheticizations of paranoia. On THE WIRE, an earlier example of decentralized drama that destabilizes binary distinctions of 'good and bad,' David Hodge and Hamed Yousefi note that it fits:

---

62 See on the perceived dangers of cultural Marxism within our societies: Webber, Esther/Wheeler, Brian: "What is a Trotskyist?" *BBC News*, 2016; https://www.bbc.com/news/uk-politics-37025649; Wilson, Jason: "'Cultural Marxism:' A Uniting Theory for Rightwingers Who Love to Play the Victim," *The Guardian*, 2015; https://www.theguardian.com/commentisfree/2015/jan/19/cultural-marxism-a-uniting-theo ry-for-rightwingers-who-love-to-play-the-victim

"in a long line of artistic and theoretical reflections on (and of) paranoid subjectivity since the 1960s [...] The popular television show THE WIRE is a key example, being centered on a dense web of connections which traverse the US city of Baltimore, uniting all of its diverse spheres into a violent and tragic situation that the character Omar simply calls 'the game.'"[63]

Whether in the case of GAME OF THRONES, THE WIRE, or ASSASSIN'S CREED, these aesthetics of (post-modern) conspiracy paranoia act to problematize the straightforwardness of utopian projects. That is, such aesthetics portray the (fictional) world as a complex web of contrasting utopian/dystopian interest. Rather than favouring one utopian project that is opposed to dystopian powers—the Assassin versus the Templar project—it shows the complexity of the counteracting utopian and dystopian projects—Templars see their Utopia undone by Assassins' Utopia, and so too for the mutually exclusive utopian projects of Starks, Lannisters, Targaryens, the Baltimore Police Department (think: Hamsterdam, or a safe, thriving Baltimore), Avon Barksdale, Stringer Bell, Marlo Stanfield or Omar Little. Post-modernist paranoid aesthetics enact just that: a never-ending list of actors working toward their own plural Utopoi; and nowhere does it work as well as in a complex, sprawling and ergodic game series spanning over ten years. Tellingly, it is not ASSASSIN'S CREED that is unique in its game-like structure: multiple actors followed from changing perspectives in a complex web of choices and interests. Rather, GAME OF THRONES and THE WIRE follow this game-like structure in what various others have called the "video game logic,"[64] or "ludic turn" of contemporary film and television.[65]

---

63 Hodge, David/Yousefi, Hamed: „Paranoid Subjectivity and the Challenges of Cognitive Mappig. How is Capitalism to be Represented?" *e-flux conversations*, 2015; https://conversations.e-flux.com/t/paranoid-subjectivity-and-the-challenges-of-cognitive-mapping-how-is-capitalism-to-be-represented/1080

64 Elsaesser, Thomas: "The Mind-Game Film," in: Buckland, Warren (ed.), *Puzzle Films: Complex Storytelling in Contemporary Cinema*, Oxford: Wiley-Blackwell 2009, pp. 13-41.

65 Raessens, Joost: *Homo Ludens 2.0: The Ludic Turn in Media Theory*, Utrecht: Faculteit Geesteswetenschappen 2012; see also: Simons, Jan: *Playing the Waves: Lars von Trier's Game Cinema*, Amsterdam: Amsterdam University Press 2007.

What ASSASSIN'S CREED increasingly draws, then, is a ludic postmodern picture of conspiracy that includes two interchangeable and veiled oppressors, that are equally ideological and battling each other's Utopia/dystopia on the edges of our own histories and societies. Both seek to control and to 'free' the people—whether from religion or otherwise—always in their own preferred way, and never with the people's consent. In the end, potentially 'Everything is true,' while nothing is permitted.

LITERATURE

Aarseth, Espen J.: *Cybertext: Perspectives on Ergodic Literature*, Baltimore: JHU Press 1997.

Apperley, Thomas/Justin, Clemens: "The Biopolitics of Gaming: Avatar-Player Self-Reflexivity in Assassin's Creed II," in: Kapell, Matthew (ed.), *The Play Versus Story Divide in Game Studies Critical Essays*, Jefferson: McFarland 2015, pp. 110-124.

Aupers, Stef: "'Better Than the Real World.' On the Reality and Meaning of Online Computer Games," *Fabula* 48, no. 3-4 (2007), pp. 250-269.

Barber, Malcolm: *The New Knighthood: A History of the Order of the Temple*, Cambridge: Cambridge University Press 2012.

Berg, Lawrence D.: "Between Modernism and Postmodernism," *Progress in Human Geography* 17.4 (1993), pp. 490-507.

Boletsi, Maria: *Barbarism and its Discontents*, Stanford: Stanford University Press 2013.

Bosman, Frank G.: "'The Lamb of Comstock.' Dystopia and Religion in Video Games," *Online. Heidelberg Journal of Religions on the Internet* 5 (2014), pp. 162-182.

Bruce, Steve: *God Is Dead: Secularization in the West*, Vol. 3, Oxford: Blackwell 2002.

Clegg, Stewart R./Kornberger, Martin: "Modernism, Postmodernism, Management and Organization Theory," *Post Modernism and Management* 21 (2003), pp. 57-88.

Curry, Michael R.: "Postmodernism, Language, and the Strains of Modernism," *Annals of the Association of American Geographers* 81, no. 2 (1991), pp. 210-228.

de Wildt, Lars/Aupers, Stef: "Bibles and BioShock: Affording Religious Discussion on Video Game Forums," *Proceedings of the Annual Symposium on Computer-Human Interaction in Play* (2017), pp. 463-475.

de Wildt, Lars/Aupers, Stef: "Playing the Other: Role-Playing Religion in Videogames," *European Journal of Cultural Studies* (2018).

de Wildt, Lars/Aupers, Stef: "Pop Theology: Forum Discussions on Religion in Videogames," *Information, Communication & Society* (2019), pp. 1-19.

de Wildt, Lars et al.: "(Re-)Orienting the Video Game Avatar," *Games and Culture* (OnlineFirst).

de Wildt, Lars: "Entwining the National and Personal: Art Spiegelman's Post-9/11 Shapeshifting," in: Folio, Jessica/Luhning, Holly (eds.), *Body Horror and Shapeshifting: A Multidisciplinary Exploration*, Leiden: Brill 2013, pp. 123-136.

de Wildt, Lars: "On the Subject of Play: Digital Game-Play as Models of Ideologies," 2014, Leiden University; https://openaccess.leidenuniv.nl/handle/1887/28571

Demurger, Alain: *Jacques de molay: le crépuscule des templiers*, Payot 2002.

Demurger, Alain. *The Last Templar: The Tragedy of Jacques de Molay, Last Grand Master of the Temple*, Profile 2004.

Dinicola, Nick: "The 'Assassins' Religion," *Pop Matters*, 2010; https://www.popmatters.com/118104-rationalizing-faith-in-assassins-creed-2496143914.html.

Dobbelaere, Karel/Voyé, Liliane: "Religie en kerkbetrokkenheid: ambivalentie en vervreemding, " *Verloren zekerheid De Belgen en hun waarden, overuigingen en houdingen*, Tielt: Lannoo 2001, pp. 117-152.

Dobbelaere, Karel: "Some Trends in European Sociology of Religion: The Secularization Debate," *Sociology of Religion* 48, no. 2 (1987), pp. 107-137.

Dobbelaere, Karel: "Towards an Integrated Perspective of the Processes Related to the Descriptive Concept of Secularization," *Sociology of Religion* 60, no. 3 (1999), pp. 229-247.

Dray, Colin: "Look at You, You Big Silly, Says Assassin's Creed 3," *Pop Matters*, 2015; https://www.popmatters.com/194103-assassins-creed-man-against-the-machine-2495523043.html

Durkheim, Emile: *De la division du travail social*, Quadrige: Presses Universitaires de France 1991.

Eagleton, Terry: *Reason, Faith, and Revolution: Reflections on the God Debate*, New Haven: Yale University Press 2009.

El-Nasr, Magy Seif et al.: "Assassin's Creed: A Multi-Cultural Read," *Loading...* 3/2 (2008), pp. 1-32.

Elsaesser, Thomas: "The Mind-Game Film," in: Buckland, Warren (ed.), *Puzzle Films: Complex Storytelling in Contemporary Cinema*, Oxford: Wiley-Blackwell 2009, pp. 13-41.

Farca, Gerald. *Playing Dystopia: Nightmarish Worlds in Video Games and the Player's Aesthetic Response*, Bielefeld: transcript 2018.

Ferns, Christopher S.: *Narrating Utopia: Ideology, Gender, Form in Utopian Literature*, Liverpool: Liverpool University Press 1999.

Fish, Stanley: "Don't Blame Relativism," *The Responsive Community* 12, no. 3 (2002), pp. 27-31.

Galloway, Alexander: "Warcraft and Utopia," *Ctheory* 2/16 (2006).

Haber, John: "The Postmodern Paradox," *Haber Arts: Art Reviews from Around New York*; https://www.haberarts.com/postdox.htm

Habermas, Jürgen: "Notes on Post-Secular Society," *New Perspectives Quarterly* 25, no. 4 (2008), pp. 17-29.

Habermas, Jürgen: „Die Dialektik der Säkularisierung," *Blätter für deutsche und internationale Politik*, 4 (2004), pp. 33-46.

Hammar, Emil Lundedal: "Counter-Hegemonic Commemorative Play: Marginalized Pasts and the Politics of Memory in the Digital Game Assassin's Creed: Freedom Cry," *Rethinking History* 21, no. 3 (2017), pp. 372-395.

Harambam, Jaron J.: *'The Truth Is Out There:' Conspiracy Culture in an Age of Epistemic Instability*, Rotterdam: Erasmus University Rotterdam 2017.

Harambam, Jaron/Aupers, Stef: "Contesting Epistemic Authority: Conspiracy Theories on the Boundaries of Science," *Public Understanding of Science* 24, no. 4 (2015), pp. 466-488.

Harvey, David: "Postmodern Morality Plays," *Antipode* 24, no. 4 (1992), pp. 300-326.

Hodge, David/Yousefi, Hamed: "Paranoid Subjectivity and the Challenges of Cognitive Mappig. How is Capitalism to be Represented?" *e-flux conversations*, 2015; https://conversations.e-flux.com/t/paranoid-subjectivity-and-the-challenges-of-cognitive-mapping-how-is-capitalism-to-be-represented/1080

Hodgson, David/Knight, David: *Assassin's Creed Limited Edition Art Book*, Roseville: Prima Games 2007.

Huntington, Samuel P.: *The Clash of Civilizations and the Remaking of World Order*, London: Simon & Schuster 1996.

Jameson, Fredric: *Postmodernism, or, the Cultural Logic of Late Capitalism*, Durham: Duke University Press 1991.

Kłosiński, Michał: "Games and Utopia," *Acta Ludologica* 1, no. 1 (2018), pp. 4-14.

Knight, Peter (ed.): *Conspiracy Nation: The Politics of Paranoia in Postwar America*, New York: NYU Press 2002.

Markocki, Miłosz: "Creating Utopian or Dystopian Worlds in Digital Games," *More After More* (2016), pp. 118-133.

Marx, Karl/Engels, Friedrich: "Manifest der Kommunistischen Partei," in: *Marx-Engels: Werke* 4, 1848, pp. 459-493.

Melley, Timothy. *Empire of Conspiracy: The Culture of Paranoia in Postwar America*, Ithaca: Cornell University Press 2000.

Milner, Jarred: "Review: Assassin's Creed Unity," *SA Gamer*, 2014; https://sagamer.co.za/review-assassins-creed-unity-xbox-one

Norris, Pippa/Inglehart, Ronald: *Sacred and Secular: Religion and Politics Worldwide*, Cambridge: Cambridge University Press 2011.

Parker, Martin: "Human Science as Conspiracy Theory," *The Sociological Review* 48.2 (2000), pp. 191-207.

Partridge, Christopher: *The Re-Enchantment of the West,* Vol. 2, London: A&C Black 2006.

Quake, John: "Assassin's Creed 2 Review," *Rebel Gaming Canada*, 2017; https://www.rebelgamingcanada.com/assassins-creed-2-review/

Raessens, Joost: *Homo Ludens 2.0: The Ludic Turn in Media Theory*, Utrecht: Faculteit Geesteswetenschappen 2012.

Reparaz, Mikel: "Assassin's Creed Review," *Gamesradar*, 2007; https://www.gamesradar.com/assassins-creed-review/

Rosenberg, Adam: "Assassin's Creed 3: Liberation Review: Flawed, But Realized Potential," *Digital Trends*, 2012; https://www.digitaltrends.com/gaming/assassins-creed-3-liberation-review-realized-potential/

Rothstein, Edward: "Moral Relativity is a Hot Topic? True. Absolutely," *New York Times* 7 (2002), p. 13.

Schaap, Julian/Aupers, Stef: "'Gods in World of Warcraft Exist:' Religious Reflexivity and the Quest for Meaning in Online Computer Games," *New Media & Society* 19, no. 11 (2017), pp. 1744-1760.

Shaw, Adrienne: "The Tyranny of Realism: Historical Accuracy and Politics of Representation in Assassin's Creed III," *Loading...* 9/14 (2015), pp. 4-24.

Simons, Jan: *Playing the Waves: Lars von Trier's Game Cinema*, Amsterdam: Amsterdam University Press 2007.

Stempel, Carl et al.: "Media Use, Social Structure, and Belief in 9/11 Conspiracy Theories," *Journalism & Mass Communication Quarterly* 84, no. 2 (2007), pp. 353-372.

Totilo, Stephen: "The Controversial Assassin's Creed III Is More Impressive in 2019," *Kotaku*, 2019; https://kotaku.com/the-controversial-assassin-s-creed-iii-is-more-impressi-1833676354

Tulloch, Rowan: "Ludic Dystopias: Power, Politics and Play," *Proceedings of the Sixth Australasian Conference on Interactive Entertainment* (2009), pp. 1-4.

Wallis, Roy/Bruce, Steve: "Secularization: The Orthodox Model," in: Bruce, Steve (ed.), *Religion and Modernization: Sociologists and Historians Debate the Secularization Thesis*, Oxford: Oxford University Press 1992.

Webber, Esther/Wheeler, Brian: "What is a Trotskyist?" *BBC News*, 2016; https://www.bbc.com/news/uk-politics-37025649

Weber, Max: *Wissenschaft als Beruf*, Vol. 1., Berlin: Duncker & Humblot 1919.

Wilson, Bryan R.: *Religion in Secular Society*, London: Penguin 1969.

Wilson, Jason: "'Cultural Marxism:' A Uniting Theory for Rightwingers Who Love to Play the Victim," *The Guardian*, 2015; https://www.theguardian.com/commentisfree/2015/jan/19/cultural-marxism-a-uniting-theory-for-rightwingers-who-love-to-play-the-victim

Wood, Michael James/Douglas, Karen M.: "'What About Building 7?' A Social Psychological Study of Online Discussion of 9/11 Conspiracy Theories," *Frontiers in Psychology* 4 (2013).

Gamography

Assassin's Creed (Ubisoft 2007, O: Ubisoft Montreal)
Assassin's Creed II (Ubisoft 2009, O: Ubisoft Montreal)
Assassin's Creed III (Ubisoft 2012, O: Ubisoft Montreal)
Assassin's Creed III: Liberation (Ubisoft 2012, O: Ubisoft Sofia)
Assassin's Creed IV: Black Flag (Ubisoft 2013, O: Ubisoft Montreal)
Assassin's Creed Odyssey (Ubisoft 2018, O: Ubisoft Quebec)
Assassin's Creed Origins (Ubisoft 2017, O: Ubisoft Montreal)
Assassin's Creed Rogue (Ubisoft 2014, O: Ubisoft Sofia)
Assassin's Creed Syndicate (Ubisoft 2015, O: Ubisoft Quebec)
Assassin's Creed: Unity (Ubisoft 2014, O: Ubisoft Montreal)
BioShock (2K Games 2007, O: 2K Boston)
BioShock: Infinite (2K Games 2013, O: Irrational Games)
Black & White (Electronic Arts 2001, O: Lionhead Studios)
Brink (Bethesda Softworks 2011, O: Splash Damage)
Cart Life (Richard Hofmeier 2010, O: Richard Hofmeier)
Dishonored (Bethesda Softworks 2012, O: Arkane Studios)
Fallout (Interplay Productions 1997, O: (Interplay Productions)
Half-Life (Sierra 1998, O: Valve)
SimCity (Maxis 1989, O: Maxis)
World of Warcraft (Blizzard Entertainment 2004, O: Blizzard Entertainment)

Beyond the Holonovel
The Holographic Interactive Digital Entertainment Utopia of STAR TREK

TONGUC IBRAHIM SEZEN

INTRODUCTION

The long running science fiction franchise STAR TREK, which spreads over multiple TV series, theatrical movies, countless games, comics, and novels has been called a classical utopian narrative and praised for its optimistic political and technological visions for humanity's future.[1] Despite been criticized for overstating the role of technological advancement in human development,[2] it has also been listed amongst major science fiction franchises presenting influential design fictions of speculative technologies.[3] STAR TREK's 'predictions' include now widely used electronic devices such as smart

---

1 Isaacs, Bruce: "A Vision of a Time and Place: Spiritual Humanism and the Utopian Impulse," in: Kapell, Matthew Wilhelm (ed.), *Star Trek as Myth: Essays on Symbol and Archetype at the Final Frontier*, Jefferson: McFarland 2010, pp. 182-196.
2 Kapell, Matthew Wilhelm: "Speakers for the Dead: Star Trek, the Holocaust, and the Representation of Atrocity," in: Kapell, Matthew Wilhelm (ed.), *Star Trek as Myth: Essays on Symbol and Archetype at the Final Frontier*, Jefferson: McFarland 2010, pp. 67-79.
3 Shedroff, Nathan/Noessel, Christopher: *Make It So: Interaction Design Lessons from Science Fiction*, New York: Rosenfeld Media 2012.

phones and tablets, and up and coming technologies such as consumer 3D printing and smart glasses. One such influential speculative concept depicted in STAR TREK has been the immersive holographic interactive entertainment platform, the holodeck. Using detailed audio-visual and material mimicry and advanced computing, the holodeck was shown to be capable of creating illusions of realistic multisensory environments populated by seemingly sentient beings occupying playful or dramatic roles within various interactive scenarios. While STAR TREK's holodeck was following an almost a century old science-fiction trope of virtual reality systems creating worlds indistinguishable from lived reality, its depiction distinguished itself from the usually deceptive and addictive portrayal of such systems seen in previous speculative fiction.[4] Just like the franchise itself, STAR TREK's holodeck was an interactive digital entertainment utopia for the late 20th century audiences.

THE UTOPIAN FUTURE OF STAR TREK

To understand the holodeck and the fictional holographic entertainment utopia built around it, we must first understand the social and technological utopia in which it emerged. The fictional future chronicled in multiple STAR TREK productions starts approximately in the early 22nd century and ends by the end of the 24th century. In these three centuries humanity transforms from an obscure species at the edge of self-destruction into one of the leading members of an advanced and peaceful multi-species coalition, the United Federation of Planets, ruling over a sizeable portion of the Milky-Way Galaxy. Reflecting the humanist ideals of the STAR TREK creator Gene Rodenberry,[5] the utopian future society of the Federation is shaped by paradigm shifts and advances which differentiates it from ours in multiple ways: The first contact with an alien species right after the third world war triggers the unification of humanity under a world culture in which racism, sexism, and

---

4   Wolf, Mark J.P.: "Virtual Worlds," in: Mark J.P. Wolf (ed.), *The Routledge Companion to Imaginary Worlds*, New York: Routledge 2018, pp. 192-197.
5   Copson, Andrew: "Die humanistischen Werte von Star Trek," in: Bauer, Michael C. (ed.), *Neue Welten – Star Trek als humanistische Utopie?*, Berlin: Springer 2019, pp. 9-12.

religious divisions cease to exist.⁶ Allied with other species, humans advance in areas such as interstellar travel, advanced computing, and conversion of matter and energy. They gain access to new natural resources and increase productivity through technologies which can synthesize goods instantaneously. New economic and social policies providing equitable distribution of almost unlimited material wealth are enacted and raise the living standards of Federation citizens. Humanity leaves poverty behind and transforms into a post-scarcity civilization.⁷ With individual possession losing its importance, humans start to seek psychological fulfillment and intellectual improvement over material gain.⁸

Most of the main characters depicted in STAR TREK productions are members of the Starfleet, the exploration and defense branch of the Federation. They are bright, physically fit, and well-educated. Besides being good in their jobs they are also highly intellectual and well-versed in arts and culture.⁹ In his book *Star Trek: Parallel* Narratives, Chris Gregory calls Starfleet officers "virtual 'Renaissance' men and women"¹⁰ and continues:

> "Throughout STAR TREK there is an emphasis on the highly 'cultured' nature of Federation life. Starfleet officers often know the works of the great writers, dramatists and composers intimately, and the names of many present and past artistic and scientific figures are frequently evoked. It appears that what today is regarded as 'high culture' is now the culture of all."¹¹

These highly cultured men and women are sent to years long exploration missions in deep space, during which they remain isolated from the rest of the galaxy for long periods of time. To compensate potential psychological

---

6   Gregory, Chris: *Star Trek: Parallel Narratives*, London: Palgrave Macmillan 2000.
7   Saadia, Manu: *Trekonomics: The Economics of Star Trek*, San Francisco: Pipertext 2016.
8   Murphy, Jason/Porter, Todd: "Recognizing the Big Picture: Why We Want to Live in the Federation," in: Decker, Kevin S./Eberl, Jason T. (eds.), *Star Trek and Philosophy: The Wrath of Kant*, Chicago: Open Court: 2008, pp. 147-160.
9   Ibid.
10 C. Gregory: *Star Trek: Parallel Narratives*, p. 146.
11 Ibid.

risks evoked by being enclosed, in the 23rd century the Federation equips its starships with onboard entertainment facilities such as libraries, sporting areas, arboretums as well as multiple dining options, various games, and musical instruments.[12] By the late 24th century though, Starfleet engineers (and STAR TREK producers) start to explore new interactive digital entertainment options for their crews.

THE VISION BEHIND THE HOLODECK

The notion of a regularly visited "simulated outdoor recreation area" onboard the USS Enterprise, the first one of the hero-ships of the STAR TREK universe where most of the action takes place, was proposed by Gene Roddenberry in 1968 during the development of the third season of STAR TREK: THE ORIGINAL SERIES (1966-1969), but was never used due to budgetary constraints.[13] According to the official STAR TREK franchise website, startrek.com, the concept than evolved during a demo meeting Roddenberry had in 1973 with the inventor Gene Dolgoff, who was an expert of 3D imaging, optics, and holography.[14] In a 2014 interview with the website Dolgoff described the meeting as follows:

"I introduced the concept that I'd come up with, which was matter holograms. At that point, holograms were used to generate three-dimensional images, but you could pass your hand through the images. So, with matter holograms, I'd realized that matter is made up of interference patterns of energy as well, and so you could actually record a hologram of the structure of matter and then reproduce the matter in the same way. So I then explained to Gene, not only is this the basis to teleportation in the future, but you could make a holographic environment in which people could interact with the

---

12 Johnson, Shane: *Star Trek: Mr. Scott's Guide to the Enterprise*, New York: Pocket Books 1987.
13 Solow, Herbert/Justman, Robert H.: *Inside Star Trek: The Real Story*, New York: Pocket Books 1996.
14 N.N.: "Meet the Man Behind the Holodeck, Part 1," *startrek.com*, 2014; https://www.startrek.com/article/meet-the-man-behind-the-holodeck-part-1

objects and the scenes and everything, and create a recreation room, a training room, an area that could be for entertainment."¹⁵

In 1974, STAR TREK: THE ANIMATED SERIES (1973-1974) second season episode THE PRACTICAL JOKER featured such a recreation room onboard the USS Enterprise which could simulate pre-programmed holographic environments. These environments were naturalistic sceneries including a beach and a forest which could be activated and changed by the crewmembers within seconds. In line with Dolgoff's matter hologram concept, they featured not only visual and audio elements but were also tangible. Crewmembers could touch trees, walk on fallen branches, feel the wind on their faces, and were affected by the changes in the temperature. Besides the elements and plants, animals were also seen been simulated in the background, but the complexity of their behavioral patterns were not explored in the episode.

By mid-1980's Roddenberry began with the pre-production of a new STAR TREK TV series which would eventually become STAR TREK: THE NEXT GENERATION. Inspired by the immersive projection rooms seen in the 1973 science fiction film SOYLENT GREEN, Robert H. Justman, the supervising producer of the show, had proposed to introduce a special area onboard the new USS Enterprise-D, where crewmembers could psychically connect with their home planets to overcome the psychological stresses caused by living in enclosed environments for longer periods of time.¹⁶ But unlike the confining projection in SOYLENT GREEN, Justman had envisioned that the series would "explore all the dramatic possibilities inherent therein."¹⁷ *The Star Trek: The Next Generation Writers/Directors Guide*, an internal reference document written to familiarize prospect production staff to the general concepts and setting of the new series was one of the first documents describing the new concept and officially naming it as the holodeck:¹⁸

---

15   Ibid.
16   Altman, Mark A./Gross, Edward: *The Fifty-Year Mission: The Complete, Uncensored, Unauthorized Oral History of Star Trek: The Next 25 Years, From the Next Generation to J.J. Abrams*, New York: Thomas Dunne Books 2016.
17   Ibid., p. 58-59.
18   Roddenberry, Gene: *The Star Trek: The Next Generation Writers/Directors Guide*, unpublished internal document, USA 1987.

"The Enterprise's holodecks can duplicate with startling reality almost any landscape or seaworld complete with winds, tides, precipitation, and whatever. These decks are much used in both education and recreation and are even more important in preventing crew and families from feeling like they are living 'contained and limited lives.' In the holodecks almost any kind of recreation, training, or exercise can be simulated."[19]

The holodeck was officially introduced to TV audiences in the first episode of STAR TREK: THE NEXT GENERATION (1987-1994). In early episodes, it was treated as a novelty or a gimmick but following the award-winning first season episode THE BIG GOODBYE its potential as key story element was discovered by the writers of the show.[20] Throughout the series, the holodeck was used regularly, with an increasing complexity and dramatic depth in its depiction and continued to be featured prominently in STAR TREK: THE NEXT GENERATION spin-off TV series', STAR TREK: DEEP SPACE NINE (1993-1999), and STAR TREK: VOYAGER (1995-2001). It also appeared in four sequel movies featuring the cast of STAR TREK: THE NEXT GENERATION released between 1994 and 2002. While later installments of the franchise have featured various holographic technologies, as of early-2019, no major STAR TREK production since 2002 used or referred the concept again (except for one STAR TREK: ENTERPRISE (2001-2005) episode[21] which story took place during the 7th season of STAR TREK: THE NEXT GENERATION).

The holodeck was a digital entertainment vision created in a specific historical period, both in STAR TREK's fictional universe and in the real one. The one and a half decade the holodeck was seen on analog TV screens coincided with the development of the World Wide Web, the growth and collapse of the dot-com bubble, release of pioneering hypertext fictions, fourth and fifth generations gaming consoles, the prominence of point-and-click adventures and isometric RPGs in the video games market, the emergence of RTSs and FPSs as popular video game genres, the formation of ESRB, IGDA, and ELO, the early concerns and discussions on games and violence

---

19 Ibid., p. 22.
20 Pearson, Roberta/Messenger Davies, Máire: *Star Trek and American Television*, Berkeley: University of California Press 2014.
21 STAR TREK: ENTERPRISE: THESE ARE THE VOYAGES... (USA 2005, D: Allan Kroeker).

in the USA,[22] and the release of milestone video games such as CIVILIZATION (1991), MYST (1993), TOMB RAIDER (1996), THE SIMS (2000), DEUS EX (2000), and GRAND THEFT AUTO III (2001). STAR TREK writers at the time were not only aware of these developments in digital entertainment, they also competed in the market by contributing to video games under the STAR TREK brand, some of which even featured playable versions of the holodeck.[23] Yet, like many speculative technologies seen on STAR TREK, the vision of the holodeck did not just reflect the concepts and concerns of its time, and more than a decade after the last episode it was seen on, it continues to be credited by scientists and practitioners as a source of inspiration.[24]

THE HOLODECK AS A UTOPIA

Reflecting the design-oriented fan culture formed around the STAR TREK franchise,[25] various speculative aspects of the holodeck, such as "holodeck matter" and "force fields," have been described in detail in official paratextual in-universe reference books.[26] The technology behind the concept was also studied in terms of scientific accuracy and probability[27] and deemed by some so beyond our present science that it was almost impossible to discuss

---

22 Sezen, Tonguc Ibrahim/Sezen, Digdem: "Dijital Oyun Tarihinin Dönüm Noktaları," in: Unal, Gulin Terek/Batı, Ugur (eds.), *Dijital Oyunlar*, Istanbul: Derin Yayınları 2011, pp. 249-284.
23 STAR TREK: KLINGON (Simon & Schuster 1996, O: Simon & Schuster).
24 Jordan, Philipp/Auernheimer, Brent: "The Fiction in Computer Science: A Qualitative Data Analysis of the ACM Digital Library for Traces of Star Trek," in: Ahram, Tareq/Falcão, Christianne (eds.), *Advances in Intelligent Systems and Computing*, Berlin: Springer 2018, pp. 508-520.
25 Rehak, Bob: *More Than Meets the Eye: Special Effects and the Fantastic Transmedia Franchise*, New York: New York University Press 2018.
26 Sternbach, Rick/Okuda, Michael: *Star Trek: The Next Generation Technical Manual*, New York: Pocket Books 1991.
27 Siegel, Ethan: *Treknology: The Science of Star Trek from Tricorders to Warp Drive*, Minneapolis: Voyageur Press 2017.

it intelligently.[28] In this regard, there were also scholars and practitioners who warned against using the holodeck as a reference point: Michael Heim mentioned it as a source of unrealistic public expectations in virtual reality (VR) research back in 1994[29] and Warren Spector warned the game industry against building a hype for the current generation of VR technologies by referencing the holodeck, as it would be unfruitful.[30] According to Andrew Hutchison, the main reason holodeck would not work as a reference point was not its failure as a fictional technology, but instead its successes as one. It was developed to perform a specific narrative function in a TV series and not as a demo piece for VR technology, thus its possible usage in the future could not be predicted.[31] Nevertheless, the holodeck did play a prominent role in academic discussions on its relevance as a utopia for interactive digital entertainment.

In her seminal book *Hamlet on the Holodeck*, Janet H. Murray had used the concept as a cultural reference point for a possible future convergence of computation and storytelling,[32] and described the holodeck as "a universal fantasy machine, open to individual programming: a vision of the computer as a kind of storytelling genie in the lamp."[33] In her book, Murray focuses on "holonovels," which the in-universe reference book *The Star Trek Encyclopedia* describes as literary holodeck programs, in which users take the roles

---

28 Lasbury, Mark E.: *The Realization of Star Trek Technologies*, Berlin: Springer 2017.

29 Heim, Michael: *The Metaphysics of Virtual Reality*, Oxford: Oxford University Press 1994.

30 Spector, Warren: "Holodeck: Holy Grail or Hollow Promise? Part 1," *gamesindustry.biz*, 2013; https://www.gamesindustry.biz/articles/2013-07-31-holodeck-holy-grail-or-hollow-promise-part-1

31 Hutchison, Andrew: "Back to the Holodeck: New Life for Virtual Reality," *Proceedings of DIMEA 2007: Second International Conference on Digital Interactive Media in Entertainment and Arts*; http://doi.acm.org/10.1145/1306813.1306838

32 Murray, Janet H.: "How Close Are We to the Holodeck?," *Clash of Realities Keynote, Cologne Game Lab 2015*; http://penlab.gatech.edu/wp-content/uploads/sites/9/2018/09/MurrayHowCloseHolodeck.pdf

33 Murray, Janet H.: *Hamlet on the Holodeck: The Future of Narrative in Cyberspace*, Cambridge: The MIT Press 1997, p. 15.

of the protagonists or other major characters.[34] Murray underlines holonovels' ties to genre fiction and discusses one particular example inspired by gothic fiction featured in several episodes of STAR TREK: VOYAGER. The holonovel ends with the protagonist leaving it to relieve herself from her emotionally loaded attachment to her character's holographic love interest. She later concludes,

"the holonovel offers a model of an art form that is based on the most powerful technology of sensory illusion imaginable but is nevertheless continuous with the larger human tradition of storytelling, stretching from the heroic bards through the nineteenth-century novelists."[35]

In 2002, criticizing Murray's reading of the STAR TREK: VOYAGER episodes, Marie-Laure Ryan uses the term "internal-ontological interactivity"[36] to describe the user experiences on the holodeck:

"Here the players are cast as characters situated in both the time and the space of the fictional world. The actions of the players determine the fate of their character (avatar in the technical jargon) and, by extension, the fate of the fictional world. Every run of the system produces a new life and consequently a new life story for the avatar. This narrative is created dramatically, by being enacted, rather than diegetically, by being narrated."[37]

One of the core problems with internal-ontological interactivity on the holodeck according to Ryan is, the limitations it has as a first-person narrative experience. In a later publication she explains, "not every type of character and consequently not every type of plot lends itself to the first-person perspective of interactive drama,"[38] and continues, "the personal experience of

---

34 Okuda, Michael/Okuda, Denise: *The Star Trek Encyclopedia*, New York: Pocket Books 1999.
35 J.H. Murray: *Hamlet on the Holodeck*, p. 26.
36 Ryan, Marie-Laure: "Beyond Myth and Metaphor: Narrative in Digital Media," *Poetics Today* 23:4 (2002), pp. 581-609.
37 Ibid., p. 601.
38 Ryan, Marie-Laure: *Avatars of Story*, Minneapolis: University of Minnesota Press 2006, pp. 124-125.

many fictional characters is so unpleasant that users would be out of their mind—literally as well as figuratively—to want to live their lives in the first-person mode."[39] For Ryan, the protagonist's actions in STAR TREK: VOYAGER, leaving the simulation instead of enduring the possibly painful consequences of her actions, demonstrates the weakness of the holodeck as an interactive digital narrative platform.

Another critique on the first-person perspective of the holodeck is made by Brian Upton. According to him, the limitation of the experience of playing a character in a holonovel becomes apparent when users try out new roles. Unlike stock characters such as Sherlock Holmes, whose peculiarities and constraints are known, acting out an unknown character might prove to be difficult and even problematic for many:[40]

"A holodeck would be a great place to play laser tag, or to act out your sexual fantasies. But it would be a lousy place to tell a story, because there is no mechanism for establishing the internal constraints that define the protagonist. It resembles a storytelling medium within an episode of Star Trek only because we are watching actors working from a script—a set of constraints. In the real world, such an experience would feel aimless and pointless."[41]

According to Upton such an experience based on improvisation would only be appealing for a specific group of users who are used to prepare for their roles, such as historical re-enactors and fans of tabletop role-playing games.[42] But even these types of users, who enjoy changing ludic identities may find the holodeck limiting. As Souvik Mukherjee points out, the holodeck does not allow all types of complex identity play available even in contemporary video games; in Mukherjee's words, "intriguingly enough, the STAR TREK TV series or the movies do not have any cross-gender activity on the holodeck."[43]

---

39 Ibid.
40 Upton, Brian: *The Aesthetic of Play*, Cambridge, Mass.: The MIT Press 2015.
41 Ibid, p. 276.
42 Ibid.
43 Mukherjee, Souvik: *Video Games and Storytelling: Reading Games and Playing Books*, New York: Palgrave Macmillan 2015, p. 184.

Of course, neither of these analyses are directly targeting the holodeck. Their readings of the fictional platform are reflections about the potential of narrative in digital interactive entertainment and the study of video games. In this regard, Murray's work may be seen at least partially responsible for triggering the so called "ludology-narratology debate" in video game studies[44] since it inspired others, such as pioneering video game scholar Espen Aarseth to take position against her readings of the holodeck.[45] While this particular "debate" may be settled down for now, Murray's vision and Ryan's criticism on holonovels are still used as a starting point for discussing the potential of video games, as seen in Jesper Juul's exploration of tragedy and responsibility in video game form.[46] In interactive digital narrative studies on the other hand the holodeck vison has been embraced[47] and attempts were made to test the promise of the holodeck with today's technology.[48] In this regard, in one of her later publications, while still calling it a yet unachievable model, Ryan had acknowledged holodeck's individual features as valid goals to be pursued by the developers of interactive narratives.[49] These features according to Ryan were (1) "natural interface," or being capable of interacting with the virtual world in exactly the same way as interacting with the real world; (2) "integration of user action within the story," or the contribution of each user interaction to the forward movement of the

---

44 Mäyrä, Frans: *An Introduction to Game Studies*, London: SAGE Publications 2008.
45 Aarseth, Espen: "Genre Trouble," *Electronic Book Review*, 2004; https://electronicbookreview.com/essay/genre-trouble/
46 Juul, Jasper: *The Art of Failure: An Essay of the Pain of Video Games*, Cambridge, Mass.: The MIT Press 2013.
47 Koenitz, Hartmut et al.: "Introduction: Perspectives on Interactive Digital Narrative," in: Koenitz, Hartmut et al. (eds.): *Interactive Digital Narrative: History, Theory and Practice*, New York: Routledge 2015, pp. 1-8.
48 Cavazza, Marc et al.: "Madame Bovary on the Holodeck: Immersive Interactive Storytelling," *Proceedings of the 15th ACM international conference on Multimedia*; http://citeseerx.ist.psu.edu/viewdoc/download?doi=10.1.1.385.2249&rep=rep1&type=pdf
49 Ryan, Marie-Laure: *Narrative as Virtual Reality 2: Revisiting Immersion and Interactivity in Literature and Electronic Media*, Baltimore: Johns Hopkins University Press 2015.

plot; (3) "frequent interaction," or the system's capability to accept constant user input, and finally (4) "dynamic creation of the story," or a user's ability to affect the flow and outcome of the story through her every actions.[50] Ryan's proposed goals display the challenges the holodeck vision puts in front of scholars and practitioners of interactive digital narratives. But while the holonovel was the most publicized and discussed form of entertainment seen performed on the holodeck, it was not the only one. As Steven E. Jones points out, "despite all its imagined sophistication, the holodeck [was] essentially a futuristic video game platform,"[51] a multiform entertainment platform displaying multiple interactive scenarios to be precise. And a proper understanding of the holodeck as a utopia for holographic interactive digital entertainment requires the acknowledgment of all its features as well.

BEYOND THE HOLONOVEL

If we leave serious uses such as training simulations and various deceptions on the holodeck caused by malfunctions or alien interferences aside, the total number of various holographic entertainment programs featured or mentioned in the 526 STAR TREK episodes and four STAR TREK movies released between 1987 and 2002 turns out to be 114. A cumulative investigation of all these scenarios instead of focusing only on selected holonovels, provides us a detailed map of the wider holographic entertainment utopia as imagined by STAR TREK writers and producers. During the investigation, besides the episodes themselves, the fan-written STAR TREK wiki *Memory Alpha*[52] and a fan-run online screenplay collection with a custom search tool[53] were also used as secondary resources. Even if they not necessarily provide concrete reference points for possible future directions in video game and interactive digital narrative design, the findings nevertheless revealed a much more familiar entertainment ecology.

---

50 Ibid.
51 Jones, Steven E.: *The Meaning of Video Games: Gaming and Textual Strategies*, New York: Routledge 2008, p. 117.
52 N.N.: *Star Trek Wiki*, 2003; https://memory-alpha.fandom.com/wiki/Portal:Main
53 N.N.: *Chrissie's Transcripts Site*, 2019; http://www.chakoteya.net/

As the most discussed holographic entertainment form of the 24th century, the holonovels were indeed featured prominently in STAR TREK and were given considerable screen time.[54] Some appeared even in multiple episodes. Yet, surprisingly the total number of individual holonovels seen on multiple STAR TREK productions was just twelve. In other words, their prominence came from their quality rather than their quantity. Besides their minority as a product branch within the whole holographic entertainment ecology, the investigation generally reflected the findings of the academic research summarized above.

Most of the holonovels are literary adaptations or homages based on genre fiction and traditional legends. This prominence of linear stories as source materials for interactive holonovels suggests the existence of an advanced interactive narrative adaptation engine, or the possibility of a simpler adaptation approach and process which closely follows the narrative structure of the original work. Holonovels are rarely experienced fully and seldom reach one of their intended ends. Due to the plot twists in the episodes, they usually end prematurely or become a dangerous trap for crewmembers. They are never seen replayed and thus, assessing their level of narrative complexity is nearly impossible.

From STAR TREK's twelve holonovels, we see only two fully played out scenarios, albeit with jumps and cuts. In-universe, these are written by STAR TREK: VOYAGER's holographic character the Doctor and described as personal pieces. The first one is a political story on the oppression of the holograms by the humans[55] and the second one, while not called a holonovel on screen, is a drama on the loss of a family member.[56] Both experiences are quite linear and direct their protagonists through external factors to tragic and painful ends. In this regard they present how tragic stories may be experienced in holodeck's first-person perspective.

In line with Justman's original proposal for the concept, the most common use of the holodeck was visiting virtual environments for recreational purposes. In 15 years, 44 environmental simulations were shown or men-

---

54 Stoppe, Sebastian: "Getting Immersed in Star Trek: Storytelling Between True and False on the Holodeck," *Science Fiction Research Association Review* 316 (2016); http://ul.qucosa.de/api/qucosa%3A20883/attachment/ATT-0/
55 STAR TREK: VOYAGER: AUTHOR, AUTHOR (USA 2001, D: David Livingston).
56 STAR TREK: VOYAGER: REAL LIFE (USA 1997, D: Anson Williams).

tioned on screen. These environments could be divided under three categories based on their characteristics. The first environmental simulations seen in STAR TREK were the so-called "patterns of natural environments"[57] or unnamed and unpopulated exotic locations such as forests, deserts, and meadows which were visited for relaxation. While the name "pattern" suggests a possible procedural generation process, since such locations were always shown only once, it's impossible to prove this speculation.

Another popular category among environmental simulators were recreations of famous locations such as real-world museums, restaurants, and tourist attractions, which were visited by crewmembers for authentic experiences. Simulated in their current or past states they were populated by period-appropriate characters. While these locations were not designed to offer specific first-person narrative experiences, traces of environmental storytelling practices were seen in some episodes. Crewmembers could observe emotional conversations of background characters[58] or interact with characters acting as well-defined local hosts.[59]

The last category of environmental simulations was reappearing fictional locations such as restaurants, bars, and even resorts or small towns. Surprisingly, these were amongst the most depicted or mentioned holodeck programs in STAR TREK. Like many holonovels they would be given screen time in multiple episodes and were featured prominently. As familiar locations they were populated by theme appropriate host characters, who not only had their own identities but also would recognize individual crewmembers and memorize their interests and interactions to build-up relationships with them.[60] Moreover, hosts were also capable of interacting with each other even though this usually would not change the status quo in the simulation. Thus, these environments were designed to provide a charming, warm and welcoming place for crewmembers to enjoy personal connections. While they were not designed for singled out narrative experiences, in rare cases,

---

57 STAR TREK: THE NEXT GENERATION: ENCOUNTER AT FARPOINT (USA 1987, D: Corey Allen).
58 STAR TREK: THE NEXT GENERATION: WE'LL ALWAYS HAVE PARIS (USA 1988, D: Robert Becker).
59 STAR TREK: VOYAGER: SCORPION (USA 1997, D: David Livingston).
60 STAR TREK: DEEP SPACE NINE: BADDA-BING, BADDA-BANG (USA 1999, D. Mike Vejar).

based on the scale, the number of active hosts and visitors, and the duration the simulation, events resembling large scale emergent stories were also depicted in some episodes.[61] In this regard, familiar location simulations can be considered amongst the most complex holodeck programs seen in STAR TREK.

Another common holodeck program type was sports simulators. From simple matches against computer-controlled opponents,[62] to play fields for team sports,[63] and natural areas for outdoor activities,[64] a total of 24 different sports simulations were mentioned or shown. These were followed by nine virtual partners with specific talents for specific hobbies such as opera singing,[65] nine erotic scenarios or sexual partners again with specific talents,[66] eight types of spa or relaxation environments with simulated specialist,[67] and three children's simulations which could be described as simplified versions of holonovels and fictional environments.[68] Finally, historical enactment programs were also shown to be somewhat popular among crewmembers. While only five individual reenactment scenarios were mentioned, they were referred in multiple episodes and constantly replayed by crewmembers.[69] Interestingly these crewmembers were shown even to enjoy losing battles and eager to replay the challenge. Unfortunately, because such scenarios are only mentioned and never seen on the screen it's impossible to investigate them further.

---

61 STAR TREK: VOYAGER: SPIRIT FOLK (USA 2000, D: David Livingston).
62 STAR TREK: THE NEXT GENERATION: CODE OF HONOR (USA 1987, D: Russ Mayberry).
63 STAR TREK: DEEP SPACE NINE: TAKE ME OUT TO THE HOLOSUITE (USA 1998, D: Chip Chalmers).
64 STAR TREK: THE NEXT GENERATION: TRANSFIGURATIONS (USA 1990, D: Tom Benko).
65 STAR TREK: VOYAGER: THE SWARM (USA 1996, D: Alexander Singer).
66 STAR TREK: DEEP SPACE NINE: THE EMPEROR'S NEW CLOAK (USA 1999, D: LeVar Burton).
67 STAR TREK: DEEP SPACE NINE: A MAN ALONE (USA 1993, D: Paul Lynch).
68 STAR TREK: VOYAGER: ONCE UPON A TIME (USA 1998, D: John Kretchmer).
69 STAR TREK: DEEP SPACE NINE: THE CHANGING FACE OF EVIL (USA 1999, D: Mike Vejar).

Conclusion

While not each contemporary interactive digital entertainment form had a mirror image in STAR TREK's future, its holographic interactive entertainment utopia was not so different from our entertainment ecology in terms of its diversity. Despite its well-deserved prominence both on screen and in academic research, the holonovel was just only one of those offerings.

Reflecting the core feature of the platform, creating virtual spaces, it was mainly used for activities defined by space. But as the franchise evolved and different STAR TREK shows presented different requirements, these spatial experiences evolved as well. STAR TREK: THE NEXT GENERATION's earlier mainly empty environmental simulations were in time given cultural contexts. STAR TREK: DEEP SPACE NINE's darker and to some degree serialized storylines required more character development than any other STAR TREK show at the time, thus regularly visited entertainment venues with complex, self-aware holographic hosts were introduced. STAR TREK: VOYAGER's crew was stranded on the other side of the galaxy and required to escape to familiar locations from time to time, thus their environmental simulations began more and more to resemble theme parks and run for longer times, which led to emergent behaviors. While simpler holographic spaces continued to be seen, by the end of the 24th century there was a tendency towards "storified" spaces which required less dramatic agency from the users compared to holonovels, but nevertheless could offer dramatic situations.

The high number of sports simulations seen in STAR TREK was not surprising. Sport is a popular leisure activity today and will apparently be so in the 24th century. A sports simulation on the holodeck would require the recreation and balancing of the physical components in the holographic form but beyond that would basically be an implementation of the rules. Beyond their functional requirements, holographic opponents in sports games and other virtual partners in hobby, relaxation and erotica simulations could be programmed with different characteristics as well. Opponents displaying determination and partners encouraging crewmembers were not uncommon.

All in all, maybe because of their expected users' cultured nature, STAR TREK's holodeck simulations were displaying a tendency towards cultural context and narrative tones. In this regard, the holonovel was the perfect form for STAR TREK's crewmembers even if they preferred popular and genre-driven content and indulged other simulations as well. We will never fully answer theoretical questions regarding the design and functionality of holonovels, since we never witnessed one fully performed on screen, let aside replayed. The holonovel and the holodeck in general was a not so concrete utopia which took the shape of whatever the writers of STAR TREK needed it to take. Nevertheless, it was still a utopia and what STAR TREK producers had shown was enough to both inspire and confuse contemporary scholars and practitioners and will continue to do so.

LITERATURE

Aarseth, Espen: "Genre Trouble," *Electronic Book Review*, May 21, 2004; https://electronicbookreview.com/essay/genre-trouble/

Altman, Mark A./Gross, Edward: *The Fifty-Year Mission: The Complete, Uncensored, Unauthorized Oral History of Star Trek: The Next 25 Years, From the Next Generation to J.J. Abrams*, New York: Thomas Dunne Books 2016.

Cavazza, Marc et al.: "Madame Bovary on the Holodeck: Immersive Interactive Storytelling," *Proceedings of the 15th ACM international conference on Multimedia*; http://citeseerx.ist.psu.edu/viewdoc/download?doi=10.1.1.385.2249&rep=rep1&type=pdf

Copson, Andrew: "Die humanistischen Werte von Star Trek", in: Michael C. Bauer (ed.), *Neue Welten – Star Trek als humanistische Utopie?*, Berlin: Springer 2019, pp. 9-12.

Gregory, Chris: *Star Trek: Parallel Narratives*, London: Palgrave Macmillan 2000.

Heim, Michael: *The Metaphysics of Virtual Reality*, Oxford: Oxford University Press 1994.

Hutchison, Andrew: "Back to the Holodeck: New Life for Virtual Reality," *Proceedings of DIMEA 2007: Second International Conference on Digital Interactive Media in Entertainment and Arts*; http://doi.acm.org/10.1145/1306813.1306838

Isaacs, Bruce: "A Vision of a Time and Place: Spiritual Humanism and the Utopian Impulse", in: Kapell, Matthew Wilhelm (ed.), *Star Trek as Myth: Essays on Symbol and Archetype at the Final Frontier*, Jefferson: McFarland 2010, pp. 182-196.

Johnson, Shane: *Star Trek: Mr. Scott's Guide to the Enterprise*, New York: Pocket Books 1987.

Jones, Steven E.: *The Meaning of Video Games: Gaming and Textual Strategies*, New York: Routledge 2008.

Jordan, Philipp/Auernheimer, Brent: "The Fiction in Computer Science: A Qualitative Data Analysis of the ACM Digital Library for Traces of Star Trek," in: Ahram, Tareq/Falcão, Christianne (eds.), *Advances in Intelligent Systems and Computing*, Berlin: Springer 2018, pp. 508-520.

Juul, Jasper: *The Art of Failure: An Essay of the Pain of Video Games*, Cambridge, Mass.: The MIT Press 2013.

Kapell, Matthew Wilhelm: "Speakers for the Dead: Star Trek, the Holocaust, and the Representation of Atrocity," in: Kapell, Matthew Wilhelm (ed.), *Star Trek as Myth: Essays on Symbol and Archetype at the Final Frontier*, Jefferson: McFarland 2010, pp. 67-79.

Koenitz, Hartmut et al.: "Introduction. Perspectives on Interactive Digital Narrative," in: Koenitz, Hartmut et al. (eds.), *Interactive Digital Narrative: History, Theory and Practice*, New York: Routledge 2015, pp. 1-8.

Lasbury, Mark E.: *The Realization of Star Trek Technologies*, Berlin: Springer 2017.

Mäyrä, Frans: *An Introduction to Game Studies*, London: SAGE Publications 2008.

Mukherjee, Souvik: *Video Games and Storytelling: Reading Games and Playing Books*, New York: Palgrave Macmillan 2015.

Murphy, Jason/Porter, Todd: "Recognizing the Big Picture: Why We Want to Live in the Federation," in: Decker, Kevin S./Eberl, Jason T. (eds.), *Star Trek and Philosophy: The Wrath of Kant*, Chicago: Open Court: 2008, pp. 147-160.

Murray, Janet H.: *Hamlet on the Holodeck: The Future of Narrative in Cyberspace*, Cambridge, Mass.: The MIT Press 1997.

Murray, Janet H.: "How Close Are We to the Holodeck?," *Clash of Realities Keynote, Cologne Game Lab 2015*; http://penlab.gatech.edu/wp-content/uploads/sites/9/2018/09/MurrayHowCloseHolodeck.pdf

N.N.: *Chrissie's Transcripts Site*, 2019; http://www.chakoteya.net/

N.N.: "Meet the Man Behind the Holodeck, Part 1," *startrek.com*, 2014; https://www.startrek.com/article/meet-the-man-behind-the-holodeck-part-1

N.N.: *Star Trek Wiki*, 2003; https://memory-alpha.fandom.com/wiki/Portal:Main

Okuda, Michael/Okuda, Denise: *The Star Trek Encyclopedia*, New York: Pocket Books 1999.

Pearson, Roberta/Messenger Davies, Máire: *Star Trek and American Television*, Berkeley: University of California Press 2014.

Rehak, Bob: *More Than Meets the Eye: Special Effects and the Fantastic Transmedia Franchise*, New York: New York University Press 2018.

Roddenberry, Gene: *The Star Trek: The Next Generation Writers/Directors Guide*, unpublished internal document, USA 1987.

Ryan, Marie-Laure: "Beyond Myth and Metaphor: Narrative in Digital Media," *Poetics Today* 23:4, (2002), pp. 581-609.

Ryan, Marie-Laure: *Avatars of Story*, Minneapolis: University of Minnesota Press 2006.

Ryan, Marie-Laure: *Narrative as Virtual Reality 2: Revisiting Immersion and Interactivity in Literature and Electronic Media*, Baltimore: Johns Hopkins University Press 2015.

Saadia, Manu: *Trekonomics: The Economics of Star Trek*, San Francisco: Pipertext 2016.

Sezen, Tonguc Ibrahim/Sezen, Digdem: "Dijital Oyun Tarihinin Donum Noktalari," in: Unal, Gulin Terek/Bati, Ugur (eds.), *Dijital Oyunlar*, Istanbul: Derin Yayinlari 2011, pp. 249-284.

Shedroff, Nathan/Noessel, Christopher: *Make It So: Interaction Design Lessons from Science Fiction*, New York: Rosenfeld Media 2012.

Siegel, Ethan: *Treknology: The Science of Star Trek from Tricorders to Warp Drive*, Minneapolis: Voyageur Press 2017.

Solow, Herbert/Justman, Robert H.: *Inside Star Trek: The Real Story*, New York: Pocket Books 1996.

Spector, Warren: "Holodeck: Holy Grail or Hollow Promise? Part 1," *gamesindustry.biz*, 2013; https://www.gamesindustry.biz/articles/2013-07-31-holodeck-holy-grail-or-hollow-promise-part-1

Sternbach, Rick/Okuda, Michael: *Star Trek: The Next Generation Technical Manual*, New York: Pocket Books 1991.

Stoppe, Sebastian: "Getting Immersed in Star Trek: Storytelling Between True and False on the Holodeck," *Science Fiction Research Association Review*, 316, 2016; http://ul.qucosa.de/api/qucosa%3A20883/attachment/ATT-0/

Upton, Brian: *The Aesthetic of Play*, Cambridge, Mass.: The MIT Press 2015.

Wolf, Mark J.P.: "Virtual Worlds," in: Mark J.P. Wolf (eds.), *The Routledge Companion to Imaginary Worlds*, New York: Routledge 2018, pp. 192-197.

Filmography

Soylent Green (USA 1973, D: Richard Fleischer)
Star Trek: Enterprise: These Are The Voyages... (USA 2005, D: Allan Kroeker)
Star Trek: The Animated Series: The Practical Joker (USA 1974, D: Bill Reed)
Star Trek: Deep Space Nine: A Man Alone (USA 1993, D: Paul Lynch)
Star Trek: Deep Space Nine: Badda-Bing, Badda-Bang (USA 1999, D: Mike Vejar)
Star Trek: Deep Space Nine: Take Me Out To The Holosuite (USA 1998, D: Chip Chalmers)
Star Trek: Deep Space Nine: The Changing Face Of Evil (USA 1999, D: Mike Vejar)
Star Trek: Deep Space Nine: The Emperor's New Cloak (USA 1999, D: LeVar Burton)
Star Trek: The Next Generation: Code Of Honor (USA 1987, D: Russ Mayberry)
Star Trek: The Next Generation: Encounter At Farpoint (USA 1987, D: Corey Allen)
Star Trek: The Next Generation: Transfigurations (USA 1990, D: Tom Benko)
Star Trek: The Next Generation: We'll Always Have Paris (USA 1988, D: Robert Becker)
Star Trek: Voyager: Author, Author (USA 2001, D: David Livingston)
Star Trek: Voyager: Once Upon A Time (USA 1998, D: John Kretchmer)
Star Trek: Voyager: Real Life (USA 1997, D: Anson Williams)
Star Trek: Voyager: Scorpion (USA 1997, D: David Livingston)
Star Trek: Voyager: Spirit Folk (USA 2000, D: David Livingston)
Star Trek: Voyager: The Swarm (USA 1996, D: Alexander Singer)

Gamography

CIVILIZATION (MicroProse 1991, O: MicroProse)
DEUS EX (Eidos Interactive 2000, O: Ion Storm)
GRAND THEFT AUTO III (Rockstar Games 2001, O: DMA Design)
MYST (Brøderbund 1993, O: Cyan)
STAR TREK: KLINGON (Simon & Schuster 1996, O: Simon & Schuster)
THE SIMS (Electronic Arts 2000, O: Maxis)
TOMB RAIDER (Eidos Interactive 1996, O: Core Design)

Utopias of Digital Games

Feminist Interventions for Better Futures of Digital Games

ALISON HARVEY

INTRODUCTION: WHITHER UTOPIA?

When I was invited to speak on the topic of "Playing Utopia: Futures in Digital Games," I experienced two conflicting responses. There was firstly a sense of curiosity about the potential of thinking about games and feminism from this conceptual approach. But there was also an overriding sensation of scepticism, deriving from the feminist political economy perspective I take on the games industry and in particular the organization of its workforce. Specifically, I questioned how utopia could relate to the vivid portrait of the global labour force entailed in contemporary games development Michael Thomsen paints.[1] In his article, he outlines the working practices of outsourced games work in firms in Brazil, China, Serbia, and Taipei, with a focus on the workers of Virtuos Limited in Shanghai. Virtuos has become one of the largest outsourced game development companies in the world, providing 3D art, level design, and programming for games including STAR WARS BATTLEFRONT II (2017), MARVEL VS. CAPCOM: INFINITE (2017), and CALL OF DUTY: BLACK OPS 3 (2015). In this story, Thomsen describes the work space's "agricultural symmetry",[2] with teams and leads

---

1 Thomsen, Michael: "The Universe Has Been Outsourced," *The Outline*, February 6, 2018; https://theoutline.com/post/3087/outsourcing-blockbuster-video-games-made-in-china-horizon-zero-dawn?zd=1&zi=gjogtqmv
2 Ibid.

lined up neatly in rows, surrounded by decor made up of an eclectic mix of Western iconography to remind the workers of the market they are producing for.

These spatial configurations of games development—along increasingly transnational and fragmented supply chains in the Global South (as explored in Fung's research)[3] and in mundane, neon-lit offices that could literally be anywhere (quite distinct from the playful work spaces discussed by Johnson)[4]—sit uneasily alongside the perfect alternative societies and places of literary Utopias. In Thomas More's[5] original formulation of Utopia, such imagined spaces are both 'good places' and also 'no places,' impossible fantasies that are potentially dangerous for the escapist tendencies they embody.

Literary-informed approaches to understanding video game utopias (and dystopias) are not uncommon within game studies, either implicitly or explicitly.[6] Given their spatial dynamics and the world-building element of many games,[7] such place-based forms of analysis come as no surprise. This research has been valuable for understanding the latent ideology within the mass cultural form of many digital games. For instance, in their analysis of BIOSHOCK INFINITE (2013), Óliver Pérez-Latorre and Mercè Oliva[8] contrast the dystopian narrative of the game with its mechanics, which encode a straightforward set of neoliberal values familiar from many mainstream games. This includes an emphasis on the entrepreneurial self, monitoring and improving one's quantitatively-assessed biopower, consumerism and rampant consumption, individualism over collective power, and of course, zero-

---

3   Fung, Anthony Y.H.: "Comparative Cultural Economy and Game Industries in Asia," *Media International Australia* 159 (2016), pp. 43-52.
4   Johnson, Robin S.: "Toward Greater Production Diversity: Examining Social Boundaries at a Video Game Studio," *Games and Culture* 8 (2013), pp. 136-160.
5   More, Thomas: *Utopia*, Mineola, New York: Dover Publications, 1997.
6   See for example Aldred, Jessica/Greenspan, Brian: "A Man Chooses, A Slave Obeys: *BioShock* and the Dystopian Logic of Convergence," *Games and Culture* 6 (2011), pp. 479-496; Henthorne, Tom: "Cyber-Utopias: The Politics and Ideology of Computer Games," *Studies in Popular Culture* 25 (2003), pp. 63-76.
7   Wolf, Mark J.P.: *Building Imaginary Worlds: The Theory and History of Subcreation*, New York City, New York: Routledge 2012.
8   Pérez-Latorre, Óliver/Oliva, Mercè: "Video Games, Dystopia, and Neoliberalism: The Case of *Bioshock Infinite*," *Games and Culture*, OnlineFirst (2017).

sum, meritocratic competition. Their critique echoes the earlier insights of Julian Stallabras,[9] who argues that in the perfectly functioning markets of the game world, the only dream in the 'good place' is of fully rational capitalist forces. These conservative visions of what fantastic realms might comprise of, simulations of frictionless control and efficiency, lead Paolo Pedercini to posit that "computer games are the aesthetic form of rationalization,"[10] supported by the hegemonic norms of goal-oriented gameplay. As his discussion of the rise of social games including but not limited to FARMVILLE (2009) and mobile apps demonstrates, the instrumentalization of actions within these kinds of simulations can lead to an objectification and exploitation of both non-player characters and other users we relate to in these networks.

Furthermore, as a growing body of postcolonial research in game studies indicates, these dynamics of domination, exploitation, and control in tandem with open worlds seem to enable above all the proliferation of imperialist and colonial missions, relations, and norms. The CIVILIZATION (1991-) series is an obvious example, but as Souvik Mukherjee[11] notes, colonial norms in games pervade spatial representations as highlighted by the widespread use of maps, the common dynamics of colonizer/colonized in games often linked to militarist storylines, and in the construction of the "Other" that is so dominant in ludic narratives.

As this brief overview demonstrates, the normative values simulated and represented in games may reproduce and reify hegemonic systems of exploitation and exclusion, including neoliberal capitalism, (neo-)imperialism, and hypermilitarism. Video games, as highlighted by research on online gaming spaces in particular,[12] can also perpetuate dystopian realities for women,

---

9   Stallabras, Julian: "Just Gaming: Allegory and Economy in Computer Games," *New Left Review* 198, March/April (1993); http://web.stanford.edu/class/history34q/readings/Cyberspace/StallabrasJustGaming.html

10 Pedercini, Paolo: "Videogames and the Spirit of Capitalism," *Indiecade East*, February 14, 2014; http://www.molleindustria.org/blog/videogames-and-the-spirit-of-capitalism/

11 Mukherjee, Souvik: "Playing Subaltern: Video Games and Postcolonialism," *Games and Culture* 13 (2018), pp. 504-520.

12 Cote, Amanda C.: "I Can Defend Myself: Women's Strategies for Coping with Harassment While Gaming Online," *Games and Culture* 12 (2016), pp. 136-155; Cross, Katherine: "Ethics for Cyborgs: On Real Harassment in an 'Unreal' Place,"

people of colour, and other marginalized communities in the sexist, racist, and otherwise oppressive norms circulating therein. Scholarship on representation in games[13] demonstrates that the simulated societies within games consistently mirror and recreate the interlocking systems of oppression Elisabeth Schüssler Fiorenza[14] calls kyriarchy, referring to the intersectional nature of sexist, racist, ableist, classist and other exploitative structures. The fiercely defensive GamerGate campaign against women in particular and inclusivity more broadly[15] indicates that such simulations are an (increasingly contested) utopia for some, but certainly not all.

GAMES ARE DYSTOPIAS

The link between game worlds and game cultures brings us back to the conclusion of Stallabras' prescient analysis of games worlds. He posits:

"there is a tenebrous dance of the utopian and the apocalyptic, an ambiguity which it is tempting to resolve by saying that they present the apocalypse as Utopia. If this is so, it is because the absolutes of destruction and death are sought as an escape from

---

Loading... The Journal of the Canadian Game Studies Association 8 (2014), pp. 4-21; Gray, Kishonna L.: "Intersecting Oppressions and Online Communities: Examining the Experiences of Women of Color in Xbox Live," *Information, Communication & Society* 15 (2012), pp. 411-428.

13 Kennedy, Helen W.: (2002.) "Lara Croft: Feminist Icon or Cyberbimbo? On the Limits of Textual Analysis," *Game Studies* 2 (2002); http://www.gamestudies.org/0202/kennedy/; Lynch, Teresa et al.: "Sexy, Strong, and Secondary: A Content Analysis of Female Characters in Video Games Across 31 Years," *Journal of Communication* 66 (2016), pp. 564-584.

14 Schüssler Fiorenza, Elisabeth: *Wisdom Ways: Introducing Feminist Biblical Interpretation*, Ossining, New York: Orbis Books 2001.

15 Braithwaite, Andrea: "It's About Ethics in Games Journalism? Gamergaters and Geek Masculinity," *Social Media + Society* 2 (2016), pp. 1-10; Gray, Kishonna L. et al.: "Blurring the Boundaries: Using Gamergate to Examine 'Real' and Symbolic Violence against Women in Contemporary Gaming Culture," *Sociology Compass* 11 (2016), pp. 1-8.

the virtuality and artificiality of everyday life. While this is only achieved in a digital simulation, its effects may spill back into the real world."[16]

The norms of video game development discussed at the start of this chapter clearly validate such an assertion. For instance, the controversy around the 100-hour work weeks necessitated by the release of RED DEAD REDEMPTION 2 (2018) uncomfortably reminds us of the exploitation that runs through games worlds beyond the simulated realm.[17] Whatever element of games you study or work with, it has become almost impossible to look away from the distinctly dystopian realities associated with the production of this cultural form. Indeed, the field of game studies has consistently detailed how the industrial but also technological, cultural, and aesthetic context of this major media form encapsulate, reify, and exemplify exploitative and exclusionary norms within contemporary capitalism.

For example, in their book *Digital Play*, Stephen Kline, Nick Dyer-Witheford, and Greig de Peuter[18] argue that games are the ideal commodity of the post-Fordist economy. In the intervening fifteen years this industry has come to act as a canary-in-the-coalmine for trends in creative and cultural work, media production, and the tech industry, particularly in terms of flexible specialization as demonstrated by the games outsourcing Michael Thomsen investigates. The 'passion' so heavily emphasized in labour discourse, from job descriptions to justifications for ungodly working hours, sets the tone for affective calls to 'do what you love.' This in turn entails that games workers and those training to become them love the increased personal risk, precarity, and self-exploitation[19] entailed in what Gina Neff[20] calls venture labour.

---

16 J. Stallabras: "Just Gaming."
17 Partin, Will: "Red Dead Redemption 2 and the Problems with Creative Work," *The Outline*, October 22, 2018; https://theoutline.com/post/6437/red-dead-redemption-2-crunch-outsourcing-labor?zd=1&zi=3zj4poia
18 Kline, Stephen et al.: *Digital Play: The Interaction of Technology, Culture, and Marketing*, Montreal, QC: McGill-Queen's University Press 2003.
19 Harvey, Alison: "Becoming Gamesworkers: Diversity, Higher Education, and the Future of the Game Industry," *Television and New Media*, forthcoming.
20 Neff, Gina: (2012.) *Venture Labor: Work and the Burden of Risk in Innovation Industries*, Cambridge, MA: The MIT Press 2012.

In later work, Nick Dyer-Witheford and Greig de Peuter refer to video games as the "exemplary media of empire."[21] They examine how the origins of games in military-based partnerships and their expansion within the context of post-industrial capitalism's emphasis on immaterial labour is replicated in the organization of the industry. This includes its approach to accumulation based on a range of forms of cognitive exploitation, such as stringent claims to IP rights, and their design of games that make "becoming a neoliberal subject fun."[22]

The 2018 firing of two ArenaNet employees over their Twitter engagement in non-working hours for a failure to "uphold [...] standards of communicating with players"[23] indicates another element of contemporary gameswork, the feminization of the workforce. Donna Haraway[24] uses this concept not to denote how many women are working in an industry, because the research also tells us that this not the case.[25] Instead, this refers to how in new relations of production and reproduction, workers become increasingly vulnerable and exploited, based on contracts, mobile by necessity. This concept also indicates how knowledge and service-based work entail affective interactions such as relationship-building, care, and emotional labour. In other words, the feminization of work occurs when it becomes like that associated with the attributes of women's work historically- immaterial, precarious, affective, and largely invisible in discourses of formalized work. The affective element, in addition to passionate self-exploitation at work, indicates how workers engage in emotional labour, which "requires one to induce or suppress feeling in order to sustain the outward countenance that produces

---

21 Dyer-Witheford, Nick/de Peuter, Greig: *Games of Empire: Global Capitalism and Video Games*, Minneapolis/London: University of Minnesota Press 2009, p. xxix.
22 Ibid, p. xxx.
23 Alexander, Julia/Kuchera, Ben: "ArenaNet's Firings Reinforced Gaming Culture's Worst Impulses," *Polygon*, July 10, 2018, np; https://www.polygon.com/2018/7/10/17550276/guild-wars-2-arenanet-firings-jessica-price-gamergate
24 Haraway, Donna: "A Cyborg Manifesto: Science, Technology, and Socialist-Feminism in the Late Twentieth Century," in: *Simians, Cyborgs and Women: The Reinvention of Nature*, London/New York: Routledge 1991, pp. 149-182.
25 Prescott, Julie/Bogg, Jan: *Gender Divide and the Computer Game Industry*, Hershey, PA: IGI Global, 2014.

the proper state of mind in others."[26] The firing of Jessica Price and Peter Fries for failing to manage the feelings of social media users in their off-hours is the consequence of not providing the expected emotional labour entailed in the feminization of gameswork.

In this way, we see that games reify exploitative, conservative, and destructive norms in their design and their production, but also in their engagement with the cultures in and around them. The relationship between GamerGate and the rise of the so-called alt-right demonstrates how these dystopian norms spill out from games into broader culture. Kristin Bezio notes that the language and imagery that developed as part of this harassment campaign against women is now deployed to silence progressive figures and voices in American politics, including the use of pejorative framings of 'safe spaces,' 'social justice warriors,' and 'snowflakes.'[27] This discourse, rhetoric, and affect has had broader uptake in British, French, Hungarian, Brazilian, Bulgarian, and Polish politics, among others.[28] The anger expressed by these largely young white men, in the pursuit of purity and a return to a 'better' time and place, can be contextualized within the socio-economic losses posed by the feminization of labour under global neoliberal capitalism but is more effectively mobilized by those with the most privilege and power for their own ends.

While 2018's '#boycottACE' campaign saw games academia galvanizing against Steve Bannon as the keynote speaker at the International Conference on Advances in Computer Entertainment Technology,[29] the reality is

---

26 Hochschild, Arlie Russell: *The Managed Heart: Commercialization of Human Feeling*, Berkeley, CA: University of California Press, 1983, p. 7.

27 Bezio, Kristin M: "Ctrl-Alt-Del: GamerGate as a Precursor to the Rise of the Alt-Right," *Leadership* 14 (2018), pp. 556-566.

28 See for example Jenkins, Simon: "Fear and Anger won the Election in Brazil. It's a Wake-up Call to the World," *The Guardian*, October 29, 2018; https://www.theguardian.com/commentisfree/2018/oct/29/brazil-election-far-right-democracy-social-media; Schaeffer, Carol: "How Hungary Became a Haven for the Alt-Right," *The Atlantic*, May 28, 2017; https://www.theatlantic.com/international/archive/2017/05/how-hungary-became-a-haven-for-the-alt-right/527178/

29 Matsakis, Louise: "The Weird Saga of the Gaming Conference Hosting Steve Bannon," *Wired*, October 31, 2018; https://www.wired.com/story/steve-bannon-gaming-conference-saga/

that, as a field, game studies was not active or outspoken enough in 2014, something many should reflect on seriously given how this has catalyzed and normalized alt-right discourse, community, and ideology.

In sum, the context for thinking about utopia is quite bleak in games, from within play spaces and communities to across the spaces of production and scholarship. It is important that we reflect on this as the first step in what utopian thinking can allow. The field of utopian studies and the role of utopia in sociological thought is a good port of call for inspiration in this regard.

Utopian Impulses and Critique

In this body of work, literary utopias or the idea of a utopia as a blueprint for prescribing more perfect worlds are not, by and large, the key focus. Instead, the emphasis in this scholarship is on utopia as an impulse as per Fredric Jameson's formulation.[30] This refers to utopia as a critical and transformative drive providing a distance from hegemonic structures to imagine alternatives holistically, an analytical rather than descriptive mode. The work of Ruth Levitas[31] is especially powerful for thinking this way, as she posits utopia as a method that provides a lens on how we as scholars can engage with the public and work towards the goal of transformation and the making of a better world.

The pressing political and economic concerns I have indicated in games do not negate the power of utopian methods but instead provide their grounds. These realities necessitate action for change and demonstrate that while some will dismiss utopias as impossible, what is actually impossible is for us to continue on with the exploitative and destructive status quo. Utopian thinking is a modality for considering sustainable lives for everyone and the social and economic systems that will enable this. As Levitas says,

---

30 Jameson, Fredric: "Reification and Utopia in Mass Culture," *Social Text* 1 (1979), pp. 130-148.
31 Levitas, Ruth: *Utopia as Method: The Imaginary Reconstitution of Society*, Basingstoke, Hampshire: Palgrave Macmillan 2013.

"the core of utopia is the desire for being otherwise, individually and collectively, subjectively and objectively. Its expressions explore and bring to debate the potential concerns and contexts of human flourishing. It is thus better understood as a method than a goal."[32]

She refers to this method as the imaginary reconstitution of society (IROS).

This expression of utopian thinking and methods chimes with the aims of the feminist, political economy perspective from which I operate. Within both of these conceptual approaches, critical analysis is not simply about unpacking the conditions of domination and the structures that sustain it but also about imagining the possibilities for transformation and dismantling of these systems. Ending the discussion with the dystopian conclusion, a solely negative analysis, is insufficient. As Carmen Sirianni says, "a critical theory must justify its normative basis and attempt to elaborate the social possibilities of the human species if it is to have either explanatory or emancipatory power."[33] Our scholarship, then, must make a gesture towards utopian possibilities. As with all texts and practices in media culture, games are not simple ideological tools but are imbued with complex and contradictory meanings. Therefore, as Douglas Kellner argues about mass culture,[34] the study of games entails an approach that balances consideration of both ideology and utopia.

Such an approach is enabled by a feminist perspective on games that considers the systemic nature of inequalities in this cultural form, and then imagines what could be otherwise. A great deal of the ethos of IROS resonates with the ethics and politics of feminist theory and methods, such as the emphasis on reflexivity, partiality, and critical engagement with difference.[35] IROS also challenges hegemonic notions of epistemology, questioning

---

32 Ibid., p. xi.
33 Sirianni, Carmen: "Production and Power in a Classless Society: A Critical Analysis of the Utopian Dimensions of Marxist Theory," in: *Unfinished Business: Twenty Years of Socialist Review*, London, UK: Verso Books 1991, pp. 33-82, here p. 279.
34 Kellner, Douglas: *Media Culture: Cultural Studies, Identity and Politics Between the Modern and the Postmodern*, London: Routledge 1995.
35 Haraway, Donna: "Situated Knowledges: The Science Question in Feminism and the Privilege of Partial Perspective," *Feminist Studies* 14 (1988), pp. 575-599.

conservative definitions of what constitutes both research and ways of knowing. Levitas argues that utopian thinking already exists beyond Western-sanctioned knowledge production,[36] and its embrace might therefore be seen as part of the agenda of decolonizing the academy advocated by postcolonial scholars (Bhambra, Gebrial & Nişancıoğlu).[37]

Feminist game studies has a strong history of enacting utopia thinking in diverse ways. In the remainder of this contribution, I will highlight some of this work before turning to how such insights are more generalizable and indeed urgent for the field of game studies.

THE UTOPIAN DRIVE OF FEMINIST GAME STUDIES

An invaluable concept for transformative action in games is that of 'the hegemony of play' as articulated by Fron, Fullerton, Morie & Pearce.[38] Theorizing the norms and values of the games discussed earlier as the product of dynamic interrelations between commerce, technology, and culture, this feminist artist-activist-research collective points to not only the multiple sites where marginalization occurs but also possible points of disruption of these hegemonic practices. Their work is therefore generative of ways of conceptualizing the multi-sited reification of video games as 'boy's toys,' even as play has become mainstream. It is also productive for imagining forms of intervention in this exclusionary domain.

Accounts of the trajectory of interventionist work related to games, gender, and its intersections with race, sexuality, and age in particular[39] provide

---

36 R. Levitas: *Utopia as Method*.
37 Bhambra, Gurminder K. et al. (eds.): *Decolonising the University*, London, UK: Pluto Press 2018.
38 Fron, Janine et al.: "The Hegemony of Play," Paper presented at the annual meeting for the Digital Games Research Association, Tokyo, Japan, September 24-28, 2007.
39 See Richard, Gabriela T.: "Gender and Gameplay: Research and Future Directions," in: Bigi, Benjamin/Stoppe, Sebastian (eds.), *Playing with Virtuality: Theories and Methods of Computer Game Studies*, Frankfurt a.M.: Peter Lang Academic 2013, pp. 269-284; Jenson, Jennifer/de Castell, Suzanne: "Gender,

glimpses of how feminist work has engaged with better futures of digital games along these lines for some time. This has included educational initiatives creating spaces for girls to play and design games,[40] socially progressive business practices aimed at fostering inclusion by developing new kinds of products, including games for girls,[41] research revealing the erasure of women from the history of games and their ever-present contributions to the field,[42] and critical artistic work shifting the ways games are designed and played.[43]

At the forefront of this work today is the international research network ReFIGuring Innovation in Games (ReFIG), the evolution of Jennifer Jenson and Suzanne de Castell's research and leadership on the preceding Feminist in Games project. Its mission statement—"promoting diversity and equity in the game industry and culture and effecting real change in a space that has been exclusionary to so many"[44]—indicates the ways in which critique is tightly linked to action. Its network of collaborators, including academics, artists, studios, and community organizers, engage in research and activism related to Games Culture, Games Industry, Informal Education, and Formal Education, focusing on enacting change and making interventions into inequalities and exclusionary norms. This network is attuned to entangled sites where gendered power relations are reified and perpetuated, and the intersectional nature of exclusion. And from the very beginning of its formation it

---

Simulation, and Gaming: Research Review and Redirections," *Simulation & Gaming* 41(2010), pp. 51-71.

40 Dahya, Negin et al.: "(En)gendering Videogame Development: A Feminist Approach to Gender, Education, and Game Studies," *Review of Education, Pedagogy and Cultural Studies* 39 (2017), pp. 367-390; Kafai, Yasmin B.: "Gender Play in a Tween Gaming Club," in: Yasmin B. Kafai et al. (eds.), *Beyond Barbie and Mortal Kombat: New Perspectives on Gender and Gaming*, Cambridge, Mass.: The MIT Press 2008, pp. 111-124.

41 Laurel, Brenda: *Utopian Entrepreneur*, Cambridge, Mass.: The MIT Press 2001.

42 Nooney, Laine: "A Pedestal, A Table, A Love Letter: Archaeologies of Gender in Videogame History," *Game Studies* 13 (2013); http://gamestudies.org/1302/articles/nooney

43 Flanagan, Mary: *Critical Play: Radical Game Design*, Cambridge, Mass.: The MIT Press 2009.

44 See http://www.refig.ca/

has been deeply invested in supporting projects that identify possible points of disruption, potential change, and coordinated action in games-based institutions and relations. This work in 'inventing equity'[45] has entailed challenges to the way that game jams are organized,[46] how inclusion in e-Sports tournaments may be fostered,[47] and which games are canonized within the field of game studies.[48]

In parallel with this active collective of international researchers is a growing body of work highlighting the largely obscured queer potentialities within games,[49] the diversity of masculinities in games,[50] and the ways that game design and culture exclude people of colour.[51] The accessibility of games for those with disabilities[52] and the decolonization of games[53] are also active areas of engagement, and in many cases this work happens in partnerships between academics and other stakeholders, with a focus on connecting these initiatives with wider publics.

In my own work with ReFIG, the focus has been on those who create games. Within the sphere of mainstream games production, the 'creative elite' who develop digital play experiences is notoriously nondiverse, with

---

45 Jenson, Jennifer/de Castell, Suzanne: "Tipping Points: Marginality, Misogyny, and Videogames," *Journal of Curriculum Theorizing* 29 (2013), pp. 72-81, here p. 79.

46 Kennedy, Helen W.: "Game Jam as Feminist Methodology: The Affective Labours of Intervention in the Ludic Economy," *Games and Culture* 13 (2018), pp. 708-727.

47 Taylor, T.L.: "Gender & Esports Tournaments: Best Practices Recommendations," White Paper for AnyKey, 2017; http://www.anykey.org/wp-content/uploads/Gender-best-practices.pdf

48 Chess, Shira/ Paul, Christopher A.: "The End of Casual: Long Live Casual," *Games and Culture* 14 (2019), pp. 107-118.

49 Ruberg, Bonnie/Shaw, Adrienne (eds.): *Queer Game Studies*, Minneapolis, Minnesota: University of Minnesota Press 2017.

50 Taylor, Nicholas/ Voorhees, Gerald (eds.): *Masculinities in Play*, London, UK: Palgrave Macmillan 2018.

51 K. L. Gray.: "Intersecting Oppressions."

52 See for example https://ablegamers.org/; https://www.specialeffect.org.uk/

53 Nixon, Sarah: "Decolonizing Gaming: Examining Indigenous Portrayals in Video Games," *NYMG*, November 28, 2018; https://www.nymgamer.com/?p=4096

women making up only 19 % and BAME individuals only 4 % of the UK games workforce,[54] numbers that also do not reflect rampant occupational segregation with more women represented in sales, management, and marketing roles than design or programming positions.[55] As recent news from Riot Games[56] and revelations of massive gender pay gaps in the UK industry[57] indicates, those women who have managed to break into the industry face structural sexism and discrimination when they do join the workforce.

Given how the global games industry and its strikingly homogenous workforce mirrors the imagined hardcore gamer's presumed identity, the sphere of production represents a promising site for challenging exclusionary norms. My own work has considered game-making from the viewpoints of both independent, community organizations and formal higher education, considering how games talent is engendered. With Stephanie Fisher[58] and

---

54 Densham, Sophie: "10 300 now Employed in Games in UK; 19 % are Women," *UKIE*, April 27, 2016; https://ukie.org.uk/news/2016/04/10300-now-employed-games-uk-19-are-women

55 Prescott, Julie/Bogg, Jan: "Segregation in a Male-Dominated Industry: Women Working in the Computer Games Industry," *International Journal of Gender, Science and Technology* 3 (2011), pp. 206-227.

56 D'Anastasio, Cecilia: "Inside The Culture Of Sexism At Riot Games," *Kotaku*, July 8, 2018; https://kotaku.com/inside-the-culture-of-sexism-at-riot-games-1828165483

57 Batchelor, James: "69 % of Large UK games Firms have Bigger Gender Pay Gap than National Average," *Gamesindustry.biz*, April 5, 2018; https://www.gamesindustry.biz/articles/2018-04-04-gender-pay-gaps-revealed-across-leading-uk-games-firms

58 Fisher, Stephanie/ Harvey, Alison: "Intervention for Inclusivity: Gender Politics and Indie Game Development," *Loading...Journal of the Canadian Game Studies Association* 7 (2013), pp. 25-40; Harvey, Alison/Fisher, Stephanie: "Making a Name in Games: Immaterial Labour, Indie Game Design, and Gendered Social Network Markets," *Information, Communication, and Society* 16 (2013), pp. 362-380; Harvey, Alison/Fisher/Stephanie: "Everyone Can Make Games!: The Post-Feminist Context of Women in Digital Game Production," *Feminist Media Studies* 15 (2015), pp. 576-592; Harvey, Alison/ Fisher, Stephanie: "Growing Pains: Intergenerational Feminisms in Digital Games," *Feminist Media Studies* 16 (2016), pp. 648-662.

Tamara Shepherd,[59] I have engaged in feminist participatory action research[60] in collaboration with Dames Making Games in Toronto and Pixelles in Montreal, two organizations that have over the last eight years created manifold opportunities for girls and women to get involved with game-making to various ends. In this way, they have transformed their local communities but also on a broader level shifted the conversation about diversity and inclusion in game development, providing alternatives to many of the cultural norms around game creation normalized within the hegemony of play. Such action is particularly valuable given that within formalized games education the status quo is largely maintained as talent is trained up for work in an industry that is understood as punishing but also unmovable.[61]

Across its active history, feminist game studies has critiqued the status quo of games and highlighted ways of shifting the hegemony of play for more inclusive and sustainable practices moving forward. While not always articulated (or perceived) in this way, feminist game studies is premised on a utopian methodology, driven by the desire to transform inequitable systems for better futures for all.

CONCLUSION – TOWARDS BETTER FUTURES IN DIGITAL GAMES

The dark realities discussed at the start of this chapter urgently indicate that utopia as method is not only accessible to all but also imperative in our given context. In a reality of nightmarish crunch and a context of development that as Amy Hennig says is "an arms race that is unwinnable and is destroying

---

59 Harvey, Alison/Shepherd, Tamara: "When Passion isn't Enough: Gender, Affect and Credibility in Digital Games Design," *International Journal of Cultural Studies* 20 (2016), pp, 492-508.

60 Feminist participatory action research engages with a challenge or issue in collaboration with communities, with research conducted iteratively WITH rather than ON participants to address the problem. For more on this method, see Frisby, Wendy et al.: "The 'F' Word has Everything to do with it: How Feminist Theories Inform Action Research," *Action Research* 7 (2009), pp. 13-29.

61 A. Harvey: "Becoming Gamesworkers."

people,"[62] we cannot play or research neutrally. Games are not culturally, socially, economically, or politically innocent, and neither is game studies.

Challenges to the hegemony of play are certainly not limited to feminist work. The authors and researchers cited earlier in the discussion of games dystopias largely all evince utopian thinking as well, concluding their critiques with insights into better possible futures of games. Dyer-Witheford & de Peuter note that the exemplary nature of games includes their potential for 'games of multitude,' including playful experiences, cultures, and practices that challenge, subvert, and create alternatives to this dominant order.[63] They reflect on the potential of activist game mods, machinima, and independent games as well as counter-play practices where the gamer resists and refuses empire in their play. A key example of alternative practice is the Molleindustria project led by Pedercini, who in addition to his own games exploring labour and alienation points to the radical potential of storytelling and physicality in games as a counterbalance to computationally-delimited game worlds. He points to J.S. JOUST (2011), SPACE TEAM (2012), and CART LIFE (2010) as exemplars of these alternatives.[64] Pérez-Latorre & Oliva also see independent games like these as well as LIMBO (2010) and JOURNEY (2012) as providing subversive alternatives to the latent ideology of mainstream games.[65]

Utopia as method therefore does not necessarily entail participatory action research nor a feminist or political economy frame. Recall, it is a holistic approach, one that might implicate our practices of knowledge production on various levels, from our citational politics to where we draw our attention in our research design to how we conclude, by either highlighting the negative or showcasing subversive alternatives.

To that end, I want to conclude by reflecting on the future of game studies and the value of utopian thinking in our work. In a climate where it is easy to purchase and flaunt a T-shirt that reads the "The Future is Female," even

---

62 Quoted in M. Thomsen, "The Universe has Been Outsourced."
63 N. Dyer-Witheford/G. de Peuter: *Games of Empire*.
64 P. Pedercini: "Videogames and the Spirit of Capitalism."
65 O. Pérez-Latorre/M. Oliva: "Video Games, Dystopia, and Neoliberalism."

as ecological[66] and economic[67] destruction is normalized we need to probe the deeper meaning of this statement. Does it refer to the growing precarity, self-exploitation, and risk entailed in the feminization of work? Does it indicate wider and deeper inequalities for all reflecting the historically marginalized and oppressed status of women globally? To resist these trends in contemporary capitalism entails an embrace of utopia as a method, including in game studies.

Utopias as method is not prescriptive but attuned to, to paraphrase and synthesize the scholarship cited throughout this chapter, re-orientation and revolution, problem-making rather than problem-solving, sustainability and flourishing, better and more inclusive worlds, and the imagination of better futures. Feminist, queer, and anti-racist scholarships also demonstrates that an attunement to love, joy, and hope are also valuable for transformative thinking. This goes beyond the feminist frames I have reviewed. As Ruth Levitas says, "explicit alternative scenarios for the future are fundamental to *any kind of democratic debate.*"[68]

For those who feel discouraged about the power and potency of games work, recall the role played by GamerGate in politics mentioned earlier. Consider also recent attacks on the University, such as the ban on gender and migration studies in Hungary[69] and the raids on classrooms in Brazil.[70] These

---

66 Carrington, Damien: "Plummeting Insect Numbers 'Threaten Collapse of Nature'," *The Guardian*, February 10, 2019; https://www.theguardian.com/environment/2019/feb/10/plummeting-insect-numbers-threaten-collapse-of-nature

67 Elliott, Larry: "World's 26 Richest People Own as much as Poorest 50 %, says Oxfam," *The Guardian*, January 21, 2019; https://www.theguardian.com/business/2019/jan/21/world-26-richest-people-own-as-much-as-poorest-50-percent-oxfam-report

68 R. Levitas: *Utopia as Method*, p. xviii, emphasis my own.

69 Oppenheim, Maya: "Hungarian Prime Minister Viktor Orban bans gender studies programmes," *Independent*, October 24, 2018; https://www.independent.co.uk/news/world/europe/hungary-bans-gender-studies-programmes-viktor-orban-central-european-university-budapest-a8599796.html

70 Smith, Amy Erica: "Brazilian Media Report that Police are Entering University Classrooms to Interrogate Professors," *Vox*, November 1, 2018; https://www.vox.com/mischiefs-of-faction/2018/10/26/18029696/brazilian-police-interrogate-professors

are chilling but also potentially electrifying occurrences highlighting how fascist forces fear the academy and the work of critical scholars. There must therefore be something threatening to destructive hegemonic rule about what we do in our teaching and research, and we need to rediscover and embrace that power.

Within games specifically and digital cultures more broadly, we are witnessing tremendous grassroots action towards transformation, including discussions of universal basic income, four-day work weeks, and unionization.[71] We are not without hope in this context.

Whatever one's particular approach to thinking about sustainability, justice, and equity in society, our greatest threat is the distinctly anti-utopian ethos of hegemonic political discourse and culture. Conservative politics seek to nullify social change and frame it as irresponsible at best or terroristic at worst. We must then first disrupt what is taken-for-granted, and open our minds to the idea that we as a field have a role to play in better futures.

LITERATURE

Aldred, Jessica/Greenspan, Brian: "A Man Chooses, A Slave Obeys: *BioShock* and the Dystopian Logic of Convergence," *Games and Culture* 6 (2011), pp. 479-496.

Alexander, Julia/Kuchera, Ben: "ArenaNet's Firings Reinforced Gaming Culture's Worst Impulses," *Polygon*, July 10, 2018; https://www.polygon.com/2018/7/10/17550276/guild-wars-2-arenanet-firings-jessica-price-gamergate

Batchelor, James: "69 % of Large UK games Firms have Bigger Gender Pay Gap than National Average," *Gamesindustry.biz*, April 5, 2018; https://www.gamesindustry.biz/articles/2018-04-04-gender-pay-gaps-revealed-across-leading-uk-games-firms

Bezio, Kristin M: "Ctrl-Alt-Del: GamerGate as a Precursor to the Rise of the Alt-Right," *Leadership* 14 (2018), pp. 556-566.

---

[71] Colwill, Tim: "Game Developers Need to Unionize," *Polygon*, January 16, 2019; https://www.polygon.com/2019/1/16/18178332/game-developer-union-crunch

Bhambra, Gurminder K. et al. (eds.): *Decolonising the University*, London, UK: Pluto Press 2018.

Braithwaite, Andrea: "It's About Ethics in Games Journalism? Gamergaters and Geek Masculinity," *Social Media + Society 2* (2016), pp. 1-10.

Carrington, Damien: "Plummeting Insect Numbers 'Threaten Collapse of Nature'," *The Guardian*, February 10, 2019; https://www.theguardian.com/environment/2019/feb/10/plummeting-insect-numbers-threaten-collapse-of-nature

Colwill, Tim: "Game Developers Need to Unionize," *Polygon*, January 16, 2019; https://www.polygon.com/2019/1/16/18178332/game-developer-union-crunch

Cote, Amanda C.: "I Can Defend Myself: Women's Strategies for Coping with Harassment While Gaming Online," *Games and Culture* 12 (2016), pp. 136-155.

Cross, Katherine: "Ethics for Cyborgs: On Real Harassment in an 'Unreal' Place," *Loading... The Journal of the Canadian Game Studies Association* 8 (2014), pp. 4-21.

Dahya, Negin et al.: "(En)gendering Videogame Development: A Feminist Approach to Gender, Education, and Game Studies," *Review of Education, Pedagogy and Cultural Studies* 39 (2017), pp. 367-390.

D'Anastasio, Cecilia: "Inside The Culture Of Sexism At Riot Games," *Kotaku*, July 8, 2018; https://kotaku.com/inside-the-culture-of-sexism-at-riot-games-1828165483

Densham, Sophie: "10 300 now Employed in Games in UK; 19 % are Women," *UKIE*, April 27, 2016; https://ukie.org.uk/news/2016/04/10300-now-employed-games-uk-19-are-women

Dyer-Witheford, Nick/de Peuter, Greig: *Games of Empire: Global Capitalism and Video Games*, Minneapolis/London: University of Minnesota Press 2009.

Elliott, Larry: "World's 26 Richest People Own as much as Poorest 50 %, says Oxfam," *The Guardian*, January 21, 2019; https://www.theguardian.com/business/2019/jan/21/world-26-richest-people-own-as-much-as-poorest-50-per-cent-oxfam-report

Fisher, Stephanie/Harvey, Alison: "Intervention for Inclusivity: Gender Politics and Indie Game Development," *Loading...Journal of the Canadian Game Studies Association* 7 (2013), pp. 25-40.

Flanagan, Mary: *Critical Play: Radical Game Design*, Cambridge, Mass.: The MIT Press 2009.

Frisby, Wendy et al.: "The 'F' Word has Everything to do with it: How Feminist Theories Inform Action Research," *Action Research* 7 (2009), pp. 13-29.

Fron, Janine et al.: "The Hegemony of Play," Paper presented at the annual meeting for the Digital Games Research Association, Tokyo, Japan, September 24-28, 2007.

Fung, Anthony Y.H.: "Comparative Cultural Economy and Game Industries in Asia," *Media International Australia* 159 (2016), pp. 43-52.

Gray, Kishonna L.: "Intersecting Oppressions and Online Communities: Examining the Experiences of Women of Color in Xbox Live," *Information, Communication & Society* 15 (2012), pp. 411-428.

Gray, Kishonna L. et al.: "Blurring the Boundaries: Using Gamergate to Examine 'Real' and Symbolic Violence against Women in Contemporary Gaming Culture," *Sociology Compass* 11 (2016), pp. 1-8.

Haraway, Donna: "Situated Knowledges: The Science Question in Feminism and the Privilege of Partial Perspective," *Feminist Studies* 14 (1988), pp. 575-599.

Haraway, Donna: "A Cyborg Manifesto: Science, Technology, and Socialist-Feminism in the Late Twentieth Century," in: *Simians, Cyborgs and Women: The Reinvention of Nature*, London/New York: Routledge 1991, pp. 149-182.

Harvey, Alison/Fisher, Stephanie: "Making a Name in Games: Immaterial Labour, Indie Game Design, and Gendered Social Network Markets," *Information, Communication, and Society* 16 (2013), pp. 362-380.

Harvey, Alison/Fisher/Stephanie: "Everyone Can Make Games!: The Post-Feminist Context of Women in Digital Game Production," *Feminist Media Studies* 15 (2015), pp. 576-592.

Harvey, Alison/Fisher, Stephanie: "Growing Pains: Intergenerational Feminisms in Digital Games," *Feminist Media Studies* 16 (2016), pp. 648-662.

Harvey, Alison/Shepherd, Tamara: "When Passion isn't Enough: Gender, Affect and Credibility in Digital Games Design," *International Journal of Cultural Studies* 20 (2016), pp. 492-508.

Harvey, Alison: "Becoming Gamesworkers: Diversity, Higher Education, and the Future of the Game Industry," *Television and New Media*, forthcoming.

Henthorne, Tom: "Cyber-utopias: The Politics and Ideology of Computer Games," *Studies in Popular Culture* 25 (2003), pp. 63-76.

Hochschild, Arlie Russell: *The Managed Heart: Commercialization of Human Feeling*, Berkeley, CA: University of California Press, 1983.

Jameson, Fredric: "Reification and Utopia in Mass Culture," *Social Text* 1 (1979), pp. 130-148.

Jenkins, Simon: "Fear and Anger won the Election in Brazil. It's a Wake-up Call to the World," *The Guardian*, October 29, 2018; https://www.theguardian.com/commentisfree/2018/oct/29/brazil-election-far-right-democracy-social-media

Jenson, Jennifer/de Castell, Suzanne: "Gender, Simulation, and Gaming: Research Review and Redirections," *Simulation & Gaming* 41 (2010), pp. 51-71.

Jenson, Jennifer/de Castell, Suzanne: "Tipping Points: Marginality, Misogyny, and Videogames," *Journal of Curriculum Theorizing* 29 (2013), pp. 72-81.

Johnson, Robin S: "Toward Greater Production Diversity: Examining Social Boundaries at a Video Game Studio," *Games and Culture* 8 (2013), pp. 136-160.

Kafai, Yasmin B.: "Gender Play in a Tween Gaming Club," in: Yasmin B. Kafai et al. (eds.), *Beyond Barbie and Mortal Kombat: New Perspectives on Gender and Gaming*, Cambridge, Mass.: The MIT Press 2008, pp. 111-124.

Kellner, Douglas: *Media Culture: Cultural Studies, Identity and Politics between the Modern and the Postmodern*, London: Routledge 1995.

Kennedy, Helen W.: "Lara Croft: Feminist Icon or Cyberbimbo? On the Limits of Textual Analysis," *Game Studies* 2 (2002); http://www.gamestudies.org/0202/kennedy/

Kennedy, Helen W.: "Game Jam as Feminist Methodology: The Affective Labors of Intervention in the Ludic Economy," *Games and Culture* 13 (2018), pp. 708-727.

Kline, Stephen et al.: *Digital Play: The Interaction of Technology, Culture, and Marketing*, Montreal, QC: McGill-Queen's University Press 2003.

Laurel, Brenda: *Utopian Entrepreneur*, Cambridge, Mass.: The MIT Press 2001.
Levitas, Ruth: *Utopia as Method: The Imaginary Reconstitution of Society*. Basingstoke, Hampshire: Palgrave Macmillan 2013.
Lynch, Teresa et al.: "Sexy, Strong, and Secondary: A Content Analysis of Female Characters in Video Games Across 31 Years," *Journal of Communication* 66 (2016), pp. 564-584.
Matsakis, Louise: "The Weird Saga of the Gaming Conference Hosting Steve Bannon," *Wired*, October 31, 2018; https://www.wired.com/story/steve-bannon-gaming-conference-saga/
More, Thomas: *Utopia*, Mineola, New York: Dover Publications, 1997.
Mukherjee, Souvik: "Playing Subaltern: Video Games and Postcolonialism," *Games and Culture* 13 (2018), pp. 504-520.
Nixon, Sarah: "Decolonizing Gaming: Examining Indigenous Portrayals in Video Games," *NYMG*, November 28, 2018; https://www.nymgamer.com/?p=4096
Neff, Gina: *Venture Labor: Work and the Burden of Risk in Innovation Industries*, Cambridge, Mass.: The MIT Press 2012.
Nooney, Laine: "A Pedestal, A Table, A Love Letter: Archaeologies of Gender in Videogame History," *Game Studies* 13 (2013); http://gamestudies.org/1302/articles/nooney
Oppenheim, Maya: "Hungarian Prime Minister Viktor Orban bans Gender Studies Programmes," *Independent*, October 24, 2018; https://www.independent.co.uk/news/world/europe/hungary-bans-gender-studies-programmes-viktor-orban-central-european-university-budapest-a8599796.html
Partin, Will: "Red Dead Redemption 2 and the Problems with Creative Work," *The Outline*, October 22, 2018; https://theoutline.com/post/6437/red-dead-redemption-2-crunch-outsourcing-labor?fbclid=IwAR1JS4Gj-b8HLJZijKrB2GZ5i1WR9VqLC6sVaVeV5784g7_2_DNKzcGs24&zd=2&zi=vc5hlegw
Pedercini, Paolo: "Videogames and the Spirit of Capitalism," *Indiecade East*, February 14, 2014; http://www.molleindustria.org/blog/videogames-and-the-spirit-of-capitalism/
Pérez-Latorre, Óliver/ Oliva, Mercè: "Video Games, Dystopia, and Neoliberalism: The Case of Bioshock Infinite," *Games and Culture*, OnlineFirst (2017).

Prescott, Julie/Bogg, Jan: "Segregation in a Male-Dominated Industry: Women Working in the Computer Games Industry," *International Journal of Gender, Science and Technology* 3 (2011).

Prescott, Julie/Bogg, Jan: *Gender Divide and the Computer Game Industry*, Hershey, PA: IGI Global 2014.

Richard, Gabriela T.: "Gender and Gameplay: Research and Future Directions," in: Bigi, Benjamin/Stoppe, Sebastian (eds.), *Playing with Virtuality: Theories and Methods of Computer Game Studies*, Frankfurt a.M.: Peter Lang Academic 2013, pp. 269-284.

Ruberg, Bonnie/Shaw, Adrienne (eds.): *Queer Game Studies*, Minneapolis, Minnesota: University of Minnesota Press 2017.

Schaeffer, Carol: "How Hungary Became a Haven for the Alt-Right," *The Atlantic*, May 28, 2017; https://www.theatlantic.com/international/archive/2017/05/how-hungary-became-a-haven-for-the-alt-right/527178/

Schüssler Fiorenza, Elisabeth: *Wisdom Ways: Introducing Feminist Biblical Interpretation*, Ossining, New York: Orbis Books 2001.

Sirianni, Carmen: "Production and Power in a Classless Society: A Critical Analysis of the Utopian Dimensions of Marxist Theory," in: *Unfinished Business: Twenty Years of Socialist Review*, London, UK: Verso Books 1991, pp. 33-82.

Smith, Amy Erica: "Brazilian Media Report that Police are Entering University Classrooms to Interrogate Professors," *Vox*, November 1, 2018; https://www.vox.com/mischiefs-of-faction/2018/10/26/18029696/brazilian-police-interrogate-professors

Stallabras, Julian: "Just Gaming: Allegory and Economy in Computer Games," *New Left Review* 198, March (1993); http://web.stanford.edu/class/history34q/readings/Cyberspace/StallabrasJustGaming.html

Taylor, Nicholas/ Voorhees, Gerald (eds.): *Masculinities in Play*, London, UK: Palgrave Macmillan 2018.

Taylor, T.L.: "Gender & Esports Tournaments: Best Practices Recommendations," White Paper for AnyKey (2017); http://www.anykey.org/wp-content/uploads/Gender-best-practices.pdf

Thomsen, Michael: "The Universe Has Been Outsourced," *The Outline*, February 6, 2018; https://theoutline.com/post/3087/outsourcing-blockbuster-video-games-made-in-china-horizon-zero-dawn?zd=1&zi=gjogtqmv

Wolf, Mark J.P.: *Building Imaginary Worlds: The Theory and History of Subcreation*, New York City, New York: Routledge 2012.

Gamography

BIOSHOCK INFINITE (2K Games, 2013, O: Irrational Games)
CALL OF DUTY: BLACK OPS III (Activision, 2015, O: Treyarch)
CART LIFE (O: Richard Hofmeier, 2010)
CIVILIZATION (MPS Labs, 1991, O: MicroProse)
FARMVILLE (Zynga, 2009, O: Zynga)
JOURNEY (Sony Computer Entertainment, 2012, O: Thatgamecompany)
J.S. JOUST (O: Douglas Wilson, 2011)
LIMBO (Playdead, 2010, O: Playdead)
MARVEL VS. CAPCOM: INFINITE (Capcom, 2017, O: Capcom)
RED DEAD REDEMPTION 2 (Rockstar Games, 2018, O: Rockstar Studios)
SPACE TEAM (Henry Smith, 2012, O: Sleeping Beast Games)
STAR WARS BATTLEFRONT II (Electronic Arts 2017, O: EA Dice)

Ludopian Visions
On the Speculative Potential of Games in Times of Algorithmic Work and Play[1]

ANNE DIPPEL

Media theory and critical theory both engage with the relations between ideology and technology. Media theory constitutes itself around the assumption that media technologies 'format' or even 'determine our situation.'[2] Critical theory aims to question ideologies by analyzing the dominating structures and power relations behind them. While the underlying paradigms of media theory had been developed within the framework of war technologies—Alan Turing's machine, Claude Shannon's communication theory, or Norbert Wiener's idea of cybernetics—, critical theory, as conducted by Walter Benjamin amongst others, had emerged out of the engagement with social and cultural developments in an ever more technologized modern world. Here, Georg Wilhelm Friedrich Hegel, Karl Marx, Sigmund Freud amongst others, served as patrons of thought in questioning the existing power relations. My aim in this essay is to bring those two theoretical approaches together in order to ask whether computers and computer games may open up spaces of possibility to envision utopian societies.

I am developing the concept of ludopia by re-reading Walter Benjamin's Second Version of his famous piece on "The Work of Art in the Age of Its

---

1 I want to thank Sonia Fizek for her invaluable help in revising and partially translating this essay.
2 Kittler, Friedrich A.: *Grammophon, Film, Typewriter*, Munich: Fink 1986, p. 5.

Technological Reproducibility;"[3] especially his concept of *Spiel* "understood in its multiple German meanings as 'play,' 'game,' 'performance,' and 'gamble.'"[4] I want to map out ludopian visions in two very different spheres:

- Algorithmic Workspaces: the sphere of digital work environments in high-energy physics that create multiple spaces for play
- Algorithmic Playspaces: the sphere of digital games that address the need for utopias in criticizing post-capitalist working conditions

I will argue that algorithms and digital infrastructures—however confining—not only make us perform within but allow us to outperform and transgress current power relations. Digitality and play (ludopias) open up possibilities to speculate about potential futures and bring a grain of optimism into the vision of failed encoded utopian spaces.[5]

ENVISIONING LUDOPIAS VIA BENJAMIN'S CONCEPT OF 'SPIEL'

Usually, Walter Benjamin is considered one of the gloomiest amongst critical theory thinkers, leaving little room for change and treating the past as a display of the human incapacity to create a world of justice and enlightened freedom. Similarly to Karl Marx, in his attempt to grasp the capitalist mode of production, Benjamin directed his vision towards a possible future of exploitation augmenting capitalism and as such preventing it from its own destruction. Benjamin's dystopian visions seem to resound in the neoliberal

---

3   Benjamin, Walter: "The Work of Art in the Age of Its Technological Reproducibility: Second Version," in: Jennings, Michael W./Eiland, Howard (eds.), *Selected Writings 3: 1935-1938,* Harvard: Harvard University Press 2006, pp. 101-133.
4   Hansen, Miriam Bratu: "Room-for-Play. Benjamin's Gamble with Cinema," *October* 109 (2004), pp. 3-45, here p. 6.
5   Galloway, Alexander: *Protocol. How Control Exists after Decentralization*, Cambridge, Mass.: MIT Press 2006.

paradigms we are currently experiencing. In the 21st "ludic century"[6] capitalism is further enhanced in a new medium: the computer game.

Despite the usually austere tone, Benjamin's essay could be read as an attempt to envision the revolutionary capacity of art, and by extension the potential of media technology to confront the fascistic abuse of modern media for totalitarian aesthetics.[7] Although the technological conditions fostered and fueled fascist modes of exploitation of collectivities, Benjamin endowed a grain of hope for mankind by ushering the concept of *Spiel* as crucial for a critical theoretical aesthetic. The possibility to imagine, expressed within *Spiel* and through the act of *spielen*, is the starting point for any subversion of existing conditions. It may even pave the way to revolution. Miriam Bratu Hansen interprets it as a crucial theory and:

"[…] an alternative mode of aesthetics on a par with modern, collective experience, an aesthetics that could counteract at the level of sense perception, the political consequences of the failed—that is, capitalist and imperialist, destructive and self-destructive—reception of technology."[8]

Benjamin follows a tradition of German Enlightenment, which locates human's capacity of change in will[9] and play (*spielen*),[10] defining it as the "*Ur-phenomenon* of all artistic activity."[11] By repeating things over and over again in play, and subsequently turning these experiences of mastery into a

---

6 Zimmerman, Eric: "Manifesto for a Ludic Century," in: Deterding, Sebastian/Walz, Steffen P. (eds.), *The Gameful World: Approaches, Issues, Applications*, Cambridge, Mass.: MIT Press 2014, pp. 19-22.

7 Benjamin, Walter: "Das Kunstwerk im Zeitalter seiner technischen Reproduzierbarkeit," in: Benjamin, Walter, *Werke und Nachlaß. Kritische Gesamtausgabe*, Band 16, Berlin: Suhrkamp 2013 [1936], p. 1.

8 M.B. Hansen: "Room-for-Play," pp. 3-45.

9 Kant, Immanuel: *Kritik der reinen Vernunft*, Frankfurt a.M.: Suhrkamp 1974 [1781], p. A 803/B831.

10 Schiller, Friedrich: *Über die ästhetische Erziehung des Menschen in einer Reihe von Briefen, Fünfzehnter Brief*, München 1963 [1801].

11 W. Benjamin: "The Work of Art in the Age of Its Technological Reproducibility," p. 368; see also M.B. Hansen: "Room-for-Play," p. 15.

narrative, we are able to reimagine and in effect, create entire events anew.[12] This happens not only on the level of action (playing, gaming, gambling, and performing) but also on the level of technology itself. If we reframe technology as a "toy," expanding on Benjamin's argument, we no longer remain at the mercy of algorithmic architectures but can use the emerging digital tools, logics and infrastructures as "sites of conflict,"[13] seeing in them cultural implements that expand the human power of imagination. It is useful to take the Benjaminian "class character" as an example here. By realizing the toy's "class character," we are able to see beyond its purely aesthetic value, consciously rejecting or acting upon it. This can also happen, for instance, in the moment of refusal to succumb to gender-specific aesthetic (e.g., pink dolls for girls and blue cars for boys), which re-plays the dominant relations in a society. A similar realization by rejecting socially dominant patterns may apply to post-industrial work environments or repetitive play rhythms perpetuated in digital environments (the contemporary mobile gaming sector entertains a post-industrial mode of play). In the case of technologically and systemically complex systems (working conditions and games), such a realization requires a very different form of literacy; perhaps not even critical media literacy or ludic literacy[14] but an algorithmic one. It is extensively more difficult to locate or specify the algorithmic 'sites of conflict' as seen in the polyphonic discourse in media theory[15] or the confusion in digital legislation (e.g., EU's "article 13" directive and the use of the so-called content recognition algorithms).

---

12 Benjamin, Walter: "Spielzeug und Spielen," in: Adorno, Theodor W. et al. (eds.), *Gesammelte Schriften, Band 2*, Frankfurt a.M.: Suhrkamp 1991 [1928], pp. 127-131; English: Benjamin, Walter: "Toys and Play: Marginal Notes on a Monumental Work," in: *Selected Writings 2, Vol 1: 1927-1930*, Harvard: Harvard University Press 1999, pp. 117-121.

13 Ibid. p. 120.

14 For ludoliteracy see: Zagal, José P.: *Ludoliteracy: Defining, Understanding, and Supporting Games Education*, Halifax: ETC Press 2010.

15 Engemann, Christoph/Sudmann, Andreas (eds.): *Machine Learning – Medien, Infrastrukturen und Technologien der künstlichen Intelligenz*, Bielefeld: transcript 2018; Sudmann, Andreas (ed.): *The Democratization of Artificial Intelligence*, Bielefeld: transcript 2019.

Despite the ever more growing complexity of digital simulations as opposed to analog representations Benjamin refers to in his essay (film and visual art), his concept of *Spiel* remains a promising starting point and a lens to locate the 'sites of conflict' and question complex power relations. Perhaps, the complexity of the system itself may be playfully subverted in order to represent a particular social dynamic. I want to see play as a mode of experience,[16] which may serve as a condition for creativity, social empowerment, and change, an argument I will expand in the later parts of this essay.

ALGORITHMIC WORKSPACES

Somber visions of the algorithmic future seem to be dominating recent debates in anthropology as well as science and technology studies. One of the most illustrative arguments is that of Nick Seaver's on social and software architectures:

"[...] social architectures, software architectures, and physical architectures echo each other. Walking into a tech company's offices today, one can conjure the feeling of walking into the software itself, as though the building and the people in it—their positions, their interactions, the flow of information—were programs transcoded into social space."[17]

A matrix-like concept of a social space founded on the logics of code taps into (perhaps unconsciously) a very Kittlerian tradition of media theory, which sets cultural and social foundations in 'media a priori.' Such a vision leaves little, if any, room for speculation or change. A social utopia finds it hard to nest itself in a system of its own oppression. But Seaver's argument, however attractive, is also deeply problematic.

---

16 Stevens, Philipp: "Play and Work: A False Dichotomy?" In: Schwartzmann, Helen B. (ed.), *Play and Culture*, New York: Westpoint 1980, pp. 316-323; Malaby, Thomas M.: "Anthropology and Play: The Contours of Playful Experience," *New Literary History* 40/1 (2009), pp. 205-218.
17 Seaver, Nick: "What Should an Anthropology of Algorithms Do?" *Cultural Anthropology* 33/3 (2018), pp. 375-385.

Above all, most code architecture is temporal and as such much more volatile than any modern architectonic structure, unless we consider America's 'tech-world' workspaces and their cities a universal model, where architectonical structures seem to come and go depending on the shape of the new technological frontier. It is hard, if not reductionist, to imagine the Boolean logic (true or false) implemented directly into a complex work environment; or if-then-else conditional statements as the basis for decision making while moving through an architectural space. As many beautiful anthropological arguments, Seaver's concept seems to be a seductive rhetorical trick that illustrates the importance of algorithms in today's digital workspace. Millions of diverse programmers around the world surely cannot be held accountable for creating dystopian physical working environments, many of which predate the digital era. In many ways, algorithms are running on pre-digital modern network infrastructures. Old factories and bakeries of yesterday house server farms of today, which in turn house the algorithmic data. Analyzed media archeologically and historically, the 19th century factory and a weaving machine are as much influencing today's algorithmic ecology as algorithms are in turn shaping the postmodern workspace.

I want to challenge Seaver's hypothesis referring to my own fieldwork—a modest witnessing[18]—of algorithmic workspaces, done amongst high-energy physicists at the Center for Nuclear Research (CERN) at the border of Switzerland and France near Lake Geneva since 2013. One of the most significant insights I have gained through interviews and participant observation is that media theory often tries to impose reasonable doubts on what can be assumed as 'reality' with the help of simulation. Physicists and computer scientists may hope to find an algorithmic ultimate solution to the world's complex problems, while at the center of their daily enterprise lies measurement: much of their everyday research procedure boils down to 'hunting bugs' in the never-ending lines of code. Computers have become a core part of high-energy physics ever since the H-bomb was built: In the 1970s the first fully digital experiments were conducted, and in the 1980s computer simulation became the gold standard of measurement within the field. In the 1990s, when the Large Hadron Collider with its grand scale experiments (ATLAS, CMS, LHCb and Alice) started off, the "meeting rooms had turned

---

18 Haraway, Donna J.: *Modest_Witness@Second_Millennium. FemaleMan_Meets_ OncoMouse: Feminism and Technoscience*, New York: Routledge 1997.

blue," as one of my physicist informants put it, referring to the ubiquitous use of personal computers screens in everyday work. The research site at CERN is constantly evolving, on the level of the experiment's digital as well as analog infrastructure.

However, none of these physical architectures have been designed in accordance with code architecture, neither the existing social architectures. The architecture of code, *organizing* the work of physicists, constantly changes; older physicists need to adapt to new programming languages as well as code organization techniques. CERN is not a monogenerational object. It is a 'living' institution employing people from their early twenties beyond their retirement age. Often, the older generation of physicists feels deprived of their status, stating that new languages are hard to learn, or that they even lost without contact to code management. Younger physicists, on the other hand, complain that the previous code infrastructure is too "complicated" for collaborative work. Older physicists see their ways as much more straightforward. In these spaces, where transgenerational work on code forces the younger ones to understand the ways of their older peers, while the older ones need to constantly keep up with the new developments, the algorithms are producing new forms of hierarchies that seem to favor the newly arriving ones. If the physical architecture mimics anything, it is not code, but the imaginary inspired by science fiction and popular culture. If there were a place where software architecture mirrored a socio-spatial environment, it would have to be CERN. Instead, what one can observe is the allegedly confining algorithmic culture intertwined with playfulness.

There is a whole realm of playful social infrastructure that unfolds in those workspaces, which at first glimpse do not differ from average modern offices equipped with tables, sockets, internet access points, heaters, and lights. The offices are not only inhabited by physicists, but more surprisingly by 'dead' objects left behind by previous generations of CERNies: cartoon jokes, tags and toys. One of my favorite offices belongs to a sixty-year-old physicist and one in his late twenties. The first has chosen Obelix as his 'totem," the latter Homer Simpson. Both comic figures are quite similar—resilient, resistant, good-hearted, and quite naïve, but always on the winning side of things. The urge to transform the otherwise exchangeable workspace into a personal room seems vital. One could see playfulness as a long-term strategy of survival in a highly competitive and bureaucratic environment. The figure of Homer Simpson may be regarded as a form of ludic subversion, mocking the seriousness of being at CERN. In their daily work, physicists face lots of pressure, posed by technical aspects of the experiment, time management issues as well as the communication strategy of the largest collaborative science project on planet Earth. Toy figures are oftentimes a ludic or playful way to escape the pressure of a world, all the while ironically working with very ludic form of simulation (the Monte Carlo randomized algorithms which also run the Las Vegas gambling infrastructure).

Physicists tend not only to personalize their spaces; they keep the memory of those who had been there before. As I have shown elsewhere,[19] physicists deploy ludic ways to deal with frictions between the social, economic, and technological. The implementation of ludic objects, even playful uses of language are deeply encoded in the physics work culture, to play upon the digital metaphor.

Utopian aspects may also be observed in highly neoliberal work spaces. At the Large Hadron Collider (LHC) of CERN particles collisions are performed to gain an understanding of the origins of the universe. On a theoretical level, this project is deeply utopian. Like a child grasping for the moon, physicists stretch out for the origin of stars.[20] In order to achieve their goal, they live in entangled worlds of ludic architectures, coding the behavior of particles and of the detector in the C++ language. Physicists are 'utopianists' *avant la lettre*. Even the nerdy joke culture that one can observe in everyday talk and self-fashioning, fits into the utopian and ludic tradition of this digital scientific tribe. Work, when creative and experimental, turns out to be playful.

---

19 Dippel, Anne: "Das Big Data Game. Zur spielerischen Konstitution kollaborativer Wissensproduktion in der Hochenergiephysik am CERN," *NTM* 4 (2017), pp. 485-517.

20 See Benjamin, Walter: *Das Passagen-Werk. Gesammelte Schriften Band V*, Frankfurt a.M.: Suhrkamp 1982; English: Benjamin, Walter/Tiedemann, Rolf (eds.): *The Arcades Project*, New York: Belknap Press, p. 361; see also M.B. Hansen: "Roomfor-Play," p. 20.

ALGORITHMIC PLAYSPACES

The question whether digital games can be conceptualized as spaces of utopia not only rests upon their technologically confined complexity but depends on how utopia itself is defined. Ernst Bloch, for instance, sees utopia as a program, a vision of a new society or an impulse referring to action.[21] Media theorist Alexander R. Galloway expands on Bloch in "Warcraft and Utopia."[22] His is an argument for the impossibility of digital ludic utopias as written in code:

"[...] virtual worlds are always in some basic way the expression of utopian desire, and in doing so they present the very impossibility of imagining utopia; this is not simply a kneejerk ontological paradox, that code utopias, being immaterial, formal, and virtual, are by definition not 'real,' but that the very act of creating an immaterial utopian space at the same time inscribes a whole vocabulary of algorithmic coding into the plane of imagination that thereby undoes the play of utopia in the first place."[23]

Not all voices in games criticism are as uniformly dystopian. Michał Kłosiński, for instance, questions Galloway by pointing to his algorithmic determinism, which renders the discussion about the possibility of utopias within the digital world futile in the first place. Nevertheless, as he argues, what digital games are capable of—despite their code-related infrastructural confinement—is a utopian satire, that is a "non-existent society described in considerable detail and normally located in time and space that the producer/developer intended a contemporaneous player to view as a criticism of that contemporary society."[24] Such a conceptualization of "ludopias" requires a different theoretical framework to that of Bloch's or Galloway's. To argue for the possibility of utopias in games, Kłosiński leans on Ruth Levitas' utopian architecture and juxtaposes it against the concept of the magic

---

21 Bloch, Ernst: *The Principle of Hope*, Cambridge, Mass.: MIT Press 1995 [1954].
22 Galloway, Alexander: "Warcraft and Utopia," *Ctheory* 2/16 (2006); https://journals.uvic.ca/index.php/ctheory/article/view/14501/5342
23 Ibid. p. 6.
24 Kłosiński, Michał: "Games and Utopia", *Acta Ludologica* 1/1 (2018), pp. 4-14, here p. 8.

circle, which "delimits a space for thinking about rebuilding the world and reorganizing the social institutions that function within this world."[25]

EVERY DAY THE SAME DREAM (2009) by the game collective LaMolleindustria is a very illustrative example of how ludopian visions may be achieved in digital games. The developers identify themselves as creators of "radical games against the tyranny of entertainment." In game design, they see a potential for carving out spaces for social criticism; Benjaminian 'sites of conflict' we could argue. Their games take a variety of critical topics on board, such as: terrorism, petroleum industry, the Anthropocene or alienating modes of work. All their games deal with critical topics, going beyond the representational or visual layer, instead of using the game's procedurality[26]—the ability to execute a series of encoded rules—to lay bare the workings of the criticized system. By playing through conflicts and problems of the current global condition, the player becomes aware of these. They might even come up with daring concepts to solve them. In this sense, LaMolleindustria is not only exemplifying a Benjaminian aesthetics but putting procedural rhetorics[27] into ludic practice. I do not want to delve deeper into Bogost's concept here, but its relevance in envisioning ludopias should not be downplayed. The capacity of games to develop a persuasive argument on the level of their procedurality serves as a counterargument to Galloway's impossibility of utopias in encoded systems. So, let's see how it is done in EVERY DAY THE SAME DREAM.[28]

The player's goal is to find a solution to escape the everyday grey monotonous work life pattern by solving riddles. They take on the role of an 'Everyman' whose life is an illustration and an allegory of capitalist working conditions. Once the alarm kicks off, they are out of bed, showering, dressing and passing their wife wordlessly. Everyday fresh coffee is served in the kitchen before the character embarks on his usual journey to work. They are

---

25 Ibid. p. 11; Levitas, Ruth: *Utopia as Method. The Imaginary Reconstitution of Society*, London: Palgrave Macmillan 2013.

26 Murray, Janet H.: *Hamlet on the Holodeck. The Future of Narrative in Cyberspace*, Cambridge, Mass.: MIT Press 1997.

27 Bogost, Ian: *Persuasive Games. The Expressive Power of Video Games*, Cambridge, Mass.: MIT Press 2007.

28 The game seems to be inspired by Hariton Pushwagner's famous graphic novel *Soft City* (2008).

driving a vehicle, accompanying swarms of other vehicles, all moving lethargically and half-autonomously from left to right. Finally, they reach their workspace, look for the cubicle amongst other cubicles, just to make it to the end of the working day (or play session), take the same route back home, and wake up to fresh coffee the next morning. The cycle repeats like a mantra in every level, with tiny variations built in, creating a space of possibility to play oneself out of the black and white automated reality. The player needs to watch out for colorful objects in the otherwise grey game in order to accept the invitation to subvert the usual order of things. Seeing beyond the usual game may amount to noticing a leaf on a tree or accompanying a homeless person, usually ignored in the heat of the routine.

EVERY DAY THE SAME DREAM is a playful invitation to reflect work in industrialized and automated times. It urges to ask how social and algorithmic architectures in the capitalist everyday interfere with each other by merging game worlds and the actual lives of those who play these worlds. The game's narrative, although lulling the player to sleep, is compelling as it relies on the repetition of gaming actions, which perfectly mimic the dullness of alienating working conditions. Computer games as procedural machines are a particularly fitting form to criticize the execution of automatic rules. This is where the rigid logic of code transforms into a powerful argument. If an image is worth a thousand words, then a procedure may be worth a thousand moving images. Within a game, a complex idea is not only portrayed but also performed or played out in a complex system of relations.

If we follow Marx in locating utopia as a space of possibility that is planted in the seeds of presence, then utopian particles are to be traced in the here and now. According to this logic, what needs to be changed must be detectable at the moment. Utopia is no Phoenix mysteriously from the ashes, where new society concepts are to be found. Utopias are then not so much living in imagined science fiction spaces but partially existing in present conditions. Games may provide for hopeful tools to simulate utopias emerging from current states (compare to the concept of *emergent gameplay*). Satirical procedural utopias such as EVERY DAY THE SAME DREAM might serve as powerful catalysts to reflect and rethink ethical, aesthetic, and economic societal values. Digital games are more than a medium; they may be seen as architecture, bureaucracy, experience, objects of affect and emotion; even as works of art.

LUDOPIAN VISIONS AT WORK AND PLAY

The relation between work and digital play has been very well studied in the last two decades. It has taken many shapes, emerging from such concepts as playbour, gamification or workification.[29] In the design world, games have been announced as tools for change, deployed to solve the world's biggest challenges.[30] There are gloomier approaches as well, which envision games as "factories of the future."[31] If we look at most current commercial digital games, we could identify in them five definitions of modern work as analyzed by Marie Jahoda:[32]

---

29 Kücklich, Julian: "Precarious Playbour: Modders and the Digital Games Industry", *fibreculture* (2006); http://journal.fibreculture.org/issue5/kucklich_print.html; Rey, PJ: "Gamification and Post-fordist Capitalism", in: Deterding, Sebastian/Walz, Steffen P. (eds.), *The Gameful World: Approaches, Issues, Applications*, Cambridge, Mass.: MIT Press 2014, pp. 277-296; Dippel, Anne: "Arbeit", in: Rautzenberg, Markus et al. (eds.), *Philosophie des Computerspiels*, Stuttgart: Metzler Verlag 2018, pp. 123-148; Dippel, Anne/Fizek, Sonia: "Ludification of Culture. The Significance of Play and Games in Everyday Practices of the Digital Era," in: Koch, Gertraud (ed.), *Digitalisation. Theories and Concepts for the Empirical Cultural Research*, London: Routledge 2017, pp. 276-292; Dippel, Anne/Fizek, Sonia: "Laborious Playgrounds: Citizen Science Games as New Modes of Work/play in the Digital Age," in: René Glas et al. (eds.), *The Playful Citizen: Civic Engagement in a Mediatized Culture*, Amsterdam: Amsterdam University Press 2018, pp. 255-271; Rauch, Eron: "Workification. Warum sich Spiele manchmal wie Arbeit anfühlen – und was wir dagegen tun können", *WASD* 12 (2017); https://wasd-magazin.de/wasd-12/leseprobewarum-sich-spielemanch mal-mit-arbeit-anfuehlen-und-was-wir-dagegen-tun-koennen/; Zichermann, Gabe/Linder, Joselin: *The Gamification Revolution: How Leaders Leverage Game Mechanics to Crush the Competition*, New York: McGraw Hill 2012.

30 McGonigal, Jane: *Reality is Broken. Why Games Make Us Better and How They Can Change the World*, New York: Penguin Books 2011.

31 Fizek, Sonia: "All work and no play: Sind Computerspiele die Fabriken der Zukunft?" *TUMULT* 3 (2015), pp. 89-93.

32 Bleckmann, Paula et al.: "Der virtuelle Geist des Kapitalismus oder: warum exzessives Computerspielverhalten Arbeit ist," *Zeitschrift für Qualitative Forschung* 113, 1-2 (2012), pp. 235-261.

1. Imposition of a rigid time structure
2. Extension of range of social experiences into areas that are less emotionally charged than family life
3. Participation in collective goals or efforts
4. Allocation of status and identity through occupation
5. Requested regular activity[33]

Is there any place for ludopian spaces in games seen from such an angle? Or are we to accept computer games as machines reproducing neoliberal concepts, be it in their production process or play patterns?

I would like to end with a more optimistic vision, arguing for the possibility of ludic utopias. As Benjamin's writings illustrate, utopias are dependent on the 'ur-phenomenon' of play. In other words, each utopia carries in itself an aspect of play. The argument can also be reversed, so that games and play are seen as spaces for emerging utopias. It should come as no surprise then that the medium of computer games has the capacity to allow its players to, e.g. critically rethink the capitalist values by experiencing them in a whole new dimension.

In his analysis conducted in the 1930s, Benjamin shows how via mass production art loses its aura, uniqueness, and connection to any tradition. At first glance, a similar parallel could be drawn to video games. Players from all over the world, whether in Japan, India, or Europe, can participate in the ubiquitous gaming experience. However, those experiences of immersion (sometimes a collective one) bring about unique spaces and conjure up entire social worlds. Video games seem to be re-introducing the aura, re-attaching "the technique of reproduction to the reproduced object and to the domain of tradition."[34] We can go even one interpretive step further and see the utopian impulse of video games in the aura of the collective and yet individualistic experience. The spaces where gaming takes place—home, street, work—turn each moment into a unique gameplay session as opposed to the aesthetic dispositive of mainstream cinema, which tries to recreate a similar ambiance in every movie theatre regardless of its location.

---

33 Jahoda, Marie: *Wieviel Arbeit braucht der Mensch? Arbeit und Arbeitslosigkeit im 20. Jahrhundert*, Basel: Weinheim 1983, p. 99.
34 W. Benjamin: "The Work of Art in the Age of Its Technological Reproducibility," p. 4.

The aura of games shared like a magic performative object rather than mechanically copied may contribute to the idea of societal change since it creates collectivity and allows to experience utopian worlds as a commonality. The level of creativity in games is opening up new horizons. Games are a chance to understand society by their repetitive nature; doing a thing over and over again until we master even the most frightening fundamental experiences. This may result in a deeper understanding of society and create a chance to deal consciously with its conflicts, without having to live through the same moment all over again (EVERY DAY THE SAME DREAM). In a Benjaminian sense, the repetitiveness of games may help the players to put the experience into a story to be mastered, and not repeated yet again, because we've already played through it. Such a realization may take many repetitions, also virtual ones.

Playing, according to Benjamin, asks for: mastery of elementary social skills as a precondition for playing with natural forces. Just as the child who is learning to grasp stretches out his hand for the moon as it would for a ball, so humanity, in its efforts at innervation, sets its sights as much on presently still utopian goals as on goals within reach.[35]

Cultural scientist Miriam Bratu Hansen expands on Benjamin, explaining that the act of grasping utopias is a playful one. It may be observed in film, which Hansen refers to as "second technology."[36] Within such technologies, we observe: "the unfolding of work in play."[37] They "function not unlike the moon for which the child reaches while it learns to grasp."[38] Miscognition, according to Hansen, is a creative process. In games, which could be considered a third technology, due to their interactive character, players constantly keep misrecognizing the world in creative ways.

The old modes of production may be still reflected in the way many games 'work,' and old 'traditions' may still be at work in many video games. But new worlds, envisioning other ideas of society, are in the making. Think of the rich global avant-garde and independent game design scene, growing with each year. A hopeful example for the conclusion is the LITTLE BROTHER

---

[35] Ibid. p. 360; see also M.B. Hansen: "Room-for-Play," p. 19.
[36] Ibid, p. 20
[37] W. Benjamin: "The Work of Art in the Age of Its Technological Reproducibility," p. 361.
[38] M.B. Hansen: "Room-for-Play," p. 20.

2984 (2017), a game in which different tribes and nations celebrate an ethnic concept of community, humans are decentered, and since they are coming to another planet, they themselves are the aliens (not the colonizers). Games like LITTLE BROTHER 2984 and EVERY DAY THE SAME DREAM are spaces to rethink the society. They are not a refuge but a remedy. They serve as a 'pharmakon' to neutralize the effects of technology and social normativity.[39]

With Benjamin, computer games may be seen as spaces of friction between fun and frustration. In such an understanding, games turn away from a representational concept of art and become reflective spaces, as theatre for Bertolt Brecht or film for Harun Farocki. This shift from a representational aesthetic to a reflective one opens a gate to possible worlds and utopias. To think reflectively is to change existing conditions, with an awareness of the most prevalent societal conflicts.

LITERATURE

Benjamin, Walter: "The Work of Art in the Age of Its Technological Reproducibility: Second Version," in: Jennings, Michael W./Eiland, Howard (eds.), *Selected Writings 3: 1935-1938*, Harvard: Harvard University Press 2006, pp. 101-133.

Benjamin, Walter: "Das Kunstwerk im Zeitalter seiner technischen Reproduzierbarkeit," in: *Walter Benjamin, Werke und Nachlaß. Kritische Gesamtausgabe,* Band 16, Berlin: Suhrkamp 2013 [1936].

Benjamin, Walter: "Spielzeug und Spielen," in: Adorno, Theodor W. et al. (eds.), *Gesammelte Schriften, Band 2*, Frankfurt a.M.: Suhrkamp 1991 [1928], pp. 127-131.

Benjamin Walter: "Toys and Play: Marginal Notes on a Monumental Work," in: *Selected Writings 2, Vol 1: 1927-1930*, Harvard: Harvard University Press 1999, pp. 117-121.

Benjamin, Walter/Tiedemann, Rolf (eds.): *The Arcades Project*, New York: Belknap Press.

---

39 Derrida, Jacques: "Plato's Pharmacy," in: *Dissemination*, Chicago: University of Chicago Press 1981, pp. 63-171; Stiegler, Bernard: *What Makes Life Worth Living: On Pharmacology*, Cambridge: Polity Press 2010.

Benjamin, Walter: *Das Passagen-Werk. Gesammelte Schriften Band V*, Frankfurt a.M.: Suhrkamp 1982.

Bloch, Ernst: *The Principle of Hope*, Cambridge, Mass.: MIT Press 1995 [1954].

Bleckmann, Paula et al.: "Der virtuelle Geist des Kapitalismus oder: warum exzessives Computerspielverhalten Arbeit ist," *Zeitschrift für Qualitative Forschung* 113, 1-2 (2012), pp. 235-261.

Bogost, Ian: *Persuasive Games. The Expressive Power of Video Games*, Cambridge, Mass.: MIT Press 2007.

Derrida, Jacques: "Plato's Pharmacy," in: *Dissemination*, Chicago: University of Chicago Press 1981, pp. 63-171.

Dippel, Anne: "Das Big Data Game. Zur spielerischen Konstitution kollaborativer Wissensproduktion in der Hochenergiephysik am CERN," *NTM* 4 (2017), pp. 485-517.

Dippel, Anne: "Arbeit," in: Rautzenberg, Markus et al. (eds.), *Philosophie des Computerspiels*, Stuttgart: Metzler Verlag 2018, pp. 123-148.

Dippel, Anne/Fizek, Sonia: "Ludification of Culture. The Significance of Play and Games in Everyday Practices of the Digital Era," in: Koch, Gertraud (ed.), *Digitalisation. Theories and Concepts for the Empirical Cultural Research*, London: Routledge 2017, pp. 276-292.

Dippel, Anne/Fizek, Sonia: "Laborious Playgrounds: Citizen Science Games as New Modes of Work/Play in the Digital Age," in: Glas, René et al. (eds.), *The Playful Citizen: Civic Engagement in a Mediatized Culture*, Amsterdam: Amsterdam University Press 2018, pp. 255-271.

Engemann, Christoph/Sudmann, Andreas (eds.): *Machine Learning – Medien, Infrastrukturen und Technologien der künstlichen Intelligenz*, Bielefeld: transcript 2018.

Fizek, Sonia: "All work and no play: Sind Computerspiele die Fabriken der Zukunft?" *TUMULT* 3 (2015), pp. 89-93.

Galloway, Alexander: *Protocol. How Control Exists after Decentralization*, Cambridge, Mass.: MIT Press 2006.

Galloway, Alexander: "Warcraft and Utopia," *Ctheory* 2/16 (2006); https://journals.uvic.ca/index.php/ctheory/article/view/14501/5342

Hansen, Miriam Bratu: "Room-for-Play. Benjamin's Gamble with Cinema," *October* 109 (2004), pp. 3-45.

Haraway, Donna J.: *Modest_Witness@Second_Millennium. FemaleMan_ Meets_OncoMouse: Feminism and Technoscience*, New York: Routledge 1997.

Jahoda, Marie: *Wieviel Arbeit braucht der Mensch? Arbeit und Arbeitslosigkeit im 20. Jahrhundert*, Basel: Weinheim 1983.

Kant, Immanuel: *Kritik der reinen Vernunft*, Frankfurt a.M.: Suhrkamp 1974 [1781].

Kittler, Friedrich A.: *Grammophon, Film, Typewriter*, München: Fink 1986.

Kłosiński, Michał: "Games and Utopia", *Acta Ludologica* 1/1 (2018), pp. 4-14.

Kücklich, Julian: "Precarious Playbour: Modders and the Digital Games Industry", *fibreculture* (2006); http://journal.fibreculture.org/issue5/kucklich_print.html

Levitas, Ruth: *Utopia as Method. The Imaginary Reconstitution of Society*, London: Palgrave Macmillan 2013.

Malaby, Thomas M.: "Anthropology and Play: The Contours of Playful Experience," *New Literary History* 40/1 (2009), pp. 205-218.

McGonigal, Jane: *Reality is Broken. Why Games Make Us Better and How They Can Change the World*, New York: Penguin Books 2011.

Murray, Janet H.: *Hamlet on the Holodeck. The Future of Narrative in Cyberspace*, Cambridge, Mass.: MIT Press 1997.

Pushwagner, Hariton: *Soft City*, New York: New York Review Comics 2008.

Rauch, Eron: "Workification. Warum sich Spiele manchmal wie Arbeit anfühlen – und was wir dagegen tun können," *WASD*, 12 (2017); https://wasd-magazin.de/wasd-12/leseprobewarum-sich-spiele-manchmal-mit-arbeit-anfuehlen-und-was-wir-dagegen-tun-koennen/

Rey, PJ: "Gamification and Post-fordist Capitalism", in: Deterding, Sebastian/Walz, Steffen P. (eds.), *The Gameful World: Approaches, Issues, Applications*, Cambridge, Mass.: MIT Press 2014, pp. 277-296.

Schiller, Friedrich: *Über die ästhetische Erziehung des Menschen in einer Reihe von Briefen*, München 1963.

Seaver, Nick: "What Should an Anthropology of Algorithms Do?" *Cultural Anthropology* 33/3 (2018), pp. 375-385.

Stevens, Philipp: "Play and Work: A False Dichotomy?" in: Schwartzmann, Helen B. (eds.): *Play and Culture*, New York: Westpoint 1980, pp. 316-323.

Stiegler, Bernard: *What Makes Life Worth Living: On Pharmacology*, Cambridge: Polity Press 2010.
Sudmann, Andreas (eds.): *The Democratization of Artificial Intelligence*, Bielefeld: transcript 2019.
Zagal, José P.: Ludoliteracy: *Defining, Understanding, and Supporting Games Education*, Halifax: ETC Press 2010.
Zichermann, Gabe/Linder, Joselin: *The Gamification Revolution: How Leaders Leverage Game Mechanics to Crush the Competition*, New York: McGraw Hill 2012.
Zimmerman, Eric: "Manifesto for a Ludic Century," in: Deterding, Sebastian/Walz, Steffen P. (eds.), *The Gameful World: Approaches, Issues, Applications*, Cambridge, Mass.: MIT Press 2014, pp. 19-22.

Gamography

Every day the Same Dream (LaMolleindustria 2009, O: LaMolleindustria)
Little Brother 2984 (Yang Myung-jin 2017, O: Yang Myung-jin)

Playful Utopias

Sandboxes for the Future

HARTMUT KOENITZ

SIMULATION AND (SAFE) FAILURE

Video games have been described as the *Art of Simulation*[1] and the *Art of Failure*.[2] These descriptions are not exclusive. Together, they illustrate functions which distinguish video games from other mediated forms. Games allow us to simulate complex situations and experiment with it, to play 'as if' and try out different strategies. A crucial element of this playful process is that we can fail without danger, in a safe space. These characteristics make video games especially valuable in in the light of the many challenges societies are facing in the 21st century, from the refugee crisis to global warming.

Indeed, the potential for video games as tools to represent and understand serious topics has long been a subject of discussion, with Ian Bogost's coinage of "persuasive games"[3] and his investigation of a specific procedural rhetoric being an important milestone. This line of research and game design practice has mostly focused on awareness and change, on drawing attention

---

1   Aarseth, Espen J.: "Genre Trouble. Narrativism and the Art of Simulation," in: Wardrip-Fruin, Noah/Harrigan, Pat (eds.), *First Person: New Media as Story, Performance, and Game*, Cambridge, Mass.: MIT Press 2004, pp. 45-55.
2   Juul, Jesper: *The Art of Failure*, Cambridge, Mass.: MIT Press 2012.
3   Bogost, Ian: *Persuasive Games: The Expressive Power of Videogames*, Cambridge, Mass.: MIT Press 2007.

to societal issues and how existing situations might be altered, for example in terms of improving civic engagement.[4] These are important functions, yet games can also be oriented towards the future. In particular, they can take the role of 'sandboxes' in which we can build what we can describe as utopias—considerable improvements over the current situation—and test them before they can fail in the real world.

To illustrate this point, I will now consider the complexity of societal challenges and then turn to games and critically reflect on their ability to address societal challenges. Next, I will introduce strategies for improving the impact of such works. Finally, I will frame some serious games as a stepping stones towards more utopian games and then consider scenarios for sandboxes for the future.

SOCIETAL CHALLENGES

What are the challenges, we might be able to address with games? When we look around in this moment in history, we might concede that we live in an era of uncertainty. The effects of a rise in populism in Western democracies, of climate change, and of a worldwide migration movement will continue to challenge established ways of how we have organized our societies, economies and outside relations. The question is no longer whether change will come, but what kind of change it will be and what level of control and what kind of instruments we still have to organize the transition. And in a sense, we should not be surprised about this development—there have been plenty of warnings, from the worldwide grassroots environmental protection movements starting in the 1960s to the high-level association of the Club of Rome and its warnings about the limits of economic growth in 1972.[5] Indeed, already 40 years ago, in 1979, Jean-Francois Lyotard described the postmodern

---

4   Kahne, Joseph et al.: *The Civic Potential of Video Games*, Cambridge, Mass.: MIT Press 2009; Neys, Joyce/Jeroen, Jansz: "Engagement in Play, Engagement in Politics: Playing Political Video Games," in: Glas, René et al. (eds.), *The Playful Citizen. Civic Engagement in a Mediatized Culture*, Amsterdam: Amsterdam University Press 2018, pp. 36-55.

5   Meadows, Dennis L. et al.: *The Limits to Growth*, New York: Universe Books 1972.

condition we live under as the end of "Grand Narratives,"[6] the loss of coherence and certainty provided by uncontested institutions (the state, the churches, national histories) and their associated majority narratives. Lyotard's diagnosis in 1979 was groundbreaking and visionary—however, the full effect of the issues he diagnoses only become visible now, as we experience how many certainties seem to be slipping away on an almost daily basis.

Yet, the postmodern condition is not simply a dystopia, it is also a description of plentitude[7] and resilience. Donald Trump does not speak for the USA anymore in the same way John F. Kennedy might still have been able to in the 1960s. This is evident for example in Trump's announcement to leave the Paris climate accord, which was quickly followed by numerous counter-announcements by local and state governments in the US, pledging their continued adherence to the agreement. This example does not only show the diversity of political perspectives in the US, it is also a testimony to the fact that even the head of government of the supposedly most powerful country in the world no longer commands the power to prevent dissenting voices from being heard and broadcast worldwide.

THE COMPLEXITY OF ISSUES

The disappearance of simple grand narratives also has to do with our growing awareness of the complexity of many issues. What is actually better for the environment? Many times, the answer is not obvious and we cannot be sure. Is eating meat worse than driving a car? Giving the environmental impact of the meat industry, we can imagine that a vegetarian sports car driver might have less impact on the environment than their bicycling, meat-eating neighbor. Yet, what about if we only eat organically produced meat? How does that change the impact on the environment and our example of the sports car driver and the now organic meat-eating bicycling neighbor? The answer certainly is complicated and might depend on many factors—What kind of sports car? What distance is the car driven? At what speed? What amount of

---

6   Original 1979 in French, first English translation: Lyotard, Jean-François: *The Postmodern Condition*, Minneapolis: University of Minnesota Press 1984.
7   Bolter, Jay David: *The Digital Plenitude*, Cambridge, Mass.: MIT Press 2019.

meat does the neighbor eat? Which kind of meat? How does the neighbor get the meat? Is it delivered to their house or picked up at a local store?

Even if we would be able to quantify this comparison and find a clear answer, what would that actually tell us about the total environmental impact of these two imaginary people? What have we been missing? And—maybe most importantly—if we are either of these people, what is the most impactful change we can make?

A recent report by a team at Carnegie Mellon University serves as a concrete example in regards to the real-world complexity of the use of seemingly environmentally-friendly technologies by pointing out that even the time of day used for charging an electrical vehicle can have considerable impact on the overall emissions, as night-time power in some US states is produced exclusively by coal-firing electricity plants.[8] Another report[9] concludes that given the differences in the available energy mix in different US states, an electrical car might be best for the environment in states with predominantly sustainable energy production, but in other areas, a hybrid car would produce lower emissions, with its mix of battery-powered operation for short distances and a gas-powered engine for longer distances. In fact, the report warns of the negative effects of electrification without changes to power generation:

"Driving an electric car in China, where coal is by far the largest power plant fuel, is a catastrophe for climate change. And if the coal plant lacks pollution controls—or fails to turn them on—it can amplify the extent of smog, acid rain, lung-damaging microscopic soot and other ills that arise from burning fossil fuels. The same is true in other major coal-burning countries, such as Australia, India and South Africa."[10]

The longer-term implications of these reports are quite clear—worldwide power generation needs to move to sustainable, renewable energy. However,

---

8 Weis, Allison et al.: "Emissions and Cost Implications of Controlled Electric Vehicle Charging in the U.S. PJM Interconnection," *Environ. Sci. Technol.* 49/9 (2015), pp. 5813-5819.

9 Biello, David: "Why Charging an Electric Car at Night Is Worse for the Environment," *PBS*, May 12, 2016; https://www.pbs.org/newshour/science/why-charging-an-electric-car-at-night-is-worse-for-the-environment

10 Ibid.

the difficulty is in the complexity for individual decisions in the more immediate future.

What I am trying to show with my discussion connecting mobility and diet is that in order to understand the actual environmental impact of a particular human existence we need to account for many, often interrelated factors. Attempting to do so as an individual can appear to be an insurmountable challenge, even if reliable data is available and accessible. This is where games come into the picture. Computer games as simulations can provide an interface to large collections of data and provide playful ways to interact with them. Sim-type games like SIM CITY (1989) and THE SIMS (2000) are examples that show the potential of this approach, although they do not qualify as representations of the real world since they are using proprietary, undisclosed and most likely vastly simplified data models.

For the games I am envisioning here, the underlying data models would have to be carefully selected and ideally independently verified, for example by a board of scientists.

Provided this verification step is implemented, we can potentially benefit from using games to explore complex topics such as the individual environmental impact in three strategic manners: first, by 'packaging' serious topics in a way that is accessible and not overwhelming, second, by raising awareness for the complexity of many issues surrounding us and third, by allowing players to experiment with decisions based on complex underlying relations and rules.

REALITY CHECK

While these strategies might seem convincing in general, a reality check is necessary in order to understand the actual impact of serious games. Recently, van 't Riet et al.[11] reminded us that the effectiveness of serious games has rarely been verified, pointing to a similar judgment nearly a decade

---

11 van 't Riet, Jonathan et al.: "Investigating the Effects of a Persuasive Digital Game on Immersion, Identification, and Willingness to Help," *Basic and Applied Social Psychology* 40/4 (2018), pp. 180-194.

earlier[12] and little progress since. Unfortunately, the results of their study of AGAINST ALL ODDS (2005)—a game designed to increase empathy for refugees—is a clear warning in this regard as it shows no advantage over traditional forms of storytelling in creating empathy: "The results of the present research serve as a warning that, notwithstanding their theoretical merit, not every persuasive game will be more persuasive than traditional, noninteractive media."[13]

This finding parallels the somber atmosphere at the 2017 "Persuasive Gaming in Context" conference,[14] where both Ian Bogost and Miguel Sicart pointed out the limited success of persuasive games and instead emphasized the potential of play as an activity.

The underlying question here is whether the potential of serious games was overstated or whether the actual challenge is in understanding the potential better in terms of possible effects on the audience, in terms of conceptual framing, and in regards to concrete design approaches. For example, in discussing their own findings van 't Riet et al. point to the results obtained by a different study[15] that showed no effect of a serious game directly after the experience, but a significant one three weeks later. More work is certainly necessary to understand if this finding of a more long-term effect is only a particular occurrence or more common. Equally, conceptual framing, and concrete design approaches in serious games require continued attention.

STRATEGIES FOR IMPROVEMENT

Joost Raessens, investigating ecologically-themed games, argues that while many existing games have focused on raising awareness by presenting scientific facts, most have failed to provide a positive perspective on how to

---

12 Peng, Wei et al.: "The Effects of a Serious Game on Role-Taking and Willingness to Help," *Journal of Communication* 60/4 (2010), pp. 723-742.
13 van 't Riet, Jonathan et al.: "Investigating the Effects of a Persuasive Digital Game," p. 192.
14 http://persuasivegaming.nl/persuasive-gaming-conference/
15 Ruggiero, Dana: "Spent: Changing Students' Affective Learning Toward Homelessness Through Persuasive Video Game Play," *CHI 2014*, New York: ACM 2014, pp. 3423-3432.

address the situation: "strategies other than presenting 'facts only' might indeed convince people to change their behavior regarding ecological issues."[16] Raessens presents a three-part strategy to address this challenge, based on the framework of Per Espen Stoknes.[17] Concretely, Raessens proposes the following:

1. emphasize closeness/relatedness of a global issue to a particular player
2. provide a hopeful perspective and frame a difficult topic as a positive opportunity and finally
3. make the topic compatible with the existing value system of the player

Raessens sees these strategies as being realized in the online experience COLLAPSUS (2010) a production by Dutch company Submarine Channel, applying what Raessens deems to be a mixture of elements from games, documentaries, and storytelling techniques. This description puts the categorization of the work as 'game' in doubt, and Raessens himself is careful to classify the work as an "interactive experience" and remarks that the work is "usually presented as a game."[18]

Given the connection to documentary practices and storytelling, COLLAPSUS is more in line with descriptions of interactive digital narratives (IDN),[19] a cross-cutting perspective that explicitly combines several of the elements described by Raessens, expressed for instance by Roth and me previously: "IDN is an umbrella term that encompasses a range of manifestations, including video games, interactive documentaries, installation pieces,

---

16 Raessens, Joost: "Collapsus, or How to Make Players Become Ecological Citizens," in: Glas, René et al. (eds.), *The Playful Citizen. Civic Engagement in a Mediatized Culture*, Amsterdam: Amsterdam University Press 2018, pp. 92-120, here p. 94.
17 Stoknes, Per E.: *What We Think About When We Try Not to Think About Global Warming*, Chelsea: Green Publishing 2015.
18 J. Raessens: "Collapsus," p. 94.
19 Koenitz, Hartmut et al.: *Interactive Digital Narrative: History, Theory, and Practice*, New York: Routledge 2015.

and AR/VR experiences."[20] Perspectives investigating IDN[21] can thus provide a backdrop to analyze such a work and the considerations that inform its design. I am making this point not for categorial reasons but to emphasize the specific status of COLLAPSUS and its apparent success in attaining its goals in contrast to the issues with serious games reported in the preceding section. In other words: the strategies described by Raessens are successfully implemented in COLLAPSUS with the help of specifically narrative approaches.

TOWARDS UTOPIAN SANDBOXES

Addressing societal issues with interactive works is not only a question of specific design strategies, but also one of topic and perspective. A specific advantage of video games and interactive digital narratives is that they are not bound by the restrictions of the real world, yet can simulate probable scenarios with great detail. Many serious video games have focused on dystopian perspectives and concrete problems, to educate its audiences about

---

20 Roth, Christian/Koenitz, Hartmut: "Towards Creating a Body of Evidence-based Interactive Digital Narrative Design Knowledge: Approaches and Challenges," *AltMM 17. Proceedings of the 2nd International Workshop on Multimedia Alternate Realities*, New York: ACM 2017, pp. 19-24, here p. 19.

21 Murray, Janet H.: *Hamlet on the Holodeck: The Future of Narrative in Cyberspace*, New York: Free Press 1997; Louchart, Sandy/Aylett, Ruth: "Narrative Theory and Emergent Interactive Narrative," *International Journal of Continuing Engineering Education and Life Long Learning* 14/6 (2004), pp. 506-518; Mitchell, Alex/McGee, Kevin: "Reading Again for the First Time: A Model of Rereading in Interactive Stories," in: Oyarzun, David et al. (eds.), *Interactive Storytelling: 5th International Conference, ICIDS 2012, Proceedings*, Berlin/Heidelberg: Springer 2012, pp. 202-213; Koenitz, Hartmut et al.: "Interactive Narrative Design Beyond the Secret Art Status: A Method to Verify Design Conventions for Interactive Narrative," *Materialities of Literature* 6/1 (2018), pp. 107-119; Eladhari, Mirjam P.: "Re-Tellings: The Fourth Layer of Narrative as an Instrument for Critique," in: Rouse, Rebecca et al. (eds.), *Interactive Storytelling—11th International Conference on Interactive Digital Storytelling, ICIDS 2018, Proceedings*, Berlin/Heidelberg: Springer 2018, pp. 65-78.

inequality (AYITI: THE COST OF LIFE, 2006), consumerism (MCDONALD'S VIDEO GAME, 2006), oppression (PAPERS, PLEASE, 2013), and depression (DEPRESSION QUEST, 2013). Yet, there are also games that give us a kind of utopia, a 'blank slate' to experiment and literally 'play with', that allow us to make a string of decisions and see the results of our actions. Many society-building games fall in this category, from BLACK AND WHITE (2001), to CIVILIZATION (1991), but also simulation games like THE SIMS, STARDEW VALLEY (2016) and specialized titles like FARMING SIMULATOR (2008).

I propose to expand this strategy further and consider games as vessels for utopias, as playful explorations for *trying out what could be*, instead of *changing what is*. We need not only tools to help with current problems, but also to consider a future worth working towards. Indeed, this is a perspective recently proposed in regards to social media by Susana Tosca, in a call to "open up for a utopian picture, in which users are invited to formulate their own visions."[22] Tosca is inspired in her approach by Ruth Levitas' book *Utopia as Method. The Imaginary Reconstitution of Society*,[23] who positions utopias as an instrument to imagine future societies. Levitas identifies three ways in which utopias work as a method: archeological (identifying the positive roots and images embedded in a society), ontological (what behaviors and traits are encouraged and rewarded or oppressed) and architectural (imaginations of possible future scenarios). The latter mode is particularly relevant for the present discussion and Levitas' description is therefore reproduced here in full: "The third [aspect] is an architectural mode—that is, the imagination of potential alternative scenarios for the future acknowledging the assumptions about and consequences for the people who might inhabit them."[24]

This is the place for games, as architectural utopias, as means to consider how we might want to live in the future, taking into account what we know about the limits of economic growth, available resources, climate change, environmental impact and worldwide migration. I understand 'utopias' here not in a purely positivistic manner, but as playgrounds that also allow for failure. Provided that, by focusing on the future in utopian games, instead of

---

22 Tosca, Susana: "Utopian Social Media," *Digital Creativity* 30/2 (2019), pp. 93-106, here p. 93.
23 Levitas, Ruth: *Utopia as Method*, London: Springer 2013.
24 Ibid., p. 153.

the present and the past, we can gain a positive vision that can guide our behavior in the years to come.

I like to finish this section by providing three concrete ideas for utopian sandboxes:

1. *Sustainable Civilization*: A game similar to the CIVILIZATION series, but facing the challenges of climate change, increasing population, dwindling resources and an economic model built on ongoing growth. Unlike in Civilization, the winning condition would not be one of dominance or superiority over competitors, but of achieving sustainability understood as an equilibrium that is robust enough to withstand continuous challenges.
2. *No Man's Earth*: A game where the player character is an alien archeological time traveler who finds a devasted planet earth in the future. The player can travel back in time, to our present, and make societal changes before returning to their time and observing the effects of the changes. In the best of circumstances, the player finds that earth's population has evolved and consequently survived.
3. *Balance of Local Power*: This game would allow the player to explore different economic concepts and political structures in a local community evolving for 50 years into the future. This game is less focused on environmental issues and more on what kind of power relations evolve from economic and structural decisions. The game's microcosm could turn into a totalitarian regime or a society based on respect and solidarity.

Conclusion

In this paper, I have considered the complexity of many contemporary societal challenges and how games can help to address them. As there is well-founded doubt regarding the effectiveness of serious games, I have turned to Raessens' improvement strategies and pointed out a connection with perspectives on interactive digital narratives. Next, I have discussed the ability of interactive digital works to simulate future scenarios and introduced the concept of utopian sandboxes. Finally, I have discussed potential concepts for such utopian sandboxes. Many more such utopian games are possible. It is time that we realize this potential and make use of it. Still today, interactive digital forms are often only seen in contrast to traditional forms: Are games better at creating empathy than a documentary movie? A better question is to ask: What can interactive digital forms do that traditional forms cannot? One answer is to provide us with utopian sandboxes.

LITERATURE

Aarseth, Espen J.: "Genre Trouble. Narrativism and the Art of Simulation," in: Wardrip-Fruin, Noah/Harrigan, Pat (eds.), *First Person: New Media as Story, Performance, and Game*, Cambridge, Mass.: MIT Press 2004, pp. 45-55.

Biello, David: "Why Charging an Electric Car at Night Is Worse for the Environment," *PBS*, May 12, 2016; https://www.pbs.org/newshour/science/why-charging-an-electric-car-at-night-is-worse-for-the-environment

Bogost, Ian: *Persuasive Games: The Expressive Power of Videogames*, Cambridge, Mass.: MIT Press 2007.

Bolter, Jay David: *The Digital Plenitude*, Cambridge, Mass.: MIT Press 2019.

Eladhari, Mirjam P.: "Re-Tellings: The Fourth Layer of Narrative as an Instrument for Critique," in: Rouse, Rebecca et al. (eds.), *Interactive Storytelling—11th International Conference on Interactive Digital Storytelling, ICIDS 2018, Proceedings*, Berlin/Heidelberg: Springer 2018, pp. 65-78.

Juul, Jesper: *The Art of Failure*, Cambridge, Mass.: MIT Press 2012.

Kahne, Joseph et al.: *The Civic Potential of Video Games*, Cambridge, Mass.: MIT Press 2009.

Koenitz, Hartmut et al.: *Interactive Digital Narrative: History, Theory, and Practice*, New York: Routledge 2015.

Koenitz, Hartmut et al.: "Interactive Narrative Design Beyond the Secret Art Status: A Method to Verify Design Conventions for Interactive Narrative," *Materialities of Literature* 6/1 (2018), pp. 107-119.

Levitas, Ruth: *Utopia as Method*, London: Springer 2013.

Louchart, Sandy/Aylett, Ruth: "Narrative Theory and Emergent Interactive Narrative," *International Journal of Continuing Engineering Education and Life Long Learning* 14/6 (2004), pp. 506-518.

Lyotard, Jean-François: *The Postmodern Condition*, Minneapolis: University of Minnesota Press 1984.

Meadows, Dennis L. et al.: *The Limits to Growth*, New York: Universe Books 1972.

Mitchell, Alex/McGee, Kevin: "Reading Again for the First Time: A Model of Rereading in Interactive Stories," in: Oyarzun, David et al. (eds.), *Interactive Storytelling: 5th International Conference, ICIDS 2012, Proceedings*, Berlin/Heidelberg: Springer 2012, pp. 202-213.

Murray, Janet H.: *Hamlet on the Holodeck: The Future of Narrative in Cyberspace*, New York: Free Press 1997.

Neys, Joyce/Jeroen, Jansz: "Engagement in Play, Engagement in Politics: Playing Political Video Games," in: Glas, René et al. (eds.), *The Playful Citizen. Civic Engagement in a Mediatized Culture*, Amsterdam: Amsterdam University Press 2018, pp. 36-55.

Peng, Wei et al.: "The Effects of a Serious Game on Role-Taking and Willingness to Help," *Journal of Communication* 60/4 (2010), pp. 723-742.

Raessens, Joost: "Collapsus, or How to Make Players Become Ecological Citizens," in: Glas, René et al. (eds.), *The Playful Citizen. Civic Engagement in a Mediatized Culture*, Amsterdam: Amsterdam University Press 2018, pp. 92-120.

Roth, Christian/Koenitz, Hartmut: "Towards Creating a Body of Evidence-based Interactive Digital Narrative Design Knowledge: Approaches and Challenges," *AltMM 17. Proceedings of the 2nd International Workshop on Multimedia Alternate Realities*, New York: ACM 2017, pp. 19-24.

Ruggiero, Dana: "Spent: Changing Students' Affective Learning Toward Homelessness Through Persuasive Video Game Play," *CHI 2014*, New York: ACM 2014, pp. 3423-3432.

Stoknes, Per E.: *What We Think About When We Try Not to Think About Global Warming*, Chelsea: Green Publishing 2015.

Tosca, Susana: "Utopian Social Media," *Digital Creativity* 30/2 (2019), pp. 93-106.

van 't Riet, Jonathan et al.: "Investigating the Effects of a Persuasive Digital Game on Immersion, Identification, and Willingness to Help," *Basic and Applied Social Psychology* 40/4 (2018), pp. 180-194.

Weis, Allison et al.: "Emissions and Cost Implications of Controlled Electric Vehicle Charging in the U.S. PJM Interconnection," *Environ. Sci. Technol.* 49/9 (2015), pp. 5813-5819.

Gamography

AGAINST ALL ODDS (UNHCR 2005, O: UNHCR)
AYITI: THE COST OF LIFE (GameLab 2006, O: GameLab)
BLACK AND WHITE (Electronic Arts 2001, O: Lionhead Studio)
CIVILIZATION (MicroProse 1991, O: MicroProse)
COLLAPSUS. ENERGY RISK CONSPIRACY (Tommy Pollatta 2010, O: Tommy Pollatta)
DEPRESSION QUEST (The Quinnspiracy 2013, O: The Quinnspiracy)
FARMING SIMULATOR (Excalibur Publishing 2008, O: Giants Software)
MCDONALD'S VIDEO GAME (La Molleindustria 2006, O: La Molleindustria)
PAPERS, PLEASE (3909 LLC 2013, O: 3909 LLC)
STARDEW VALLEY (ConcernedApe 2016, O: ConcernedApe)
THE SIMS (Electronic Arts 2000, O: Maxis)
SIM CITY (Maxis 1989, O: Maxis)

Building Utopia, Brick by Brick?
Selling Subversiveness in LEGO DIMENSIONS

HANNS CHRISTIAN SCHMIDT

INTRODUCTION:
BUILDING UTOPIAN DISCOURSES AROUND LEGO

According to the Danish toy company Lego, creating your own world is child's play. Equipped with the right amount of plastic bricks and a fair bit of imagination, children should be able to construct their very own spaces of the imagination: places that were literally non-existent before and are therefore 'utopian' (no-places) in the original sense of the word. Furthermore, these worlds can also be considered utopian in the more common and idealistic sense: Through the activity of building with bricks, children participate in a behavior that might be regarded as highly desirable for the 'betterment' of our society. The media scholar David Gauntlett, for example, emphasizes this normative aspect of 'valuable play' when he describes Lego not only as 'a tool for thinking and creativity,' but also as one for nothing less than 'changing the world.' In his paper of the same title, he suggests that

"[1] LEGO building helps people to step into the world of making, and this is a vital shift in terms of a person's sense of self in the world—being a creator, not just a consumer. These small steps are significant [...] and contribute to a necessary shift in our culture towards a greater sense of creative ownership, and engagement with our environment; [2] LEGO play builds the sense in which things can be constructed, deconstructed, reviewed and changed, not simply by thinking about them, but by actually making them and changing them; [3] The LEGO ecosystem [...] includes [and fosters,

HCS] extensive networks of users to learn and to exchange knowledge and inspiration."[1]

Not only do these assumptions sound quite optimistic, but they are also debatable from more critical points of view. One could, for example, consider how franchised Lego sets might 'colonize the imagination'[2] of children with products from the cultural industries[3]—as it is arguably the case with the LEGO STAR WARS or LEGO HARRY POTTER-themes. One could also point towards Lego's presentations of female characters in its FRIENDS-sets and observe how their depiction of girls is used to sell the other Lego themes solely as 'boys' toys' (although there has been a lot of improvement in this regard in the last years).[4] And, finally, if you observe the very act of building itself, this activity is still highly dependent on your private reservoir of bricks and your ability to combine all of its special pieces in a functional way. This is poignantly summarized by Kevin Schut:

"The space-themed LEGO sets I grew up playing with are a little paradoxical. The galaxy beyond our atmosphere lacks any limits, yet this particular plastic toy, with its geometrically perfect rows of bumps, is all about boundaries. The possible configurations of LEGO blocks is nearly infinite—as evidenced by my children cheerfully mixing and matching my thirty-year-old set of pirates knights, and astronauts whenever we visit my parents—but the blocks themselves are rigid and perfect. They can only

---

1   Gauntlett, David: "The LEGO System as a Tool for Thinking, Creativity, and Changing the World," in: Wolf, Mark J.P. (ed.), *LEGO Studies. Examining the Building Blocks of a Transmedial Phenomenon*, Hoboken: Taylor and Francis 2014, pp. 189-205, here p. 11.
2   Eder, Jens: "Transmediale Imagination," in: Hanich, Julian/Wulff, Hans J. (eds.), *Auslassen, Andeuten, Auffüllen: Der Film und die Imagination des Zuschauers*, München: Wilhelm Fink 2012, pp. 207-238, here p. 225.
3   See, for example, Cross, Gary S: *Kid's Stuff: Toys and the Changing World of American Childhood*, Cambridge, Mass.: Harvard University Press 1997.
4   Sarkeesian, Anita: "Lego & Gender Part 1: Lego Friends/Lego & Gender Part 2: The Boys Club," *feministfrequency*, 2012; https://feministfrequency.com/tag/lego-friends

click together in very specific formations. My gray space cruiser, in other words, is a set of unchangeable parts that suggest a universe free of restrictions."[5]

In this sense, the assigned cultural value of Lego has always been part of a larger debate. It revolves around ideologies that are highly critical of today's convergent media industries as well as the educational possibilities of toys in general. Instead of partaking in this debate and claiming a stance towards one position or the other, this contribution aims to show what happens when analog Lego play becomes digital—and how the utopian ideals of enabling creativity and imagination through play are transported and altered along the way. The question of whether Lego bricks are still a tool for 'changing the world' or rather one that simply fosters commodification and therefore might actually limit the imaginative potential of children is, as it turns out, not only answered in Lego's P.R.-campaigns and partnerships with educators but also in the fictional stories the company provides. These stories are distributed in a transmedial way and emphasize a certain, quite specific mode of playfulness that can be read as a distinct argument in the debate about the pedagogic benefits of Lego bricks. Echoing Henry Jenkins' concept of transmedial storytelling,[6] these stories become a puzzle piece in Lego's larger efforts across media to reframe the discourse about itself; creating a narrative that does not only employ the act of physical worldbuilding but also very much the concept of brand building in the same regard.

ENTER LEGO DIMENSIONS: WHAT HAPPENS IF A CONSTRUCTION TOY BECOMES DIGITAL?

To show how Lego tries to reframe the debate, I will take a closer look at LEGO DIMENSIONS, a serialized, hybrid toys-to-life-game that was launched in 2015 and ceased its development in 2018. Typically, most Lego games are also licensed games based on large entertainment properties such as STAR

---

5 Schut, Kevin: "The Virtualization of LEGO," in: Wolf, Mark J.P. (ed.), *LEGO Studies. Examining the Building Blocks of a Transmedial Phenomenon*, Hoboken: Taylor and Francis 2014, pp. 227-240, here p. 227.

6 Jenkins, Henry: *Convergence Culture. Where Old and New Media Collide*, New York/London: New York University Press 2008.

WARS and are developed by the British game company Traveller's Tales. As shown by Kinder[7] and Jenkins,[8] video games have always been an important part of the construction of transmedial worlds and building media franchises,[9] but only a fraction of licensed games provides a satisfying gaming experience for the recipients as well. The reasons for this lie not only in production-related and logistical problems that make cooperation between game developers and film and television studios difficult[10] but also in the fact that many games concentrate too much on the mere repetition of set pieces, the depiction of familiar characters and already known narrative sequences.[11] As a result, they are often too much orientated on pre-established narrative material that does not translate well to the medial—that is, the ludic—affordances of digital games (e.g., interaction with game mechanics). In this regard, Lego is quite a special case: Even though new iterations of the LEGO STAR WARS and LEGO HARRY POTTER game series appear quite regularly, they are not simply adaptations of a given source material, but also an adaptation of a construction toy for kids. Jonathan Smith, Traveller's Tales former lead designer, speaks of a certain design philosophy he had in mind while his company created the first licensed Lego games; a philosophy that seems to be an important aspect of how physical Lego play could be translated to digital Lego play: "The titles [of former digital Lego Games, HCS] signposted some of the themes and qualities that the team were attempting to develop. This was a particular kind of freedom; a permission to play."[12]

---

7   Kinder, Marsha: *Playing with Power in Movies, Television, and Video Games: From Muppet Babies to Teenage Mutant Ninja Turles*, Berkeley: University of California Press 1991.
8   H. Jenkins: *Convergence Culture*.
9   Johnson, Derek: *Media Franchising. Creative License and Collaboration in the Culture Industries*, New York: New York University Press 2013.
10 Elkington, Trevor: "Too Many Cooks. Media Convergence and Self-Defeating Adaptations," in: Perron, Bernad/Wolf, Mark J.P (eds.), *The Video Game Theory Reader 2*, New York: Routledge 2009, pp. 213-235.
11 Schmidt, Hanns Christian: "Playing with Stories, Playing in Worlds. Transmedial Approaches to Video Games," in: Freyermuth, Gundolf S. et al. (eds.): *Clash of Realities 2016/2017*, Bielefeld: transcript 2018, pp.175-193.
12 Smith, Jonathan quoted in Newman, James/Simons, Iain: "Using the Force. Lego Star Wars: The Video Game. Intertextuality, Narrative, and Play," in: Page, Ruth/

Even though the "permission to play" can definitely be found in these games, they do not really resemble the type of play that is typical when kids actually build something out of Lego bricks. As Kevin Schut notes:

"Although most LEGO games fit into the action category, they are, in a sense, all puzzle games: until players solve this or that challenge, they cannot advance to the next one. [...] When a puzzle or challenge in a video game cannot be re-imagined or wished away, it has a kind of solidity that makes conquest of it deeply satisfying. So, there is a kind of tradeoff here: in virtual form, LEGO becomes less of a free-form open toy, and more a rigid, goal-directed item."[13]

That also means that Traveller's Tales' Lego games stray further away from the construction possibilities that the physical Lego toy is known for: "LEGO has traditionally sat near the paidea [sic] site of the continuum, going virtual has pulled the former toy in the direction of the ludus game,"[14] Schut writes, employing of Roger Caillois' classical cultural taxonomy of play.[15] What is clearly adapted to the game world though, are the *aesthetics* of the physical Lego materiality: the possibilities of modifying certain assets of the level architecture, the way Lego characters keep falling apart and effortlessly reassemble themselves, and the characteristic clicking noises of interlocking plastic bricks. However, by transporting Lego games in the ludus direction, the act of constructing something freely also becomes an act of deconstructing—or rather one of destroying: While players can indeed build something in these games from time to time (by simply holding down a single button),

"a large part of the game is destroying any and every object lying around; [...] LEGO objects are [...] all breakable, and when they explode, they spray out a shower of little round 'stud' pieces, which the player collects, and which form a kind of score for the level."[16]

Thomas, Bronwen (eds.), *New Narratives. Stories and Storytelling in the Digital Age*, Lincoln: University of Nebraska Press 2011, pp. 239-254, here p. 250.
13 K. Schut: "Virtualization of Lego," p. 236.
14 Ibid., p. 231.
15 Caillois, Roger: *Man, Play, and Games*, Chicago: University of Illinois Press 2001.
16 K. Schut, "Virtualization of Lego", p. 233.

Judging from the tradeoff Schut observes, the Lego games make it fairly easy for a critic of the Lego phenomenon to see them as examples for the cultural-industrial argument: Even though Schut's final statement ("as LEGO is virtualized, we gain and lose something")[17] appears to be quite neutral, the comparison between those two forms of Lego play allows for a clear judgement: A series of fairly simple digital puzzle games, in which everything has to be beaten to pieces, seems to be much less pedagogically valuable than a toy that may playfully convey an understanding of technical processes—and ultimately could even 'change the world,' as Gauntlett understands it.

OPERATING THE REMEDIATION MACHINE

Is LEGO DIMENSIONS any different in this regard? First of all, LEGO DIMENSIONS is not based on a single license, but 25 licenses from all kind of different media platforms. The main storyline revolves around the sinister fictional character Lord Vortech, a powerful interdimensional being who is obsessed with the plan of realizing his very own Utopia. Vortech plans to seize the dominion over Lego's 'multiverse' and to 'unify' all of its different dimensions—the various Lego licensed storyworlds based on already existing intellectual properties (e.g., the fictional version of GHOSTBUSTERS' New York City or Springfield, the hometown of the SIMPSONS family). To achieve his goal, Vortech tries to steal the magical 'foundation elements' from these worlds—which are basically plot devices, such as the One Ring from THE LORD OF THE RINGS or Dorothy's shoes from THE WIZARD OF OZ—that will give Vortech the power to alter time and space itself. By traveling through the various dimensions, he also opens up a dimensional rift that results in a clash and a chaotic mash-up of all the different storyworlds. This calls the caped crusader Batman, the underground rebel Wildstyle from the LEGO MOVIE and the wizard Gandalf from THE LORD OF THE RINGS to the plan to stop the villain.

LEGO DIMENSIONS is a so-called toys-to-life-game that consists of an 'actual' Lego set and a digital game. The Starter Pack represents a dimensional portal and the three Lego minifigures mentioned above. Those characters are meant to be put on a so-called "toypad," which can be connected to a

---

17 Ibid., p. 238.

Playstation 3 or 4, a Nintendo Wii U or Xbox One console via a NFC connection. The physical Lego figures standing on the toypad appear as virtual avatars in the digital space and can be navigated through various levels.

The Lego portal, which has a virtual pendant in an interdimensional space within the virtual world, serves as a hub in the game area—as a center from which the protagonists can enter different storyworlds and go on various missions. Apart from engaging in the main story mission, there is also the possibility to buy additional expansion packs from other licensed properties to unlock more game content and have more characters with different skills at your proposal. In playfully switching characters in different settings, you could argue that they actually become rather "[digital] bricks than [...] filmic texts; the playful subversions that arise from mixing and matching characters and scenes are transferred from the bedroom floor to the screen."[18]

Figure 1: LEGO DIMENSIONS

Source: Screenshots from LEGO DIMENSIONS and amazon.com

---

18 J. Newman/I. Simons: "Using the Force," p. 247.

However, the supposed variety of possible combinations is strongly tied to the player's purchasing power: At the height of LEGO DIMENSIONS popularity in 2017, 56 sets were available, which were launched on the market within a total of nine different time frames (so-called waves). The price of these sets was between 8-15 € for a Fun Pack, about 20-25 € for a Team Pack, 20-30 € for a Level Pack and up to 40 € for a Story Pack—and a test run at the online market Amazon showed that the costs for all packs were 925,54 € (the exclusive minifigures Green Arrow and Supergirl not included, because they are only available in console bundles). These packs were based on 25 different intellectual properties, consisting of a comic franchise (DC Comics: characters like Batman, Superman and Wonder Woman), 13 film franchises (LORD OF THE RINGS, THE LEGO MOVIE, THE LEGO BATMAN MOVIE, THE GOONIES, HARRY POTTER, GHOSTBUSTERS, E.T., GREMLINS, JURASSIC WORLD, BACK TO THE FUTURE, MISSION: IMPOSSIBLE, BEETLEJUICE, THE WIZARD OF OZ), seven TV franchises (THE SIMPSONS, DOCTOR WHO, THE A-TEAM, SCOOBIE-DOO!, POWER PUFF GIRLS, KNIGHT RIDER, ADVENTURE TIME), three computer game franchises (PORTAL, MIDWAY ARCADE, SONIC THE HEDGEHOG), two Lego themes (LEGENDS OF CHIMA, NINJAGO) and with LEGO CITY: UNDERCOVER even an adaptation of a Lego game based on a Lego theme that has been translated back to the world of LEGO: DIMENSIONS.

It should not come as a surprise that the story of the main campaign is filled to the brim with characters, set pieces, musical cues, quotes and references from the aforementioned entertainment properties; from the Land of Oz to Superman's Metropolis, the western town of Hilldale from BACK TO THE FUTURE II and even to the Aperture Labs from the video game series PORTAL, in which the game's villain GLaDOS is visited by HAL 9000 from Stanley Kubrick's 2001: A SPACE ODYSSEY. The main attraction of the game lies above all in the oftentimes surprising ways in which these references are put together. This is something that was described by Umberto Eco as the joy we receive from engaging into an intertextual dialogue:

"One of the procedures typical of postmodern narrative has been used frequently in the field of mass communication: the ironic quotation of the commonplace (topos). [...] The viewer has to recognize many things here: [...] she must have, in short, not only a knowledge of the text, but also a knowledge of the world and the circumstances surrounding it. Such phenomena of 'intertextual dialogue' were once typical of experimental art and, assuming a model reader, culturally highly refined. The fact that similar strategies have become common property in today's media world leads us to the insight that the media both presuppose and pass on ownership of pieces of information already conveyed through other media."[19]

However, if players are unfamiliar with the narrative worlds depicted here—if they are, in a way, popculturally illiterate—then there is not too much left to enjoy: The gameplay and the tasks that have to be mastered are quite easy to handle without the required encyclopedic knowledge. They are structurally just like the well-known and recurring patterns which are firmly anchored in the Traveller's Tale other Lego games—use a skill of one character at the push of a button, construct an object at the push of a button, place an object on the toypad and use the object that appears with the constructed object, find a switch, etc. Those challenges not only prove to be repetitive but are also often only inspired by the original narrative worlds on a mere surface level; a surface so thin it ultimately could be received as "uninteresting ornament and gift wrapping,"[20] as the game studies scholar Markku Eskelinen once famously condemned all games that are in his opinion too focused on narrative and aesthetics.

On the other hand, the ornamental 'gift wrapping' in LEGO DIMENSIONS, in particular, is too elaborated that it could be simply ignored in any meaningful analysis: This seems to be clearest at the SCOOBY-DOO MYSTERY MANSION MASH UP-level, in which the game demonstrates that it is not only interested in a mere *narrative* remix of existing story parts, but is also highly determined to make the aesthetic surface as interesting as possible. In the level mentioned, the graphical style switches from rendered polygons to a Cel-Shading graphics filter. That way, it creates a distinct cartoon aesthetic that not does not only stand out from the rest of the game but also orients itself on its very specific point of reference—the 'Saturday morning cartoons' by the American cartoon studio Hanna-Barbera of the 1960s. But apart from the graphical style that depicts a wide range of standardized familiar tropes—like the typical interior of a cartoonish haunted house with all of its scary oil paintings, secret passages, skeletons, spiderwebs and the occasional

---

19　Eco, Umberto: *Streit der Interpretationen*, Berlin: Philo-Verlag 2005, pp. 91-94; translated by HCS.

20　Eskelinen, Markku: "The Gaming Situation," *Game Studies*, 2001; http://www.gamestudies.org/0101/eskelinen/

torture tool—this includes also the sound: by heavily drawing from Hanna-Barbera's original archive of sound effects (like Scooby Doo's chattering teeth when he is afraid), LEGO DIMENSIONS demonstrates that it plays both with intertextual quotations as well with certain styles of depiction that we know from other media. LEGO DIMENSIONS, in this sense, also becomes a remediation machine, using different medial styles to impress its audience.[21]

Despite all the self-aware media-aesthetic takeovers and pop-cultural reminiscences, the MYSTERY MANSION MASHUP level remains committed to the same basic gameplay formula: it is still a typical Lego game from Traveller's Tales, in which you have to smash every object to pieces along the way. This changes when LEGO DIMENSIONS switches from depicting linear narratives like films and TV-series to emulating another media genre: the video game.

In the main story campaign of LEGO DIMENSIONS, there are two video game properties that have been adapted: Valve's PORTAL and four classic arcade games from the publisher Midway that have been compiled to an overall 'video game level' called *All Your Bricks Are Belong to Us*, referencing a well-known quip from gaming culture. While the PORTAL level is not really interesting in terms of game mechanics, the Midway Arcade level offers a break out from the standardized game formula: When Gandalf, Wyldstyle and Batman enter the level, we witness first of all a change of the perspective. From the previous isometric view, the image now tilts into a side view that reminds of the representation of 2D game worlds. Meanwhile, a battle takes place in the sky between spaceships, which retro gaming fans will recognize as the starting scenario of the computer game DEFENDER (1980) due to the graphic design language and sound effects, blending the cube-like appearance of the plastic bricks almost perfectly with the pixel graphics of the classic video game.

After rescuing five astronauts, the protagonists are taken to a new level and find themselves in a labyrinth lined with stone floor tiles, teeming with monsters and treasure chests. A noisy computer announcement declares, "Friends can join in any time," which, in connection with the level design, already indicates to the audience that this game must be GAUNTLET (1985). To get to the next level section, treasures and keys have to be collected,

---

21 Bolter, Jay David/Grusin, Richard: *Remediation. Understanding New Media*, Cambridge, Mass.: MIT Press 2000.

monsters have to be killed, and the exit of the labyrinth has to be found. The dungeons, the respawn points, the accumulation and movement of enemy hordes and the goals to be achieved represent the typical GAUNTLET starting situation in terms of gameplay. Thus, some mechanical features of the arcade game are actually integrated into LEGO DIMENSIONS and could be seen as 'true to the original.' In this respect, it is worth noting that due to the 'Legoness' of the level architecture, players are allowed to cheat: By activating on the toypad a Lego vehicle that can fly—such as Batman's airplane, the Batwing—players can hover over the walls and reach the exit much quicker.

Once this area is completed, a dimension gate opens to a third level section, in which the characters must win a race in order to advance the plot: It's an emulation of the game SUPER SPRINT (1986), in which the mechanics of the original game are faithfully adapted (with the difference that the camera is a little bit closer to the characters in comparison to the original). Like in the section before, players are able to 'cheat' and can eliminate the traction of the cars (which makes them hard to control) by summoning another Lego vehicle, like the much more powerful Batmobile.

Figure 2: Arcade level in LEGO DIMENSIONS *(left to right):* DEFENDER, GAUNTLET, SUPER SPRINT, ROBOTRON: 2084

Source: Screenshots from LEGO DIMENSIONS

After the race is finished, a last mini-game has to be played: the multi-directional shooter ROBOTRON 2084 (1982). Here, too, the camera remains in the bird's eye view, but the characters themselves, who until then had always been shown in a correct spatial 3D-representation, are tilted to the side, creating a flat and simple 2D-impression. This way, the character representation corresponds to a characteristic graphic element of an older arcade shooter. The level section also adopts other visual and sound effects from the source material (including the psychedelic box effect, flickering in unusual, bright colors when an astronaut is rescued from the enemy robots). However, in the last wave of opponents, figures from other franchises are teleported into the level section (such as the Cybermen from DOCTOR WHO), drawing again from the characteristic mash-up-elements that are an essential part of LEGO DIMENSIONS' formula.

The level sections described here show how LEGO DIMENSIONS—as a relatively recent video game—integrates other, much older games into its own system of intertextual, aesthetic and mechanic gameplay. In addition to the numerous references to the peculiar aesthetics of the classic arcade games, it becomes that LEGO DIMENSIONS does not only emulate or adapt the other properties but also 'overwrites' them with a standardized Lego-ness. The distinction Smith made in relation to the LEGO STAR WARS games—"This isn't the game of the movie. This is the game where you play with the movie"[22]—also applies to the other games: Here, we do not only play DEFENDER, GAUNTLET, SUPERSPRINT or ROBOTRON 2084, but we are actually invited to toy with the mechanics of the classic arcade games and find ways of exploiting them by using its distinct Lego-ness. The consequence of this is that LEGO DIMENSIONS becomes a sort of super-structure, one that modifies and preserves those older games within Lego's own specific language of form and assimilates other media seamlessly into its own larger concept.

BREAKING THE RULES OF IMAGINATION?

In this way, LEGO DIMENSIONS demonstrates how ludus and paidia can be integrated to different degrees into a Lego game. Due to the game mechanics

---

22 J. Smith quoted in J. Newman/I. Simons: "Using the Force," p. 251.

that Traveller's Tales' Lego games are known for the rule-based ludus aspect clearly prevails most of the time. However, the paidia-dimension is present, too—albeit rather in a figurative sense and on the story level.

This is well in accordance with the other parts of the larger transmedial universe of the Lego franchise. If it is considered as a storytelling medium, LEGO DIMENSIONS clearly takes some of its most important thematic cues from the recent iterations of the animated theatrical films: As you can see within THE LEGO MOVIE (2014), THE LEGO BATMAN MOVIE (2017) as well as THE LEGO NINJAGO MOVIE (2017), all these stories reach their dramatic climaxes when the boundaries of narrative conventions are broken, the implicit rules of storyworlds are suspended, and the fourth wall is torn down. In the transition to the third act, THE LEGO MOVIE, for example, becomes a meta-story about nothing less than the act of playing itself. By incorporating live-action footage into the otherwise computer-animated film, the movie turns out to be a story sparked from the imagination of a kid all along. It is the result of an act of free, associative and chaotic play that takes place in a father's hobby cellar that teems with artistically stunning Lego constructions that are not allowed to be touched. What happens in the movie can be interpreted as a lively debate about what modes of play are actually 'allowed' (or socially accepted)—with anarchic bottom-up-players on one side and commercially-oriented and order-loving top-down-players on the other. Nevertheless, Batman, whose character in the LEGO BATMAN MOVIE appears to be all the previous cinematic iterations of the comic figure at once, is not only a dazzling media- and self-parody, but it is also a statement for the playful opening of canon boundaries: In the showdown of the movie, we see not only many of the villains of the DC universe but also famous villains from very different film, television, and literary contexts—from Agent Smith from THE MATRIX, Sauron from THE LORD OF THE RINGS to Count Dracula and Medusa. And in THE NINJAGO MOVIE, the 'ultimate weapon' is not a dangerous laser beam, but merely a conventional laser pointer that functions as a bait for a 'real' cat. The laser pointer causes the animal, which is fully engaged in the frenzy of its own play, to casually crush whole Lego skyscrapers while hunting for the red light spot.

LEGO DIMENSIONS fully embraces the spirit of its transmedial siblings from the cinema screen. However, while free play with standardized, prefabricated material does take place in the game, it tends to happen mostly on the narrative level (and with very little exceptions the game also embraces mechanics from older arcade games). The kind of free play proposed by the story is not a type of play that is made available for the players themselves, but rather for the authors and producers of the game, who play with license agreements on an intertextual, a media-aesthetic and occasionally also on a ludic level. In this sense, LEGO DIMENSIONS at best *suggests* that it is a good thing to break the rules of imagination, but it is not really good at granting this freedom to its audience. Hence, paidia is not formally transposed into the game, but rather *imitated* on a story level—and thus represents a form of mimicry, to remain in Caillois' terminology. In other words, LEGO DIMENSIONS shows how the Lego company wants to be perceived: Not only as a toy for free play but also as a tool that helps to spark creativity and to encourage a certain way to engage with the world. And of course, worlds *are* actually changed by playing with Lego—but at least in LEGO DIMENSIONS, it is not for the player to decide how.[23]

Nevertheless, it might be the material hybridity of LEGO DIMENSIONS that could provide a starting point for a productive mode of appropriation. Arguably the most interesting aspect of the game may not take place within the virtual Lego world itself, but when players tear open a bag of plastic blocks to actually build the tangible Lego constructions depicted on the screen. The game does invite to a material mode of appropriation that eludes the manufacturer and the licensor, and which—drawing from on Seth Giddings'

---

23 It is particularly interesting in this respect that Lego's failure in not seizing this mode of free playing in digital realms may also explain the development of one of the most successful contemporary video games of all times: MINECRAFT (2011). After all, MINECRAFT is nothing more than a virtual Lego construction kit—with an inexhaustible supply of building blocks. In the game, raw materials can be extracted ("mine") and processed into other objects ("craft"). MINECRAFT is fundamentally characterized by a kind of editor or building block style: there are (practically) no concrete game goals, rather the program relies almost exclusively on the creativity of the players. And of course, the irony of it all: Lego already licensed MINECRAFT as a physical construction theme. Lego's very own MINECRAFT-clone, LEGO WORLDS, has been launched in 2017 but lacks the licensed content LEGO DIMENSIONS wants the players to 'break the rules' with.

assumption of Lego play as essentially being "dark play" with "bright bricks"[24] —is in no way predictable. Where the actual gameplay is still very strongly regulated by license agreements, the physical part of the game may relocate it near an idea that media scholar Giddings' describes with the image of the Lego box:

"The ubiquitous box, then, is by no means merely for storage—as well as an evocative object in its own right, it was, and is, integral to modes of construction and play; a technology in itself, holding all the pieces but also randomly generating suggestions for unexpected juxtapositions and new lines of flight for the imagination. [...] 'The Box' as an evocative focus for a multiplicity of memories, and the well-spring from which many LEGO play events emerge, and its collection or absorption of numerous sets, negates critique of themed sets and instructions as constraining. Not only does the box mix up initially distinct sets, it often originates in, or has incorporated, LEGO from older siblings, relatives or buildings."[25]

Back in the box, it is exactly where inconsistencies may become productive again—and where players (which are children, most of all) are not dependent on partaking in an intertextual dialogue in order to 'get the jokes' from a story someone else is telling them. Instead, through physical Lego play, children may become able to operate the remediation machine themselves. In this sense, all the references mentioned above could also be understood as an instruction manual teaching kids to throw away the instruction manual; an encouragement, an invitation—or even as a sort of learning platform for the productive appropriation of prefabricated elements of our transmedial convergent culture. By making fun of the essential parts and characters of these worlds, by smashing its various parts together and combining them in unforeseen ways, children could learn something about our media culture along the way. These learning processes may be part of something that many cultural critics would probably recognize as an important component of a distinct form of media literacy: a *Lego Literacy* if you will. After all, there is

---

24 Giddings, Seth: "Bright Bricks, Dark Play: On the Impossibility of Studying LEGO," in: Wolf, Mark J.P. (ed.), *LEGO Studies. Examining the Building Blocks of a Transmedial Phenomenon*, Hoboken: Taylor and Francis 2014, pp. 241-67.
25 Ibid., p. 257-260.

probably no marketing agency in the world that could predict what children will actually do with a physical dimensional portal.

Literature

Bolter, Jay David/Grusin, Richard: *Remediation. Understanding New Media*, Cambridge, Mass.: MIT Press 2000.
Caillois, Roger: *Man, Play, and Games*, Chicago: University of Illinois Press 2001.
Cross, Gary S: *Kid's Stuff: Toys and the Changing World of American Childhood*, Cambridge, Mass.: Harvard University Press 1997.
Eco, Umberto: *Streit der Interpretationen*, Berlin: Philo-Verlag 2005.
Eder, Jens: "Transmediale Imagination," in: Hanich, Julian/Wulff, Hans J. (eds.), *Auslassen, Andeuten, Auffüllen: Der Film und die Imagination des Zuschauers*, München: Wilhelm Fink 2012, pp. 207-238.
Eskelinen, Markku: "The Gaming Situation," *Game Studies*, 2001; http://www.gamestudies.org/0101/eskelinen/
Elkington, Trevor: "Too Many Cooks. Media Convergence and Self-Defeating Adaptations," in: Perron, Bernad/Wolf, Mark J.P (eds.), *The Video Game Theory Reader 2*, New York: Routledge, 2009, pp. 213-235.
Gauntlett, David: "The LEGO System as a Tool for Thinking, Creativity, and Changing the World," in: Wolf, Mark J.P. (ed.), *LEGO Studies. Examining the Building Blocks of a Transmedial Phenomenon*, Hoboken: Taylor and Francis 2014, pp. 189-205.
Giddings, Seth: "Bright Bricks, Dark Play: On the Impossibility of Studying LEGO," in: Wolf, Mark J.P. (ed.), *LEGO Studies. Examining the Building Blocks of a Transmedial Phenomenon*, Hoboken: Taylor and Francis 2014, pp. 241-67.
Jenkins, Henry: *Convergence Culture. Where Old and New Media Collide*, New York/London: New York University Press 2008.
Johnson, Derek: *Media Franchising. Creative License and Collaboration in the Culture Industries,* New York: New York University Press 2013.
Kinder, Marsha: *Playing with Power in Movies, Television, and Video Games: From Muppet Babies to Teenage Mutant Ninja Turles*, Berkeley: University of California Press 1991.

Newman, James/Simons, Iain: "Using the Force. Lego Star Wars: The Video Game, Intertextuality, Narrative, and Play," in: Page, Ruth/Thomas, Bronwen (eds.), *New Narratives. Stories and Storytelling in the Digital Age*, Lincoln: University of Nebraska Press 2011, pp. 239-254.

Sarkeesian, Anita: "Lego & Gender Part 1: Lego Friends / Lego & Gender"/ "Part 2: The Boys Club," *feministfrequency*, 2012; https://feministfrequency.com/tag/lego-friends/

Schmidt, Hanns Christian: "Playing with Stories, Playing in Worlds. Transmedial Approaches to Video Games," in: Freyermuth, Gundolf S. et al. (eds.): *Clash of Realities 2016/2017*, Bielefeld: transcript 2018, pp. 175-193.

Wolf, Mark J.P. (ed.): *LEGO Studies. Examining the Building Blocks of a Transmedial Phenomenon*, Hoboken: Taylor and Francis 2014.

FILMOGRAPHY

THE LEGO BATMAN MOVIE (USA 2017, D: Chris McKay)
THE LEGO MOVIE (USA 2014, D: Phil Lord & Chris Miller)
THE LEGO NINJAGO MOVIE, (USA 2017, D: Charles Bean, Paul Fisher, Bob Logan)

GAMOGRAPHY

DEFENDER (Williams Electronics 1980, O: Williams Electronics)
GAUNTLET (Atari 1985, O: Atari)
LEGO DIMENSIONS (Warner Bros. Interactive Entertainment 2015, O: Traveller's Tales)
MINECRAFT (Mojang/Microsoft 2011, O: Mojang)
ROBOTRON 2084 (Williams Electronics 1982, O: Vid Kidz/Williams Electronics)
SUPER SPRINT (Atari 1986, O: Atari)

We have won this battle ;)
Modding and Swapping as a Utopian Video Game Practice

THOMAS HAWRANKE

> These marginal events and occurrences, these wondrous acts of transgression, are absolutely vital because they give us hope, true or false; they remind us that it is possible to regain control, however briefly, to dominate that which dominates us so completely.[1]

INTRODUCTION

In this contribution, I will have a look at the utopian potential of modding. Modding is a bundle of practices that alter an existing video game, bringing one's own creations into the industrially produced game space. The paper starts with an example that will show different aspects of modding, followed by two image sequences which highlight both the critical potential as well as the creation of utopian spaces within video game worlds. I conclude by seeing this utopian potential as a fundamental aspect of video games, one that marks their core modus operandi and brings forward the specificity of the medium.

---

1 Aarseth, Espen J.: "I Fought the Law: Transgressive Play and the Implied Player," in: Digital Games Research Association (DiGRA) (eds.), *Proceedings of DiGRA 2007 Conference. Situated Play*, 2007, pp. 130-133, here p. 133.

Modding

I will begin with a description of the first scenes of a YouTube video[2] in which the creator made heavy use of different modifications to tell a story. The underlying setting for the video is the vast city of Los Santos and the rural sites of Blain County, both part of the blockbuster video game GRAND THEFT AUTO V (2013, GTAV). In the beginning the video shows the date June 15, 2017 while the melody of Mozarts *Lacrimosa,* performed by Tony Cello sets in. This is followed by a fade in of a text:

> Take Two Interactive announces war against OpenIV by declaring it illegal.
> The mods lose their powers and jobs and are soon pursued by Take Two.

In the next scene we see Mario, the main character of Nintendo's SUPER MARIO franchise sitting at the side of the road in the rain, leaning his back against a building and crying. The camera moves slowly and steadily towards the crying Mario. In the next shot we see Cat Woman, Spider Man (both from the Marvel Universe) and Juliet Starling (from the video game LOLLIPOP CHAINSAW, 2012) hanging around at an urban street corner by night. A black car approaches the characters and the camera shifts focus to the number plate with the insignia of Take Two, the publisher of the GRAND THEFT AUTO video game series. Two scenes later, a Stormtrooper from the STAR WARS movies stands at the side of a rural street and tries to hitchhike. Once more, the black car stops in front of the Stormtrooper and—in a long shot—the camera reveals a crashed Tie Fighter starship with another Stormtrooper standing beside and Darth Vader sitting under a rainbow-colored umbrella.

In the following sequences this order repeats itself: Characters from different IP (intellectual property) Universes are picked up by the black car. Finally, all characters are collected in a bus and taken to a prison. On its way the bus passes by a sign with the lettering "Modschwitz," a terrible, inappropriate holocaust-relativizing reference to the Nazi extermination camp in World War II located in Poland. A small boy witnesses the bus driving through the gates of the prison and leaves the scene shortly after. Suddenly, the music stops and the boy runs through the rain and into a barber shop in the city, where he meets different characters of the GTAV world. After this

---

2   https://www.youtube.com/watch?v=x7-WJvGC6D8

sequence, the image fades to black and recording of a telephone call with the support hotline of Rockstar (the developer of GTAV) is played, where one of the main characters of GTAV insults a technical support assistant. In the last sequence of the video a scroll-down through an internet thread titled "RockstarGames Talks Publisher into Leaving GRAND THEFT AUTO VModders Alone" is shown.

In four and a half minutes the video gathers multiple aspects of the practice this paper will be dealing with. By modding a video game, the modders create new content or migrate existing content to a particular game space. This mod-practice is cross-referential, which means that sometimes textures, characters, vehicles or even complete settings are taken from one pop-cultural product and implemented into another.[3] In the example above, the characters from different franchises, like STAR WARS, DRAGON BALL, and Marvel are merged together within the world of GTAV. The external character models are treated like the models included in the original game, they are influenced by the gravity of the world, the lightning or the collision detection. To be more specific, the added characters take up a preexisting space within the data structure of the game. When the game engine loads the assets of the game into the random-access memory of the computer to assemble the game world, the modified data is handled just in the same way as every other data that comes with the game. It simply takes the place of an existing model, which is dismissed from the world when the mod is installed.

Models, textures, audio files, etc. are exported from other existing media like games, movies, comics etc. via specific software or are built from the core in general purpose 2D or 3D Editing Software and then imported into the data structure of the game. As seen in the example, the user can install a variety of mods and finds all the changes present at the same time when starting the modified game.

The creator of the video described above lists 21 mods that were used, ranging from the more obvious character mods like Darth Vader or

---

3   Besides this, mods are often based on historical or contemporary media, like a drawing of a World War II-Rifle that is used as a prefiguration for a 3D-model, original audio files from a political speech that become in-game voices, or photographs of a graffiti implemented as wall textures. For cultural reference in modding see: Newman, James: *Playing with Videogames*, London/New York: Routledge 2008, p. 171.

Spiderman to software-mods that e.g. enable the staging of these characters within the game world.[4] It is complicated to classify the multitude of different mods and the list of different superior mod-categories depends on the author's view on the topic.[5] In the research about modding it is somehow common sense that mods are linked to game content.[6] A definition by Peter Christiansen extends this idea and includes tools in his more general classification: "Game modifications can be artwork, skins (graphic look), tools, total game transformations, new code, or, perhaps less clearly, games ported to other platforms by fans."[7]

The example of the YouTube clip stretches this classification even further: Mods were used to grant the user the possibility of using the game as a cinematic tool. The corresponding practice is called "machinima making," which Henry Lowood defines as followed:

"The word 'machinima' was derived from 'machine cinema.' A more apt derivation might be 'machine animation.' [...] It means making animated movies in real-time with the software that is used to develop and play computer games."[8]

There is a close connection between modding and machinima making, because the real-time filmmakers not only use mods but also create software-modifications themselves to implement their practice. The maker of the YouTube clip uses mods to stage modified data (the characters) within the world or to apply preexisting animation data from GTAV to these models. When Spiderman rubs himself against the lamp pole in the already described scene of the movie, the animation is derived from other characters of GTAV.

---

4 A precise list of the used mods can be accessed via the commentary field of the YouTube clip.
5 J. Newman: *Playing with Videogames*, pp. 160-161.
6 Laukkanen, Tero: *Modding Scenes—Introduction to User-created Content in Computer Gaming*, Tampere: Tampere University 2005, pp. 30-59.
7 Champion, Erik: *Game Mods. Design, Theory and Criticism*, Pittsburgh, Pa.: ETC Press 2012, p. 12.
8 Lowood, Henry: "High-Performance Play: The Making of Machinima," in: Clarke, Andy/Mitchell, Grethe (eds.), *Videogames and Art*, Chicago: Intellect 2007, pp. 59-79, here p. 60.

Mods are sometimes modified themselves, such as when the modder uses a preexisting mod and adds his personal changes. This one-sided collaboration matures into a real division of labor in bigger mod projects. By doing so, the different mod teams mirror and mimic the general production pipeline of the video game industry, which means that often whole mod teams work on one mod, splitting the labor into different areas of expertise such as 3D modelling, 2D texturing, animation, visual effects, sounds, narration and so on.[9] Therefore, modding is also a highly cooperative online practice in which different modders work together, share knowledge and distribute their creations for free via the infrastructures of the internet. Anyone who has a copy of the original game (official or unofficial) can install the mod. Dan Pinchbeck describes the benefit of modding efforts from the perspective of the publisher:

"Mods can be freely distributed and shared, with developers and publishers understanding that these communities and experiences add significant value and shelf life to their products, introduce new users to their games, uncover new talent, and break new ground in terms of experimentation and optimization."[10]

However, there is also a downside to this: By further developing the content of a 'finished' industrial product, modders are undergoing free and unpaid labor. In the debates around modding this circumstance is referred to as playbour, a term coined by Julian Kücklich.[11] Here, all the risks of innovation lie on the shoulders of free working modders, who do not have any involvement in the financial success achieved through their actions. They spend time training themselves, producing additional content, optimizing the game— and all of this for free. Furthermore, by signing the end user license agreement of a game, all the rights of intellectual property of content produced

---

9   Beil, Benjamin: "Vom Castle Smurfenstein zum LittleBigPlanet. Modding, Leveleditoren und Prosumenten-Kulturen," in: Abresch, Sebastian et al. (eds.), *Prosumenten-Kulturen*, Siegen: universi 2009, pp. 191-214, here p. 193.

10 Pinchbeck, Dan: *Doom. Scarydarkfast*, Ann Arbor, MI: University of Michigan Press 2013, p. 119.

11 Kücklich, Julian: "Precarious Playbour: Modders and the Digital Games Industry," in: *The Fibreculture Journal* 5 (2005); http://five.fibreculturejournal.org/fcj-025-precarious-playbour-modders-and-the-digital-games-industry/

through modding are automatically transferred to the holder of the IP.[12] In the history of modding, the laws of intellectual property were always used against the communities: Not only do they lack any rights to their own creations, modding teams are also prosecuted because of copyright infringements—like for example the ones in the YouTube video where Marvel characters were implemented into GTAV. Game companies can freely decide, which content they will implement in the next iteration of the game, which content they will support and which they will prohibit.[13] There is no discussion, only a few lawsuits.

However, there are a couple of examples in which the industry tried to foster the financial success further and where the mod community shreds these ambitions into pieces with massive protest.[14] As Pinchbeck states, the mod communities are vital for the evolution of a game and the gaming industry is aware of the power these communities hold. Nevertheless, if money becomes a factor, developers and mod communities fight each other. Communities often assert their authority with prohibition, review-bombing or hate speech in attempts to revert changes the game industry has made to further commercialize modding activities.

This cat-and-mouse game is also the last piece needed to understand the nature of the YouTube clip from the beginning of this paper and has

---

12 Postigo, Hector: "Video Game Appropriation Through Modifications. Attitudes Concerning Intellectual Property Among Modders and Fans," in: *Convergence: The International Journal of Research into New Media Technologies* 14 (2008), pp. 59-74.

13 Modding happens under three general community-publisher-relationships: In officially sanctioned modding, the publisher/developer supports modding activities, where in unsanctioned modding communities, the practice is prohibited. Between those poles there is a very unclear third type: In unofficially-sanctioned modding communities the publisher/developer forbids modding, but do not enforce this prohibition. See also: Hawranke, Thomas: *Modding. Künstlerische Forschung in Computerspielen*, Weimar: Bauhaus-University 2018, pp. 84-94.

14 One example for this is the effort of Valve to sell mods via the Steam platform. This change was withdrawn from the company after a massive protest from the gamer community where for example games of that company where downrated through the Steam platform: https://www.gamestar.de/artikel/steam_workshop, 3085192.html

something to do with the motivation of people modifying existing games. Based on empirical data, some research on the motivations of modders has identified common goals, such as e.g. making the games their own, improving job opportunities, outlive creativity, teamwork, fun, nostalgia, approval of others.[15] However, the motivation behind the video is a different one: protest. The date depicted at the beginning of the video coincides with the specific moment in time in which the publisher of GTAV Take Two forced the developer of OpenIV to disable his tool. OpenIV is a software, developed by Nizhniy Novgorod and the main access to the data structure of GTAV.[16] It decrypts the binary files of the game, has a couple of editors and viewers to manipulate this data and encrypts the modifications back into the file structure of the game.[17] All the modified characters in the video clip are brought into the world of GTAV by using OpenIV. By cutting the unofficially sanctioned support of OpenIV, Take Two ended the possibility to mod GTAV. Existing mods could not be installed and the creation of new mods was simply not possible anymore. The video clip is a reaction to this event.

But why cut off a lively mod community that enhances a commercial product for free? Like in all the great battles between the mod community and the game industry, one answer to this is rather simple: because of money. In the weeks before the shutdown, people hacked the financial system of GTA ONLINE. The online version comes with the main title GTAV and creates a multi-user online experience. Part of it is an in-game purchase system, in which 'real' is transformed into 'virtual' money that can be used to buy shiny cars, new outfits and nice equipment for your avatar. A hack in the

---

15 Katharina-Maria Behr gatherers different studies on player motivations, including research from Sotamaa, Olli: "Computer Game Modding, Intermediality and Participatory Culture," Lecture at: The Nordic Vetwork Innovating Media and Communication Research, Sonderborg, Denmark 2003, H. Postigo: "Video Game Appropriation Through Modifications," and Theodorsen, Jesper: *Participatory Culture on Web 2.0: Exploring the Motives for Modding Video Games*,Master Thesis, University of Amsterdam 2008. See: Behr, Katharina-Maria: *Kreativer Umgang mit Computerspielen. Die Entwicklung von Spielmodifikationen aus aneignungstheoretischer Sicht*, Boizenburg: vwh 2010, p. 65.

16 http://openiv.com/

17 On a more detailed description and the use of the *OpenIV* tool see: T. Hawranke: *Modding*, pp. 189-190.

system caused Take Two to lose profit, because it produced a giant amount of free money that could now be spent on virtual goods.[18] To put this in an simpler way: Take Two lost control over parts of their own product, so the publishers shut down the mod tool to prevent further damage. One important detail about this is that you cannot log into GTA ONLINE if you have modified the data of your copy of the game with the mod tool OpenIV.[19] Following the false accusations against the GTAV mod community the modders started to protest: They review-bombed GTAV to only 24 % positive reviews on the Steam platform, they wrote outraged comments in threads, prank-called the support hotline of the developer Rockstar Games and produced videos as a form of protest, like the one described at the beginning of this article.[20] The video makers reacted to the accusation of the violation of the terms of use of the game with copyright infringements. They used mods to stand up for their right to mod.

This procedure is rather common within modding communities, from the use of copyright infringements in GTAV to protest-sign-mods in the video game SKYRIM (2011).[21] The practice of modding has a critical potential to it that might be derived from the uncertain legal situation most mod teams are operating within, from copyright-infringements, discontent over unpaid labor and finally to the ambivalent relationship between the community and the industry.

Around the year 1999, the practice of modding was conquered by digital artists and there was somehow a naïve hope that these artists would intensify the critical potential of modding.[22] On the following pages I will have a look at one artistic mod project in which the artists use a specific strategy to both form protest in and extend the work to an alternative gaming experience. This

---

18 For the outcome of some of the lawsuits against those hackers see: https://www.gtaboom.com/rockstar-gta-online-hack-case/

19 http://openiv.com/?cat=23&paged=2

20 For some examples see: https://gtaforums.com/topic/889348-take-two-vs-modding/page/61/?tab=comments#comment-1069656426

21 http://steamed.kotaku.com/steams-most-popular-skyrim-mod-is-a-protest-against-pai-1700486550

22 In a personal observation Olli Sotamaa describes 2003 the absence of intellectual criticism within the creations of modding communities. O. Sotamaa: "Computer Game Modding, Intermediality and Participatory Culture," p. 6.

example anticipates the idea of the utopian potential of modding practices I will subsequently describe, linking the critical potential as a starting point to create one's own utopian space through modding actions.

SWAPPING

In July 1999, Anne-Marie Schleiner created the first exhibition in which community mods and art mods were curated together.[23] Schleiner preferred the internet as an exhibition space over a classical offline gallery situation, as it was connected both to the acceptance of the internet as a medium and as a more democratic art space.[24] Through its selection of modifications "Cracking the Maze: Game Plug-ins and Patches as Hacker Art" demonstrated the affinity between the gaming and the artist community, where the exhibition space encompassed modifications from both spheres. The exhibition could be accessed online, where a dedicated space was designed to hold the mod data, GIF-Animations and additional texts. To perceive the mods, one had to install them on a computer and within the file structure of the original game. One of the modifications manipulated the appearance of the player characters in QUAKE (1996). The FEMALE SKIN PACK EXCERPTS by Sonya Roberts is a collection of texture files that transform the bulky male characters of QUAKE into so called "frag queens" (bulky female avatars).

In the history of modding there is a large number of so-called "skin modifications." They are all based on the replacement of existing textures by drawing over the skins of the available characters. For the game engine the data remains the same. As part of the exhibition, Sonya Roberts created a zip-file with various skin modifications: From a leather wearing "Dominatrix" to a "Cutie Girl" (both skins from the modder Dan Bickell) with hot pants, sneakers, sunglasses and a grey sweater. By installing the skin, the appearance of the male player model switches to the designs of the female skin packs.

For Schleiner, the FEMALE SKIN PACK EXCERPTS were a protest against the mediated image of women in video games. Aside from a few exceptions,

---

23 http://switch.sjsu.edu/archive/CrackingtheMaze/note.html
24 http://www.gamescenes.org/2009/12/interview-annemarie-schleiners-cracking-the-maze-1999-10-years-later.html

most of the player characters in video games were male at the time. By overwriting the male content with the female data, the skin packs created the possibility to run, jump and shoot as a woman. Following Schleiner, it was due to the efforts of these skin modifications that id Software integrated the choice between genders as a feature in QUAKE 2 (1997). Schleiner describes this official design of the female avatar model from QUAKE 2 as a curvier and somehow more elegant model, which reproduces an attribution towards a discriminating division between bulky male and slender female body forms that fosters a stereotypic view of the world.[25] In contrast, Roberts' skin modifications in QUAKE were queer hybrids in which images of characters with female attributes were stretched over a masculine geometry to form strong and dangerous looking women.

The swapping of gender through modifications facilitates a critical perspective on the status quo of gender representation in particular games and gaming culture in general. By creating a gender alternative, the author's critique is not only stated but presents already a solution through its practice. The competitive arenas of QUAKE become an alteration that creates a new space where the predefined meaning of the content shifts towards an individual view. By changing one tiny asset of the game, the world itself is transformed.

Swapping is neither limited to 2D images nor to a specific game. It is rather a simple way to modify all kinds of game worlds and could be seen as a universal, critical, and transformative sub-practice of modding.[26] Many things can be swapped: vehicles, character models, textures, sound, etc.[27] While the texture files in the FEMALE SKIN PACK EXCERPTS were overdrawn by the modders, swapping also includes the substitution of one file with another. Following the idea of changing the gender, the modder simply takes

---

25 Schleiner, Anne-Marie: *Ludic Mutation: The Player's Power to Change the Game*, Amsterdam: University of Amsterdam 2012, p. 51.
26 On the implication of a technical and aesthetical quality of swaps see: T. Hawranke: *Modding*, pp. 102-105.
27 For the idea of swapping as a gameplay element see: Abend, Pablo: "'Greetings Arma fans. I submit to you this humble contribution to the mod-a-verse.' Modding als kritische Aneignungspraxis digitaler Spiele", in: Goethe-Institut (eds.), *Games and Politics. Eine interaktive Ausstellung des Goethe-Institut in Kooperation mit dem ZKM*, München: Goethe-Institut 2016, pp. 63-70.

the 3D model of a female character in the data structure, renames it into a corresponding male model and then overwrites the original file with the renamed one. In doing so, the game engine will render every iteration of the male model as a female one. Through this intervention within the data structure of the game, everything else is maintained just as it was before. It does not create errors but produces tiny disruptions within the overall staging of the game world, its storyline and its atmospheres. Depending on the swapped data, one will ideally end up with female characters that are equipped with 'boy toys' and are moving in a way one would culturally perceive as masculine. Interestingly, when doing it the other way around—overwriting the female characters with male models—one can dismantle the staging of gender stereotypes and it becomes clear, for example, how sexist the focus of the camera really is. By creating what seems to be a small disruption within the ideological order inscribed in the game, aspects become evident that were rather subliminal before.

The practice of swapping is a common approach within modding scenes, switching for example the model of a gun with another weapon. But swapping also means that one can modify aspects of the world represented in the game into something that is more fitting to the individual's perspective—and by doing so, perhaps draw the image of a better future for oneself. By swapping the race, the class or the gender of a character, the game world might become a place that is more suitable to the representation of diversity. One could say that the responsibility to integrate a more diverse world view lies in the hands of the developers. This may be true, but modding enables the users to establish a richness in perspectives and details that goes beyond the developers' capacities. These actions can most certainly inspire the gaming industry to implement changes in their upcoming versions of games. In that way, modding and swapping are practices that might change the future of video games in general. It lies in the hands of the users.

What follows are two image sequences that depict alterations to existing video game worlds. Both are based on the modification of the corresponding games through model swaps. And in both cases the modification renders a complete, alternative world. The first sequence shows, in tradition of the FEMALE SKIN PACK EXCERPTS, a swap in gender in METAL GEAR SOLID 5: THE PHANTOM PAIN (2015, MGSV: TPP). The second is based on a human-animal swap in GTAV. The images are meant as peepholes into parallel game worlds and maybe into a possible future.

SWAPPING FOR A BETTER WORLD

100 % Gender Swap in MGSV:TPP

The video game MGSV:TPP was released in September 2015 by the publisher Konami Digital Entertainment. It is the ninth installment to the METAL GEAR SOLID franchise, written and designed by Hideo Kojima and his company Kojima Productions. The game got very positive reviews, won several gaming awards, and was a commercial success with 6 million copies sold till December 2015.[28] MGSV:TPP is an action-adventure stealth game, which is played in a third-person perspective. The storyline takes place in 1984 where the protagonist Punished "Venom" Snake builds up and leads a mercenary force against the Patriots organization. The game is set in Afghanistan during the Soviet-Afghan War and in the Angola-Zaire border region during the Angola Civil War.[29] The primary source for MGSV:TPP mods is the Nexusmods website, a repository for modifications for different games.[30] Today, there are around 580 mods for MGSV:TPP, ranging from small visual enhancements to tools for encryption/decryption of the game data. The modding software is developed by the community, because there is no official mod support by the publisher/developer. Modding is forbidden but tolerated by the holder of the rights.

The image sequence (Fig. 1-12) is based on a mod done by me in the year 2018, where I swapped around 2100 files. Within the modification I transposed all the male models of the entire game with female ones and vice versa. The result is a variant of the game, where female characters drive the course of the action and are centered within the world with all its male agency. The image sequence shows the original and the modified staging of two cinematic sequences within the game.

---

28 https://www.ign.com/articles/2016/01/29/metal-gear-solid-5-the-phantom-pain-shipped-over-6-million-copies

29 https://www.ign.com/wikis/metal-gear-solid-5-the-phantom-pain/Story#Prior_to_Phantom_Pain

30 https://www.nexusmods.com/

50 % Human-Animal Ped Swap in GTAV

GTAV was developed by Rockstar North and published by Take-Two Interactive in 2013. Like the previous game, GTAV is also part of series of games which started in 1997 with GRAND THEFT AUTO developed by DMA Design for MS-DOS and consoles. The release of the fifth installment was both critically acclaimed and financially successful. As of April 2019, the game has sold 110 million copies.[31] GTAV is an action-adventure game set in the virtual city of Los Santos and Blain County. It is an open world game where players complete a list of different missions that they can freely choose from. The game world is viewed from the first-person or third-person perspective. The story unfolds by playing three different characters who are interconnected through criminal activities.

The mod community of GTAV is like the one in the previous example, supported neither by the developer nor the publisher. To get access to the game data the already mentioned software OpenIV is used. One of the main hubs for mod distribution is the website gta5-mods.com where mods are collected under different categories, like for example "vehicles," "weapons," "scripts," etc. In April 2019, the total number of GTAV-modifications available on the site was 18.480.[32] The image sequence (Fig. 13-24) is based on a mod that I created as part of my practice-based Ph.D. in 2017, in which I swapped "ped" ("pedestrians") characters in GTAV. These characters are controlled by the game engine. For the swap I extracted the model of a chimpanzee and overwrote half of the pedestrians with this model. As the image sequence depicts, the city of Los Santos is now a shared space of human and non-human animals.[33]

---

31 https://www.gamesindustry.biz/articles/2019-05-13-grand-theft-auto-v-has-sold-110m-copies
32 https://www.gta5-mods.com/all/latest-uploads
33 I produced a machinima of the modified setting called GRAND APE TOWN: https://vimeo.com/185806151

Figure 1-3: Metal Gear Solid V: The Phantom Pain

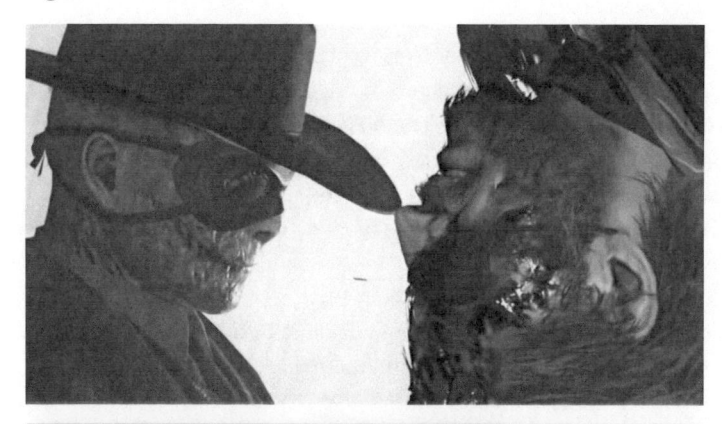

Source: Screenshots from Metal Gear Solid V: The Phantom Pain

Figure 4-6: METAL GEAR SOLID V: THE PHANTOM PAIN, 100 % Gender Swap

Source: Screenshots from METAL GEAR SOLID V: THE PHANTOM PAIN (modified)

Figure 7-9: METAL GEAR SOLID V: THE PHANTOM PAIN

Source: Screenshots from METAL GEAR SOLID V: THE PHANTOM PAIN

Figure 10-12: METAL GEAR SOLID V: THE PHANTOM PAIN, 100% Gender Swap

Source: Screenshots from METAL GEAR SOLID V: THE PHANTOM PAIN (modified)

Figure 13-15: GRAND THEFT AUTO V, 50 % Human-Animal Ped Swap

Source: Screenshots from GRAND THEFT AUTO V (modified)

Figure 16-18: GRAND THEFT AUTO V, 50 % Human-Animal Ped Swap

Source: Screenshots from GRAND THEFT AUTO V (modified)

Figure 19-21: GRAND THEFT AUTO V, 50 % Human-Animal Ped Swap

Source: Screenshots from GRAND THEFT AUTO V (modified)

Figure 22-24: GRAND THEFT AUTO V, *50 % Human-Animal Ped Swap*

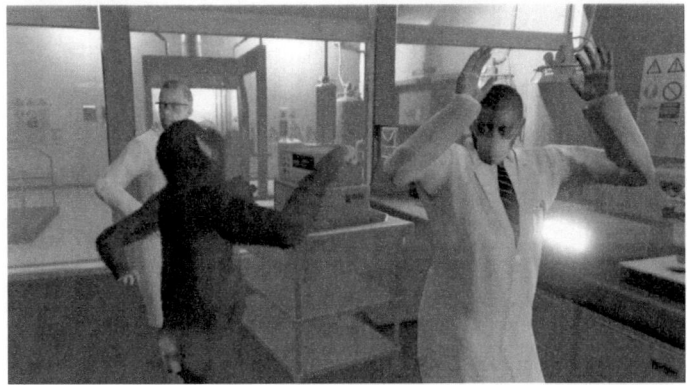

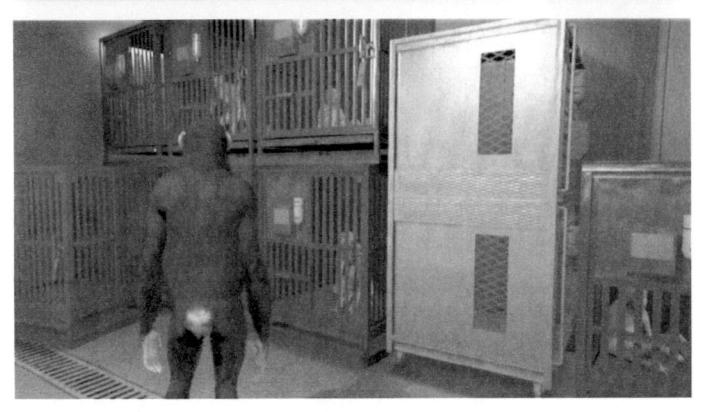

Source: Screenshots from GRAND THEFT AUTO V (modified)

UTOPIAN VIDEO GAME PRACTICES

Alongside its realized game space, every existing game also has an infinite amount of unrealized game worlds.[34] There are multiple practices that evoke these un-rendered worlds. I will refer to the following bundle of actions as utopian video game practices. Crucial to this demonstration is the fact that video games can be appropriated by its users.

Video games as artifacts are surrounded by a flexibility in interpretation.[35] This means that apart from its intended use, the player can use and interpret it in other ways. The YouTube video from the beginning of this paper e.g. shows that its creator used the video game space of GTAV not as an interactive game but as a cinematic environment. Furthermore, by installing different mod tools he transformed the game into a cinematic tool itself. Playing suddenly becomes acting and directing. This circumstance changes the relationship between the individual and the artifact itself, which is fundamental to the idea of appropriation.[36] The practice of appropriation in video games is not limited to modding. There are many other ways to transform the game into something new, e.g. by trying to reach the goal of the game in the smallest amount of time, speedrunners redesign the game space into competitive arenas.[37] Other players use the existing game space as a substructure for their own narrations or to turn the game into a simulation

---

34 Butler, Mark: *Would you like to play a game? Die Kultur des Computerspielens*, Berlin: Kadmos 2007, p. 90.

35 Knorr, Alexander: "Die Deutungsoffenheit der Quelle," in: Lutterbeck, Bernd et al. (eds.), *Open Source Jahrbuch 2007. Zwischen freier Software und Gesellschaftsmodell*, Berlin: Lehmanns Media 2007, pp. 59-72, here p. 67.

36 Knorr, Alexander: "Game Modding. Die soziokulturelle Aneignung digitaler Spielräume," in: Bukow, Gerhard C. et al. (eds.), *Raum, Zeit, Medienbildung. Untersuchungen zu medialen Veränderungen unseres Verhältnisses zu Raum und Zeit*, Wiesbaden: Springer VS 2012, pp. 135-153, here p. 9.

37 For a detailed analysis of speedrunning see: T. Hawranke: *Modding*, pp. 45-57. For a conceptional view on speedruns see: Scully-Blaker, Rainforest: "A Practiced Practice: Speedrunning Through Space With de Certeau and Virilio," in: *Game Studies* 14/1 (2014); http://gamestudies.org/1401/articles/scullyblaker

by defining strict rules.[38] Basic to all these actions is the flexibility in the utilization of the game. In 3D video games this is already provided by the freedom of movement itself.[39]

When designing a video game, the creators have to find a good balance between freedom of the players and the rigidity of the game world. When playing a 3D exploration game, the freedom of spatial movement is key to the concept of the game. Exploration requires the player to feel that there is a whole universe to discover and not a confined area governed by predefined actions and restricting rulesets. By giving up parts of the authority over the space, the designers make the game more flexible and more permissive towards the invention of new spatial actions. Practices like glitching for example use this freedom to trespass barriers within the game that are normally unpassable.[40] With this flexibility in mind, the amount of possible ways to appropriate the game increases.

The implied player, as Espen Aarseth argues, gives us a clue of what actions the designer has anticipated for the game: "The implied player, then, can be seen as a role made for the player by the game, a set of expectations that the player must fulfill for the game to exercise its effect."[41] The idea behind utopian practices contains all the possible actions beyond those anticipated by the designers. In lieu of exercising its effects, utopian practices create new effects through its actions. The sum of both, the implied and the utopian actions, would be the totality of all possible actions within the game. Therefore, utopian practices are connected to everything that is possible, yet some of it remains unrealized.

Now, let me return to the specific practice this article focusses on. By modding a video game, the modder can create one of these unrealized gaming

---

38 Christopher Livingston defines his own set of rules and uses modifications to further enhance the video game *The Elder Scrolls 4: Oblivion* into a simulation. For a detailed description of the project see: T. Hawranke: *Modding*, pp. 40-43.

39 Nitsche, Michael: *Video Game Spaces. Image, Play, and Structure in 3D Game Worlds*, Cambridge, Mass.: The MIT Press 2008, p. 28.

40 For a detailed description what a glitch in video games is and how people us them to their advantage see: Meades, Alan F.: "Why We Glitch: Process, Meaning and Pleasure in The Discovery, Documentation, Sharing and Use of Videogame Exploits," in: *Well Played* 2 (2013), pp. 79-98.

41 E. Aarseth: "I Fought the Law," p. 132.

ideas hidden in the game.[42] In fact the research into the motivations behind modding includes the desire to enhance the existing game, to make it better.[43] To be clear, this primarily means making it look better. But one can adapt this idea to a more general proposition: Modding gives us the possibility to make the game better for us, which has nothing to do with the graphical quality. By modding an existing game one can transform its meaning towards something that is more suitable for us as individuals. If we do not want to see another action game where male characters are wielding guns, we can change it to something else. If we want to see video games that focus on the representation of animal agency, we can create it. This is not meant to dismiss the gaming industry of their responsibility to transport a more diverse view in their games, but again, it could be a starting point for change. In the history of modding there are always examples of successful mods that were absorbed by the gaming industry.[44] Or others, in which the modders themselves transformed the mod into a commercially successful game.[45] In the eyes of the publisher, mods can be seen as test environments for future ideas. The key to generate new and unique concepts, mechanics, gameplays and styles is the fact that there is no pressure to create financial success: "Many in the mod community were and still are fiercely noncommercial, and this gives the scene its punk ethos and arguably protects the petri dish of outlaw experimentation we find."[46] The publishers look at the production of modifications inside their mod communities very carefully, because they are aware of the possibility of finding new and unique ideas and potentially new talents for their future production pipelines.

Besides this potential to influence the production of commercial games, the utopian practice of modding shows something else. In the way the communities interact with the product, they define a very unique aspect of the video game itself: that the raw material from which the game is made is

---

42 Bojahr, Philipp: "Störungen des Computerspielens," in: GamesCoop (eds.), *Theorien des Computerspiels*, Hamburg: Junius 2012, pp. 147-178, here p. 174.
43 J. Theodorsen: *Participatory Culture on Web 2.0*, p. 36.
44 Two famous examples are DOTA 2 (2013), which is the successor of the modification DEFENSE OF THE ANCIENTS, and COUNTER-STRIKE (2000) based on a HALF-LIFE mod.
45 An example for this is the mod and video game DEAR ESTHER (2012).
46 D. Pinchbeck: *Doom*, p. 124.

accessible for its users and that the technology to compose a potential game world is the game itself. When we have a look at the two image sequences of this article, we see that the modified content is integrated into the world nearly perfectly. Some things might be a bit off: In the MGSV:TPP-Swap there are sunglasses that don't really fit the swapped model, whereas in the GTAV-Swap the chimpanzees float a few centimeters above the ground. Apart from this, they are integrated into the world just like the original content of the game. By changing the raw material of the game and its inherent order and by entering the modified game world afterwards, our own creations are blended into the world by the game and its game engine. In order to create something new out of the existing, one must only copy, rename and overwrite the game data. The rest will happen by itself. When talking about the media specificity of video games, there is always the reference to its interactive quality. Modding shows that the interaction is rooted deeply within the technology itself. In that way, it is the medium itself that calls for its corresponding utopian practices—one only has to assert a level of control over the existing system.

In the quote at the beginning of this article, Espen Aarseth claims that transgressive play let us regain control over the game. This idea refers to the action of playing and encompassing the already mentioned variety in different playing behaviors, like glitching, speedrunning, cheating, etc. For Aarseth this regain of control can be seen as a "symbolic gesture of rebellion against the tyranny of the game"[47] and in this sense it can be understood as a critical video game practice in general. The concept can be easily adapted to the idea of utopian practices in video games. From the FEMALE SKIN PACK EXCERPTS by Sonya Roberts to the Swaps in MGSV:TPP and GTAV: All of these modifications have in common that they originate from a critique towards the existing representation of race, class and gender in video games. The urge to create a somehow better future is deeply rooted in the absence of present alternatives. We are called upon to act ourselves. We have to interact with the products of the industry to form something out of it that renders a world more pleasing for us. In order to do so the gaming industry has to give up parts of their control over the products and the modders have to accept this shift in power to create something visionary. Aside from the 'punk ethos' and the outlaw experimentations mentioned by Pinchbeck, modding already

---

47 E. Aarseth: "I Fought the Law," p. 132.

has the potential to become an exercise in creating alternative futures. As an utopian practice and in opposition to corporate media dynamics, modding can generate a world only made for you.

LITERATURE

Aarseth, Espen J.: "I Fought the Law: Transgressive Play and The Implied Player," in: Digital Games Research Association (DiGRA) (eds.), *Proceedings of DiGRA 2007 Conference. Situated Play*, 2007, pp. 130-133.

Abend, Pablo: "'Greetings Arma fans. I submit to you this humble contribution to the mod-a-verse.' Modding als kritische Aneignungspraxis digitaler Spiele", in: Goethe-Institut (eds.), *Games and Politics. Eine interaktive Ausstellung des Goethe-Institut in Kooperation mit dem ZKM*, München: Goethe-Institut 2016, pp. 63-70.

AX System: "What really happened with OpenIV [GTA V]," 2017; https://www.youtube.com/watch?v=x7-WJvGC6D8

Behr, Katharina-Maria: *Kreativer Umgang mit Computerspielen. Die Entwicklung von Spielmodifikationen aus aneignungstheoretischer Sicht*, Boizenburg: vwh 2010.

Beil, Benjamin: "Vom Castle Smurfenstein zum LittleBigPlanet. Modding, Leveleditoren und Prosumenten-Kulturen," in: Abresch, Sebastian et al. (eds.), *Prosumenten-Kulturen*, Siegen: universi 2009, pp. 191-214.

Bojahr, Philipp: "Störungen des Computerspielens," in: GamesCoop (eds.), *Theorien des Computerspiels*, Hamburg: Junius 2012, pp. 147-178.

Butler, Mark: *Would you like to play a game? Die Kultur des Computerspielens*, Berlin: Kadmos 2007.

Champion, Erik: *Game Mods. Design, Theory and Criticism*, Pittsburgh, Pa.: ETC Press 2012.

Gerencser, Aron: "Rockstar Wins $150,000 GTA Online Hack Case," 2019; https://www.gtaboom.com/rockstar-gta-online-hack-case/

GooD-NTS: "Take Two vs. Modding," 2017; https://gtaforums.com/topic/889348-take-two-vs-modding/page/61/?tab=comments#comment-1069656426

Grayson, Nathan: "Steam's Most Popular Skyrim Mod Is A Protest Against Paid Mods," 2015; http://steamed.kotaku.com/steams-most-popular-skyrim-mod-is-a-protest-against-pai-1700486550

GTA5-Community: "GTA5-Mods," 2019; https://www.gta5-mods.com/all/latest-uploads

Hawranke, Thomas: *Modding. Künstlerische Forschung in Computer-spielen*, Weimar: Bauhaus-University 2018.

IGN Team: "Prior to Phantom Pain," 2015; https://www.ign.com/wikis/metal-gear-solid-5-the-phantom-pain/Story#Prior_to_Phantom_Pain

Jansson, Mathias: "Interview: Anne-Marie Schleiner's Cracking the Maze (1999)—A Decade Later," 2009; http://www.gamescenes.org/2009/12/interview-annemarie-schleiners-cracking-the-maze-1999-10-years-later.html

Knorr, Alexander: "Die Deutungsoffenheit der Quelle," in: Lutterbeck, Bernd et al. (eds.), *Open Source Jahrbuch 2007. Zwischen freier Software und Gesellschaftsmodell*, Berlin: Lehmanns Media 2007, pp. 59-72.

Knorr, Alexander: "Game Modding. Die soziokulturelle Aneignung digitaler Spielräume," in: Bukow, Gerhard C. et al. (eds.), *Raum, Zeit, Medienbildung. Untersuchungen zu medialen Veränderungen unseres Verhältnisses zu Raum und Zeit*, Wiesbaden: Springer VS 2012, pp. 135-153.

Kücklich, Julian: "Precarious Playbour: Modders and the Digital Games Indus-try," in: *The Fibreculture Journal* 5 (2005); http://five.fibrecultur ejournal.org/fcj-025-precarious-playbour-modders-and-the-digital-game s-industry/

Laukkanen, Tero: *Modding Scenes—Introduction to User-created Con-tent in Computer Gaming*, Tampere: Tampere University 2005.

Lowood, Henry: "High-Performance Play: The Making of Machinima," in: Clarke, Andy/Mitchell, Grethe (eds.), *Videogames and Art*, Chicago: Intellect 2007, pp. 59-79.

Meades, Alan F.: "Why We Glitch: Process, Meaning and Pleasure in the Discovery, Documentation, Sharing and Use of Videogame Exploits," in: *Well Played* 2 (2013), pp. 79-98.

Newman, James: *Playing with Videogames*, London/New York: Routledge 2008.

Nitsche, Michael: *Video Game Spaces. Image, Play, and Structure in 3D Game Worlds*, Cambridge, Mass.: The MIT Press 2008.

Passalacqua, Michael: "Metal Gear Solid 5: The Phantom Pain Shipped Over 6 Million Copies," 2016; https://www.ign.com/articles/2016/01/29/metal-gear-solid-5-the-phantom-pain-shipped-over-6-million-copies

Pinchbeck, Dan: *Doom. Scarydarkfast*, Ann Arbor, MI: University of Michigan Press 2013.
Postigo, Hector: "Video Game Appropriation Through Modifications. Attitudes Concerning Intellectual Property Among Modders and Fans," in: *Convergence: The International Journal of Research into New Media Technologies* 14 (2008), pp. 59-74.
Ritter, Tobias: "Steam Workshop. Massive Kritik an Bezahl-Mods für Skyrim," 2015; https://www.gamestar.de/artikel/steam_workshop,3085192.html
Schleiner, Anne-Marie: "Curators Note. Cracking the Maze," 1998; http://switch.sjsu.edu/archive/CrackingtheMaze/note.html
Schleiner, Anne-Marie: *Ludic Mutation: The Player's Power to Change the Game*, Amsterdam: University of Amsterdam 2012.
Scully-Blaker, Rainforest: "A Practiced Practice: Speedrunning Through Space With de Certeau and Virilio," in: *Game Studies* 14/1 (2014); http://gamestudies.org/1401/articles/scullyblaker
Sotamaa, Olli: "Computer Game Modding, Intermediality and Partici-patory Culture," Lecture at: The Nordic Vetwork Innovating Media and Communication Research, Sonderborg, Denmark 2003.
Theodorsen, Jesper: *Participatory Culture on Web 2.0: Exploring the Motives for Modding Video Games*, Master Thesis, University of Amsterdam 2008.
Valentine, Rebekah: "Grand Theft Auto V Has Sold Nearly 110m Copies," 2019; https://www.gamesindustry.biz/articles/2019-05-13-grand-theft-auto-v-has-sold-110m-copies

GAMOGRAPHY

DEAR ESTHER (The Chinese Room 2012, O: The Chinese Room)
DOTA 2 (Valve 2013, O: Valve)
COUNTER-STRIKE (Sierra 2000, O: Valve)
HALF-LIFE (Sierra 1998, O: Valve)
GRAND THEFT AUTO V (Rockstar Games 2013, O: Rockstar North)
LOLLIPOP CHAINSAW (Warner Bros. Interactive Entertainment 2012, O: Grasshopper Manufacture)

METAL GEAR SOLID V: THE PHANTOM PAIN (Konami 2015, O: Kojima Productions)
SKYRIM (Bethesda 2011, O: Bethesda)
QUAKE (GT Interactive 1996, O: id Software)
QUAKE 2 (Activision 1997, O: id Software)

The Utopia of Getting Over It

BENJAMIN BEIL

Figure 1: At the foot of a mountain…

Source: GETTING OVER IT WITH BENNETT FODDY (2017)

At the foot of a mountain sits a man in a big black metal cauldron. Only the upper half of his body is visible, and it is unclear how his legs fit inside the pot, or if he even has legs at all. The scene is accompanied by a voice-over commentary by Bennett Foddy, the creator of the game. He reveals to us that the name of the almost-silent protagonist of GETTING OVER IT is Diogenes, a name chosen quite appropriately. The ancient Greek philosopher Diogenes from Sinope decided to live with as few things as possible, one of them being a very big pot. The oversized Yosemite hammer that the man holds in his hands is not historically documented.

However, the hammer is important. It is wielded, using mouse and keyboard, to grip objects and move the man in the cauldron up the mountain. The controls are imprecise and seem inconsistent. Whether this is a shortcoming or a quality of the game, will be discussed later. Players have only one task: to climb the huge mountain, a mountain that seems to consist of nothing but trash, an arbitrary collection of prefabricated elements, taken from the collection of a level editor. GETTING OVER IT is "a game of disposable content."[1] Even the avatar is a stock model, more precisely, *Model No. 1* from the Adobe Fuse library, as Bennett Foddy explained during a Let's Play video.[2]

GETTING OVER IT WITH BENNETT FODDY is a strange game, at first glance unprepossessing, technically unfinished, and above all far too difficult. But it is also, at least for an indie title, an extraordinarily successful game that enjoys great popularity.

"If you're aware of GETTING OVER IT WITH BENNETT FODDY, it's probably the result of a streamer or YouTuber playing through the game. That's not a bad thing. It's clearly one of the reasons the game has been as successful as it has. But it also gives the game something of a reputation of being a game designed for streaming online, merging GOAT SIMULATOR style absurdist humor with a sort of infuriating difficulty […]. It would be easy to dismiss GETTING OVER IT as a quirky game tailor-made to get attention by having YouTubers get angry and scream at a naked man in a pot for a few hours. But I think there's more going on here. The game makes it pretty clear, it's something of a meditation on challenge, difficulty, failure, suffering, pain, and what they mean."[3]

It is not a new insight that games are meditations on these categories. A ludic goal can fulfill its rewarding function only if failure is possible. Roger Caillois' famous definition describes play as an "uncertain activity," because "[a]n outcome known in advance, with no possibility of error or no surprise,

---

1 Franklin, Chris (ErrantSignal): "Getting Over It (Spoilers?)," 2018; https://www.youtube.com/watch?v=DCcA4FyWeXI
2 Rogers, Tim: "We Made the Developer of Getting Over It Play His Own Infuriating Game," *Kotaku*, 2017; https://kotaku.com/we-made-the-developer-of-getting-over-it-play-his-own-i-1821193180
3 C. Franklin: "Getting Over It."

clearly leading to an inescapable result, is incompatible with the nature of play."[4]

Jesper Juul has dedicated a small monograph to *The Art of Failure* in video games, mainly dealing with what he calls "the paradox of failure."[5] His study opens with three observations:

"1. We generally avoid failure. 2. We experience failure when playing games. 3. We seek out games, although we will likely experience something that we normally avoid."[6]

A central strategy for Juul in dealing with this paradox is to face failure and finally master a game through ongoing (more or less) hard training:

"My argument is that the paradox of failure is unique in that when you fail in a game, it really means that *you* were in some way inadequate. Such a feeling of inadequacy is unpleasant for us, and it is odd that we choose to subject ourselves to it. However, while games uniquely induce such feelings of being inadequate, they also motivate us to play *more* in order to escape the same inadequacy, and the feeling of escaping failure (often by improving our skills) is central to the enjoyment of games. Games promise us a fair chance of redeeming ourselves. This distinguishes game failure from failure in our regular lives: (good) games are designed such that they give us a fair chance, whereas the regular world makes no such promises."[7]

However, does this argument apply to GETTING OVER IT? Surely, players can get better at this game. The inaccurate controls and the danger of losing all your progress through even the smallest mistake, however, seem to stand in the way of the promise of "a fair chance of redeeming ourselves." But does this make GETTING OVER IT a bad game?

---

4 Caillois, Roger: *Man, Play, and Games*, Chicago: University of Illinois Press 2001, p. 7.
5 Juul, Jesper: *The Art of Failure. An Essay on the Pain of Playing Video Games*, Cambridge, Mass.: The MIT Press 2008, p. 1. See also: Herte, Michelle: *Forms and Functions of Endings in Narrative Digital Games*, PhD Thesis, University of Cologne 2019.
6 J. Juul: *The Art of Failure*, p. 33.
7 Ibid., p. 7.

THE ART OF DIFFICULTY

For Juul, a well-dosed challenge is part of every 'good' game:

"We are motivated to play when something is at stake. It seems that the more time we invest into overcoming a challenge (be it completing a game, or simply overcoming a small subtask), the bigger the sense of loss we experience when failing, and the bigger the sense of triumph we feel when succeeding. Even then, our feeling of triumph can quickly evaporate if we learn that other players overcame the challenge faster than we did. To play a game is to make an emotional gamble: we invest time and self-esteem in the hope that it will pay off."[8]

In this spirit, designing a fair (good) game seems primarily a careful balancing of failing and winning conditions. And thus, the simple answer to the question of what defines the art of failure in video games, is that there are different forms of failure, and, of course, different kinds of triumphs.

In terms of the latter, Juul differentiates between three types of goals in video games: *completable*, *transient*, and *improvement goals*.[9] Completable goals are found in "mostly linear" story-driven games that "can be completed once and for all."[10] A transient goal can be to win a single round; the success is, therefore, "tied to that specific game session:"[11] "Winning a match in SUPER STREET FIGHTER IV (2010) only means that we have won *this* match."[12] An improvement goal is a "compromise"[13] of a completable and a transient goal, e.g., beating the high score in an arcade game. An improvement goal can act as a completable goal, but by reaching it, it is immediately replaced with a new challenge: beating the new high score. "Such improvement goals concern our ongoing personal struggles for improvement, and can by definition never be reached."[14]

---

8   Ibid., pp. 13-14.
9   Ibid., p. 83.
10   Ibid., p. 85.
11   Ibid.
12   Ibid.
13   Ibid.
14   Ibid., pp. 85-86.

When it comes to losing, a distinction between failure and punishment is essential. Does a false step result in the loss of a few seconds or several minutes of progress? Are there other forms of punishment, e.g., the loss of equipment or experience points? In recent years, games like SUPER MEAT BOY (2010) and the DARK SOULS (2011-) series have led to controversial discussions about the 'right' level of difficulty and how this level has changed over the years with games opening up to a wider (mainstream) audience. Whether games have really become easier or more difficult over time seems to be a too general and therefore rather pointless question. More interesting, however, is the question in which way the level of difficulty has changed.

"In the early history of video games, the dominant way to deal with failure was the arcade model with its limited number of failures per game. During the 1990s and 2000s, single-player games gradually began giving players unlimited lives. [...] Yet the fact that we are given infinite retries also means that we now fail more frequently than we used to, even though we often describe newer games as easy. The combination of more failures and smaller punishments adds up to more frequent opportunities for having failure force us to reconsider our strategies, to learn from our mistakes."[15]

A recurring argument in this debate is that games must be fair and learnable, especially difficult games. The degree of difficulty in the DARK SOULS series, e.g., is primarily expressed by a steep learning curve: not all mechanics are explained at the beginning of the game, and safe points are far apart. The game is punishing, but it confronts players with clear 'reliable' challenges, which they will (eventually) master at some point.

As in the case of DARK SOULS, it also seems important—beyond game mechanical aspects—that the high degree of difficulty 'matches' the atmosphere of the game. DARK SOULS takes players into a sinister, threatening world, where they have to become fearless heroes fighting tirelessly against terrifying creatures—"the bigger the sense of loss [...] the bigger the sense of triumph."[16]

Though it is an extraordinarily difficult game, GETTING OVER IT seems to strangely elude this (general) discussion about the degree of difficulty of

---

15   Ibid., p. 72.
16   Ibid., p. 14.

contemporary computer games.[17] GETTING OVER IT is not a fair game and its world—a man in a cauldron climbing a mountain of trash—is neither dark nor threatening. Moreover, even the end of the hero's journey is hardly worth mentioning. At the summit of the mountain, players can expect no notable reward, no brilliant resolution of the game's mysteries, no credits, no hymns of praise—but just another self-reflexive gesture: a link to a chat room (#TopOfTheMountain), a kind of veteran meeting point. What could be a room for exchange with other 'heroes' turns out to be a largely deserted forum, filled with a mixture of meaningless comments and complaints about the game's disappointing ending.

THE UTOPIA OF GETTING OVER IT

Regarding Juul's advice for game (difficulty) design, GETTING OVER IT turns out to be not a good game for at least three reasons: First, it is not a fair game, because it does not provide reliable control options. Players will learn a few tricks, they will discover different safe and unsafe routes on their way to the summit, but the mouse and keyboard controls will remain impressive tools. Second, GETTING OVER IT is extremely punishing. Any mistake, however small, can take the avatar back to the foot of the mountain. Players can certainly perceive a form of progress by setting their individual (improvement) goals but GETTING OVER IT ultimately does not acknowledge these goals, because there is no high score list, only a mountain and a summit. And finally, GETTING OVER IT does not even reward players, at least not with a fulfilling ending.

GETTING OVER IT remains a relentless game to the very end. But is it just a game for stubborn people? Or a game for a small number of experienced players with a lot of skill (and a lot of time)? Or is it—to pick up on the suspicion from the beginning of this chapter—just a game for YouTubers, a

---

17 Bennett Foddy even gives a reason for the extreme degree of difficulty in the voice-over commentary. But can he be trusted?—"A funny thing that happened to me as I was building this mountain: I'd have an idea for an obstacle, and I'd build it, test it, and... it would usually turn out to be unreasonably hard. But I couldn't bring myself to make it easier. It already felt like my inability to get past the new obstacle was my fault as a player, rather than as the builder."

game for watching others fail? The latter reason is certainly not wrong. Schadenfreude is a design feature that should never be underestimated. But in addition to the joy of watching others fail, the countless Let's Play videos of GETTING OVER IT also do the exact opposite: They show that it is possible to reach the top of the mountain and win the game—and in this way one's own failures become all the more bitter by these triumphs of 'the others.'

However, does this mean that Bennett Foddy's talent for humiliating players extends even into the game's paratext? Chris Franklin makes a remarkable observation in his review of GETTING OVER IT: "[The game] isn't designed to be completed, even [though] technically it can be." What does this mean? It is crucial that GETTING OVER IT is not simply a paradoxical game; it is not a "Wargame," a "strange game" where "the only winning move is not to play."[18] GETTING OVER IT is rather a game for players who do not finish it, and who know perfectly well that they will never make it—but still try again and again to climb the mountain. These players know that it is possible to win the game—after all, this realization is just a Google search and a YouTube clip away—and this knowledge is essential. However, these players also know that they will never belong to the group of heroes who have documented a successful summit ascent on YouTube.

Watching speedruns of GETTING OVER IT does not, unlike in many other games, work as a walkthrough, or at least it quickly becomes clear that these videos are not suitable for getting better at the game. The opposite is the case: The virtuosity to be seen in these successful summit ascents reinforces the viewers/players in their belief that they will never be able to achieve this goal themselves. They are no summiteers—they are just ordinary players. It is precisely this knowledge, however, that makes the daily ascent, the constant trying in the face of a certain failure no less fulfilling, no less relevant—and no less heroic, as will be argued shortly.

The real players of GETTING OVER IT are no speedrunners. And they are not Diogenes either—even this detail, this misnomer, turns out to be a wrong trail that Bennett Foddy has laid out. These players are Sisyphus because GETTING OVER IT is—for most players—one thing above all: a difficult task, which they face, but which cannot be won. In this sense, GETTING OVER IT is a Utopia, a no-place.

---

18 WARGAMES (USA 1983, D: John Badham).

In his famous essay *The Myth of Sisyphus*, Albert Camus describes Sisyphus as a happy man, a man who finds fulfillment in the acceptance of his absurd existence. Sisyphus, who defied the gods, is condemned to push a rock up a mountain, and upon reaching the top, the rock always rolls down again, leaving Sisyphus to start over. Camus presents Sisyphus' endless toil as a metaphor for modern life:

"The workman of today works every day in his life at the same tasks, and this fate is no less absurd. But it is tragic only at the rare moments when it becomes conscious."[19]

For Camus, Sisyphus is not a tragic, but rather an absurd hero who lives life to the fullest, although or precisely because he is condemned to a meaningless task. That is why Camus' essay is not concerned with the punishment as such or with the moment of failure when the rock rolls back. Rather, Camus is interested in Sisyphus' thoughts when his hero is marching down the mountain, to start anew:

"I see that man going back down with a heavy yet measured step toward the torment of which he will never know the end. That hour like a breathing-space which returns as surely as his suffering, that is the hour of consciousness. At each of those moments when he leaves the heights and gradually sinks toward the lairs of the gods, he is superior to his fate. He is stronger than his rock."[20]

And so, Camus ends his essay with the famous idea of Sisyphus as a happy man:

"I leave Sisyphus at the foot of the mountain. One always finds one's burden again. [...] The struggle itself toward the heights is enough to fill a man's heart. One must imagine Sisyphus happy."[21]

1978, 36 years after Camus' *Myth of Sisyphus*, Bernard Suits published his treatise *The Grasshopper: Games, Life and Utopia*. The book is written as a Socratic dialog in which the Grasshopper explains his philosophical

---

19 Camus, Albert: *The Myth of Sisyphus*, New York: Random 1955, p. 77.
20 Ibid., pp. 76-77.
21 Ibid., p. 78.

definition of games to his students. The two most well-known concepts of Suits' study are its definition of games as "the voluntary attempt to overcome unnecessary obstacles"[22] and its coining of the term "lusory attitude,"[23] the acceptance of the rules of the game in order to engage in the activity permitted by the game. But the book also contains, as the title suggests, a definition of Utopia.[24]

The Grasshopper describes Utopia as a place where all material and intellectual needs are satisfied. Any material goods are instantly available, and all scientific knowledge is known. The Grasshopper then claims that there would be nothing left to do; even art would be pointless without the pathos of human conflict and suffering. Games are, by definition, the only things that remain: doing something inefficiently for the sake of the activity rather than the result. At the book's close, the Grasshopper wonders whether such a Utopia is really desirable, or if most people would be rather dissatisfied with activities that do not lead to any 'real' results.[25]

Suit's study ends quite abruptly with this question, and, admittedly, the question seems to burden the brief treatise with a little bit too much social-philosophical weight. Beyond this 'big metaphysical question,' however, Suit's thought experiment of Utopia provides an interesting perspective on Bennett Foddy's little playable thought experiment: Playing GETTING OVER

---

22 Suits, Bernard: *The Grasshopper. Games, Life and Utopia*, Toronto: University of Toronto Press 1978, p. 41.

23 Ibid., p. 38.

24 Interestingly, *The Grasshopper* also includes a chapter on mountain climbing (ibid., pp. 84-87). Skepticus, one of the Grasshopper's students, claims that mountain climbing is a game with no rules. The Grasshopper replies that if there was a way to simply teleport the climber to the summit, the climber would refuse. The reason for this is that the climber chose to climb the mountain 'on his/her own' (using only certain tools such as mountaineering equipment). If these rules were removed, the goal of reaching the summit would be worthless for the climber. Thereby, the 'natural rules' (or the 'natural challenges') imposed by the mountain are an essential part of the game of mountain climbing. Despite the obvious parallels to Bennett Foddy's mountain (of trash), the 'mountain climbing chapter' seems of limited interest for this essay, as it is just another example of Suit's definition of games as a "voluntary attempt to overcome unnecessary obstacles."

25 Ibid., pp. 166-178.

It is not a Utopia, but it is a remarkably consistent utopian practice in regard to its inefficiency and unnecessariness. It is just a little utopian game in an (as it seems) increasingly dystopian world, and it's certainly not a game for everyone. It is, however, a highly interesting experiment that adds a new facet to the art of failure. Even Chris Franklin, who describes his gaming experiences in a video essay, seems to have become a utopian as well as an absurd hero in the course of the game:

"I still haven't beaten [GETTING OVER IT] despite putting several hours into it. That tower of trash, that mountain of prefab assets is still there, unconquered for me. And I've lost all my progress several times at this point, but each time getting back up becomes a little bit easier. And yeah, the gameplay does taste rough and bitter and uncaring and I absolutely have to be in a certain mood to play it without just falling into frustrated despair. But […] I don't feel bad that I haven't beaten the game. It doesn't really care that I have or haven't. It'll still be there, unchanged, waiting for me, if I decide to try it again. In the meantime, the progress I have made and the progress I've lost are all mine. And there's this sort of pride in knowing that even if I am to fall from great heights, as much as the landing might sting, I've done it before, and I can do it again."[26]

Chris Franklin seems happy.

LITERATURE

Camus, Albert: *The Myth of Sisyphus*, New York: Random 1955 [1942].
Caillois, Roger: *Man, Play, and Games*, Chicago: University of Illinois Press 2001 [1938].
Franklin, Chris (ErrantSignal): "Getting Over It (Spoilers?)," 2018; https://www.youtube.com/watch?v=DCcA4FyWeXI
Herte, Michelle: *Forms and Functions of Endings in Narrative Digital Games*, PhD Thesis, University of Cologne 2019.
Juul, Jesper: *The Art of Failure. An Essay on the Pain of Playing Video Games*, Cambridge, Mass.: The MIT Press 2008.

---

26 C. Franklin: "Getting Over It."

Rogers, Tim: "We Made the Developer of Getting Over It Play His Own Infuriating Game," *Kotaku*, 2017; https://kotaku.com/we-made-the-developer-of-getting-over-it-play-his-own-i-1821193180

Suits, Bernard: *The Grasshopper. Games, Life and Utopia*, Toronto: University of Toronto Press 1978.

Filmography

WARGAMES (USA 1983, D: John Badham)

Gamography

DARK SOULS (Namco Bandai Games 2011, O: FromSoftware)
GETTING OVER IT WITH BENNETT FODDY (Humble Bundle 2017, O: Bennett Foddy)
GOAT SIMULATOR (Coffee Stain Studios 2014, O: Coffee Stain Studios)
SUPER MEAT BOY (Team Meat 2010, O: Team Meat)
SUPER STREET FIGHTER IV (Capcom 2010, O: Capcom)

Contributors

Beil, Benjamin, is Professor for Media Studies & Digital Culture at the Department of Media Culture & Theatre at the University of Cologne. Selected publications: *Avatarbilder* (Bielefeld: transcript 2012), *New Game Plus. Perspektiven der Game Studies* (co-ed., Bielefeld, transcript 2014), *Im Spielrausch. Streifzüge durch die Welten des Theaters und des Computerspiels* (co-ed., Glückstadt: vwh 2017), *Game Studies* (co-ed., Wiesbaden: Springer VS 2018). Website: http://www.mekuwi.phil-fak.uni-koeln.de/benjamin_beil.html

Czauderna, André, is an education researcher working at the Cologne Game Lab of TH Köln, where he manages and develops the study programs BA and MA Digital Games as well as teaches player research. His research interests include decision-making in strategy and management games, learning in gaming affinity spaces, educational games, and game design education. Czauderna holds a PhD from Johannes Gutenberg University Mainz. Seclected Publications: *Lernen als soziale Praxis im Internet. Objektiv hermeneutische Rekonstruktionen aus einem Forum zum Videospiel Pokémon* (Wiesbaden: Springer VS 2014); "Academic Game Design Education: A Comparative Perspective," in: *Proceedings of the Fourth Joint International Conference on Serious Games* (JCSG 2018), LNCS 11243, pp. 9-12; "Sozialwissenschaftliche Game Studies. Entwurf eines curricularen Rahmens für das Studium der Gestaltung und Entwicklung digitaler Spiele," in: B. Bartholdy/L. Breitlauch/A. Czauderna/G. S. Freyermuth (eds.): *Games studieren – was, wie, wo? Staatliche Studienangebote im Bereich digitaler Spiele* (Bielefeld: transcript 2018), pp. 129-155; "The Gameplay Loop Methodology as a Tool for Educational Game Design," in: *The Electronic Journal* *of e-Learning*, 17.3 (together with Emmanuel Guardiola). Website: https://www.th-koeln.de/personen/andre.czauderna

de Wildt, Lars, is a Ph.D. student at KU Leuven, the university where More's *Utopia* was first published in 1518. Lars until recently lived in Antwerp, where *Utopia* starts: tellingly, in front of the Cathedral. Lars' research on religion and videogames focuses on how games, players and developers play with religion in a supposedly secular age. He has been a visiting scholar at Deakin University in Melbourne and Université de Montréal, is chair of DiGRA Flanders, and has published work with *Information, Communication & Society*, the *British Journal of Sociology of Education*, the *European Journal of Cultural Studies, Games & Culture, Brill, Routledge, ACM*, and others. Website: https://www.kuleuven.be/wieiswie/en/person/00100149

Dippel, Anne, Assistant Professor at the Department of Cultural Anthropology/Cultural History of Friedrich-Schiller-University Jena. In her German book *Dichten und Denken in Österreich. Eine literarische Ethnographie* (Wien: Turia + Kant 2015), she explored how writers play with language, shaping national identities and collective memory in Austria. Her recent work focuses on high-energy physics. She asks how humans, machines and data are making (sense of) nature at the European Organization for Nuclear Research (CERN). She has been working at the cluster of excellence Image-Knowledge-Gestalt of Humboldt-University Berlin, has been visiting assistant professor at MIT, and for the time of her field work an associated member of CERN collaboration. Selected publications: "Das Big Data Game. Zur spielerischen Konstitution kollaborativer Wissensproduktion in der Hochenergiephysik am CERN," *NTM* 4/2017, pp. 485-517. "Arbeit," in: Markus Rautzenberg, Daniel Martin Feige, Michael Ostritsch (eds.): *Philosophie des Computerspiels*. Stuttgart: Metzler Verlag, pp.123-148. Website: https://www.vkkg.uni-jena.de/Seminar/Personen/Wiss_+MitarbeiterInnen/Dr_+Anne+Dippel.html

Farca, Gerald, is Professor of Game Design (Narrative Design & Game Studies) at the Macromedia University in Leipzig, Germany. He completed his Ph.D. at Augsburg University in 2017 and was a visiting lecturer & researcher at the Center for Computer Games Research at the IT University Copenhagen in 2016. Gerald specializes in the fields of game studies, narrative theory, ecocriticism, utopia/dystopia, and science fiction studies. He is also a freelance narrative consultant & writer and runs a blog on video game photography. Selected publications: *Playing Dystopia: Nightmarish Worlds in Video Games and the Player's Aesthetic Response* (Bielefeld: transcript 2018), "The Emancipated Player," *Proceedings of the First International Joint Conference of DiGRA and FGD* 13, no. 1 (2016):1-16. Website: http://www.videogamenarrative.com

Freyermuth, Gundolf S., Professor of Media and Game Studies and founding co-director at the Cologne Game Lab of TH Koeln–University of Technology, Arts and Sciences, as well as Professor of Comparative Media Studies at the ifs international film school of Cologne. Selected Publications: *Serious Games, Exergames, Exerlearning. Zur Transmedialisierung und Gamification des Wissenstransfers* (co-ed., Bielefeld: transcript 2013); *New Game Plus. Perspektiven der Game Studies. Genres, Kuenste, Diskurse* (co-ed., Bielefeld: transcript 2015), *Games | Game Design | Game Studies. An Introduction* (Bielefeld: transcript 2015); *Games studieren: was, wie, wo? Staatliche Studienangebote im Bereich digitaler Spiele (*co-ed., Bielefeld: transcript 2018). Website: www.freyermuth.com and http://www.colognegamelab.de/institute/people/gundolf-s-freyermuth/

Harvey, Alison, lecturer in Media and Communication at the University of Leicester. Research focused on issues of inclusivity and accessibility in digital culture, with an emphasis on games. Author of *Gender, Age, and Digital Games in the Domestic Context*, which was published by Routledge in 2015. Works published in a range of interdisciplinary journals, including *International Journal of Cultural Studies, Feminist Media Studies, Games & Culture, Information, Communication & Society Social Media & Society*, and *Studies in Social Justice*. Notable publications include: *Feminist Media Studies* (Cambridge: Polity, contracted); "The Fame Game: Working your Way up the Celebrity Ladder in Kim Kardashian: Hollywood," *Games and Culture* (2018), Online First.; *Gender, Age, and Digital Games in the Domestic Context* (New York: Routledge 2015). Website: https://www2.le.ac.uk/departments/media/people/dr-alison-harvey

Koenitz, Hartmut, is Professor for Interactive Narrative Design at HKU, the University of the Arts Utrecht, where he leads a research group on the topic. Current focus areas include analytical Models for Interactive Digital Narratives, Design Conventions, Pedagogy, and Representations of Complexity. Hartmut is the founding chair of ARDIN (Association for Research in Digital Interactive Narratives, ardin.online). He is the main proposer of a recently awarded COST EU grant (CA 18230) which will investigate Interactive Narrative Design for Complexity Representations. Hartmut holds a Ph.D. from the Georgia Institute of Technology and has published over 60 scholarly publications and several books, including the co-edited volume *Interactive Digital Narrative – History, Theory and Practice* (New York: Routledge 2015). Recent notable publications include: "What Game Narrative Are We Talking About? An Ontological Mapping of the Foundational Canon of Interactive Narrative Forms," *Arts* 7(4), 51 (2018); "Narrative in Video Games," *Encyclopedia of Computer Graphics and Games* (Vol. 1, Cham: Springer 2018). Hartmut is the creator of the ASAPS authoring tool, which has been used to create more than 150 works (advancedstories.net). Hartmut is also a visual artist, and his works have been shown in Atlanta, Paris, Istanbul, Seoul, Copenhagen and Porto. His latest piece, The Multiple Lives of Walter B., is a physical installation that explores virtual biographies of Walter Benjamin. Website: http://hartmutkoenitz.com

Schmidt, Hanns Christian, Ph.D., works as a research assistant at the Institute of Media Culture and Theater of University of Cologne and within the project "Literalität des Spiel(en)s – Vermittlung von Medienkompetenz im Rahmen analoger, digitaler und hybrider Spiele" ("Literacy of Play / Literacy of Games – imparting media competence within analogue, digital and hybrid games") at the Cologne Game Lab. His research interests include Game Studies, Game Literacy, Transmediality and Intermediality, Film and TV Studies, zombies, aliens and Lego bricks. Website: http://www.colognegamelab.de/institute/people/ hanns-christian-schmidt/

Sezen, Tonguc Ibrahim, is a Research Fellow at Rhine-Waal University of Applied Sciences. He holds a Ph.D. in Communications from Istanbul University, School of Social Sciences. During his doctoral studies, he visited Georgia Institute of Technology, School of Literature, Media, and Communication as a Fulbright scholar. Between 2014 and 2018 he has been an

Assistant Professor and the founding department head of the Digital Game Design Department at Istanbul Bilgi University. His research interests include cross-media narration, game design, interactive storytelling and toy studies. Website: https://de.linkedin.com/in/tonguc-ibrahim-sezen-dr-habil-0012756